Ethics and Time in the Philosophy of History

Also available from Bloomsbury:

Biopolitics After Neuroscience, by Jeffrey P. Bishop,
M. Therese Lysaught and Andrew A. Michel
Debating New Approaches to History, edited by Marek Tamm and Peter Burke
Rethinking Historical Time, edited by Marek Tamm and Laurent Olivier
The History and Ethics of Authenticity, by Kyle Michael James Shuttleworth

Ethics and Time in the Philosophy of History

A Cross-Cultural Approach

Edited by
Natan Elgabsi and Bennett Gilbert

BLOOMSBURY ACADEMIC
LONDON • NEW YORK • OXFORD • NEW DELHI • SYDNEY

BLOOMSBURY ACADEMIC
Bloomsbury Publishing Plc
50 Bedford Square, London, WC1B 3DP, UK
1385 Broadway, New York, NY 10018, USA
29 Earlsfort Terrace, Dublin 2, Ireland

BLOOMSBURY, BLOOMSBURY ACADEMIC and the Diana logo are trademarks of
Bloomsbury Publishing Plc

First published in Great Britain 2023
This paperback edition published in 2024

Copyright © Natan Elgabsi, Bennett Gilbert and Contributors, 2023

Natan Elgabsi and Bennett Gilbert have asserted their right under the Copyright,
Designs and Patents Act, 1988, to be identified as Editors of this work.

For legal purposes the Acknowledgements on p. xi constitute an extension
of this copyright page.

Cover image: Wooden Boats On A Lake (© EyeEm / Alamy Stock Photo)

All rights reserved. No part of this publication may be reproduced or transmitted
in any form or by any means, electronic or mechanical, including photocopying,
recording, or any information storage or retrieval system, without prior
permission in writing from the publishers.

Bloomsbury Publishing Plc does not have any control over, or responsibility for, any third-party websites referred to or in this book. All internet addresses given in this book were correct at the time of going to press. The author and publisher regret any inconvenience caused if addresses have changed or sites have ceased to exist, but can accept no responsibility for any such changes.

A catalogue record for this book is available from the British Library.

A catalog record for this book is available from the Library of Congress.

ISBN: HB: 978-1-3502-7909-4
PB: 978-1-3502-7913-1
ePDF: 978-1-3502-7910-0
eBook: 978-1-3502-7911-7

Typeset by Deanta Global Publishing Services, Chennai, India

To find out more about our authors and books visit www.bloomsbury.com and sign up for
our newsletters.

Contents

Notes on Contributors — vii
Acknowledgments — xi

Introduction

Temporal Humanity: Involvement with Ethics and Time Across Cultures *Natan Elgabsi and Bennett Gilbert* — 3

Section I History as Ethics

1 Past Deeds and the On-going Work of History *Réal Fillion* — 25
2 The Time of Ghosts and the Ghosts of Time *Ethan Kleinberg* — 40
3 Gifts from the Dead: Heritage and the Ligatures of History *Hans Ruin* — 53
4 Multilayered Temporalities Underlying Transitional Justice: Rethinking Resentment and Melancholia from Jean Améry and Walter Benjamin *Rafael Pérez Baquero* — 69

Section II Agency, Relativity, and Affect

5 The Relativism of Historical Distance and the Contextual Constitution of Agency *Nora Hämäläinen* — 89
6 Heroism, Self-determination, and Magnanimity: Hegel and Brandom on Self-conscious Agency *Chiel van den Akker* — 105
7 Farness and Immemorial Time: An Ontology of Vestiges *Roberto Wu* — 122

Section III Mortality and Personal Identity

8 Neither to Be, Nor Not to Be: The Interrelation of Life and Death in Tanabe's Later Philosophy of Death *Takeshi Morisato* — 141
9 Arresting Time's Arrow: Death, Loss, and the Preservation of Real Union *Megan Fritts* — 158
10 Heidegger's Process Metaphysics of Personhood *Anne Sophie Meincke* — 173

Section IV Reconsidering Ontology

11 "When the Time Is Right . . ." In the Māori World *Georgina Tuari Stewart* — 195
12 Levinas on Time: The Ethical Import of our Existential Chronological Inconsistency *Benda Hofmeyr* — 210

13 Historical Time, Collective Memory, and the Finitude of Historical Understanding *Jeffrey Andrew Barash* 225

14 The Time of History *Jan-Ivar Lindén* 239

Section V Concluding Reflections from Existential Anthropology

15 The Death of the Angel: In Search of a Tango of Temporal Humanity *Ruth Behar* 257

Index 273

Contributors

Chiel van den Akker is Lecturer in Historical Theory at the Department of Art and Culture, History and Antiquities at The Free University of Amsterdam, The Netherlands. He is the author of *The Modern Idea of History and its Value: An Introduction* (2020) and *The Exemplifying Past: A Philosophy of History* (2018), both published by Amsterdam University Press. He recently edited *The Routledge Companion to Historical Theory* (2022). His interests are in German idealism, neo-pragmatism, history-didactics, and narrativist philosophy of history.

Jeffrey Andrew Barash is Emeritus Professor of Philosophy at the University of Amiens, France. His publications include: *Martin Heidegger and the Problem of Historical Meaning* (2003), and *Collective Memory and the Historical Past* (second paperback edition, 2020). He has edited the book *The Social Construction of Reality: The Legacy of Ernst Cassirer* (2008). Forthcoming books are *Shadows of Being: Encounters with Heidegger in Political Theory and Historical Reflection* and *Historical Reflection and the Polemics of Political Myth in the Twentieth Century*.

Ruth Behar is the James W. Fernandez Distinguished University Professor of Anthropology at the University of Michigan, Ann Arbor, USA, and a member of the American Academy of Arts & Sciences. Born in Havana, Cuba, she grew up in New York. As a cultural anthropologist, she is the author of several books, including *The Vulnerable Observer: Anthropology that Breaks Your Heart* (1996), *An Island Called Home: Returning to Jewish Cuba* (2007), and *Traveling Heavy: A Memoir in Between Journeys* (2013). Also a writer of young adult books, Behar has written the novels, *Lucky Broken Girl* (2017) and *Letters from Cuba* (2020). Behar is the recipient of a MacArthur Fellows Award and was named a "Great Immigrant" by the Carnegie Corporation.

Natan Elgabsi is a Postdoctoral Researcher in Philosophy at Åbo Akademi University, Finland. The title of his dissertation is *Literacy, Historiography, and the Ethics of Writing About the Absent Other* (Åbo Akademi, 2022). His research interests are existential questions of responsibility and understanding in the philosophy of historical and anthropological writing; the philosophy and phenomenology of writing broadly conceived; the relationship between epistemology and ethics in the human sciences, including moral psychology and the sociology of biological anthropology.

Réal Fillion is Emeritus Professor of Philosophy at the University of Sudbury, Canada. He is the author of *Multicultural Dynamics and the Ends of History: Exploring Kant,*

Hegel, and Marx (2008), *Foucault and the Indefinite Work of Freedom* (2012), and *The Elective Mind: Philosophy and the Undergraduate Degree* (2021), all published by the University of Ottawa Press.

Megan Fritts is Assistant Professor of Philosophy at University of Arkansas at Little Rock, USA. Her research interests focus on questions in philosophy of action, applied ethics, and nineteenth-century philosophy. She is the author of "Reasons Explanations (of Actions) as Structural Explanations," (2021) and "Evidence Through a Glass, Darkly" (2021).

Bennett Gilbert is adjunct Assistant Professor at Portland State University, USA, where he teaches philosophy, history, and philosophy of history. He is the author of *A Personalist Philosophy of History* (2019) and of *Power and Compassion: On Moral Force Ethics and Historical Change* (forthcoming), as well as numerous papers. Besides moral philosophy and philosophy of history, his interests include a broad range of the history of ideas, notably around the beginnings of print in Europe and at the turn of the eighteenth century.

Benda Hofmeyr is Full Professor of Philosophy at the University of Pretoria, South Africa. Her research interests fall within the broad ambit of contemporary Continental philosophy (especially thinkers following in the wake of Heidegger with emphasis on post-structuralism and phenomenology) with an enduring fascination for the inextricable entanglement of the ethical and the political. Apart from numerous articles and book chapters, she is author of *Ethics and Aesthetics in Foucault and Levinas* (2005), and editor of *Radical Passivity: Rethinking Ethical Agency in Levinas* (2009) and *The Wal-Mart Phenomenon: Resisting Neoliberal Power Through Art, Design and Theory* (2008). Most recently she published *Foucault and Governmentality: Living to Work in the Age of Control* (2022).

Nora Hämäläinen is Senior Researcher of Philosophy at the Centre for Ethics as Study in Human Value at the University of Pardubice, Czech Republic. Her research interests include ethics, moral personhood, moral change, moral anthropology, philosophy and literature, and philosophical method. She is the author of *Literature and Moral Theory* (Bloomsbury, 2015), *Descriptive Ethics: What does Moral Philosophy Know about Morality* (2016), and *Är Trump Postmodern: En essä om sanning och populism* (Förlaget M, 2019), and co-editor of *Language, Ethics and Animal Life: Wittgenstein and Beyond* (Bloomsbury, 2012) and *Reading Iris Murdoch's Metaphysics as a Guide to Morals* (2019).

Ethan Kleinberg is Class of 1958 Distinguished Professor of History and Letters at Wesleyan University and Editor-in-Chief of *History and Theory*. Kleinberg's scholarly work spans across the fields of history, philosophy, comparative literature, and religion. He is the author of *Generation Existential: Heidegger's Philosophy in France 1927–61* (2006), *Haunting History: For a Deconstructive Approach to the Past* (2017), and *Emmanuel Levinas's Talmudic Turn: Philosophy and Jewish Thought* (2021). His current book project focuses on what he calls "temporal anarchy"—the unrestrained mingling of past, present, and future—which can lead to an understanding of history that points us toward critical political and ethical action.

Jan-Ivar Lindén is Senior Researcher of Philosophy at Heidelberg University, Germany, and at the University of Helsinki, Finland. He is Director of the Centre for Historical Ontology. Recent publications are *Prolegomena zur historischen Ontologie* (2019), *Aristotle on Logic and Nature* (2019), and *To Understand What Is Happening: Essays on Historicity* (2021), as well as a work in Swedish on paradise and modernity (*Paradis och modernitet*, 2020). Currently he is working on the Swedish edition of Aristotle's *Metaphysics*.

Anne Sophie Meincke is Senior Research Fellow and Lecturer of Philosophy at the University of Vienna, Austria. Her research interests focus on metaphysics, philosophy of biology, philosophy of mind and action, and nineteenth- and twentieth-century European philosophy. She has published on personal identity, biological identity, process ontology, agency, and dispositions, thereby combining "analytic" and "continental" approaches. Her latest article is "One or Two? A Process View of Pregnancy" (2021).

Takeshi Morisato is Lecturer of Non-Western Philosophy at the University of Edinburgh, Scotland. He currently serves as the editor of the *European Journal of Japanese Philosophy* (EJJP), the book series, "Studies in Japanese Philosophy" and "Asian Philosophical Texts". Additionally, he works as the regional editor of the "Bloomsbury Introduction to World Philosophies" (Bloomsbury) and the associate editor of the *Journal of East Asian Philosophy*. His publications include, *Faith and Reason in Continental and Japanese Philosophy* (Bloomsbury, 2019) and *Tanabe Hajime and The Kyoto School* (Bloomsbury, 2021). His research interests are metaphysics, philosophy of religion, the Kyoto School, metaxology, and world philosophies.

Rafael Pérez Baquero is Assistant Professor in Philosophy at the University of Murcia, Spain. His research interests focus on philosophy of history, memory studies, and transitional justice. His last publication was the book *Trauma, recuerdo y duelo: Una aproximación filosófica a las relaciones entre memoria e historia* (2021).

Hans Ruin is Professor of Philosophy at Södertörn University, Sweden. He is founder of the Södertörn philosophy department in 1999, co-founder of the Nordic Society for Phenomenology (and President 2014–2017). From 2010 to 2015 he was director of a multidisciplinary six-year research program "Time, Memory, and Representation." He serves as co-editor of the Swedish edition of Nietzsche's *Collected Works*. His recent books are *Being-with-the-dead: Burial, Ancestral Politics, and the Roots of Historical Consciousness* (2019); *Between Reduction and Reflection: Introduction to Husserl's Phenomenology* (in Swedish, 2020); and *In the Shadow of Reason: Essays on Nietzsche's Philosophy* (in Swedish, 2021).

Georgina Tuari Stewart is Associate Professor in Te Ara Poutama at Auckland University of Technology, Aotearoa (New Zealand). She is the author of the book *Māori Philosophy: Indigenous Thinking from Aotearoa* (Bloomsbury, 2020) that expounds a critical or Kaupapa Māori approach to investigating Māori knowledge. Stewart is also co-editor of the premier academic education journal of Aotearoa (New Zealand), *New Zealand Journal of Educational Studies*, and associate editor of the leading national science journal, *Journal of the Royal Society of New Zealand* and of the international journal *Educational Philosophy and Theory*.

Roberto Wu is Professor of Philosophy at Federal University of Santa Catarina, Brazil, and President of the Brazilian Society of Rhetoric (2021–2023). His research focuses on hermeneutics, phenomenology, rhetoric, philosophy of technology, and decoloniality. He is author of numerous papers and book chapters on Heidegger, Gadamer, and Levinas; and co-editor (with Cláudio Reichert do Nascimento) of *Pensar Ricoeur: Vida e Narração* (2016). He is currently working on a book concerning farness that is related to the chapter in this volume.

Acknowledgments

The rudimentary ideas for a joint project at the intersection of ethics and the philosophy of history sparked to life for us during a conference at the Centre for Philosophical Studies of History at the University of Oulu in 2017. Having presented at the same panel on ethics, we decided to elaborate these, in our view, underdeveloped concerns under the concept of an existential philosophy of history, derived from our own separate works in philosophical hermeneutics and personalism. In early 2020—feeling the ever so strong absence of the value of ethical life in philosophical discourse—we decided to try to initiate a volume consisting of a variety of existential perspectives that most strongly speak to the concerns that we esteem. This is the brief story of this book.

The present initiative to show the richness and depth of an existential approach in various areas of the philosophy of culture and history could not have been possible without all our colleagues and friends here who support and contribute to this work. Indeed we must recognize right at the start the extraordinary efforts of our contributors, as well as the efforts of those many scholars whom we have had the fortune to be in contact with during the course of this project. They all have had to persevere through illness, hospitalization, job insecurity, actual job loss, childbirth, home teaching, moving house, and family crises, as well as through the Covid-19 pandemic. The chapters in this book have their own inner histories; they do not spring to life without human labor and struggle. This must be said, for it is often one of those things that are left unsaid. We are immensely grateful to these scholars for their perseverance and cooperation in making this collection of their papers. Despite their being absorbed by numerous other tasks and concerns, they have patiently responded to our sometimes stubborn demands. In addition, they all have shown a love of this field of inquiry and collegial openness to writing papers to the highest standard.

We have also benefited from the friendly assistance of our editors at Bloomsbury Academic, Jade Grogan and Suzie Nash; and from a number of anonymous third-party readers whom we have consulted in the course of editing. We are very grateful for their advice and professionality.

One does nothing well without the support of colleagues. These include all the researchers and artists at the department of Philosophy at Åbo Akademi University, particularly Hugo Strandberg, Camilla Kronqvist, Ylva Gustafsson, Åsa Slotte, Alexander Öhman, Jonas Ahlskog, Göran Torrkulla, and Kalle Pihlainen; Otso Kortekangas at the department of History of Science, Technology, and Environment at the Royal Institute of Technology in Stockholm; Andreas Granberg at the department of Nordic History at Åbo Akademi University; Yrsa Neuman at the Open Science and Library administration of Åbo Akademi University; Professors Maurice Hamington, John Ott, and Albert Spencer of Portland State University; and Professor Allen Megill at the University of Virginia; the administrative staffs of the History and Philosophy

Departments, and of the University Studies Program at Portland State; and its indefatigable librarians, as well as many students. One does nothing without the support of friends. These include Nicholas Begley, Tommy Bourgeois, Jan Carpenter, Ülker Gokberk, Alex Pierson, and Finn Turner. And one does nothing at all without the inspiration of one's partners, Ada Elgabsi and Damien Jack.

Georgina Tuari Stewart's chapter includes words in Māori that are not italicized out of respect for the cultural political status of the Māori in Aotearoa (New Zealand). Ruth Behar's essay was presented at the Aboagora symposium, Turku, Finland, on August 18, 2011, and published as "The Death of the Angel: Reflections on the Relationship between Enlightenment and Enchantment in the Twenty-first Century," in *Temenos: Nordic Journal of Comparative Religion*, vol. 47, no. 1 (2011), 77–96. It is here reused by Behar with permission of The Finnish Society for the Study of Religion.

Introduction

Temporal Humanity

Involvement with Ethics and Time Across Cultures

Natan Elgabsi and Bennett Gilbert

Ethics and time are central to any vision of life and to every cultural worldview, guiding the life of works, rests, and days. The various traditions of our human world testify to the multitude of ways whereby ethics and time have been both vital parts of people's lives and the subject of speculative fascination. Fables and histories, as well as arts and crafts, are often responses to this temporal implication that a cultural tradition involves. Numerous ethical and temporal elements form a world in which a person is born and into which that person is existentially drawn. As we live in a situation, we also write and think from it. This life within is where thoughts belong.[1]

Thinking from where we stand in our own lives about ethics and time beyond the particularity of cultural traditions is a ravaging task. Frequently we find it a challenge to move outside of our presuppositions in a meaningful way. We lose sight of how our concepts steer us and how they can lock us into certain positions. Our inherited ideas might have a history of reification and conflict that we must do justice to whenever we lean on them.[2] Universalizing ideas of ethics and time are no exception. The struggle to reach beyond what is culturally particular can make us fail in realizing that such endeavors are also embedded in a tradition that all people do not necessarily share. For philosophical ethics this has become what Simon Critchley calls "the vast question," namely:

> can ethics be both generalizable and subjectively felt, both universalizable and rooted in our moral selfhood, or are these two halves of a dialectic that cannot be reconciled?[3]

This is a piercing question. Somehow we must be more humble in facing the truth that people live and see the world with their own eyes. Somehow we must see that other persons' "many interests and understandings of time," as Fredrik Barth says, "brings along that their life and reality will be essentially different from our own."[4] Differences and similarities between people often reside in the ways in which each person imagines her own and other's particular lives related to the temporality of a greater, interconnected whole. Cultural endowments and enculturation are sometimes very strong roots for these lived, ethical variations. In our philosophical attempts at coming to terms with the question of universality and selfhood, we will find ourselves at a disturbing nexus of ethics, culture, and time that will not leave us unengaged.

The hazards of a dialectical engagement between universality and ethical selfhood are ever tangible. Georgina Tuari Stewart shows in this volume that totalizing concepts not sensitive to cultural differences can very easily be oppressive. The normativity of "clock and calendar time" in the wake of a still persistent colonial clash of worldviews is, as Stewart argues from a Māori perspective, a concrete reality in societies in which colonial heritages and stigmatization are deeply integrated in people's daily lives. The politics of time—dominated by modern concepts aligned with an often dehumanizing ideology of productivity—is a social reality involving the stakes of oppression and recognition of the values of indigenous peoples, who wish to continue living a life in a traditional way. In the concrete social context of Aotearoa (New Zealand) certain universalizing ideas are directly congruent with historical oppression. How can we still continue to bear these manifestly problematic ideas? Perhaps the hermeneutic insight asked for through the challenge of postcolonial critique and cross-cultural philosophy, is precisely, as A. Raghuramaraju argues, to understand better where we ourselves stand in our inquiries when we say "we" and "they." We are responsible for reiterating and reusing the ideas of a "we" that we live with and imagine we share. But the "we" that we thought was uniform, perhaps never was so; and this insight destabilizes us.[5] If ethics and time should be regarded as anthropological universals, it becomes certainly imperative to support this notion of humanity that stresses the voice of cultural traditions that do not necessarily share "Western"[6] conceptions of time and ethics, realizing that these values and ways of life can be places of age-old dispute. We are also often torn between worldviews; and we can have a variety of incompatible visions of life, a kind of liminal experience that is all too familiar. Giving voice to cultural traditions on their own terms involves, as Stewart says, "the slippery path between romanticism and imperialism," which above all is a warm call for existential situatedness and conceptual clarity, the kind of self-awareness from which a friendly cultural crossing can spring.[7]

In the Western philosophical traditions, from which we as editors of this work write, one could delineate explicit connections between ethics and time that concern the historicity and temporality of humanity. One way to understand this notion of the temporality of humanity is, with Paul Ricoeur, to start with the sense that part of our self-understanding concerns our implication in temporal structures that are internal to the practical "language of 'doing something.'"[8] Ethics and time are thus directly bound together. Ricoeur expands Augustine's reflection on temporal existence in *Confessions*, particularly his notion of *distentio animi*, through Aristotle's central argument in *Poetics* that *mimesis* is an imitation of action by the means of a plot. This way temporality and its subsequent ethical demand on our apprehension are internal both to action and to the stories we tell.[9] We grasp, Ricoeur says, human activity under temporal conditions. The language of action supervenes on temporality. Temporal existence, in turn, requires us "to recognize in action temporal structures that call for narration,"[10] which furthermore means that narration brings us back to an apprehension of our own temporal implication. In this way, time, action, and narrative identity merges. As an "I" in acting needs a place to act here and now, there is no action without a temporally extended "I" who acts. There is no action without a prior context and a posterior consequence. This is the situation of the temporal self, which involves an ethics of personal integrity. For, as Ricoeur says in a related discussion, in ethics it is the "I" who must be able to act, who cannot lose the capacity to do something "on behalf of others" or "out of *regard* of others."[11] The violation of this capacity for action is, in some respects, a denial of temporality, which takes an ethical detour as the experience of "a violation of self-integrity."[12] Temporal distention constituting agentive capability is internally connected to the ethics of the self, universalized to a philosophy of action.

In Ricoeur's philosophical anthropology, the temporality of an agentive "I," in turn, merges with the temporality of humanity through the stories we tell about those time-bound implications in which we realize ethical situatedness. The result is what Ricoeur calls "historical time," in which our "narrative being" stands at the level of action because our relations to one another, our social life, is narrativized.[13] The "call for narration" then stems from temporality as the mode of our existence in which we act. This is how the language of action is connected to the language of storytelling and description that we use in our lived acts of remembering and interpreting what is done and what has happened. The agentive view exemplified by Ricoeur is thus one way of explicating the relationships between temporality and ethics, and it can be enlarged by other experiences and examples from various traditions and life contexts.

Many of the contributors to this volume stress those dimensions of the relationship between ethics and time that differ (sometimes quite radically) from this agentive vision of the capability of an "I," extended onto "historical time." They do so from a variety of predicaments and experiences. Narrating historically cannot be well conceived, as Rafael Pérez Baquero argues in his paper, without being challenged by personal experiences and feelings, even those that are hardest to bear. Historical temporality ruthlessly concludes that wounds heal in time, that traumas are worked through, and that persons who cannot go on in time are to be regarded as weak, anachronistic, or even pathological subjects that prevent social reconciliation. The melancholic wish to undo time, to "make whole what has been smashed,"[14] not as a wish to gather the pieces and move on but rather as a wish for it to never have happened to anyone at all, is, as Pérez Baquero shows, the way ethics counteracts history. Resentful and melancholic subjects, who live on in time but who are dead inside, are the living testimonies of what historical time can neither do justice to nor heal.

In a different dissent from the agentive view, Megan Fritts in her paper argues that something other than the active and evanescent present might add a decisive hope to our ethical stance. If our lives are marked by relations to each other, the loss of one part in that relation is a severe loss of our selfhood. This relation between persons is not circumscribed as agentive and is not necessarily dependent on a before and after death. It places another temporality into view. Still, mortality as such testifies that our humanity is temporal; the immanence of nothingness is conclusive for us, as Takeshi Morisato claims in his study of Tanabe Hajime. The question is, how do we continue to live with the dead in a social life that is shared? The relation between life and death is, in Morisato's reading of traditional Buddhist texts, not an either-or question; the one we commemorate is "not to be spoken as (it is) life, and not to be spoken as (it is) death." The generational, social life that is aware of our interwoven existence will not speak of the other in the coffin in that way. Finitude, as Anne Sophie Meincke argues, also structures our continuous personal identity as a process in which we learn who we are. In her view this is a matter of organic self-stabilization, and not necessarily a question of narrativity or agency. The past—a life with the dead, a life with those having been—presses back on us in a way that should have the capacity to liberate us from a too narrow presentist understanding. And we need to ask, with Ethan Kleinberg, do the ghosts enjoin us into an ethical relationship with the past?

The historicization of ethical life can have many implications of these sorts. Some of these implications split up universalizing views of ethics and time and touch upon a traditional metaphysical struggle in Western thought, namely the debate over the temporalization of ethics, which has often concerned how to understand the supposedly universal ethical essence of humanity. The struggle is over the question of whether the ethical essence of humanity changes in concert with the ways in which manners and moral norms evolve.[15] Immanuel Kant's and Johann Gottfried Herder's opposing views are in many ways characteristic of the metaphysical divide that has continued to inform the modern philosophical and anthropological ideas about the temporality of humanity. In contrast to enlightenment philosophers such as Voltaire, Herder contended in his "philosophy of the history of humankind" that historically and geographically different people were not immoral savages, but rather that all peoples and tribes strive toward actualizing the potentiality of their "humanity" in their own distinct ways, gathered by the tribes' own life of familial entanglements and compassion to one another.[16] Kant, in turn, counteracted this tribalism in several texts (and with increasing directness in his later years), most prominently by explicating "a universal history with a cosmopolitan aim," suggesting that humankind en masse needs to strive toward realizing how a life in reason obliges any human being to acknowledge the moral imperative.[17] In Kant's view this progressive realization of the ethical demands of a life in reason is also the answer to the question, "What is enlightenment?"[18] G. W. F Hegel, among many philosophers who inherited ideas from Kant and Herder, developed moral progress in a way that suggested the liberatory potential of life lived according to the historical trajectory of self-conscious reason.[19]

These concerns with the historicity of the ethical life and character of humanity—and with how the ideas of moral progress and ethical ideality should be understood—are also the original concerns of the concept of a *philosophy of history*. In a variety of ways, historicization through a philosophy of history forms a challenge to the metaphysical concept of humanity often understood in Western theological and philosophical traditions as having an atemporal and ethical essence. The biblical narrative that humans are formed to the image of God but have fallen, or the contention of Thomas Hobbes that we are essentially *homo homini lupus* but find mutual benefit and create social contracts for increasing cooperation, are examples of metaphysical ideas about the atemporal essence of humanity that are challenged by a more profound historicity in the wake of the clash between enlightenment and proto-romantic thinkers.[20]

The historization of ethics, as Knud Ejler Løgstrup puts it in his critique of historical relativity, means that "we learn from history that the morality and order we know today have not always existed."[21] Through an understanding of time, Løgstrup continues, we may see that "our morality and order too will totter," sometimes inviting the consequence "that when we learn that that which is good today was bad two hundred years ago, then we are no longer in duty bound to do that which is good today."[22] A further possible implication related to the historicity of ethical life is our tendency to think that we can "at any time do away with our morality and order and replace it with another."[23] Løgstrup anticipates irresponsible attitudes connected to the historization of ethics. But then we need to ask if a consequent form of indifference truly is the mode that a temporal consciousness invites. The contributors of this volume show that historization does not necessarily invite irresponsibility. The relationship to time established by universals, though necessary to ethical thought, must be rooted in our relationship to the variety of cultural and historical circumstances of individuals and of collectives.[24] As Benda Hofmeyr suggests in her paper, the contradictions of our temporal existence can lead to pathological concepts of time exactly because we do not live in only one temporal relation. Far from leading to indifference, an understanding of this risk for "chronopathology" can sharpen our ethical sensitivity. To be a *temporal humanity* means exactly to be subject to variation and change in a way that can break up simplified, metaphysical uniformities of human nature.

And yet along with this, temporalization can be a basis for grasping a generalized ethical character for humanity, whether in permanent or transitory forms. As Jan-Ivar Lindén shows in his discussion of historical ontology, we seek meaningfulness through the identity and change patterns of historical awareness. To try to elucidate the temporality of humanity by reflecting on ethics and time from a variety of perspectives is, as we have noted, inevitably challenged by these difficult modes of our existence. But it is also to recognize that whether we historicize in terms of permanence or transition or in terms of continuity or discontinuity, we do it as responsive selves discursively relating to a transgenerational world in which temporally other persons are already there. Historicization calls us into an understanding of ourselves in this relationship with absent, often dead others. "If," Løgstrup says, "we were to lose the tradition in which we were reared and which has shaped us, we would lose ourselves."[25] Such loss means that a loss of ethical-temporal implication is a loss of where we stand, the loss of a past we cannot disavow and ought not cease to respond to—a responsibility to the other to which temporality binds us that is re-actualized in our personal lives. For Løgstrup the ethical demand we face is not circumscribed by our subjectivity. Instead, it is an absolute reality of our interpersonal relationship because it comes not only from outside us but also from before us—from the time before that in which we live and the subjectivity with which we face the world present to each of us.[26] What can there be prior in time to the subjective moral agent? The answer is simple but immense: the demand comes from those who lived before us, actualized in what has been thought and done.[27] The population of these others extends to the whole humankind that is the most utterly and weightily real care and concern.[28]

Such precedence is the context in which we live. The passage of time yielding precedence becomes the tradition in which we find or face ethical obligation to others. The vital retention of this tradition as ethical responsiveness through the temporality of narration thus centers upon ethical self-understanding—a kind of advanced storytelling about who we are. Hans Ruin's essay demonstrates the continuing pressure of keeping hold of the past at the highest possible level. But is this the task of a science? The heritage industry, as Ruin shows, is an endeavor that is not always a responsible retention of tradition. We let a new genealogical science driven by antiquarian satisfactions preserve the past so that it should not vanish, but its objects are placed in the biobanks or museums as curiosities for a presentist ego. In our techno-scientific culture it is indeed easy to think that the human ethical character—as both a final goal and a supreme puzzle—requires a synthesis of the *theoria* that a scientific worldview has at disposal. In more than one way this is a misunderstanding. Insofar as the fundamentals of human existence interweaves not only the knowledge production of a scientific worldview but all kinds of knowledge that transpire in different ways of life, the human sciences address something uniquely vast and not easily or simply connected to our own involvement.

Still, the wisdom about human life that is sought in the human sciences is often expected to become an absolute, atemporal, object, as if it were the object of a science that we can peel apart and explain without realizing that the object is neither amoral nor atemporal. It would not even always be right to call the human phenomena that we relate to in the human sciences objects of inquiry as they are entangled in other real persons often living or having lived in other cultural and temporal circumstances. That is to say, as Ruth Behar shows in her existential-anthropological reflection that concludes this book, we will stand in relation to vulnerable persons with whose lives we become involved through our listening and our telling of their stories.[29]

A relationship with the people we come to write about can arise from differing kinds of temporal sharedness, such as temporal distance or proximity. Temporal distance, Nora Hämäläinen claims in this volume, can be "helpful for making philosophical sense of the complexities, tensions, and dynamics of past as well as present moral lives." Withholding judgmental attitudes in favor of engaging with the concrete difficulties that other persons experience in their lived circumstances can shed new light on our own ethical and temporal situation. This attitude is not only crucial for the human sciences but is also ethically important in our concrete lives with other persons. We have a situatedness that we cannot disavow. But temporal implication in terms of distance, as Réal Fillion and Roberto Wu argue here, can also be an ethical pressure, even if the distant call springs from a particular historical event that intertwines our own life; or concerns the general ethical call from the immemorial past with regard to what has happened. These are ways in which we hear an ethical call—a murmur—that addresses us from afar. In our lives it calls us to respond to another who has lived. It calls us to ethical action and justice and to seeking how we should continue to live with these voices.

In this light, one could say that we chase an illusion about absolute objects under the conditions of ceaseless change with which transient circumstances challenge us. Whenever we take on knowledge as having the character of absoluteness, it is absoluteness itself that becomes a problem. It is the supreme entrainment into which understanding ourselves pulls us that leads to that confusion which is generated by inquiries aiming at the absolute. Reflecting on this issue, Hans-Georg Gadamer asks,

> Is not the very concept of an "absolute object" a contradiction in terms? Neither the biological nor the physical universe can, in fact, deny its concrete existential relativity.[30]

Speaking of the "absolute" primarily refers to the factual and neutral objectivity for which empirical investigation aims, and yet it also must refer to any system of universal logical explanation. The "object," in turn, refers to that to which we address inquiry and understanding, since Gadamer also argues that no existent can be an object in itself unless it is an object of understanding. In this sense no knowledge of the world around us and of ourselves can be an absolute object of science because any such study is undertaken from the human perspective, or more exactly, from the perspective of a person inquiring. Our understanding of our world has therefore the open-ended incompleteness of our self-knowledge and necessarily the ethical involvement of relationality.[31]

Gadamer's striking name for what the universe itself cannot deny is "its concrete existential relativity." Whose relativity is this, and why does he talk about the universe as an agent? It is the concept of the absolute object of which the concrete existential relativity cannot be denied. The agent, however, is not the universe but is the human implicated in the physical and biological world, whose most earnest claim to an absolute position is belied by the relativity of humanity—that is, by our contingency and fragility. This existentially relative "object"—that is, the subject of history—is in ceaseless change through which it experiences the fundamentals of its existence. These, in turn, though relative in the sense of being specific to individuals, to collectives, and to society, and interwoven among human lives and groups in various ways, are absolute in the sense of being parts of a whole in which one person's life, or the life of a social world, or life as such must be understood.

The historical-hermeneutic account invites a different sense of absoluteness and objectivity from the customary scientific ideas suggesting that objectivity is detached from ethical engagement and is a view from nowhere.[32] Objective knowledge is in most accounts said to have absolute value without regard to the human standpoint by which we must face the people we live with. Ethical understanding, in turn, is inconceivable without that standpoint, and yet at the same time it is also inconceivable without some capacity to bring rational judgment to bear on the varied specifics of human affairs.[33] From this standpoint we do not seek to grasp a timeless objectivity, but rather to live and be nourished by the fraught temporality that involves ourselves extended by action over time to our predecessors and successors as well as to our contemporaries in the next hours of the life we jointly live. We act as limited and finite beings, and yet we also surmount time by persisting in reflection on the lessons our fragility teaches us over generations. Today the dynamics of the collective identity and action that collective memory supports are, as Jeffrey Barasch argues in his contribution, more fraught and deeply stressed than ever, leading to the need for a new approach. And as Chiel van den Akker concludes, the domain of our collective ethical responsibility now extends to a nearly overwhelming, very demanding universality. Understanding the fundamentals of being human comprises both living as humans and then in time reflecting on our living.

Philosophy of history is conventionally divided into the speculative and the critical or, in other formulations, the speculative/metaphysical, and the empirical/epistemological forms.[34] But the kind we explore throughout this volume is different from both of these, as it has neither a speculative-metaphysical nor an empiricoepistemological point of reference. It is existential and responds to core problems at the intersection of time, culture, and ethics. What we have brought forward in this introduction is our view that ethical deliberation and life essentially involves *temporal* understanding and self-knowledge. But we have also shown that discourses on temporality inevitably involve *ethical* self-knowledge, in the sense of how we should understand ourselves in a larger whole. Recent scholarly discourses sometimes touch upon this issue but often abandon it in favor of detached epistemic questions that do not recognize ethical situatedness, spoken and lived as if they were situated nowhere. The contributors of this volume, by contrast, take our existential situation as the sole possibility for ethical and temporal reflection. If it is the case that ethical and temporal self-knowledge are intimately connected, it means, on the one hand, that ethical reflection stands in need of historical understanding in terms of reflective hermeneutic consciousness that is subject to interpretative sensitivity. On the other hand, this means that historical understanding, or a temporal understanding in general, is also dependent upon deeper insights from philosophical ethics about how we should understand, describe, and narrate our relations with temporal others, over generations. Our ethical life is dynamic in general, diachronic in particular, and historical in its reality. Above all we need to recognize that our mortal ethical life is our largest historical narrative.

In the midst of the American Civil War in 1864, Emily Dickinson wrote to a friend:

> Sorrow seems more general than it did, and not the estate of a few persons, since the war began.... Every day life feels mightier, and what we have the power to be, more stupendous.[35]

Indeed, more stupendous are the evils and the good that we can do when we take in enough of the moving actuality of life so as to feel its mightiness. But have we not lost part of our sense of this today? Ethics stand in need of temporal insight and understanding both the detailed stories of lives, events, and societies and, as well, the many different metanarratives by which we live. It would include the highest-order metanarratives that inform our ethical awareness.

The fifteen contributors to this collection represent a very original and divergent spectrum when it comes to the philosophy of culture and history. The scholars work from within Western and non-Western philosophical traditions to explore four core questions that understanding this ethical-temporal implication presents:

> What is the ethical structure of historical discourse and experience?
> How does an ethical-temporal consciousness affect our agency?
> How do we think about finitude and mortality in relation to ethics?
> What is the ontology of the transgenerational reality called history?

These four questions correspond to the four substantial sections into which fourteen of the papers have been organized. The fifteenth paper forms a concluding reflection on the existential and temporal nature of doing research in the human sciences. The work of the scholars of each section, however, also exceeds these groupings: the papers in each group comment on issues arising from the questions the other groups address. All the chapters concern the ways in which humankind explores its common ethical temporality, as constituted by both universal and contingent elements. In concert in this collection, they advance the existential, phenomenological, and analytic approaches to human temporality, particularly with regard to philosophical reflection on history and historicity. They also advance questions of ethics and affect within the perspective of human temporality, and the consideration of these matters from a culturally specific to a cosmopolitan array of approaches.

* * *

Section I: What is the ethical structure of historical discourse and experience?

Realizing both temporal embeddedness and its ethical pressure on us often arises from personal, existential predicaments in our lives or in our scholarly practices. It is in the face of this concrete reality that we think and act. We are drawn into responding to the past, and we are forced to continue living inside that relation.

It is with this attitude that Réal Fillion in his "Past Deeds and the On-going Work of History," intertwines his personal experiences of living in a bilingual Canadian society and of being a scholar who discourses about the past of this society, with the acts of violence that are historically embedded in the languages of the social milieu in which people to this day live. His personal predicament of being genealogically torn between the francophone and indigenous Métis on the one hand and the anglophone foundation of the Canadian state on the other puts a stressful demand on the subject given the violence played out between these groups in the past, which culminated in the Canadian state's execution of Métis leader Louis Riel in 1885 on account of his proclaiming indigenous rights. The "murmurs" from the past that transpire in the language and the social milieu in which people live on testify to this violence on which society rests, which, according to Fillion, puts an ethical—what he calls a deconstructive—demand on our intellectual discourses of not only seeking knowledge of what has happened in the past but of responding to this violence. Being addressed by and responsibly responding to the voices from an unsettled past are internal to our ethical search for the "least violence."

The personal and societal memories that compel Fillion to responsibility toward past others are like the ghosts that, according to Ethan Kleinberg in his paper, command us to come to terms with past and future in a sustained but never-finished way. They give us a kind of knowledge that is real, though not positive; and understanding this knowledge is a task for philosophy of history that does not transgress its "proper" bounds. If it did, then the ethical demand on our knowledge of history and attitude toward it would evaporate, nor would any ethical action be required of us, even as we engaged in action with ethical consequences that we elide by confining history into the limits of a fixed past. "We clos[e] off . . . possible pasts," Kleinberg writes, "based on what we imagine to be the only pasts possible. In so doing, history is dominated by the presence of the present which tells the past what to be even as it continues to be haunted by the ghost of time." But Kleinberg wants "to reverse this movement and this temporal flow to put emphasis on the absent past that meets us . . . without reifying the reversal." His essay points us away from fixed traditional coordinates and toward different logics of history. These can enable the past to surge past our defences toward an anarchy that liberates our future.

In "Gifts from the Dead: Heritage and the Ligatures of History," Hans Ruin explores the phenomena of heritage or inheritance and, especially, how they envision ways of responding to a transgenerational bond that is inevitable in our social space with the dead. Inheritance, Ruin argues in line with Jacques Derrida, cannot in any simple way be regarded as volitional although we may have difficulties being the inheritors or even strong wishes to call people our ancestors, thus preserving certain cultural artifacts as our heritage. Ruin examines the larger cultural phenomenon of heritage through the quite recent discourse of heritage studies, which is based on institutional definitions of what the present ought to preserve. UNESCO's definitions of world heritage constitute an attitude to our inherited space as a response to what seems to vanish with an escalating rapidity. But, Ruin claims, these discourses also rest on an inherent "schizophrenic relation" to our past, "as both that from which the present is escaping in order to reach forward into the new and as that for which the present sees itself as responsible in order that it does not disappear in the process." We must learn to handle this schizophrenia in face of a transgenerational entanglement we cannot escape from. Ruin anatomizes the responsibilities that having a past imposes on a society.

Rafael Pérez Baquero shows an excruciatingly hard but real aspect of these responsibilities. In "Multilayered Temporalities Underlying Transitional Justice: Rethinking Resentment and Melancholia from Jean Améry and Walter Benjamin," he examines the temporal and ethical foundations on which transitional justice initiatives are grounded. In the aftermath of atrocities, reparations politics and transitional justice initiatives are sought to create a place for reconciliation so that the society can be restabilized and move on. In the wake of post–Second World War atrocities this process is usually called *Vergangenheitsbewältigung* and designates a sense of working through a traumatic past. Pérez Baquero argues that the temporality and ethics underlying transitional justice initiatives can be fundamentally challenged by the traumatic experiences that the victims have lived through. His examples are Jean Améry's expression of resentment and Walter Benjamin's melancholia. In the process of transitional justice these resentful and melancholic subjects are often regarded as "living anachronisms" who are "stranded in the past," thus preventing social reconciliation by their very inability to let go of the past. Pérez Baquero emphasizes our need to pay further attention to what it means in ethical terms that there are wounds that time cannot heal, and that transitional justice initiatives as a response to the past thus can bear a dimension of irresponsibility with regard to the victims.

* * *

Section II: How does an ethical-temporal consciousness affect our agency?

Insights from historical discourse and experience also invites other types of reflections regarding ethical agency in relation to the past. These reflections concern how we should understand ethical judgement and responsibility.

In "The Relativism of Historical Distance and the Contextual Constitution of Agency," Nora Hämäläinen argues that a certain "relativism of historical distance" can be philosophically and ethically helpful in order to understand persons who live their lives in different circumstances from our own. Hämäläinen starts out her discussion from Michele Moody-Adams's critique of the ethical relativism found in concrete anthropology and in the kind of descriptive ethics that draws on historical and anthropological varieties. In contrast to Moody-Adams, Hämäläinen argues that far from constituting an ethical laxity, withholding judgmental attitudes can be a way of better seeing the struggles that persons live with in their concrete lives and contexts. She takes examples from historical fiction which historicizes in such a way as to showing an alternative ethical world, and from Veena Das's ethnographic fieldwork that closely shows what the ordinary ethical negotiation looks like within a lived context. In order to understand what people are facing, Hämäläinen contends, we must not overlook their material conditions, social relations, and the historical trajectories underpinning a way of life.

And yet human ethical judgment is a universal practice and also seems to have an inner logic driving it to universal dimensions. In "Heroism, Self-determination, and Magnanimity: Hegel and Brandom on Self-conscious Agency," Chiel van den Akker provides an interpretation of several concepts of agency introduced by G. W. F. Hegel's historical movement of Spirit. In contrast to Robert Brandom, who argues that Hegel's notion of premodern versus modern ideas of self-conscious agency—and consequently blameworthiness/responsibility (*Schuld*)—reside in the distinction between heroic deed and intentional action, van den Akker claims that the distinction between the premodern and the modern is to be understood solely with regard to the question of self-consciousness and conscience. Ancient Greek tragedy—the archetype of the portrayal of heroic deeds in the sense that the tragic agent becomes blameworthy for what he unforeseeably did put into motion—is, according to van den Akker, reminiscent of the kind of blameworthiness and responsibility one sees in present-day tragedies as well. Intentional actions, in turn, are common to people across time. What the present age can learn from the heroic deed in tragedy, however, is a sense of self-consciousness and responsibility. The magnanimous (*edelmütige*) conception of agency is, van den Akker concludes, the third stage of Spirit—a postmodern state in which we are all complexly involved in each other's doings. This means that blameworthiness and responsibility can retrospectively be induced by others far beyond the subject's intention.

Agency, one could say, is embedded in historicity. Roberto Wu takes up this problem by considering what is very "far" beyond our local perspective. In "Farness and Immemorial Time: An Ontology of Vestiges," Wu explores the phenomenology of the vestige, by arguing that "events, in contrast to mere occurrences of nature, convey expressions of alterities as vestiges" that do not make present the past but rather involve a dimension of farness. Physical remnants such a cellar of torture, Wu argues in a discussion of Brazil's dictatorial past, can have an indexical function; but this is not the same thing as considering this cellar and all traces there as vestiges. The torture room involves layers and layers of a past that are deep and unrecoverable: the tortured people, their families who cared for them, others that have lived in the same situations, and so on. "As a palimpsest with countless layers," Wu contends, "each investigation finds more and more expressions of past others." Thus the vestige belongs to a temporality that, with Emmanuel Levinas, is called the "immemorial past" and should not be conveyed as a present-at-hand or indexed through a metaphysics of presence. In line with Levinas, Wu elaborates "the experience of farness as the phenomenological counterpart for the ethical proximity with the other," with obvious ethical consequences.

* * *

Section III: How do we think about finitude and mortality in relation to ethics?

Our historical experience interweaves the abstract force, we call time, into everything that we do, especially because it brings or even supervenes on mortality. If there is an ethical structure to finitude, and to the extent that there is, it is important to engage with the existential difficulties it brings.

We come to an intensely close-up look at death, the supreme effect of time unique to each person, in the account of the thought and last days of the Japanese Buddhist phenomenologist Tanabe Hajime (1885–1962) that Takeshi Morisato provides in "Neither to Be, Nor not to Be: The Interrelation of Life and Death in Tanabe's Later Philosophy of Death." Tanabe held that death is an "indispensable moment" in constituting existence. Each person must locate the dialectical interaction of life with death in herself, so that her finitude comes to orient her toward others present and past, as well as toward herself. Morisato shows how Tanabe developed this from Zen principles and also in the context of the nuclear threat over post–Second World War Japan. For Tanabe, nothingness links us to love as it becomes self-negation and thereby compassion. Morisato shows us the rich line of thought by which Tanabe came to this understanding. But there is something here in addition to thought: Morisato narrates the remarkable manner in which Tanabe implemented these principles in his relations to others, especially his wife, at the end of his life.

When, on the other hand, one is not concerned with her own death, she nonetheless endures the loss of others at their deaths. In "Arresting Time's Arrow: Death, Loss, and the Preservation of Real Union," Megan Fritts strongly argues that the deaths of others for whom we care forces confrontation over our ethical relations with the departed that affects our understanding of the temporal continuity of our own identities. How are we now single or multiple after having fused with someone no longer living? What is the metaphysical status of this union-in-remembrance? We allow ourselves to be lost with those we have lost: this is the route that Søren Kierkegaard's knight of faith takes.

Fritts develops this conception of an impossible union into a real existential necessity by transposing it over into the metaphysics and science of time. Here, the possibility of real relations with the actual departed beloved meets our growing awareness of the possible reversibility of time. But that to which we must really attend, Fritts says, is the concrete acts of love that we can continue by faith.

Anne Sophie Meincke creates another and novel approach to the effect of finite temporality on personhood in "Heidegger's Process Metaphysics of Personhood." Holding that identity is better understood through its processual continuity than through empirical data based on the puzzles of change that arise from the traditional ontology of substance and events, she reads the Martin Heidegger of *Being and Time* as a process thinker acting in opposition to thing-ontology. This in turn leads to a striking result: the importation of Heidegger's ethics of existential authenticity, developed in opposition to depersonalization and ignited by the dynamics of "forerunning" into mortality. Meincke develops a rich picture of personal identity as self-stabilization in and against these circumstances that is deeply connected to the way in which organisms seek homeostasis in order to flourish against the fragmentation and loss of identity in inauthenticity. Thus personal identity is an authentic unfolding self-realization, to be achieved rather than given. Hence our historicity, so famously centered by Heidegger, becomes the actuality of our ethical response to time. But this form of identity must be distinguished from anything psychological or empirical. It is, instead, "resoluteness" to persist in maintaining Dasein amidst a distracting world. And it is, in Meincke's view, the interactive relations of organisms to themselves and to their societies.

* * *

Section IV: What is the ontology of the transgenerational reality called history?

History—human generational time—is necessarily a manifold, a caravanserai, an infinite tableau of particular behaviors in response to the basic conditions of our existence and their local manifestations. It is comprised of that which each generation hands down to its successors, constrained by the ways in which they remember the past, and thereby changing in accord with memory and new conditions. As ontology aims to understand existence at the highest conceptual level, it must face the complex specificity of human culture.

In "'When the time is right...' In the Māori World" Georgina Tuari Stewart starts us on the road to understanding how the thought of the Māori of Aotearoa (New Zealand) understands the roots of ethics in temporality. This grows from Māori cognitive resources and from the experiences of this people that are both ancient and also deeply affected by the colonization and repression of the last five centuries. The Māori see a genealogical structure in the universe, necessarily transgenerational; in it, we face the past forward in front of us and all around us, including in our environment. Honesty, compassion, and all right action derive from this. It is of particular interest that Stewart carefully untangles the difficulties of translation between language, cultures, and philosophical traditions necessary for understanding others. In addition, she shows all of this in the context of the place of Māori in the politics of a multicultural society, including the ways in which they achieve or cannot achieve recognition. And she brings to this a very clear and present description of her upbringing in a Māori worldview.

Another dissent from the dominant tradition of Western metaphysics arises from the work of Emmanuel Levinas, who both follows Heidegger's lines of thought and disagrees with it. Levinas's interests in time and history have grown to be of increasing interest. Here Benda Hofmeyr relies on Levinas to examine "the fundamental chronological inconsistency of the human condition" in her paper "Levinas on Time: The Ethical Import of our Existential Chronological Inconsistency." The egoist finds time to be consistent and easy, but the ethical person recognizes the responsibility to which our conflicted temporality gives rise. For us each moment interrupts and confounds the flow of formalized time with our relationship to the Other that lies in infinite time. Doing justice to the other is an ethical responsibility both at odds with time and yet also caused by time. "The instant when I am confronted with the fragility of the face of the other revealed to me in its nakedness," Hofmeyr says, "is the saying, which belongs to a time of an immemorial past. It is fundamentally the time of the moral command." But our addiction to mechanical time so traps us and alienates us from responsibility to others that it is what Hofmeyr calls our "chronopathology."

In "Historical Time, Collective Memory, and the Finitude of Historical Understanding" Jeffrey Barash carries the widening of perspective we see in Stewart's and Hofmeyr's papers to its important consequences. As thoughtful people have become more aware of the variety of perspectives on the consequences of temporality and aware as well of how limited our understanding of temporalities other than our own can be, their perception of temporality changes. This is leading to a more globalized perspective. And in turn the ways in which groups use collective memory to cohere amidst the immanence of fragmentation further alters reliance on continuities in the historical meaningfulness of existence. Transgenerational projects thus become both more insistent and more fraught as to the problematic ways in which we try to hold on to the past, the effort to come to grips with finitude as our ethical condition, and the fate of humankind. Barash presents all this through a rich survey of traditional Western ontologies of history, the work of Reinhart Koselleck and François Hartog, and the development of memory studies.

All these things taken together show us how rich the affective impact of temporal humanity on our lives is. In "The Time of History" Jan-Ivar Lindén draws out the implications of this for the understanding of our experience that the ontology of past time can give us. Affectively, we can move about in time as a hermeneutic circle in ways that are otherwise closed to us by predetermination. Although we are limited by conditions, affects deepen the intensity of our temporal experience. We find richer patterns of "lived sameness" and can guide ourselves by them, as they demand something of us. According to this historical ontology we have a sort of atemporality and a sort of freedom at hand, through the access to reality that the past gives. And this, Lindén holds, saves the many possibilities of human endeavor in accord with the real world we inhabit, know, and make.

* * *

Indeed we also bring something into the world by our own engagement, we try to respond to what it means to live with others in it. Ruth Behar's "The Death of the Angel: In Search of a Tango of Temporal Humanity" forms a concluding reflection to this volume from the perspective of an existentially engaged ethnography. It stems from her own fieldwork, conducted mainly in the Spanish-speaking world, both autobiographically and ethnographically narrated. But Behar's insights reach far beyond the dialectic between biography and ethnography. One could say that the interpersonal relations in scholarly work that we retain and come back to over a course of a life—for example through ethnographic work over many years, but also in historical and philosophical intercourse with ideas of people bygone—is part of the existential meaning of what we do in the human sciences. "We are," Behar says, "not doctors who can fix broken bones or remove cancers from anyone's brain, nor are we novelists who can sweep you off your feet with a story about an adulteress who can not decide whether it is her husband or her lover who makes her more miserable." Instead, as Behar continues,

> Our greatest asset is our compassion, our ability to enter the stories of others with such thoroughness that they come to haunt not just our waking lives but our dreams as well. Unlike novelists, our imaginations are in service to real individuals and real communities that we come to know....

The analogy for this work is the tango; to be inside a relation, swept off your feet in a moment in life. Being temporally implicated, here and nowhere else. Is this not where thoughts belong?

* * *

Human life, we have said, is lived in time. It exists amidst ethical-temporal dilemmas constituted by an intricate situation of interpenetrating and overlapping our ordering, feeling, and intelligence. In each moment of time we view the infinitesimal and innumerable movements of our percepts, and in some of those moments we re-order what we experience and grasp it into knowledge. This ethical task of seeking to understand ourselves as part of a temporal humanity might often seem to ask of us more than we are capable of giving, especially in a vast universe in which our ethical concern with regard to others seems to have no special importance. Thomas Hardy said that

> at the framing of the terrestrial conditions there seemed never to have been contemplated such a development of emotional perceptiveness among the creatures subject to those conditions as that reached by thinking and educated humanity.[36]

Any time we cross the bridge of time to those who are far away or long ago, or even break up temporality, we realize the ethical entanglements of our kinship with them. What we hold important was always, and in some ways was, first suggested by what others hold important. This is an easy thread to lose as we try to push ourselves forward. It forces us to try to learn how temporality can turn the strict logic of our rational thinking about ethics into something that connects us with others and even with nature; and to try to learn a way that is practical, tolerant, and just, and that helps us to be good as well as right. Whether we call this ethical consciousness natural, or non-natural (emergent, continuous, or even intuitive), it is *sapience*—a feature special to the ethical aspect of our experience. We then also inhabit a possibility to reach across time, to the receding splinters of the past and to the future of our posterity that we begin to determine today.

Notes

1 Wilhelm Dilthey, "The Formation of the Historical World in the Human Sciences," in *Selected Works Volume III*, ed. Rudolf A. Makkreel and Frithjof Rodi (Princeton: Princeton University Press, 2002); see for instance his famous section on reflexive awareness and autobiography, 214–25. See also Michael D. Jackson, "Where Thoughts Belongs: An Anthropological Critique of the Project of Philosophy," *Anthropological Theory* 9, no. 3 (2009): 239.
2 Seyla Benhabib, "Another Universalism: On the Unity and Diversity of Human Rights," *Proceedings and Addresses of the American Philosophical Association* 81, no. 2 (2007): 8.
3 Simon Critchley, *Infinitely Demanding: Ethics of Commitment, Politics of Resistance* (London: Verso, 2007), 25.
4 Fredrik Barth, *Andres liv–Og vårt eget [The Life of Others–And Our Own]* (Oslo: Universitetsforlaget, 1991), 125, our translation.
5 Douglas L. Berger, Hans-Georg Moeller, A. Raghuramaraju, and Paul A. Roth, "Symposium: Does Cross-Cultural Philosophy Stand in Need of a Hermeneutic Expansion?" *Journal of World Philosophies* 2, no. 1 (2017): 132–4. A similar deconstructive argument is made by Michele Moody-Adams in *Fieldwork in Familiar Places: Morality, Culture, and Philosophy* (Cambridge, MA: Harvard University Press, 1997), 66–71.
6 It should be expressly stated that "Western" in the context of this volume is not to be understood as a monolith. The concept leads us to a place where it becomes difficult for us as editors to responsibly describe a philosophy of culture that is both cross-cultural and deconstructive at the same time—namely a work in which a part of our contributors speak out of ideas that they themselves call "non-Western" in relation to other ideas that are exemplifications of "Western" thought, while yet others will disclose the multitude of temporal concepts inside "Western" and "non-Western" contexts of life. Both the cross-cultural and the deconstructive aspects are vital to the work that the contributors to this volume undertake. When we speak of "Western" we have tried to do justice to the fact that, for instance, the Māori do not experience themselves as having "Western" concepts of ethics and time linear time, "clock and calendar time," and so on, are typically practices and ideas brought about by a colonizing impact in the Aotearoa (New Zealand). We acknowledge that it can be problematic to use the notions of "Western" and "non-Western" concepts of ethics and time as they risk retaining stereotypical binaries that overshadow the fact that there are a multitude of differences inside what is sometimes labeled by those concepts. Thus, we have tried to use these concepts as sparsely as possible, minding their hazards at all times.

7. Georgina Tuari Stewart, *Māori Philosophy: Indigenous Thinking from the Aotearoa* (London: Bloomsbury, 2021), 16; Cf. Benhabib, "Another Universalism," 23.
8. Paul Ricoeur, *Time and Narrative: Volume 1*, trans. Kathleen McLaughlin and David Pellauer (Chicago: The University of Chicago Press, 1990), 54–7, quote from 57.
9. Ricoeur's line of reasoning in *Time and Narrative* seems to be an elaboration of Immanuel Kant's notion of temporality as the form of our apprehension of natural and moral causality. Cf. Immanuel Kant, "Critique of Pure Reason," in *The Cambridge Edition of the Works of Immanuel Kant: Critique of Pure Reason*, trans. and ed. Paul Guyer and Allen W. Wood (Cambridge: Cambridge University Press, 2000), A532–41/B560–9.
10. Ricoeur, *Time and Narrative: Volume 1*, 59.
11. Paul Ricoeur, *Oneself as Another*, trans. Kathleen Blamey (Chicago: The University of Chicago Press, 1994), 189.
12. Ricoeur, *Oneself as Another*, 190.
13. Ricoeur, *Time and Narrative: Volume 1*, 75. Cf. Paul Ricoeur, *Husserl: An Analysis of His Phenomenology*, trans. Edward G. Ballard (Evanston: Northwestern University Press, 1967), 111, 170–1.
14. Walter Benjamin, "Theses on the Philosophy of History," in *Illuminations*, trans. Harry Zohn, ed. Hannah Arendt (New York: Schocken Books, 2007), 257.
15. For the recent development of this growing trend within philosophical ethics, see Hanno Sauer, Charlie Blunden, Cecilie Eriksen, and Paul Rehren, "Moral Progress: Recent Developments," *Philosophy Compass* 16, no. 10 (2021): e12769.
16. See for instance Johann Gottfried Herder, *Outlines of a Philosophy of the History of Man*, trans. T. Churchill (New York: Bergman Publishers, 1800), 98–102.
17. Immanuel Kant, "Idea for a Universal History with a Cosmopolitan Aim," in *The Cambridge Edition of the Works of Immanuel Kant: Anthropology, History, and Education*, ed. Günter Zöller and Robert B. Lauden (Cambridge: Cambridge University Press, 2012), 116–9.
18. Immanuel Kant, "An Answer to the Question: What is Enlightenment?" in *The Cambridge Edition of the Works of Immanuel Kant: Practical Philosophy*, trans. and ed. Mary J. Gregor (Cambridge: Cambridge University Press, 1999), 21. See also Kant, "Idea for a Universal History," 111–2.
19. See for example G. W. F. Hegel, *Lectures on the Philosophy of World History*, trans. Hugh Barr Nisbet (Cambridge: Cambridge University Press, 2012), especially the elaborated second draft from 1830 named, "The Philosophical History of the World." In our volume, Chiel van den Akker scrutinizes morality and self-consciousness especially in connection with Hegel's philosophy of right.
20. The narratives of fallenness and social contract, of course, involve temporality in the sense that an event happens. But it could be debated if and to what extent the events of fallenness and social contract should be regarded as *deviations from* the human essence or as *changes of* the human essence. The metaphysics of original sin and social contract can indeed be understood in both ways.
21. Knud Ejler Løgstrup, *The Ethical Demand*, trans. Theodor I. Jensen, intro. Hans Fink and Alasdair MacIntyre (Notre Dame: University of Notre Dame Press, 1997), 101.
22. Løgstrup, *The Ethical Demand*, 101.
23. Løgstrup, *The Ethical Demand*, 101.
24. See for instance Benhabib, "Another Universalism," 13–9; Wim van Binsbergen, "Notes on the Fundamental Unity of Humankind," *Culture and Dialogue* 8, no. 1 (2020): 40–1.

25 Løgstrup, *The Ethical Demand*, 103.
26 This resembles Emmanuel Levinas's argument that proximity with the neighbor and responsibility refer to time immemorial. Emmanuel Levinas, *Otherwise than Being or Beyond Essence*, trans. Alphonso Lingis (Dordrecht: Springer, 1991), 47–8.
27 See also Edith Wyschogrod, *An Ethics of Remembering: History, Heterology, and the Nameless Others* (Chicago: The University of Chicago Press, 1998), 60–8.
28 This does not mean that relational ethics cannot concern a demand to care about the nonhuman world as well. See Bennett Gilbert, *A Personalist Philosophy of History* (London: Routledge, 2019), 66–8 and 70–1; and "Repairing Historicity," *Cosmos and History: The Journal of Natural and Social Philosophy* 16, no. 2 (2020): 54–75.
29 See also Ruth Behar, *The Vulnerable Observer: Anthropology That Breaks Your Heart* (Boston: Beacon Press, 1996), 1–34.
30 Hans-Georg Gadamer, *Truth and Method*, trans. Joel Weinsheimer and Donald G. Marshall (London: Continuum, 1989), 488.
31 Gadamer, *Truth and Method*, 354–5.
32 Charles Taylor, "Ethics and Ontology," *The Journal of Philosophy* 100, no. 6 (June, 2003): 309–10. See also Thomas Nagel, *The View from Nowhere* (New York: Oxford University Press, 1986), 69–71.
33 For an example of this ethical engagement in line with writing and reading history, see Marcia Sá Cavalcante Shuback, "Engaged History," in *The Ethos of History: Time and Responsibility*, ed. Stefan Helgesson and Jayne Svenungsson (New York: Berghahn, 2018), 164–7.
34 It needs to be noted that the categories of speculative/substantive philosophy of history versus critical philosophy of history are as such invented by analytically minded philosophers in the 1950s onward. As Jonas Ahlskog explains, the categorization functioned as a way of dismissing the substantive part of the philosophy of history as speculative metaphysics while the critical part was elevated to a respectable branch of epistemology. See Jonas Ahlskog, "The Idea of a Philosophy of History," *Rethinking History: The Journal of Theory and Practice* 22, no. 1 (2018): 86–104. It is in many ways an uneasy and even polemical categorization.
35 Emily Dickinson, *The Letters, Volume 2*, ed. T. H. Johnson (Cambridge: Belknap Press of Harvard University Press, 1958), 436 (#298).
36 Thomas Hardy, *Jude the Obscure* (New York: Penguin, 1998), 342.

Bibliography

Ahlskog, Jonas. "The Idea of a Philosophy of History." *Rethinking History: The Journal of Theory and Practice* 22, no. 1 (2018): 86–104.

Barth, Fredrik. *Andres liv–Og vårt eget [The Life of Others–And Our Own]*. Oslo: Universitetsforlaget, 1991.

Behar, Ruth. *The Vulnerable Observer: Anthropology That Breaks Your Heart*. Boston: Beacon Press, 1996.

Benhabib, Seyla. "Another Universalism: On The Unity and Diversity of Human Rights." *Proceedings and Addresses of the American Philosophical Association* 81, no. 2 (2007): 7–32.

Benjamin, Walter. "Theses on the Philosophy of History." In *Illuminations*, translated by Harry Zohn, edited and with an introduction by Hannah Arendt, 253–64. New York: Schocken Books, 2007.

Berger, Douglas L., Hans-Georg Moeller, A. Raghuramaraju, and Paul A. Roth. "Symposium: Does Cross-Cultural Philosophy Stand in Need of a Hermeneutic Expansion?" *Journal of World Philosophies* 2, no. 1 (2017): 121–43.

van Binsbergen, Wim. "Notes on the Fundamental Unity of Humankind." *Culture and Dialogue* 8, no. 1 (2020): 23–42.

Sá Cavalcante Shuback, Marcia. "Engaged History." In *The Ethos of History: Time and Responsibility*, edited by Stefan Helgesson and Jayne Svenungsson, 160–74. New York: Berghahn, 2018.

Critchley, Simon. *Infinitely Demanding: Ethics of Commitment, Politics of Resistance*. London: Verso, 2007.

Dickinson, Emily. *The Letters, Volume 2*. Edited by T. H. Johnson. Cambridge: Belknap Press of Harvard University Press, 1958.

Dilthey, Wilhelm. "The Formation of the Historical World in the Human Sciences." In *Selected Works Volume III*, edited by Rudolf A. Makkreel and Frithjof Rodi, 101–212. Princeton: Princeton University Press, 2002.

Gadamer, Hans-Georg. *Truth and Method*. Translated by Joel Weinsheimer and Donald G. Marshall. London: Continuum, 1989.

Gilbert, Bennett. *A Personalist Philosophy of History*. London: Routledge, 2019.

Gilbert, Bennett. "Repairing Historicity." *Cosmos and History: The Journal of Natural and Social Philosophy* 16, no. 2 (2020): 54–75.

Hardy, Thomas. *Jude the Obscure*. New York: Penguin, 1998.

Hegel, G. W. F. *Lectures on the Philosophy of World History*. Translated by Hugh Barr Nisbet. Cambridge: Cambridge University Press, 2012.

Herder, Johann Gottfried. *Outlines of a Philosophy of the History of Man*. Translated by T. Churchill. New York: Bergman Publishers, 1800.

Jackson, Michael D. "Where Thoughts Belongs: An Anthropological Critique of the Project of Philosophy." *Anthropological Theory* 9, no. 3 (2009): 235–51.

Kant, Immanuel. "An Answer to the Question: What is Enlightenment?" In *The Cambridge Edition of the Works of Immanuel Kant: Practical Philosophy*, translated and edited by Mary J. Gregor, 11–22. Cambridge: Cambridge University Press, 1999.

Kant, Immanuel. "Critique of Pure Reason." In *The Cambridge Edition of the Works of Immanuel Kant: Critique of Pure Reason*, translated and edited by Paul Guyer and Allen W. Wood. Cambridge: Cambridge University Press, 2000.

Kant, Immanuel. "Idea for a Universal History with a Cosmopolitan Aim." In *The Cambridge Edition of the Works of Immanuel Kant: Anthropology, History, and Education*, edited by Günter Zöller and Robert B. Lauden, 107–20. Cambridge: Cambridge University Press, 2012.

Levinas, Emmanuel. *Otherwise than Being or Beyond Essence*. Translated by Alphonso Lingis. Dordrecht: Springer, 1991.

Løgstrup, Knud Ejler. *The Ethical Demand*. Translated by Theodor I. Jensen. Introduction by Hans Fink and Alasdair MacIntyre. Notre Dame: University of Notre Dame Press, 1997.

Moody-Adams, Michele. *Fieldwork in Familiar Places: Morality, Culture, and Philosophy*. Cambridge: Harvard University Press, 1997.

Nagel, Thomas. *The View from Nowhere*. New York: Oxford University Press, 1986.

Ricoeur, Paul. *Husserl: An Analysis of His Phenomenology*. Translated by Edward G. Ballard. Evanston: Northwestern University Press, 1967.

Ricoeur, Paul. *Oneself as Another*. Translated by Kathleen Blamey. Chicago: The University of Chicago Press, 1994.

Ricoeur, Paul. *Time and Narrative: Volume 1*. Translated by Kathleen McLaughlin and David Pellauer. Chicago: The University of Chicago Press, 1990.

Sauer, Hanno, Charlie Blunden, Cecilie Eriksen, and Paul Rehren. "Moral Progress: Recent Developments." *Philosophy Compass* 16, no. 10 (2021): e12769.

Stewart, Georgina Tuari. *Māori Philosophy: Indigenous Thinking from the Aotearoa*. London: Bloomsbury, 2021.

Taylor, Charles. "Ethics and Ontology." *The Journal of Philosophy* 100, no. 6 (June, 2003): 305–20.

Wyschogrod, Edith. *An Ethics of Remembering: History, Heterology, and the Nameless Others*. Chicago: The University of Chicago Press, 1998.

Section I

History as Ethics

1

Past Deeds and the On-going Work of History

Réal Fillion

All of us, historians included, grow up in particular places, and are shaped by the experiences and events that shaped those places themselves, forming in each of us distinct sensibilities to the world. These sensibilities in turn give shape to the questions we pose not only in terms of the present configurations of that world, and the ethical lives they promote, but in terms that speak from the past if only we attend to them.

Introduction

I attribute the sense I have long had that the temporal dimension of my existence is distinctly historical, where making sense of it requires more than what the terms governing the present offer, to the accent in the name my parents gave me. It took quite a while to grow into the flick of its pen stroke, that otherwise satisfying second half of a check mark. In fact, I typically allowed myself to be called Ray by my English-speaking friends, most of them of francophone origin as well, simply because it was the mark of a minority status within my native Canadian province. And yet, prior to that particular adolescent self-consciousness, I enjoyed the affinity that accent had with the name of the street I grew up on, there its flourish more dramatically at its end: Taché. This is the name of the first Archbishop of Saint-Boniface; and, though I was not aware of it, the affinity actually had some depth, Taché being known for, amongst other things, identifying the scholarly potential of a young Louis Riel, the Métis leader to be discussed presently, and my own father had been singled out by the parish priest for his scholarly potential in the rural community he grew up in on land settled by his grandfather in the southern part of the relatively new province of Manitoba whose terms were negotiated under the leadership of the Métis. Here again another accent to note with its distinct historical inflection.

There was a more direct and immediate affinity with the street name itself, however, rather than with anything I could say about its bearer. Unlike most of the other streets in my neighborhood, unaccented for the most part, Taché Avenue bore its phenomenological significance for me in the very real fact that, unlike the other residential streets in my neighborhood, tucked in a bend of the Red River, it led the way to Saint-Boniface proper and what has lately been advertised as Winnipeg's

"French Quarter." I distinctly remember, as I accompanied my sister to piano lessons on Saturday mornings, being impressed by its length, well over a mile before it reached and crossed Provencher Boulevard. This latter was named after Saint-Boniface's first Bishop, whose mission beginning in 1818 was to convert Indigenous people to Catholicism thereby contributing to the somewhat fraught colonizing efforts recently underway in the area.

An Unsettled Past, or Murmurs of the Past

The Red River is never far from my mind when I am back in Saint-Boniface, retracing my steps along Taché Avenue, less because of its ancient status as a waterway and means of transportation of goods and livelihoods, than as a calming presence in a divided settlement, having often found myself along its banks as I contemplated my future. I seem to have internalized the divisions of that settlement, as two of the languages that formed its constitution continue to battle themselves out within me.

Indeed, the conflict of the two languages within me reproduces the conflicted character of the settlement itself and what is said about its past. Of course, this is not something unique to myself. We all embody within ourselves, even within our most intimate self-reflection, the expressions and words that others have used to deal with a surrounding world. As Leonard Lawlor has noted, in his book *From Violence to Speaking Out*,

> In order to hear myself speak at this very moment, I must make use of the same phonemes as I use in communication (even if this monologue is not vocalized externally through my mouth, even if it does not have the purpose of communication). It is an irreducible or essential necessity that the silent words I form contain repeatable traits. This irreducible necessity means that, when I speak to myself, I speak with the sounds of others. In other words, it means that I find in myself other voices, which come from the past: the many voices are in me. I cannot, it is impossible for me to hear myself speak all alone. There is always a very quiet "murmur" coming from the past. Others' voices contaminate the hearing of myself speaking. Just as my present moment is never immediate, my interior monologue is never simply my own.[1]

This phenomenological "necessity," as Lawlor calls it, had impressed itself upon me quite early perhaps because of the two languages I was made to speak, opening me up to the "murmurs" of the past, inviting me to attempt to render them more distinct or even simply to let their distinctiveness make itself felt, perhaps in a way more easily ignored by others whose mother tongue was the dominant language. For example, as I continue walking down Taché Avenue, I cross two busy one-way streets regulating the east/west flow through Saint-Boniface, the first called Marion Street bringing in traffic from across the river, the second called Goulet Street heading toward Winnipeg. While officially named for Maxime Goulet, who himself was named Minister of Agriculture in the Manitoba Legislature in 1880, the "murmur" of the name Goulet attaches to his brother

Elzéar. Prior to the creation of that legislature, Elzéar Goulet was part of a provisional government that constituted itself in 1869–1870 in response to what was shaping up to be a transaction between a private corporation (the Hudson's Bay Company) and the newly constituted federal state of Canada, securing for the latter the land claimed by the former, with virtually no consultation with its inhabitants. This government, under Métis's leadership, was provisional because its purpose was not to rule the territory but to interrupt the pending transaction and to voice the concerns of the actual inhabitants, most notably through a "List of Rights" to be respected by the state proposing to rule it.[2] It was, however, an armed resistance, the Métis being highly organized buffalo hunters, and Elzéar Goulet was a captain within its quasi-military configuration. But he also was a participant in what resembled court martial proceedings against an individual by the name of Thomas Scott for insubordination and rebellion against the provisional government which led to the latter's execution. While much has been written about the decision to execute Scott (and the manner in which it was done), more immediately for me, it is the "murmur" that persists from the manner in which Elzéar died that shapes my historical consciousness. Not long after the provisional government had disbanded and Canada officially recognized Manitoba as a province, he, having been struck in the head by one of the stones being pelted at him, drowned in the Red River he had plunged into in order to escape a throng of men who had identified him in a Winnipeg saloon, many of them being part of the military expedition Canada had sent to ensure the "peaceful" transition to its authority over the territory.

It seems to me that the violence evoked here—the execution and the drowning—is folded into the languages I was given to speak, shaping in so many ways the space of their utterance. To speak French or English (even to oneself as Lawlor notes) on either side of the Red River is inevitably accompanied by the murmur of these past deeds. That such past deeds linger is no doubt true in all locations, but it seems to me there is a particular haunting character to those that accompany the desire to "settle" already inhabited lands, perhaps because of their relatively recent occurrence in this part of the world, the terms of settlement still in play, as it were, even in the most random speech.

It is movement against this kind of peremptory "settler" claim and its pretension to "take possession" of lands already inhabited that helped constitute the Métis as a distinct people and nation[3] and whose resurgent Indigenous presence[4] challenges the sense of the past that animated much of the historiography I was presented with growing up. That historiography only attended sporadically to the "murmur" that otherwise accompanied my historical consciousness of my surroundings, intent as it was on establishing consistent narratives out of select archival material. If I did not become the historian I had set out to be, it was largely because of the questions left either unanswered or inadequately treated by the work I would have been expected to do, questions that, instead, I eventually began to formulate in philosophical terms.

From the Epistemological to the Ethical

The philosophical questions raised by historiography are typically epistemological, but also ontological, aesthetic, and, most importantly, ethical. That is, historiography, writing about the past, does indeed raise distinct questions about the kinds of claims that are put forward, their status, how truthful they are, what kinds of inferences that can be drawn from them, what they can "tell" us about the past, whether or not what we are saying and writing about the past is "true," whether or not it counts as "knowledge." However, importantly, these epistemological questions are connected to ontological ones about the past itself which, in no longer being (present), raises questions about its very existence or persistence outside of our efforts to know it, that is, our effort to treat things within our present as evidence of it. This in turn shows how these efforts are productive and creative and thereby betray or embrace distinct aesthetics that themselves can recast the ontological and epistemological concerns just mentioned.[5] The most important questions for me, however, the ones that come closest to addressing the "murmur" of the voices of the past implicit in the very language(s) we use to express (and even to reflect upon) ourselves, are ethical. They engage how attentiveness (or lack of it) to the past involves our relations to each other in the present (or, alternatively, how our relations to each other in the present call for an attentiveness to the past) and in that sense also contribute to shaping the future.

Indeed, I will go further here. Even the more specialized interest in what evidence of the past can be made to say rests on a fundamentally ethical relation to the lives lived in that past within the terms explored by that interest. That is, the "object" of history is not *merely* one that solicits an investigative interest; as lives once lived themselves in ethical terms, shaping their distinctive character in terms of the possibilities they offered (and denied), they address us not only cognitively but emotionally, as beings living in a distinct but related time, however indirect that relation. We are the future to their own present and past, as we ourselves presently face our own uncertain future, continuing to shape by our deeds a distinct set of possibilities for living. And it is this uncertain future, and the current shape of our ethical life (*Sittlichkeit*), the possibilities it promotes and denies, that can attune us to the "murmur" of the having-been of past lives.[6] The on-going "work" of history, I want to claim, is this limited realization of these shapes of possible ethical lives and a call to respond to the violence that accompanies them, through a commitment less to a so-called "disinterested knowledge" than to an imperative to promote what Lawlor calls the "least violence."[7]

Distinct Approaches

Ironically, this work of history as a temporally unfolding (and failing) ethical project, while easily ignored by most of us caught up in a daily busyness, can be obscured by the explicit work of historians themselves. While anything but monolithic, the work of professional historians can be seen to take on distinct priorities; and I will follow Alun Munslow in his parsing of the field into the reconstructive, constructive, and deconstructive approaches to the past.[8] It is with these approaches in mind that, as I continue my walk down Taché Avenue and come up to the Saint-Boniface Museum housed in what was once the convent of the Grey Nuns, I stop before the bust of Louis

Riel (created by the artist Réal Bérard) as it stares out across Taché Avenue and the river, inviting all who contemplate it to consider what it could be said to see.

As mentioned above, Riel was an important Métis leader in the formation of the provisional government that interrupted a transfer of claimed ownership of land from the Hudson's Bay Company to the relatively recently constituted Canadian state which led to the creation of the province of Manitoba, thus introducing a new legislative context for regulating the interactions of inhabitants and newcomers. He was also tried by the State fifteen years later for his involvement in a second Métis resistance to the manner in which the State was appropriating Indigenous lands and disrupting the lives of its inhabitants. The charge was high treason (as defined in fourteenth-century Britain), carried with it the death penalty, and the trial was held in a unilingual jurisdiction that only required six jurors, thus maximizing the chances of conviction. Riel was found guilty; the jury recommended mercy; he was nevertheless hanged on November 16, 1885.[9]

The Lure of Reconstruction

As one might expect, much has been, and continues to be, written about Riel, and not only by historians.[10] The diversity of this interest is helpful, though, as it enables us to discern better what might animate a given *historian*'s efforts. Appealing to Munslow's division, one can first appreciate, let us call it, the *reconstructive lure* of giving as complete an account as possible of the determining factors of the events surrounding both the resistance and the eventual trial and execution. I would suggest that, for historians, the lure of reconstruction is founded on the sense that the objects of investigation, belonging to the past, in being linked to things *having been done*, are amenable to this kind of forensic treatment. But of course matters are not quite so simple. Already in qualifying some of the events as a "resistance" rather than, say, a "rebellion," one is engaging issues of ethics (in the characterization of the relations involved) and ontology (determining the nature of the objects of study, what it *is* that is under investigation).[11] While most historians are surely aware of this imbrication of epistemology, ontology, and ethics, the lure of reconstructing a past "as it was" tends to cloud this issue. That is, even when they recognize the evaluative dimension to their terminological choices, their professional engagement with the material tends to emphasize the epistemic character of those choices, the yield of "knowledge" they are meant to provide in a way that insufficiently engages both ontological and ethical questions. For example, when reading such reconstructive accounts, the repeated appeal to what the evidence allows the historian to say often tends to give that evidence an unwarranted *ontological* priority, as though revealing what most significantly and effectively *was* most real, rather than merely permitting what could be *said* about what is presumed to have been the reality investigated. As Frank Ankersmit has argued quite persuasively, even as we grant a reality to the past we re-present in our historical writing, that writing does so by focusing on *aspects* of that reality and it is important not to conflate the two when we consider these ostensible re-presentations (both as writers and as readers), taking the aspects foregrounded in the re-presentation as in some sense that reality re-presented.[12] That reality is indeed *referenced*, but as a past reality it still needs the *work* of re-presentation; such work will focus on *aspects* of that reality, never fully capturing the whole to which it nevertheless refers. Similarly, while there is clearly an ethical (and political) choice in emphasizing a series of interconnected social actions as a "rebellion" rather than "resistance," a reconstructive approach tends to assume these actions are "over," in some sense completed, rather than seeing them as rendered possible by a distinct form of ethical life in the past that implicitly is connected to the ethical life supporting its very investigation and characterization.

The possibility of conflating the aspects re-presented (or, as Ankersmit insists, *presented* to the reader) with the represented reality is compounded when the inevitably lacunar nature of the evidence leads the reconstructive historian to *restrict* an appreciation of the weight of that surrounding reality, as has arguably been done with the continuing Indigenous presence in and around the "settlement" at issue here, a real presence often absent in the written record, or present in limited perspectives.[13] An example of his slippage from epistemological warrant afforded by available evidence to ontological affirmation (or denial) can be found in a discussion of Thomas Scott proposed by J. M. Bumsted, perhaps because Scott's body was actually never recovered, adding another layer of presence and absence to the historical significance of his execution.[14] Much has been said about Thomas Scott's character in the attempt to account for his execution by the provisional government, including that he was a member of the Orange Order and that he was a particularly vocal adherent to its anti-Catholic creed. Bumsted argues that there is no actual evidence that Scott was a member of the Order and makes use of this lack of evidence to make the larger point that a lack of evidence exists to support many of the things said of Scott's alleged belligerence and, indeed, racism. While his argument does a good job of reminding readers that, even if it were true that Scott's character was as despicable as often alleged, this does not account for the decision to execute him. The *effect* of basing this argument on the reconstructive premises of providing evidence for one's claims appears to be to dismiss the reality of the belligerence and, indeed, racism that one can nevertheless imagine to have saturated those tense months in the settlement, expressing itself in subsequent events like the drowning of Elzéar Goulet.

Obviously, such a dismissal was not Bumsted's purpose. My claim is merely that such a dismissal is rendered possible by the reconstructive lure of historical work intent on "setting the record straight," as it were, which assumes an authoritative record to begin with. However, any "authoritativeness" to be granted to a record needs to be established, and indeed historians contribute to such establishment through their *constructive* efforts, efforts that include challenging other efforts at establishing a record as authoritative. Bumsted's purpose becomes much clearer when we see his effort as explicitly constructive rather than allegedly reconstructive in its appeal both to "the" evidence and the *lack* of evidence to make his point. To emphasize the constructed character of a historical work is to recognize that its epistemological character—what it yields as knowledge of the past—is premised on a number of aesthetic and ethical choices that frame the presentation of those aspects of the past being foregrounded.[15] Thus, Bumsted in revisiting "the" historical record in order to test certain claims made about Thomas Scott's character in the context of his eventual execution by the provisional government explicitly frames the discussion to foreground its ethical character: the injustice of that execution. This framing follows certain aesthetic choices, challenging either the "villainous" interpretation of Scott's character found in so many narratives of this fraught period or the narrative of his stature as a "martyr," by proposing a different way to see the person of Thomas Scott as, in the tense circumstances of the unfolding events, "expendable." Bumsted, by means of this aesthetic reframing, thus effectively makes his ethical point.

At the risk of generalizing too quickly from this single example, I think it allows us to appreciate the distinctive features of both reconstructive and constructive approaches to history as these relate to the epistemological, ontological, aesthetic, and ethical dimensions involved. Reconstructive approaches are clearly epistemologically committed, intent on making use of historical records both to make and to test claims about the past. This commitment to what can be demonstrated by the appeal to such records can, however, restrict the sense of the reality of that past, as those records will always only be partial witness to that reality. This partiality is of course recognized by the reconstructive historian, and compensatory methods are developed; but, insofar as these are explicitly in the service of a basic epistemological commitment, the ontological question of the reality of the past itself tends to be subordinated to that commitment. The effect of such subordination can be that the sense of that reality contracts. The genuine *we don't know/lack the evidence to state* of the epistemologically committed historian can betray an ontologically dubious commitment to a restricted sense of the reality of the past and, in its commitment to a kind of "objectivity" or "neutrality," can lead to a disingenuous deferral of addressing questions of on-going ethical import. The ethical life that sustains the historian, in maintaining certain archives and controlling their accessibility, for example, is implicitly solicited by the past deeds under investigation, which are themselves demonstrative of the (failing) parameters of that past ethical life. Whatever temporal (in the sense of chronological) distance there might be, it is the conditions for ethical life that are at issue, even when investigative efforts strive for impartiality.

The Constructive Appeal to Aesthetics

Questions of ethical import can be foregrounded by constructive approaches to the past, but what distinguishes them, I am suggesting, is their aesthetic framing of the issues they address. Indeed, as distinct from the epistemological commitment that animates a reconstructive approach to the past, which in some sense treats the past as given, the constructive approach fully recognizes its role in *shaping* the reality of the past through its re-presentations. Precisely because the past is not (immediately) given to us, what is counted as evidence of it is taken up in a way that aims to be aesthetically *compelling*. Indeed, one might say that the constructive historian here is as aesthetically compelled as the reconstructive historian is epistemologically committed. However, because constructive historians take on the explicit responsibility of shaping the reality of the past through their efforts, their works more obviously carry with them an ethical charge, due to the aesthetic choices made in the name of the past reality. Such a charge had been especially evident to me as I contemplated historical studies because of my two languages and the unsettled settlement I grew up in. It was obvious that events were constructed differently by the two language groups, as different actors and deeds were emphasized, leading to differently accented narratives, as it were. Interestingly, within the majority language narratives, the ethical charge seemed purposely reduced (often accompanied by the epistemological commitment and appeal to the limits of a *reconstructed* past), while in the minority language narratives, the ethical charge was on the contrary more explicitly embraced as was the narrative/aesthetic of the works themselves. This is perhaps not surprising as, in the minority context, most historians saw their role as serving a distinct community of readers.

However, as Kalle Pihlainen has argued, *reading* history carries with it its own responsibility, and as readers, we should not expect simply to be served a sense of the past, just as "we" should not assume the parameters of the "we" being addressed by the historian.[16] If the constructive approach is to be aesthetically *compelling*, it must do more than merely "inform" us about the past: it must *engage* the reader. I think Pihlainen is right to suggest that it will be more effective in this if the constructive effort seeks to *disturb* the reader, or rather, it is its manner of referencing the past that creates a disturbance within the reader's present. It is this reference to past lives as actually lived (distinct actualizations of ethical life) that distinguishes the historian's creative imaginative construction from the creative imagination that fuels more purely literary works. More specifically, the disturbance provoked by the constructive reference to the past is what Pilhainen argues needs to be communicated to the reader. This reference to a past reality, Pihlainen insists, has nothing "metaphysical" about it, for the "realness of history does not come," he tells us, "from the use of historical material but from the untameability of that material by story. And this untameability, in turn, stems not from the nature of the material but from the capacities and limitations of the historical narrative, the conditions governing its story formation."[17]

If it is the "untameability" of the material of history that confronts the historian, then I have been suggesting that it is the "murmur" of the past that confronts the would-be reader of history (as a speaking ethical agent within a present confronting its past, as I have been illustrating by my walk down Taché Avenue), that is, that can motivate her to consult historians and share in the responsibility of making sense of the past (a task we are, of course, free to disregard). Here, I think, the constructive approach to history, in its effort to be aesthetically compelling, despite the efforts of theorists like Pihlainen, does not always fully take up the ethical impetus behind the shared responsibility of writers and readers of history. Part of the reason for this is that the aesthetic project of constructive history, even as it references the past, betrays a kind of ontological ambivalence about its reality as past, wary as it is of the reconstructive lure of a past as it was. And while the constructive approach is more amenable to the ethical charge of its work, it still seems to me not fully to appreciate the ethical scope of engaging with the past in its haunting presence, evident in the "murmur" surrounding the words we speak.

A Deconstructive Imperative

Here is where a *deconstructive* approach to the past and the writing and reading of history becomes especially interesting. If, as I have been suggesting, a reconstructive approach to the past is epistemologically committed, and a constructive approach is aesthetically compelled, then a deconstructive approach for its part seems to me to be primarily *ethically* motivated. That is, its primary purpose is not to pretend to know the past, nor is it to propose an aesthetic engagement with representations of it, but it is, following Ethan Kleinberg, to acknowledge how both its present absence and its absent presence continues to shape our relations.[18] This acknowledgment is effected by means of a distinct form of reading and writing texts. Kleinberg follows Derrida in describing the deconstructive approach. He writes:

> In broad strokes the deconstructive strategy is to approach a text (historical or otherwise) as a site of contestation and struggle, where one tendency in that text asserts itself as the source of order and thus establishes a hierarchy of meaning. The hierarchy is constructed in an oppositional binary that is presented as neutral and thus conceals the organizing principle (good and evil is a simple one).[19]

That is the first move. It is then followed by exposing "the binary construct and arbitrary nature of the hierarchy by revealing an exchange of properties between the two tendencies."[20] As applied to history more generally, a deconstructive approach sees the contestation and struggle in the way the presence and absence of the past in our efforts to reckon with it manifests itself in just such hierarchies, most significantly "the hierarchical order that assumes facts take priority over imagination."[21] Such an appeal to "facts" privileges the hierarchical ordering of presence over absence which Kleinberg, having identified, therefore sets out to disturb.

This intent to "disturb" the reader likens Kleinberg's approach to Pihlainen's, as described above. However, I think we can distinguish an approach that appeals to history to unsettle present understandings through the construction of aesthetically compelling narratives from one that unsettles our present understandings through the deconstruction of the texts that accrue around those past deeds that "haunt" our present. If *de*construction is a kind of "*un*doing," it is one that confronts the "done" through the very texts that record it, showing the pastness of the done not to be "done" after all, but still resonant with questions and issues to be addressed in the present "doing" of social life. In the example developed here, the "unsettled" character of a presumed settlement and the "state" responsible for it.

Just past the Saint-Boniface Museum, further down Taché Avenue, stands Saint-Boniface Cathedral, notable for its truncated bell towers and empty rose window, the building having been destroyed by fire in 1968, a newer but smaller church now rebuilt in its ruins. Louis Riel is buried on the grounds, his grave as much a tourist destination as the Cathedral itself. As mentioned above, Riel was tried and executed by the relatively recently constituted (1867) Canadian state for "high" treason, rather than treason/felony as were other participants of the Métis resistance to the manner the state was re-organizing relations to the land. The ostensible reason for using the medieval statute was that it carried with it automatically a hanging sentence, which included, technically, the drawing and quartering of the body afterwards though the latter practice had "fallen into disuse in the nineteenth century."[22] Again, the trial and execution of Riel has generated an enormous amount of literature, including various detailed reconstructions of the events leading up to it and constructions that probe its continuing significance.[23] What I would like to do in these final paragraphs is to consider briefly in a deconstructive spirit two texts that we have, transcriptions of Riel's addresses, first, to the jury prior to the verdict and, second, to the court after the verdict.[24] By deconstructive *spirit*, I mean what I take to be the primary *ethical* motivation of reading texts, as distinct from epistemologically committed or aesthetically compelled approaches, discerning in them an imperative or a reorientation to a good otherwise absent, addressing the failures of distinct forms of ethical life. They are properly "haunting" texts, extraordinary not only in the fact that Riel himself felt the need literally to *undo* his defence team's strategy of getting him acquitted for reason of insanity (he did not want to spend the rest of his life in an asylum), but also in his standing up to *speak* of the momentous events that were reshaping the lives of so many people, most dramatically the Indigenous people of that part of the world at that time. They resonate distinctly in this time and place as anyone who calls themselves "Canadian" is challenged to consider their ethical relations with contemporary Indigenous peoples when "Canada" is understood through what was evidently a kind of aspirational genocide in its formation and expansion inasmuch as it was premised on a "clearing of the plains."[25]

Addressing the "worst violence"

These addresses reveal in a remarkable manner, through Riel's extraordinary attempt, not only to be understood and to understand the events he participated in, not only to justify his actions, but to measure the weight of the deeds that constitute them as events, how his own voice was in fact attuned to the many voices that accompany our words in our efforts to speak to one another. They are deconstructive words, in a sense, that attempt to undo the manner in which a done is imposing itself on a doing, a forced conversion of a doing into a done, of a present and a future being pressed into a past to be relegated as past. In the first address to the jury, before the verdict, Riel has to undo his defence's strategy (from a defence team he nevertheless seemed to feel obliged to, given their willingness to come all the way to Regina in order to defend him) of rendering him irresponsible by reason of insanity. The address attempts to deconstruct the binaries of reason/insanity and responsibility/irresponsibility not by directly challenging the implied hierarchy of the terms but through a number of attempted reversals (it was the state which was "insane" in refusing the reasonable claims of the Métis people, and it was the state which was "irresponsible" in refusing responsible government both in itself and in the territory it claimed to govern), unsettling the coherence and legitimacy of the very framework being used to charge him. Deconstructing these binaries involved speaking of his actions in terms of his "mission" to his people who, after all, sought him out in Montana, where he was living in exile while the question of an amnesty from the Canadian government was left unanswered, and asked him to join them in expressing their grievances to a government intent on imposing a settling framework alien to their way of life (a government ostensibly on its own "mission" to settle land long considered unfavorable to its preferred agricultural mode of settlement). While the expression of those grievances had been partly heard in Manitoba fifteen years earlier, the current silence they provoked needed to be deconstructed as well, as Riel spoke not only of his personal "mission" to his people but of the timeframe within which it needed to be understood, *a timeframe that did not include a future closing off the past.* He told the jury, it "is not to be supposed that the half-breeds acknowledged me as a prophet if they had not seen that I could see something into the future."[26] And then reminds them: "We all see into the future more or less"; and, countering those who would denigrate his prophetic abilities or turn them against him, he says: "If the half-breeds had acknowledged me as a prophet, if on the other side priests come and say I am polite, if there are general officers, good men, come into this box and prove that I am polite, prove that I am decent in my manner, in combining all together you have a decent prophet."[27] The jury of six white, Protestant men found him guilty as charged (thus confirming his sanity) and may have been moved by this "decency" when they recommended clemency.

Once the verdict was pronounced, Riel would have another chance to address the court. He would do so for three hours. Whether one thinks anyone was listening,[28] or one deems, like Thomas Flanagan, that the address was "long, rambling, disorganized, sometimes almost unintelligible,"[29] it seems to me its transcription as text illustrates powerfully the fragility but courage that a voice attuned to its surrounding murmur can express, especially as it confronts what Lawlor characterizes as the "worst violence," that is, "unconditional non-passage" which translates experientially as an "unconditional non-future, a way out that is not a way in, the end."[30] Lawlor immediately goes on to write in a voice that could have been Riel's:

> We must not believe in such a final event. Instead, the thought of unconditional passage must involve a belief in the future. In French of course the word for "future" is "avenir." We must then find a way to believe, not in some other world (like heaven), but in this world of other possibilities still to come, future possibilities. We must find a way to wait and to know how to wait for a land to come and a people to come (à venir), whose coming (venir) or becoming (devenir) would make the event of another world. Not only must our thought today be one of immanence and life, not only must our thought be a thought of the outside, it must also be a thought of the messianic. What we must wait for is not the Apocalypse and certainly not for a new celestial Jerusalem . . .; we must wait for an "elsewhere," a land (une terre) whose name is still lacking.[31]

If Lawlor's "we" here is anyone today, then Riel's address can indeed be seen as "prophetic" inasmuch as it spoke to the future in this way, speaking to and with the voices of a land not yet settled by the peremptory claims of a "settler nation" with its own future of promises made with no intention of keeping them, claims that try to close off the past as past. At the risk of reviving the question of his sanity, Riel speaks not only *against* "the worst violence" being imposed on him but *for* a principle of settlement, for an ethic that, as Lawlor suggests, seeks the "least violence." Riel builds on the actual "settlement" (as agreement) that led to the creation of the province of Manitoba, where something like "one-seventh" of the lands were to be set aside for the Métis inhabitants as indigenous to those lands, acknowledging their right, acknowledging the right of all people to a "spot of land" and the value of that land. As Riel says: "We are not birds. We have to walk on the ground, and that ground is encircled of many things, which besides its own value, increases its value in another manner, and when we cultivate it we still increase that value."[32] And yet, that principle of "one-seventh" was not respected, or at least it could not withstand the thrust of dispossession that accompanied the incoming settlers, breaking it down into scrip to be sold to relieve the pressure of the onslaught. Riel, faced with a sentence of the worst violence, used his voice to speak of a different form of settlement, one that respected the principle of "one-seventh" and talked about "inviting" the other nationalities flowing into the continent, "the Italians of the States, the Irish of the States, the Bavarians of the States, the Poles of the States, the Belgians of the States, and if they come and help us here to have the seventh, we will give them each a seventh."[33] The "we" in this sentence refers no doubt to the Indigenous inhabitants of the land whose voices Riel is attempting to speak even as he struggles to speak with his own, tying the "worst violence" he is faced with to the violence accompanying a mode of settlement that premises its own future on relegating the indigenous presence to the past. As he faces his own end, he speaks. He speaks of what he had written as he awaited his trial, both the one that was winding down, moving from the doing to the done, and the one he believed would be more just, thoughts of a "peaceful emigration" and his willingness "to start the idea, and if possible to inaugurate it, but if I can't do it during my life I leave the ideas to be fulfilled in the future,"[34] intuiting here the *à venir* that forever interrupts the relegation of the past to the past.[35]

I cannot return to my hometown without revisiting Taché Avenue, its pull something other than nostalgia. No doubt because it explicitly references its own history and in that sense has shaped my own distinct historical sensibility, it nevertheless bears witness to an unsettled past and the on-going problem of the "worst violence." But in light of the Indigenous presence that preceded it, and in light of a resurgent Indigenous presence re-affirming itself not only in settler nations like Canada but all over the world, revisiting it speaks to an accompanying absence.[36] And my suggestion has been that a past that is both present and absent challenges not only the reconstructive or constructive efforts of historians and their readers, but invites, as a deconstructive approach insists, an ethical reckoning from all of us, not with that past as past, but with a future our words, like Riel's, address as well.

Notes

1 Leonard Lawlor, *From Violence to Speaking Out: Apocalypse and Expression in Foucault, Derrida and Deleuze* (Edinburgh: Edinburgh University Press, 2016), 50.
2 For a general overview, see J. M. Bumsted, *Louis Riel v. Canada: The Making of a Rebel* (Winnipeg: Great Plains Publications, 2001).

3   For a very interesting discussion of the centrality of this struggle for the Métis people, see Chris Andersen, *"Métis": Race, Recognition, and the Struggle for Indigenous Peoplehood*' (Vancouver: University of British Columbia Press, 2016).
4   For a good discussion of the notion of Indigenous resurgence, see Leanne Betasamosake Simpson, *As We Have Always Done: Indigenous Freedom through Radical Resistance* (Minneapolis: University of Minnesota Press, 2017); and for Métis nationhood, see Jean Teillet, *The North-West is Our Mother: The Story of Louis Riel's People* (Toronto: Harper Collins, 2019).
5   The aesthetic dimension of history writing is masterfully explored by Hayden White, most thoroughly in his *Metahistory: The Historical Imagination in Nineteenth-Century Europe* (Baltimore: The John Hopkins University Press, 1973).
6   I use *Sittlichkeit* in Hegel's sense of the patterns of recognition that give shape to our social lives. See G. W. F. Hegel, *Philosophy of Right* (Oxford: Oxford University Press, 1952).
7   In explicit contrast to what he calls "the worst violence" which is a violence that "strives to close off the voice that is memory, without which it is impossible to dream about a future." Lawlor, *From Violence to Speaking Out*, 286.
8   Alun Munslow, *A History of History* (London: Routledge, 2012), especially chapter three.
9   For a recent account that questions the legitimacy of the trial, see Roger E. Salhany, *A Rush to Judgment: The Unfair Trial of Louis Riel* (Toronto: Dundurn Press, 2019).
10 For an interesting account of the diversity of the interest in Riel, see Albert Braz, *The False Traitor: Louis Riel in Canadian Culture* (Toronto: University of Toronto Press, 2003).
11 As in the classic account by G. F. Stanley, *The Birth of Western Canada: A History of the Riel Rebellions* (Toronto: University of Toronto Press, 1936).
12 Frank Ankersmit, *Meaning, Truth, and Reference in Historical Representation* (Ithaca: Cornell University Press, 2012).
13 The too quick assimilation of Metis and First Nations perspectives in the "resistance" is a good example of this. See Blair Stonechild and Bill Waiser, *Loyal Till Death: Indians and the North-West Rebellion* (Toronto: Fifth House Books, 2010).
14 J. M. Bumsted, *Thomas Scott's Body and Other Essays on Early Manitoba History* (Winnipeg: University of Manitoba Press, 2000).
15 This is a point well defended by Hayden White and ably taken up recently by Kalle Pihlainen, *The Work of History: Constructivism and a Politics of the Past* (London: Routledge, 2017).
16 Pihlainen, *The Work of History*, 69.
17 Pihlainen, *The Work of History*, 69.
18 Ethan Kleinberg, *Haunting History: For a Deconstructive Approach to the Past* (Stanford: Stanford University Press, 2017).
19 Kleinberg, *Haunting History*, 15.
20 Kleinberg, *Haunting History*, 15.
21 Kleinberg, *Haunting History*, 18.
22 Bumsted, *Louis Riel v. Canada*, 274.
23 See for example, Jennifer Reid, *Louis Riel and the Creation of Modern Canada: Mythic Discourse and the Postcolonial State* (Albuquerque: University of New Mexico Press, 2008).
24 Hans V. Hansen, ed., *Riel's Defence: Perspectives on his Speeches* (Montreal & Kingston: McGill-Queen's University Press, 2014), 25–44, 45–71.

25 James Daschuk, *The Clearing of the Plains: Disease, Politics of Starvation, and the Loss of Aboriginal Life* (Regina: University of Regina Press, 2019).
26 Hansen, *Riel's Defence*, 35.
27 Hansen, *Riel's Defence*, 35.
28 Salhany, *A Rush to Judgment*, 11.
29 Hansen, *Riel's Defence*, 106.
30 Lawlor, *From Violence to Speaking Out*, 20.
31 Lawlor, *From Violence to Speaking Out*, 20.
32 Hansen, *Riel's Defence*, 54.
33 Hansen, *Riel's Defence*, 51.
34 Hansen, *Riel's Defence*, 64.
35 Hansen, *Riel's Defence*, 64.
36 See for example, Michael Asch, John Borrows, and James Tully, ed. *Resurgence and Reconciliation: Indigenous Settler-Relations and Earth Teachings* (Toronto: University of Toronto Press, 2018).

Bibliography

Andersen, Chris. *"Métis": Race, Recognition, and the Struggle for Indigenous Peoplehood*. Vancouver: University of British Columbia Press, 2014.

Ankersmit, Frank. *Meaning, Truth, and Reference in Historical Representation*. Ithaca: Cornell University Press, 2012.

Asch, Michael, John Borrows, and James Tully, ed. *Resurgence and Reconciliation: Indigenous Settler-Relations and Earth Teachings*. Toronto: University of Toronto Press, 2018.

Braz, Albert. *The False Traitor: Louis Riel in Canadian Culture*. Toronto: University of Toronto Press, 2003.

Bumsted, J. M. *Louis Riel v. Canada: The Making of a Rebel*. Winnipeg: Great Plains Publications, 2001.

Bumsted, J. M. *Thomas Scott's Body and Other Essays on Early Manitoba History*. Winnipeg: University of Manitoba Press, 2000.

Daschuk, James. *The Clearing of the Plains: Disease, Politics of Starvation, and the Loss of Aboriginal Life*. Regina: University of Regina Press, 2019.

Friesen, Gerald. *The Canadian Prairies: A History*. Toronto: University of Toronto Press, 1987.

Hansen, Hans V., ed. *Riel's Defence: Perspectives on his Speeches*. Montreal & Kingston: McGill-Queen's University Press, 2014.

Hegel, G. W. F. *Philosophy of Right*. Translated by Thomas Malcolm Knox. Oxford: Oxford University Press, 1952.

Howard, Joseph Kinsey. *Strange Empire: Louis Riel and the Métis People*. Toronto: James Lorimer, 1974.

Kleinberg, Ethan. *Haunting History: For a Deconstructive Approach to the Past*. Stanford: Stanford University Press, 2017.

Lawlor, Leonard. *From Violence to Speaking Out: Apocalypse and Expression in Foucault, Derrida and Deleuze*. Edinburgh: Edinburgh University Press, 2016.

Morton, W.L. *Manitoba: A History*. Toronto: University of Toronto Press, 1967.

Munslow, Alun. *A History of History*. London: Routledge, 2012.

Pihlainen, Kalle. *The Work of History: Constructivism and a Politics of the Past*. London: Routledge, 2017.

Reid, Jennifer. *Louis Riel and the Creation of Modern Canada: Mythic Discourse and the Postcolonial State*. Albuquerque: University of New Mexico Press, 2008.

Salhany, Roger E. *A Rush to Judgment: The Unfair Trial of Louis Riel*. Toronto: Dundurn Press, 2019.

Simpson, Leanne Betasamosake. *As We Have Always Done: Indigenous Freedom through Radical Resistance*. Minneapolis: University of Minnesota Press, 2017.

Stanley, George F. G. *The Birth of Western Canada: A History of the Riel Rebellions*. Toronto: University of Toronto Press, 1936.

Stonechild, Blair and Bill Waiser. *Loyal Till Death: Indians and the North-West Rebellion*. Toronto: Fifth House Books, 2010.

Teillet, Jean. *The North-West is Our Mother: The Story of Louis Riel's People*. Toronto: Harper Collins, 2019.

de Trémaudan, Auguste-Henri. *Histoire de la Nation Métisse dans l'Ouest Canadien*. Saint-Boniface: Les éditions du Blé, 1979.

White, Hayden. *Metahistory: The Historical Imagination in Nineteenth-Century Europe*. Baltimore: The John Hopkins University Press, 1973.

2

The Time of Ghosts and the Ghosts of Time

Ethan Kleinberg

Enter the Ghosts

We are currently living amongst the ghosts of time. There was, however, in the not so distant past, a time of ghosts. This was a time when ghosts were taken quite literally as existing, if problematic, actors in our world. On this view, and in this belief system, the past came back in the form of these haunting specters. This is to say that at that time, the past was actually allowed to come back and the ghost was the means to literally do so. But, as I stated, in our time this is not entirely or even mostly the case because "the ghost" has undergone a semantic shift such that it has become a metaphor for the presence of the past in the present. This intermingling of temporal dimensions is quite different from the time of ghosts because here, it is the ghost of times or events past that haunt us wherein the ghost becomes the means of representing an untimely cohabitation whether this manifests as trauma, collective memory, or in the sorts of fictional accounts that I find so appealing and fecund. In both cases, the confrontation with the ghost is a confrontation with the past as a moral imperative commanding one to set right an injustice or wrong from the past.

In Shakespeare's *Hamlet*, the nature of the injustice as well as Hamlet's response to it depend on how we come to the play. In the time of ghosts, "time is out of joint" because of the untimely visitor from the past providing information from another realm beyond the human world. The emphasis is on the visitor urging Hamlet to right a past wrong thus restoring the order of time. To be sure, this is a Christian ghost, a male ghost, and an aristocratic ghost. The ghost of the European patriarch if you will but a literal visitor from the past who tasks Hamlet with the restoration of his line and sovereignty. If we change our lens and view the play as indicating the ghost of time, however, something quite different is signified. Hamlet's father becomes the site of Hamlet's *own* reckoning with the past. With a past that will not leave him, invading his present and pressing on his future. Here, it is the past itself that haunts Hamlet.

Hamlet's response to the ghost of his father's command, "Remember me," can be understood in either register.

> Ay thou poor ghost, while memory holds a seat
> In this distracted globe. Remember thee?

> Yea, from the table of my memory
> I'll wipe away all trivial fond records . . .
> And thy commandment all alone shall live
> Within the book and volume of my brain. . . .[1]

In the time of ghosts, the distracted globe of which Hamlet speaks is the disordered world around him that can be set right by following the injunction of the ghost. The ghost of Hamlet's father provides instructions for the future that can repair the past. As a ghost of time, however, the distracted globe is Hamlet's head. The legitimacy or reality of the ghost is no longer necessary as the power and force of the past event resides within the psychological processes at work in Hamlet himself. The past remains within Hamlet and he cannot rid himself of it. When considering the ghosts of time, to grapple with such a spirit is the impossible task of grappling with the past itself. Hamlet here becomes the instantiation of what Nietzsche deplored as the inability to come to terms with the "it was" of time in *Zarathustra*.[2] This is why, to my mind, Hamlet speaks to us today and in a way quite different than it did to earlier audiences.

In each case, the ghost represents our awareness of, and confrontation with, the other of past persons as well as the otherness of the past, either as a literal or psychological manifestation. The ghost thus enables an ethical engagement with the past and the means to provide a moral scaffold for our future. Heeding the command of the ghost or working through its significance ostensibly provides the template to set the globe aright restoring sovereignty for the future. As we will see, however, each of these models is beholden to a set of restrictive norms, beliefs, and power dynamics that may actually derail the ethical impulse, the otherness or alterity of the past, which gives the ghost its power in its time. It is the most disturbing aspect of the ghost, its radical alterity, rather than its most comforting one, its injunction, in which the opening to an ethical relation to the past (and future) lies.

Ultimately, what is most troubling, disturbing, and powerful about the ghost is the ways in which its presence disturbs the spatiotemporal categories by which we come to make sense of the world around us. It is the past come again but emptied of its physical properties and disobedient to the rules of time and space. The ghost troubles both time and space whether as a literal *revenant* or as a metaphor for that which should no longer be with us but *is*.[3] The ghost is the site of what I call temporal anarchy, the messiness or unruliness of time and temporality (an-arkhos is without chief or ruler so it is a time without rules or measure just as in Hamlet, Denmark is without its rightful king). The ghost in this sense is a temporal (and perhaps spatial) anarchist. How this plays out is quite different depending on whether one accepts the time of ghosts or the ghost of time. I want to dwell with the ghost of time before returning to the time of ghosts and then beyond both.

Time is Out of Joint

If we accept our current metaphorical understanding of ghosts as itself conditioned by the ghost of time, we could say that the continuing existence of belief in the time of ghosts is an example of Reinhart Koselleck's *Gleichzeitigkeit des Ungleichzeitigen* (the synchronicity of the non-synchronous, or contemporaneity of the non-contemporaneous depending on which translation one follows). The prior understanding of ghosts resides amongst our current one but is out of synch. Then again, to turn things around, we could diagnose the construct of *Gleichzeitigkeit des Ungleichzeitigen* as the instantiation of our current infatuation with the ghost of time: the need to account for the past in the present and here we find our way back, or perhaps forward, to "temporal anarchy." Achim Landwehr has argued that to claim that something is "non-synchronous" means placing oneself on the side of "'progress,' 'avant-garde,' or 'elite,'" and thus reaches the conclusion: "The formula of the '*Gleichzeitigkeit des Ungleichzeitigen*' is not capable of conceptualizing the fundamental and mainly parallel coexistence of different sociocultural times, without reducing it to diachronic dissonance."[4] I agree with both aspects of his argument though I see the diachronic dissonance as an instantiation of temporal anarchy and thus a potential asset rather than liability.

Koselleck's argument about our current historical condition, and thus that the experience of time is itself historically conditioned, poses something of a conundrum because his diagnosis of the *Neuzeit* as our current condition must itself be conditioned by that historical understanding.

> The beginning of modernity (*Neuzeit*), with all the difficulties that arise out of this concept, was manifested for the first time in the Enlightenment, which had identified itself as the standard-bearer of a new time (*neue Zeit*). Behind the following historical interpretation thus stands our own present-day systematic way of formulating the questions-because the problems arising out of the concept of *Neuzeit* have become evident.[5]

Ultimately, I would like to explore whether this shift coincides with the one from the time of ghosts to the ghosts of time but I will leave it as a possibility for the moment. The temporal entanglement resides in that Koselleck's diagnosis of "our present day systematic way of formulating the questions" and thus of our current understanding of what time and history is must itself be symptomatic of that historical condition. Here, it is important to think about how Koselleck provides an anthropological or ontological account of time as well as a methodological account of time. The former is to serve as a constant that provides something of a baseline, but the latter allows us to account for the experience of time at any given historical moment. The anthropological or ontological account is thus timeless and ultimately ahistorical insofar as it is applicable at any given time or place which is at odds with Koselleck's argument that our understanding of time is historically conditioned. The two positions rest on one another even as they contradict each other.

To return to the *Gleichzeitigkeit des Ungleichzeitigen* and the ghost of time, I would like to explore two different ways in which it can be understood. In "The Eighteenth Century as Beginning of Modernity," the synchronicity of the non-synchronous is presented as moments that are chronologically simultaneous but developmentally at different stages Koselleck argues:

One could think, for instance, of the enormous precedent of scientific, and technical developments which, coming from England, spread to the United States and to many, not all, European countries and finally to Japan. Measured against such precursors or trailblazers, all the remaining countries and peoples fall into their wake and have to catch up. They appear to be lagging behind, as developing countries (something that may be completely unjustified culturally).[6]

In this instance, the totality of history is conceived in terms of progress and resultantly the inequality of the progress achieved in different parts of the world emerges which aligns with the criticisms of Koselleck's construct by Kathleen Davis, Achim Landwehr, and Dipesh Chakrabarty.[7] Because progress is regarded as a universal trait of "history" it enables a comparison in regard to different rates of development at any given moment but always in relation to a presumed totality of history and the comparison takes place on a universal/general temporal scale.

If we look at "*Begriffgeschichte* and Social History," however, we see a different possible intersection where the synchronicity of the non-synchronous refers to the way a concept can hold a "diverse strata of meaning descending from chronologically different periods."[8] This is the "synchronicity of the non-synchronous that can be contained within a concept."[9] Here we are not talking about different developmental stages taking place at the same time but strata of meaning from different times that are held within the same concept. Still, the ability to decipher and comprehend the diverse strata of meaning relies on a comparison of the differing meanings from differing times held within the concept at any given moment.

In our examples of the ghost, it could be that those who believe in the time of ghosts inhabit a world less "conceptually modern" than those who engage with the ghost of time, even though it could also be the case that the strata of meaning from different times are simultaneously held in the concept of the ghost. In the first case, different places meet within the same time while in the second case, different times meet in the same place. It is true that in each of these cases Koselleck constructs a zone of stability in which the comparison can take place and in each it is a stable moment in the present predicated on either time or space. It is a response to the ghost of time that reigns in the time of ghosts, but what continues to haunt Koselleck's model is the temporal instability and indeed malleability of the endeavor. This then begs the question as to what holds the model or provides its authority to resist the temporal anarchy of the ghost be it literal or metaphor.

Endless Mourning

Here I want to consider Walter Benjamin's account of Hamlet in *Ursprung Des Deutschen Trauerspiels* to bring Benjamin's analysis into conversation with the time of ghosts, the ghosts of time, and my own diagnosis of the state of the historical discipline in the current moment.[10] Benjamin is, of course, describing the disintegration of order set about by the killing of the King of Denmark, Hamlet's father. The fragility of that moment, the state of emergency, can be encapsulated by the realization that if one King can be killed then why not all? And the ensuing questions: What is it that actually holds sovereignty and stability and how does one restore order once order is lost? Benjamin's account takes up the ghost of time.

Benjamin sees Hamlet as being in a state of endless mourning for the death of his father, the King, which results in a state of endless consideration of what has been lost and what, if anything, can be done to rectify the situation. This ceaseless reckoning with the past and with loss deactivates the possibility for Hamlet to act in the present or for the future. As such, there can be no redemption for Hamlet or the other characters nor for the court. Even Rosencrantz and Guildenstern are dead and all the rest is silence. Hamlet's own death at the end of the play is the result of contingency, a piling up of plots and props. Schemes and orchestrations are piled upon schemes and orchestrations, none of which go to plan and none of which succeed. Hamlet's death is thus uncoupled from his purpose and this is something worth considering in a world where order has become so loose and conflict has become a mode of the interior. The redemptive promise to the ghost of Hamlet's father is a promise unfulfilled.

For us, it is the loss of order following the dissolution of the stability of historical narratives (grand or small) that has left us disoriented and disabled. If one "history" can be overthrown or called into question, why not all? Without a compass to guide us, history has lost its moral imperative, be it in pursuit of "life's lessons" or "objective truth" and thus its redemptive promise to the past is likewise a promise unfulfilled. We can consider our own moment as an extreme confrontation with the ghost of time in a state of endless mourning for the end of history. One can see this in François Hartog's *Regimes of Historicity* where he laments the arrival of a new paradigm in which memory, commemoration, heritage, and identity take the place of what had been history.[11] For Hartog, this new paradigm, to quote Aleida Assmann, "abolishes the ontological border between the past and the present and is exclusively focused on an enlarged present that is weighed down by the past and saturated with it, growing into monstrous proportions."[12] "Of course we [still] look toward the future" Hartog tells us, "but on the basis of an extended present without interruption or revolution."[13] In *Our Broad Present*, Hans Ulrich Gumbrecht diagnoses a similar deactivation of historical time with the concomitant deactivation of dynamic change. In this "ever broadening present . . . we are stuck in a moment of stagnation. Time ceases to be considered an absolute agent of change."[14] With the end of history, or the death of historical time, the categories of past and future are completely subsumed and rendered powerless by what Gumbrecht calls the "broad present" and the end of latency.[15] Finally, in *Social Acceleration* Hartmut Rosa concludes that we have entered a condition of "frenetic standstill" where nothing remains the way it is while at the same time nothing essential changes.[16]

As with Hamlet's endless state of mourning for his father's death and equally endless analysis of what should be done about it, historians and historical theorists are likewise in a state of endless mourning for the loss of history and equally endless assessment, interrogation, and analysis as to what to do about it and what it all means. The ghost of time will not leave us be and yet we seem unable to answer its call. We no longer believe in ghosts, and thus they provide no guidance from the past; but the moral compass of history has grown weak, misaligned, and unsure how to answer the ghost of time.

What has been lost, because ineffective, is the moral imperative for redemption toward which these understandings of the past once aspired.

Just as Benjamin concludes that in *Hamlet*, the edifice or staging of power becomes more important than power itself, which has now shown itself to be fragile and fleeting, so the staging of history has become more important than history itself, which has likewise shown itself to be fragile and fleeting. There is irony in the way historians and theorists of history look ceaselessly backward to the past, the way history was and the moral authority it held, as they lament its demise, end, or even death. Lacking the possibility of redemption or emancipation, what remains is a history disconnected from the future. In both Hamlet and the current historical understanding is an empty or seemingly impossible future, one without a King and the other without History, that has deactivated our ability to look forward thus compelling us to roam an ever extending present all the while plaintively and desperately looking back.

Methodologically, historians for the most part dwell in an enduring present and in this sense Hartog and Gumbrecht are correct in their diagnosis of a broad or endless present. Then again, if we follow Koselleck's analysis this has always been the case: history has always been history of the present. I want to focus on one aspect of Koselleck's claim which, I think, exposes the tension, the temporal anarchy of the ghost at work, as we saw in our discussion of *Gleichzeitigkeit des Ungleichzeitigen*. This may help us to reimagine the ghost of time beyond the collapse presented by Hartog or Gumbrecht. For Koselleck, in history of the present which is to say in all history,

> There are diachronic and synchronic dimensions at work at various temporal depths, about which historians from distant epochs can still help us gain insight for today, because history repeats itself structurally, something that is often forgotten when "singularity" is stressed.[17]

To be clear, Koselleck is speaking of "social-psychological processes that" he considers to be "constants throughout the history of events" whether past or future.[18] This account of history and human nature actually differs little from that of Thucydides in *The History of the Peloponnesian War* where he concludes that those readers

> who want to look into the truth of what was done in the past—which, given the human condition, will recur in the future, either in the same fashion or nearly so—will find this *History* valuable enough, as this was composed to be a lasting possession and not to be heard for a prize at the moment of a contest.[19]

The emphasis on the structural repetition of social-psychological processes or a permanent human condition smuggles in a transhistorical constant which allows for all aspects of the past to be explained from the vantage point of the present and even a future present. This conjuring trick allows Koselleck to master the ghost of time by creating a vector or coordinate from outside of time as it were.

In *Matter and Memory*, Henri Bergson provides an account of the phenomenon known as dèja-vu or the sense that one has previously experienced what is currently happening as if it had already taken place. On Bergson's account, what one actually experiences is not something that already happened but the contemporaneous realization that they *will* remember it. It is that recognition to come which Bergson sees as the formation of a memory of the present in real time.[20] Historians encounter something similar when they posit a permanent interpretative structure by which to decipher, interpret, and emplot the past. The sensation appears to them as a re-encounter with something that already occurred just like déja-vu. "Of course" they say, "that is the way it really happened." What they are actually experiencing is not the past as it really happened, however, but the contemporaneous realization that they are making history. Just as the experience of dèja-vu reveals the dissonance of a colliding past and present, there is a similar dissonance between the permanent structure proffered and the history presented to justify its stability. This is the place where, as in déja-vu, time is out of joint, but here it is because the historian fails to take into consideration the historical conditions of these so-called permanent structures. The historically determined conditions of possibility which restrict what we can imagine as possible pasts.[21] In so doing the historian transports their sense of what "should be" back into the past all the while ascribing a sense of permanence to these normative values. The ghost becomes a ventriloquist dummy for the historian whose own ethical injunction is provided with the trappings of authority by means of the claim to faithfully represent the commands of the past. The order we want the past to have is taken to be the order it actually had but at the expense of other possible ways of ordering or accounting for the past. Other possible commands and other possible ghosts. The matter is further complicated by the way these histories profess to guide us into the future. The events of the past here serve as justification for a lesson to be learned in the future that is unwarranted because of its relation to the present.

There is an emancipatory desire at work in these accounts no less powerful than Hamlet's own desire to set his distracted globe aright. This desire, however, remains forestalled as an emancipatory or redemptive promise unfulfilled in the endless mourning for the end of history or locked up by the transhistorical and thus changeless mechanisms intended to serve as history's cipher. In each case we encounter a closing off of possible pasts based on what we imagine to be the only pasts possible. In so doing, history is dominated by the presence of the present which tells the past what to be even as it continues to be haunted by the ghost of time. I want to reverse this movement and this temporal flow to put emphasis on the absent past that meets us, though I want to do so without reifying the reversal.

The Surge

The movement is what I call the Surge. In *Haunting History*, I describe how at any given moment a sudden surge can bring evidence of past remains to the surface.[22] In that work I use the metaphor of the ocean as the site of the Surge but one might also imagine a surge of wind, of power, or of sound. Recent films involving the supernatural, ghosts, or haunting spirits (malevolent or misunderstood) often signal the arrival of this present absence with a surge of electricity overtaxing the lights or by a surge of sound . . . sometimes even blowing the lights up and leaving us in darkness or reaching a deafening crescendo leaving us in silence. We are, by and large, afraid of surges, and I suggest that we are equally afraid of the past. This is at least a part of my argument in *Haunting History*. The instability of such open possibilities is disturbing, and conventional history often serves as an anesthetic that desensitizes us to its jarring effects. As such, conventional history does not leave the past in its otherness but always includes it in a whole calling this a historical perspective. The time of ghosts is exiled to an other side, as are other alternative relations to the past rendering the current historical moment flat, homogenous, and one-dimensional.[23]

Our encounter with the ghost of time has been for the most part about controlling the past and limiting the surge, even if the goal of such protections can be laudable when based on an emancipatory desire and promise. But as in *Haunting History*, where I demonstrate the ways that the noble goal of forging a path to the past, a *poros*, simultaneously creates an aporia, the demotion of the ghost to the realm of metaphor actually restricts our gaze and our attunement to the possible pasts and past possibles surging forth to meet us.[24] It is to these surges of the past, these ghosts, that we should be attuned. These are the histories that need to be heard, not in the purged, restricted, and methodologically homogenous version demanded by conventional history, but as histories that open space for multiple and conflicting logics of how we encounter, account for, and recount the past. A time of ghosts in contestation with the ghost of time. I am not, however, advocating a return to the time of ghosts and certainly not the ghost of a patriarchal sovereign such as Hamlet whose orders are to be unquestionably obeyed even if not enacted. This too is a restrictive harnessing of the Surge tied to a limited and limiting understanding of what the ghost is or could be. What I hope to conserve is the temporal anarchy of the ghost and the radical alterity this conveys: alternative ghosts, collective ghosts, ghosts of the future.

What I propose is a surge detector that seeks the sites of political and ethical intervention and as such engages in a different logic of history and a different mode of argument. A key question is how one pursues criticism and ethics without a normative definition of the two or having to resort to the concept of regulative ideas? I am sufficiently constructivist and Nietzschean to operate with an unbound and historically contingent understanding of ethics and ethical action. Then again, I am trying to think through the ways that the Surge either brings the past to us or helps us rise up to meet it in ways that make for ethical and political commitments—the ways we respond to the ghosts of the past literally as well as metaphorically. On this understanding there is no one normative definition or regulative guideline: thus there is the very real potential that the "ethical" or "political" intervention which prevails may not be the one which you or I would hope for. This is the danger. But is that not the case now? And would it not be better to confront this instability on the front end? The Surge is the unfettered intermingling of past, present, and future. It is free and generous and dangerous.

Attunement to the Surge enables us to reimagine the emancipatory promise of history and the possibility of redemption. This will be, and here I offer a modification of Derrida from *Specters of Marx*, a matter of thinking with new logics of history—not another history or a "new historicism," but other openings of event-ness as historicity that permits one not to renounce but on the contrary to open up access to an affirmative thinking of the emancipatory promise as promise: as promise and not as a definitive singular logic of what the past or ghost should be. Neither is this a teleology or regulatory ideal. The key to fulfilling the promise resides in the opening of access to other events in the past *as* history and other openings of event-ness *as* historicity. The Surge is a space of radical alterity and as such it is the site of ghosts and hauntings which allow historical actors from the past—different cultures, classes, times, or voices—to speak so as to unsettle any one dominant narrative or telling. The temporal anarchy of this fulfillment is that it must sustain itself as a continuous act which paradoxically can never be fulfilled.[25]

By attuning ourselves to the Surge and to these ghosts, to the ways they tear at conventional understandings of time and temporality, historians can take up their cause which is also our own. I take this to be an attunement to the past that allows such a historian or thinker to hear the call of the absent, missing, or hidden dead. In this way, the dead are not taken as persons or commodities no longer present whose properties and scope have been previously determined. Instead, the historian listens to the dead that haunt us as the presence of an absence out of time which is, as of yet, unknown and undetermined. This allows or opens space for multiple and conflicting logics of how we encounter, account for, and recount the past. The actors and vocabularies may be "unorthodox" or the accounts may be poetic, but these myriad approaches and definitions of history force us to question the dominance, politics, and ideologies behind any one variant. The anonymous nature of the Surge deprives us from taking a possessive posture in response to the past or the future. Strictly speaking it is not ours, so that here we see the possibility of an opening to the other whose past and future we are entreated to embrace. Not because it belongs to us but because we recognize they have as much right to these possessions as anyone. Rather than fight to retain "my" or even "our" past we should see the surge as pushing us toward "their" past and "their" future as temporalities to which we do and do not belong. Here I turn away from the time of ghosts and the ghost of time to imagine a ghost as "they." The ghost as an identity that does not coincide with itself and the Surge as necessarily predicated on a displacement of the self in relation to a radical and total other. The goal is to imagine what happens when we let ourselves go to think about the past and the future in accord with a totally different logic. This means letting go of all the coordinates by which we find ourselves privileged, including the external sovereignty of the time of ghosts and internal sovereignty of the ghosts of time, so as to imagine and enact an ethical relation to the past and future.

To return to the ocean metaphor, we must learn to surf the Surge. To ride with a history of differing logics and approaches to the past rather than battle against it by imposing methodological uniformity applied to an ever increasing field of areas and subjects. This attunement to the otherwise of the past will likewise be an attunement to the other in our present. As such, the past provides the call for a moral imperative in the present and for the future.

The emancipatory promise of the Surge is imbued with the potential to transform our present but only if the particular event surging from the past, now as history, is not left in the past as though the danger is over and done with or entirely appropriated by the present telling it what we want it to be. Related to this temporal shift is an emphasis on the universality of the history, the story, for a future humanity and a future beyond humanity which eclipses the particularity of any past event. This cannot be an understanding of the past in a possessive form—a restrictive "my" or "ours"—but instead a universal "they" of which we are and are not a part. This is to say, the past event can only serve us if we look beyond its particularity as past and toward its guidance toward their future. The time of ghosts retains the integrity of the particular revenant while the ghost of time extends the message and travels, as does the metaphor, beyond a particular time and place. It is not just Hamlet that must be restored but the distracted globe as well. This is a conjuring of past, present, and future that it is an exorcism of sorts. An exorcism, as Derrida says,

> not in order to chase away the ghosts, but this time to grant them the right, if it means making them come back alive, as *revenants* who would no longer be *revenants*, but as other *arrivants* to whom a hospitable memory or promise must offer welcome—without certainty, ever that they present themselves as such.[26]

In welcoming these ghosts, not as remnants of the past but as the site of emancipation, the time of ghosts haunting the ghost of time points us to what can be rather than what has already passed. It points us to the Surge, the site of dynamic temporal entanglement where the past arrives as if new, calling for intervention and engagement. The ghost imbued with a futural "they" announces a time out of joint because it awaits the work of permanent repair. The past as future, if you will, rather than a futures past.

Notes

1 William Shakespeare, "Hamlet: Prince of Denmark," in *The New Cambridge Shakespeare*, ed. Philip Edwards (Cambridge: Cambridge University Press, 2003), I.5.95–105.
2 Friedrich Nietzsche, *Thus Spoke Zarathustra*, trans. Adrian del Caro (Cambridge: Cambridge University Press, 2006), 111. "'It was': thus is called the will's gnashing of teeth and loneliest misery. Impotent against that which has been—it is an angry spectator of everything past." See Philip Edward's "'Introduction' to Shakespeare, *Hamlet, Prince of Denmark*," in *The New Cambridge Shakespeare*, ed. Philip Edwards (Cambridge: Cambridge University Press, 2003), 35–45.
3 Ethan Kleinberg, *Haunting History: For A Deconstructive Approach to the Past* (Stanford: Stanford University Press, 2017), see for example the section "The Past That Is," 134–49.
4 Achim Landwehr, "Von der 'Gleichzeitigkeit des Ungleichzeitigen,'" *Historische Zeitschrift* 295, no. 1 (2012): 19–20.
5 Reinhart Koselleck, "The Eighteenth Century as the Beginning of Modernity," in *The Practice of Conceptual History: Timing History, Spacing Concepts*, trans. Todd Pressner (Stanford: Stanford University Press, 2002), 160.
6 Koselleck, "The Eighteenth Century," 159.
7 Dipesh Chakrabarty, *Provincializing Europe: Postcolonial Thought and Historical Difference* (Princeton: Princeton University Press, 2007); Kathleen Davis, *Periodization and Sovereignty: How Ideas of Feudalism and Secularization Govern the*

     Politics of Time (Philadelphia: University of Pennsylvania Press, 2008); Landwehr, "Von der 'Gleichzeitigkeit des Ungleichzeitigen.'"
8 Reinhart Koselleck, "*Begriffgeschichte* and Social History," in *Futures Past: On the Semantics of Historical Time*, trans. Keith Tribe (New York: Columbia University Press, 2004), 90.
9 Koselleck, "*Begriffgeschichte* and Social History," 90.
10 Walter Benjamin, *Ursprung Des Deutschen Trauerspiels* (Berlin: Suhrkamp, 2000); *Origin of the German Trauerspiel*, trans. Howard Eiland (Cambridge, MA: Harvard University Press, 2019).
11 François Hartog, *Regimes of Historicity: Presentism and Experiences of Time*, trans. Saskia Brown (New York: Columbia University Press, 2015).
12 Aleida Assmann, "A Creed that had Lost its Believers? Reconfiguring the Concepts of Time and History," in *Rethinking Historical Time: New Approaches to Presentism*, ed. Marek Tamm and Laurent Olivier (London: Bloomsbury, 2019), 208.
13 Hartog, *Regimes of Historicity*, 200.
14 Hans Ulrich Gumbrecht, *After 1945: Latency as Origin of the Present* (Stanford: Stanford University Press, 2013), 200.
15 Hans Ulrich Gumbrecht, *Our Broad Present: Time and Contemporary Culture* (New York: Columbia University Press, 2015). My thanks to Juhann Hellerma for his investigation into these three thinkers in *Mapping Time: Analysis of Contemporary Theories of Historical Temporality* (doctoral dissertation, University of Tartu) (Tartu: University of Tartu Press, 2020), 22–4.
16 Hartmut Rosa, *Social Acceleration: A New Theory of Modernity*, trans. Jonathan Trejo-Mathys (New York: Columbia University Press, 2015).
17 Reinhart Koselleck, "Constancy and Change of All Contemporary Histories: Conceptual-Historical Notes," in *Sediments of Time: On Possible Histories*, trans. Sean Franzel and Stefan-Ludwig Hoffman (Stanford: Stanford University Press, 2018), 114.
18 Koselleck, "Constancy and Change," 115.
19 Thucydides, *The Essential Thucydides: On Justice, Power, and Human Nature*, ed. and trans. Paul Woodruff (Indianapolis: Hackett Publishing Co., 2021), "On Historical Method," 13 [i. 20.2–22].
20 Henri Bergson, *Matter and Memory*, trans. N. M. Paul and W. S. Palmer (New York: Zone, 1991), 139, 165. See Keith Ansell Pearson, *Bergson: Thinking Beyond the Human Condition* (London: Bloomsbury, 2018), 83.
21 Kleinberg, *Haunting History*, 137–49.
22 Kleinberg, *Haunting History*, 139.
23 See my "*One-Dimensional Man*, One-Dimensional History: Re-reading Herbert Marcuse," *Journal of the Philosophy of History* 15, no. 3 (2021): 340–60.
24 Kleinberg, *Haunting History*, 140–2.
25 Jacques Derrida, *Specters of Marx: The State of the Debt, the Work of Mourning, and the New International*, trans. Peggy Kamuf (New York: Routledge, 1994), 93–4.
26 Derrida, *Specters of Marx*, 220.

Traditional Sources

Shakespeare, William. "Hamlet: Prince of Denmark." In *The New Cambridge Shakespeare*, edited by Philip Edwards. Cambridge: Cambridge University Press, 2003.

Thucydides. *The Essential Thucydides: On Justice, Power, and Human Nature.* Edited and translated by Paul Woodruff. Indianapolis: Hackett Publishing Co., 2021.

Bibliography

Assmann, Aleida. "A Creed that had Lost its Believers? Reconfiguring the Concepts of Time and History." In *Rethinking Historical Time: New Approaches to Presentism*, edited by Marek Tamm and Laurent Olivier, 207–18. London: Bloomsbury, 2019.

Benjamin, Walter. *Origin of the German Trauerspiel.* Translated by Howard Eiland. Cambridge: Harvard University Press, 2019.

Benjamin, Walter. *Ursprung Des Deutschen Trauerspiels.* Berlin: Suhrkamp, 2000.

Bergson, Henri. *Matter and Memory.* Translated by N. M. Paul and W. S. Palmer. New York: Zone, 1991.

Chakrabarty, Dipesh. *Provincializing Europe: Postcolonial Thought and Historical Difference.* Princeton: Princeton University Press, 2007.

Davis, Kathleen. *Periodization and Sovereignty: How Ideas of Feudalism and Secularization Govern the Politics of Time.* Philadelphia: University of Pennsylvania Press, 2008.

Derrida, Jacques. *Specters of Marx: The State of the Debt, the Work of Mourning, and the New International.* Translated by Peggy Kamuf. New York: Routledge, 1994.

Edward, Philip. "'Introduction' to Shakespeare, *Hamlet, Prince of Denmark*." In *The New Cambridge Shakespeare*, edited by Philip Edwards, 35–45. Cambridge: Cambridge University Press, 2003.

Gumbrecht, Hans Ulrich. *After 1945: Latency as Origin of the Present.* Stanford: Stanford University Press, 2013.

Gumbrecht, Hans Ulrich. *Our Broad Present: Time and Contemporary Culture.* New York: Columbia University Press, 2015.

Hartog, François. *Regimes of Historicity: Presentism and the Experience of Time.* Translated by Saskia Brown. New York: Columbia University Press, 2015.

Hellerma, Juhann. "Mapping Time: Analysis of Contemporary Theories of Historical Temporality." Doctoral dissertation, University of Tartu, Tartu, 2020.

Kleinberg, Ethan. *Haunting History: For A Deconstructive Approach to the Past.* Stanford: Stanford University Press, 2017.

Kleinberg, Ethan. "*One-Dimensional Man*, One-Dimensional History: Re-reading Herbert Marcuse." *Journal of the Philosophy of History* 15, no. 3 (2021): 340–60.

Koselleck, Reinhart. "*Begriffgeschichte* and Social History." In *Futures Past: On the Semantics of Historical Time*, translated by Keith Tribe, 75–92. New York: Columbia University Press, 2004.

Koselleck, Reinhart. "Constancy and Change of All Contemporary Histories: Conceptual-Historical Notes." In *Sediments of Time: On Possible Histories*, translated by Sean Franzel and Stefan-Ludwig Hoffman, 100–16. Stanford: Stanford University Press, 2018.

Koselleck, Reinhart. "The Eighteenth Century as the Beginning of Modernity." In *The Practice of Conceptual History: Timing History, Spacing Concepts*, translated by Todd Pressner, 154–69. Stanford: Stanford University Press, 2002.

Landwehr, Achim. "Von der 'Gleichzeitigkeit des Ungleichzeitigen.'" *Historische Zeitschrift* 295, no. 1 (2012): 1–34.

Nietzsche, Friedrich. *Thus Spoke Zarathustra*. Translated by Adrian del Caro. Cambridge: Cambridge University Press, 2006.
Pearson, Keith Ansell. *Bergson: Thinking Beyond the Human Condition*. London: Bloomsbury, 2018.
Rosa, Hartmut. *Social Acceleration: A New Theory of Modernity*. Translated by Jonathan Trejo-Mathys. New York: Columbia University Press, 2015.

3

Gifts from the Dead

Heritage and the Ligatures of History

Hans Ruin

Gefährlich ist es, Erbe zu sein
—Friedrich Nietzsche, *Also sprach Zarathustra*

Introduction

In my book *Being with the Dead* I explored the interconnection between the culture of death and the origin and development of historical consciousness.[1] The term "being with the dead" was taken from Heidegger's *Being and Time*, where it is used to point out that the being-with (*Mitsein*) with the other does not cease abruptly with his or her death, but that there is a particular way of *caring* for the dead, which should not be equated with the care for inanimate objects. I develop this concept into a larger socio-ontological category, describing various ways in which such a being-with the dead is manifested through different cultural practices, not only burial rituals, but also through forms of commemoration of the dead, from ancestral piety to the scientific culture of historical research. The argument is that modern historical culture, spanning from memorial practices, historical museums, and the historical and archaeological sciences, not only grows out of this larger social-ontological territory, but that it also continues to interact with the dead in ways sometimes invisible to its practitioners. The book deploys the term "necropolitics" in order to describe the different ways in which the care for the dead can also obtain a political significance, sometimes with far-reaching consequences for the constitution and orientation of communities. The principal philosophical inspiration comes from existential ontology, deconstruction, and social ontology (Heidegger, Derrida, Schütz), but it engages a number of different disciplines, such as sociology, anthropology, archaeology, philology, historiography, and cultural memory studies.

It was only late in the writing process, when the book was already prepared for publication, that I realized that one particularly important dimension of how the relation between the dead and the living is constituted had entirely been left out of the larger picture: the phenomenon of *heritage*, or *inheritance*. The bequeathing of an inheritance is perhaps the most concrete way in which the living can aspire to reach beyond their own finitude into the life of those who come after. It is often also—reciprocally—the most immediate mode in which the living find themselves tied to or committed to the dead. The present essay is a first attempt to explore the philosophical meaning and significance of what it means to inherit within the larger framework of such a social ontology of being with the dead through a dialogue between existential phenomenology and the new discipline of *heritage studies*.[2] Through the establishment of institutions for so-called heritage management, the concept of heritage itself has obtained an increasingly important place within global cultural politics. This "heritagification" of history comes with the risk of reifying the nature of intergenerational human historical existence in ways that make us insensitive to the deeper challenges of how to share a world across generations. For this reason, it is important that we learn to situate and reflex upon the use and meaning of the concepts of heritage and inheritance within a larger context of the stretch or connectivity of history, what I in a concluding reflection also refer to as the *ligature* of history.

Terminological Interlude

The English words *inherit*, *inheritance*, and *heritage* all go back to the Latin term *heres*, designating the *heir*, with the corresponding verb *hereditare*, to inherit. It is connected to a term designating "the one left behind," as a widow or orphan. Heritage and inheritance have to do with the situation of coming *after* one who has lived and also with a just claim to a share of the life and world of those who lived before. The equivalent in ancient Greek is *kleronomos*, or simply *kleros*, as a word for *part* or *share*. The amalgam with the term *nomos* here points explicitly to having a *just* claim to a share. Someone who in Greek is *akleros* is a pauper, without a share, a "heritage-less" person.

The term also points to the basic fact that every person is situated in a generational chain, simply by virtue of being *born*. The very moment when someone is born, this person obtains the potential significance of an *heir*, of someone who *will* inherit. It is important to recall this basic and elementary meaning of the term, as situating a person within an intergenerational chain, linked to the passage of time, from birth to death. Having and becoming an heir is a general condition of mortals. And heritage is a means for life to prevail and prolong itself over and across the limit of death within a normative space of *lawfulness* but also simply as *destiny*. A child inherits from their parents, independently of whether or not he or she was made an explicit lawful heir, a *klero-nomos*. Not seldom, these processes of inheriting will be fractured, be it by unfulfilled desires, rivalries, regrets, or by an unwillingness to accept the inheritance that one has been handed. Heritage often comes with *normative* implications since it concerns questions of duty and responsibility across the limit of death. The extent to which it was from early on an important juridical-political issue can be glimpsed not least from the detailed way in which Plato addresses it in *Laws*.[3] The *biological* sense of an *inherited quality or nature* appears only in the latter half of the nineteenth century, following Charles Darwin and the subsequent rise of sociobiology. With the discovery of the genome, *heritage* has been associated even more strongly with such a biological meaning. Yet its primary sense is rooted in an intersubjective and intergenerational lifeworld, where finite beings find themselves bound not only to the dead but also to the not yet born.

Thinking Oneself as Inheritance: Derrida's Heideggerian Legacy

In June 2004, only four months before his death, which he then knew was imminent, Derrida participated in a last recorded seminar discussion with Jean-Luc Nancy and Philippe Lacou-Labarthe in Strasbourg. During this meeting, they opened the discussion—once more—around the topic of Heidegger, death, and the analysis of historicity in *Being and Time*. And once more they addressed the ominous tension between its analysis of individual mortality and collective destiny and the idea of an *authentic* historical community of a *Volk*, through which Heidegger would later also link his existential ontology to national socialism and its conservative revolutionary pathos.

But during this particular encounter their discussion took a new and different direction. After having first talked about the theme of death and mourning, Derrida—almost as if he were tired of his own discourse—instead turned the conversation toward the topics of legacy, testament, and inheritance (*téstament, héritage*).[4] As the three aging men faced death they began to confess their profound desire for *survival* and to expose their different archival efforts and strategies to secure their traces in a future to come. In Derrida's case, it led him to reflect on a phenomenon that he here chose to refer to as "exapropriation" (*exapropriation*): a parting from oneself in order to secure oneself. If his lifelong preoccupation with the question of the *trace* initially was articulated from the viewpoint of a loss that had already taken place in an irretrievable past, the thought of his own imminent destruction and disappearing now motivated him to reflect on the same logic but now from the other end, so to speak. At this point it was done in the form of an anticipation of his own possible and desired preservation through the transformation of himself into an exterior medium.

The original structure of the *trace*, as he had developed it in his early readings of Husserl, pointed toward an origin that already from its very inception was deferred from itself through its deposition in a shared means of communication and thus in a repeatable *sign*. But now he spoke instead of a particular "testamentary desire" that comes with the anticipation of death. These kinds of thoughts, he said, I call "testamentary," adding that the link between this desire and the structure of the *trace* had always "haunted" him.[5] In passing he made a reference to the famous claim in *Grammatology* that "all *graphemes* are of testamentary essence," which here in the Strasbourg conversation read: "every *trace* is of a testamentary essence" (*toute trace est d'essence testamentaire*).[6]

At the outset of *Specters of Marx*, published ten years earlier in 1993, he had recalled how the existential imperative to live also implies an imperative to address death.[7] Learning to live is learning to exist between life and death, in the existential stretch constituted by one's own life span, from not yet being born to no longer existing. But it is also to learn to live in relation to those no longer there. It was in order to describe this evasive existential in-between, that he there suggested that we think of it in terms of "the phantom" (*le fantôme*) and "spectrality" (*spectralité*). And he added that this would amount to a "politics of memory, of *inheritance*, and of generations."[8] In the Strasbourg conversation the topic was no longer primarily one of inhabiting the space of the already dead and their heritage, but instead one of grasping phenomenologically the *testamentary desire* itself, as *the will to live on*, to somehow prevail, in the awareness that this can only have the structure of an *exapropriation*. To exapropriate oneself, as a desire of a life about to disappear, is to want to become inheritance. It is a projection of oneself beyond the present, with a view toward those who will survive one's own inescapable destruction. The testamentary desire aspires to a form of afterlife with the help of the survivors, by making oneself into legacy, as gift, burden, and supplication.

In this confession of the testamentary desire from the aging Derrida we have a rare example of a speaking philosophical legacy, of a legacy that explicitly speaks of the desire that it itself is, and of the non-present presence that it is destined to become. The printed words—the graphic extension of the original recording—are that of which they simultaneously speak: materialization of a testamentary desire. But even using the word "simultaneously" is a simplification of the real situation. The preserved words carry the meaning of a moment which at the time of its deposition into a recording knew that it was destined to disappear into precisely the exterior medium that also secured its continuation. What we can read and perceive is thus at most the trace of a finite desire to continue.

The question of testament, legacy, and heritage is here exposed as an existential, a semantic, and an ontological riddle. To continue into the other, into known others, but also into unknown and perhaps yet unborn others, is to want to break the law of finitude that relegates all human life to a distinct space in time. It is to want to reach beyond the fate of death, in the awareness that this survival is conditional and that it can only happen by abandoning oneself and by letting oneself go, in other words through an exapropriation. It is done in the awareness that there is an ontological space to which one can aspire, namely to the domain of *having-been*. To live is having to die, but thereby also having to become someone who *will have lived*: in other words, to occupy the space of legacy and inheritance. Temporality and language are both partly constituted through this dual testamentary structure, of a desire to live on and an obligation to inhabit a space marked by the testamentary structure, as an integral and intersubjective dimension of finitude.

The term "having been" is taken from Heidegger, from the analysis of historicity in the second part of *Being and Time*. In his description of how the historicity of Dasein is constituted, and thus of the meaning of the historical as an experiential category, he outlines a peculiar form of reciprocity through "repetition" (*Wiederholung*) of previous possibilities for a future. It is an intersubjective dynamic that comprises both the living and the dead, as the living Dasein opens itself up to a possibility coming from Dasein "having-been," from *da-gewesene Dasein*. As Heidegger seeks to grasp the core of this interaction across the threshold of death, he also reaches for the concept of *heritage* (*Erbe*). In a section devoted to the "Essential constitution of Historicity," he defines "authentic historicity" (*eigentliche Geschichtlichkeit*) precisely in terms of a an *Erbe*: "The resoluteness in which Dasein comes back to itself discloses the actual factical possibilities of authentic existing in terms of the *heritage* which that resoluteness takes over as thrown."⁹

From the perspective of existential ontology, the phenomena of inheritance and inheriting in this philosophically elaborated form are thus not just possible outcomes or effects of the general historical nature of human existence. Instead, they are highlighted as constitutive components of the existential dynamic that makes historical awareness possible in the first place. It is as if historical time itself were opened up only through the repetition and projection of a meaning inherited from those who existed before us.

Coming from Heidegger, with his initial affirmation of conservative revolutionary politics in the Thirties, these formulations will carry an ominous tone. But the reference to history as inheritance need not imply a distinctive political or traditionalist agenda. In *Specters of Marx* Derrida speaks about how an inheritance is always radically and necessarily "heterogeneous," that it is "never gathered together, it is never one with itself, its presumed unity can only consist in the injunction to reaffirm in choosing."¹⁰ In the same text he adds: "inheritance is never given, it is always given to us as a task. It remains before us."¹¹ In this situation we are mourners of a past, but also those struggling with the past. And in perhaps the most poignant passage on this issue he writes:

> All the questions on the subject of being or of what it is to be (or not to be) are questions of inheritance. There is no backward-looking fervor in this reminder, no traditionalist flavor. Reaction, reactionary, or reactive are but interpretations of the structure of inheritance. That we are heirs does not mean that we have or that we receive this or that, some inheritance that enriches us one day with this or that, but that the being of what we are is first of all inheritance, whether we like it or know it or not.¹²

In *Specters of Marx* the context was the question of what to do with Marxism and where to find it today, in other words how to handle the legacy of Marx. It is this topic of how to carry on, as a question of how to read, understand, and what to do with what has been handed down to us, that leads him to a profound reflection on the inner and aporetic logic of inheritance as such. It points in the direction of a philosophy of history as a question of what it means to be situated within a sequence of *predecessors*. The ability to act in a responsible way for and toward a future will here rely on the ability to understand and respond to an always operative inner dynamic of inheritance.

In his book *Derrida and the Inheritance of Democracy* Samir Haddad recalls that Derrida at one point even equates deconstruction as such with inheritance.¹³ Echoing Derrida, Haddad writes that "the time of inheritance is one of disrupted linearity" and that "a legacy is always both in front of and behind the heir, since, as aporetic, it can never be located fully in a present."¹⁴ The question of inheritance and of heritage is thereby located again at the heart of the structure of historical temporality as explored by existential hermeneutics and deconstruction. As in Benjamin's *Theses on History*, it challenges a conventional chronological framework, exposing the past as an open and active promise and demand at once, and the future as its possible fulfillment. To view history and its workings in this way does not mean installing oneself in a closed-up archive or complying with an already specified order, but is instead to confront the past as both gift and interpellation, in view of a future to come. The question of what it could possibly mean to inhabit historical time in an "authentic" way will then also become a question of how to receive its inheritance.[15]

History and Heritage: The Rise of a New Discipline

A year before Derrida's Strasbourg conversation in 2004, the French historian and theorist of historiography François Hartog published a book with the title *Regimes of Historicity* (in English in 2015).[16] The principal thesis of his much-cited book is that in recent times, notably the last decades of the twentieth century, the cultural discourse of the West had experienced an unprecedented collapse in its temporal horizon toward what he calls "presentism." This development he exemplifies specifically with the rise of a cultural politics of *memory* and *heritage*. In a separate chapter devoted specifically to the concept of "heritage" and its history (*heritage*, and also *patrimoine*) Hartog recapitulates the rise of what he calls a "heritage industry" orchestrated by UNESCO and by national administrative bodies, through which "memory, heritage, history, identity, and nation were seamlessly joined in the smooth language of law."[17] He connects this changing sensibility and its institutional and political structures to a sense of disappearing, in response to which people erect signpost or "semiophores" (a term from Krzysztof Pomian) to signal an evanescent and vanishing past.[18] A previous "confidence in progress" had given way to a desire "to preserve and save," making it possible for the category of "heritage" to encompass potentially everything, both nature and culture. He connects this recent version of presentism primarily to a traumatic twentieth century that has left us "ruminating upon a past which simply won't go down." In short, he implies that there has occurred a sort of "heritage-ification" of history and of the past through which everything had been drawn into the maelstrom of an anxious present concerned only with itself and its immediate agendas.[19]

For his analysis of the increasing preoccupation with heritage and patrimony and its connection to identity and nation, Hartog cites mostly sources from a francophone discussion among historians as it had developed up until then. An important voice in these debates was Pierre Nora, who had embarked on an increasingly critical (and self-critical) scrutiny of the rise of memory and memorialization in the public debates in the years following upon the original success of his project *Lieux du Mémoir* from the early eighties onward. Hartog does not refer to Derrida or to Heidegger's deconstructive hermeneutics, whose writings on this topic never surface among his sources. His criticism is directed toward more general contemporary trends in the cultural politics of history.

Furthermore, Hartog does not seem to have been aware that a similar and parallel critical discussion had been underway already for two decades within the anglophone world. A landmark publication was David Lowenthal's *The Past is a Foreign Country* from 1985 and more importantly his sequel *The Heritage Crusade* from 1996. Especially in the latter book he argued vehemently against the political mobilization of heritage and in favor of a critical-historical approach to the past. In a preface to the second edition he describes the historian as someone who seeks to "convey a past consensually known, open to inspection and proof," whereas the heritage fashioner "seeks to design a past that will fix the identity and enhance the well-being of some chosen individual or folk."[20] According to Lowenthal, the modern world's "preoccupation with heritage" is linked to nostalgic, conservative, and neo-nationalist tendencies that emerged from the 1980s onward.[21] Just as in Pierre Nora's melancholic reflections on the loss of a natural link to the past through a living memory, Lowenthal sees that older and natural ways of relating to "tradition" and "ancestors" are being replaced today by an artificial clinging to "heritage."[22]

Lowenthal's books contributed in decisive ways to the rise of so-called "heritage studies" over the course of the last three decades. Today it has established itself as an independent academic discipline, with its journals, conferences, and academic centers of research and teaching. In 1994 the flagship *Journal of Heritage Studies* was founded, which today is accompanied by a series of journals devoted to various aspects of cultural heritage management, as well as by large companion volumes recently commissioned by several of the leading international academic publishers.[23] As a multidisciplinary study of the uses of history, heritage studies partly overlaps with memory studies, even though its researchers mostly seem to operate independently, and often seem to be unaware of one another. Whereas heritage studies is dominated by scholars from history, cultural geography, archaeology, and museology, memory studies comes mostly out of literature and language departments. In terms of theoretical background, memory studies has its principal theoretical footing in Durkheimian sociology and Maurice Halbwachs's theory of "collective memory." The theoretical foundations of heritage studies are less clear. They often take their inspiration from critical theory and Marxist sociology and social constructivism, according to which heritage amounts to the way in which "selective past material artefacts, natural landscapes, mythologies, memories and traditions become cultural, political and economic resources for the present," as the definition reads in one of the recent handbooks.[24]

When summarizing the history of heritage as such, the common procedure within the discipline would not take the route of a psychological, existential, or philosophical exploration of the term. Instead, it would normally delineate the history of state-sponsored attempts to manage historical remains. In other words, it would describe when, how, and why cultural heritage becomes a sociopolitical entity and praxis as a distinctly modern way of relating to and caring for the past within a political and administrative context. With the emergence of the modern nation states in the sixteenth century, we find the first initiatives to organize the cultivation of the nation's material-cultural past through national boards of antiquities. Following the French Revolution certain buildings were designated as national patrimony, marking the rise of a new type of politics of history, through a progressive-oriented monumentalization of the past. Napoleon's subsequent plundering of cultural treasures during his war-campaigns, notably those of the Vatican, resulted in the first attempts toward an international legal framework for repatriation of cultural property. But it is with the rise of capitalism in combination with the rapid technological transformation of the lifeworld from the mid-nineteenth century onward that the phenomenon of cultural heritage obtains the role and meaning that it still has today: as vulnerable remains from a past that needs to be cared for in order not to disappear or be destroyed by the juggernaut of modernization. The nineteenth century generated multiple such initiatives for the preservation of heritage, not only of material artifacts and buildings but also of folk culture and of nature itself, including the preservation of wildlife. The increasingly global economic system of rapid material transformation and constant increase of production for profit thus generates a characteristically schizophrenic relation to history: as both that from which the present is escaping in order to reach forward into the new and as that for which the present sees itself as responsible in order that it does not disappear in the process.

Throughout these early initiatives it was not necessarily in terms of "heritage" that the remains of the past were organized for national-political purposes. It was sometimes done in the name of national memory, or national treasures or antiquities, or simply of the cultural environment. But when the United Nations, through its cultural branch UNESCO, in 1972 passed the "Convention Concerning the Protection of the World Cultural and Natural Heritage (*patrimoine mondiale*)," the term "heritage" was raised to a new operative level on a global stage. The initiative was based on similar earlier legislative initiatives on national levels, but now with the explicit purpose of shaping an international awareness of the value of human culture at large. Today it is an almost unanimously signed convention, which has resulted in some 1,000 sites worldwide that have been selected for the status of "world heritage." Through this convention, "heritage" is now a globally recognized currency, driving initiatives to have this or that natural or man-made site recognized. The political aspiration to forge a global culture of memory and tradition has thereby also triggered an economic and political cultural competition, where "heritage" is perceived as an asset in the ongoing international rivalry among nations, alongside large sporting and cultural events, highlighting the commodification of heritage within the context of an expanding travel and tourist industry.

There is, however, another parallel sociopolitical process that is important to take into account when seeking to understand and assess the "heritage-ification" of history over the course of the last half-century: the *indigenous* and postcolonial struggles for political recognition and representation. From the late 1960s onward, first among Native Americans, and then Australian aborigines, Inuit, Sami, etc., political struggles for disenfranchised ethnic minorities and colonized populations emerged as a political movement, in which a new generation of activists sought to throw off the image of themselves as anthropological artifacts doomed to extinction or musealization. Their struggle often took the form of reclaiming agency precisely through an affirmation of their cultural *heritage*. For many of these groups, heritage was thus actualized as a source of legitimacy in political and economic struggles for resources and political influence. In this domain, heritage is still actualized as a name for a historically rooted mode of existence that cuts across the temporal limits of the present. It is a politics of heritage that refuses to let itself be defined solely by a present in which it is seen as deficient in relation to one homogenous temporal framework. As such it is an ambiguous tool, as both a means of liberation and empowerment, and as an incentive for conservative identity-politics and morals with homogenizing effects on the involved communities and their members.

Within heritage studies this dual source of the concept's modern use, can be traced in the form of a built-in dichotomy: between critical social-constructivist analyses of the uses of material and immaterial pasts and a more affirmative orientation that supports the political and communitarian potential of heritage-claims. Researchers in this field will usually maintain a neutral stance as to the validity or legitimacy of a particular heritage when it comes to the definition of the term. But such analyses can also be carried out with an explicitly critical view of the ways in which a presumably "authentic" heritage is created and shaped by actors in the present for practical political and juridical purposes.

According to one definition (as quoted above), "heritage" refers to "ways in which very selective past material artefacts, natural landscapes, mythologies, memories and traditions become cultural, political and economic resources for the present."[25] An analytical premise for this constructivist model is that things have no so-called "intrinsic" value but that they are given value according to standards of the present, a distinction which Lowenthal is apostrophized for having made. Heritage is then seen as something not existing in and of itself but as a discursive construction with material consequences.[26] In a collection of articles on heritage studies from 2015, the editors argue in a similar vein in the preface, for an understanding of heritage as "a version of the past received through objects and displays, representations and engagements, spectacular locations and events, memories and commemorations, and the preparation of places for cultural purposes and consumption."[27]

This conventional image of heritage as only a discursive construction in the present, associated with the cultural politics of modernity, was questioned by cultural geographer David C. Harvey in an influential article from 2001. Instead he stressed the need to look upon heritage in terms of long-term *processes* rather than as just strategies for managing the past within the present. Through this change of perspective it is possible to see and understand how heritage is involved precisely, as he writes, in struggles for "identity, power, and authority," especially in relation to postcolonial situations.[28] For this purpose he chose to look at what he calls "processes of heritageisation" as not restricted to any particular modern paradigm but as something that "has always been with us."[29] And instead of seeing heritage as a uniquely modern mode of interacting with the past, tied to a capitalist economy and its commodification over and against presumably older and more authentic relationships to history and the past, he suggested that heritage sites be seen as "one link in a chain of popular memory." As such they always contain an "intrinsically reflective relationship to the past." To illustrate this, he recalled examples of much earlier uses of history for identity-shaping processes, both throughout British history as well as in Roman-Christian times, where historical sites would be "re-used" and "re-interpreted" over the course of time. Inversely he suggested looking upon traditional "pilgrimage" sites as also earlier forms of commodification of the past through an amalgam of folk culture, elite interests, and commercial actors. To this he adds observations of how ancient pre-Christian monuments were both rejected and absorbed by Christian nations within a political-ideological space of heritage-ification.[30]

Harvey's analysis was important for directing the explorative field of heritage studies toward a more reflexive and hermeneutic awareness of its own domain. It showed that heritage need not simply be seen through the dichotomous lens of authentic preservation or inauthentic commodification. Instead, it can be conceived as an ongoing process of historicizing responses to the past over longer stretches of time. He ends his article by stressing that we need to "acknowledge, understand, and embrace the very long-term trajectory of the heritage phenomenon, otherwise we would not understand it at all."[31]

In a paper from one of the recent heritage studies collections, Jessica Moody builds on Harvey's analysis, arguing that the discussion concerning heritage and history within heritage studies has gradually shifted focus. Especially when viewed from the perspective of a struggle for indigenous rights, the traditional role of the historian thereby also becomes more problematic. If in Lowenthal's and Hartog's view history is posited as a clear contrast and antithesis to heritage (which is then seen as a fabricated version of history), Moody points to the fact that within the overall study of historical culture the two are now also investigated as different and parallel ways in which *the past* is represented or "construed."[32] Her basic definition of heritage is similar to the standard constructivist model, according to which "heritage is a present-day process which is used in the creation of identity" and as "a discourse about the past which is ever in fluctuation."[33] But in questioning the strict hierarchy between heritage and history, she takes a step beyond the standard model where history serves as an objective correlate.

Moody thereby also distances herself from the first generation of heritage scholars for whom heritage primarily marked a nostalgic perversion of the past for present purposes, with a mostly conservative political agenda. As historians are pulled into debates on how a particular group or phenomenon is represented, they are forced to become aware of their own role as also the creators of a living relation to the past. This is true of history when used in a pedagogical context, but it also involves the choices made in terms of what is made the topic of research and what is not.[34] Ultimately it implies ethical-political questions, in terms of which voices from the past that are recalled, listened to, and thus activated anew.

According to the standard traditional formula, history is a reconstruction of an objective past, of a *how it was*, whereas heritage would always designate the history of, by and for *someone*. But to Moody, history is seen instead as a "heritage process," as part of the more general phenomenon of the ways and means by which the past is actualized. She sees the historian as both a critical observer of heritage processes and as an actor within such processes. If the first generations of (cultural) historians who shaped the field of heritage studies saw themselves primarily as critical observers of the uses of the remains from the past, the discussion now also involves the role of historians within such processes. Through their disciplinary practices, they are drawn into enactments of the past, in struggles over legacies and inheritances, as seen not least in recent controversies over monuments and symbols of colonial histories.

Inheriting Heritage

Through the expansion of heritage studies toward a more general theorizing around how the past is maintained and lived over longer stretches of time, it reaches into the existential hermeneutic issues raised at the outset. Still, the deeper theoretical underpinnings for these new approaches are not articulated as such within the domain itself. They emerge primarily from within a need to accommodate a more positive sense of traditionalisms and identity-politics over and against the focus on contemporary use-value. In this concluding section, I return to some of the question that were raised initially in relation to Derrida and Heidegger, and indicate in what way they can contribute to elucidate the dual conceptions of heritage that are operative in the contemporary literature in the larger context of a phenomenology of history and tradition. From such an angle it is also possible to have a wider critical and self-critical discussion around the meaning and function of heritage in the contemporary situation, where it is often domesticated and instrumentalized for political and economic purposes. To put it pointedly: a theoretical challenge today is how to inherit inheritance itself.

According to the standard model, the (objective) past is what history studies in order to understand it, whereas heritage uses and molds the past for a specific present purpose. In some situations, this distinction is worth defending. It enables a critical distance to what often amounts to biased position-taking when it comes to cultural heritage, where political and economic interests generate claims of a privileged inheritance and legacy. But if we are to understand the emergence and stakes involved in the heritage-ification of history in recent decades, we also need to return to this conceptual border, to move across it and possibly to open it up in order to explore its inner anatomy. We need to take a philosophical risk in order to learn something more both about the genealogy and potential of heritage and why it remains so disputed. Here Derrida's and Heidegger's philosophical and phenomenological references to a more basic testamentary desire and to historicity as responsive repetitions are important starting points for the discussion. Through a deepened understanding of the hermeneutics of the dead and the living it is possible to contextualize these contemporary debates and their antagonisms even further.

To occupy the space of such an *inheritance* is never a neutral affair. In this predicament, the living will find themselves obliged to respond to a past as they orient themselves toward the future. As such it constitutes an ethical and political, indeed a necro-political space. It is also a hermeneutic situation in the sense that it will always have to involve the interpretation and application of given meanings. But within the current cultural-political situation, with its surge of nationalism and identity-politics that are often bound up precisely with some notion of (legitimizing) heritage, it is also important to find new ways of visualizing the inner dynamic of historical belonging without becoming complicit in potentially constraining and destructive agendas. Through the existential-phenomenological and deconstructive framework outlined at the outset, we can visualize how and why these debates and controversies are played out today, with often high stakes. It can also permit us to orient ourselves easier in the contemporary contested space of national heritage politics.

From a certain vantage point Hartog and others are correct in their critical analyses of how the temporal horizon is shrinking, into an all-consuming present, for which the past is reduced to a reservoir of intellectual and material goods to be used in the contemporary staging of cultural heritage sites, memorials, or museums. On the other hand, the deepening concerns over how the changing climate is affecting the long-term conditions for human civilization on earth opens political action and responsibility toward new and vaster historical time-scales than ever before. The most advanced technological artifacts and their long-term effects motivate a thinking in time-scales that reach across the full scope of human life on earth, most notably in the complex challenge of long-term storage of nuclear waste.[35] The rapid transformation of the earth and the biosphere, in combination with technological adventures in communication, biotechnology, and robotics, along with urbanization, indicate that humanity is passing through a phase of global history that in the longer perspective may perhaps display our scattered attempts to preserve anything at all of what is disappearing as futile responses to much larger processes of destruction and reorganization. This we cannot know. Ultimately, we too are destined to become an inheritance that will once perhaps be received, cared for or rejected, or simply forgotten by those coming after us.

In my book on our being-with the dead I sought to draw our attention toward the fact that in all our involvement with the past, in our caring for its preservation and continuation as well as in our critique and refusal to let it guide the present, we always navigate within a larger socio-ontological framework of a contested and fractured coexistence with those who are no longer there. I spoke of the *necropolitics* of historical existence. Unlike its common use in the critical literature, it was not primarily meant to designate the political control and mastery of death and dying but rather to encircle the sense and implications of how every political space as such is constituted and upheld by both the living and the dead across generations. Politics, shared organization, and action, *involve* the dead, through the ways in which the living community situates, responds to, and cares for its dead. It can have the forms of political burials and rituals of commemorations. But it can also involve precisely the different ways in which legacies are created and maintained, so as to bind the living and the dead together in mutual commitment. It is not just a question of how the living *use* the remains of the dead for this or that purpose, but of how the social bond between the dead and the living is maintained.

In thinking about this basic and yet precarious existential space it is important that we do not tie ourselves too firmly to one definitive technical terminology. Instead, it is important to keep one's philosophical attention to the matter itself, and that one is prepared to channel it along alternating conceptual trajectories. The word "heritage" carries a weight. It directs our gaze toward an inner liaison over and across generations. But in a situation, where it is being operationalized as the name for both a scientific field and as an overarching guideline for the administration of national and international cultural property and in political struggles for legitimacy, it is also important to be able to look beyond the actual concept itself.

If we turn to Jan Assmann, German Egyptologist and the pioneer of cultural memory studies, he refers instead to the phenomenon of "connective structures," the structures that bind cultures together over time. He describes how these structures constitute a "symbolic universe" in both a social and a temporal sense.[36] Through the integration into common laws, values and the memory of a shared past individual are able to identify with a plural community as a "we." The study of cultural memory thus becomes the study of the technical, symbolic, and ritual means through which the experience of such an identity and continuity is maintained. As the "primal scene of memory culture" he points to how a community does "not to allow the dead to disappear," and that "death is both the origin and the center" of memory culture."[37] In an argument that resonates well with Derrida's reflections on a "testamentary desire," he also distinguishes between two basic temporal dimensions of these practices, the "prospective" and "retrospective." In *retrospective* acts the living pay tribute to their dead and to their memory in acts that seek to preserve them for posterity. In *prospective* acts the living who face death act so as to preserve themselves across this threshold into another life or simply into another mode of existence, if only in the memories of the living and in posterity.

His colleague and spouse Aleida Assmann makes a similar point in her own book, *Cultural Memory and Western Civilization*, where she also distinguishes two principal modes in which this is manifested, both as the more "secular" aspiration to achieve recognition in the eyes of posterity, as *fama* or *kleos*, and as the more "religious" piety vis-à-vis the dead, echoing the more technical terminology of the "prospective" and the "retrospective."[38] The shaping of time along these two axes and the means employed to maintain them thus form the center of the study of "cultural memory." Especially through the work of the Assmanns, it has come to serve as a general term for *that which survives* over the course of time, through rituals, materials, and technologies, and especially through the technology of *writing*.

It is noteworthy that they hardly ever talk of "heritage," despite the obvious overlap in thematic orientation. The main framework is cultural memory as a name precisely for those "connective structures" that hold cultures together over time. Cultural memory studies and heritage studies share an interest in trying to understand how material culture with a symbolic meaning generates cultural continuity and identity over time. But depending on what words we use, and what conceptual trajectories we follow, we will have different consequences. The term heritage and inheritance, places a stronger emphasis on the internally binding nature of cultural remains. An inheritance delineates a sphere of responsibility to preserve and carry on. To refer to it as a memory places more stress on the internal preservation and on how the keeping of the past is enacted by the living in the present.

When writing this piece, I found myself drifting off in the direction of another term, that of *ligature*. The Latin verb *ligare* means to bind, tie, and hold together. The participle *ligatus* and later *ligature* is a binding. It forms part of the term *re-ligio*, in its original sense of a reconnecting, and also to *ligament*, as the joining limbs in a living body. It is used early as a metaphor for the force of a law, as an attempt precisely to bind or tie a society together but also to describe history as what unites present and past. It is created in order to unite and hold, and it can be experienced as both securing and constraining. It is a joining that covers a cut, a separation, and unity at once. Perhaps it is in the direction of such a fractured connection, as the joint that both enables and holds, that we should continue in our attempts to theorize the temporal domain of history. Through its inheritances, memories, and its interconnective structures, as well as through its responsibilities, commitments, and its interruptions, it lays a claim on us: to think of it as a situation in which we always already stand.

Notes

1. See Hans Ruin, *Being with the Dead: Burial, Ancestral Politics, and the Roots of Historical Consciousness* (Stanford: Stanford University Press, 2019).
2. A first version of this text was presented as a lecture at Wesleyan University in 2017, on the generous invitation from Ethan Kleinberg to participate in a lecture series devoted to "Rethinking Necropolitics."
3. See Plato, *Laws*, 923ff.
4. Jacques Derrida, *For Strasbourg: Conversations of Friendship and Philosophy*, ed. and trans. Pascale-Anne Brault and Michael Naas (New York: Fordham University Press, 2014).
5. As his own response to this desire, Derrida then describes how he donated his material to different archives, in the awareness that his sons did not want to preoccupy themselves with it.
6. Jacques Derrida, *Of Grammatology*, trans. Gayatri Chakravorty Spivak (Baltimore: Johns Hopkins University Press, 1998), 69; and Derrida, *For Strasbourg*, 23.
7. Jacques Derrida, *Specters of Marx*, trans. P. Kamuff (New York: Routledge, 1994).
8. Derrida, *Specters of Marx*, xvii.
9. Martin Heidegger, *Sein und Zeit* (Tübingen: Niemeyer, 2001), 383. This is the same analysis, to which Derrida and his interlocutors referred to during their last encounter.
10. Derrida, *Specters of Marx*, 16.
11. Derrida, *Specters of Marx*, 54.
12. Derrida, *Specters of Marx*, xx.
13. Samir Haddad, *Derrida and the Inheritance of Democracy* (Stanford: Stanford University Press, 2013), quoted from Derrida's *Papier machine*, 81.
14. Haddad, *Derrida*, 38.
15. For further good discussions around the topic of Derrida and the problem of tradition and legacy, see also Michael Naas, *Taking on the Tradition: Jacques Derrida and the Legacies of Deconstruction* (Stanford: Stanford University Press, 2003); Jeffrey Bennington, *Interrupting Derrida* (New York: Routledge, 2000); and Matthias Fritsch, *The Promise of Memory: History and Politics in Marx, Benjamin, and Derrida* (Albany: State University of New York Press, 2005).
16. François Hartog, *Regimes of Historicity: Presentism and Experiences of Time*, trans. Saskia Brown (New York: Columbia University Press, 2015).
17. Hartog, *Regimes*, 151.
18. Hartog, *Regimes*, 152.
19. Hartog, *Regimes*, 189.
20. David Lowenthal, *The Heritage Crusade and the Spoils of History* (Cambridge: Cambridge University Press, 1998), xi.

21 Lowenthal, *The Heritage Crusade*, v.
22 Lowenthal, *The Heritage Crusade*, 13.
23 Such as those published by Ashgate, Palgrave, Routledge, etc.
24 Brian Graham and Peter Howard, "Heritage and Identity," in *The Ashgate Research Companion to Heritage and Identity*, ed. Brian Graham and Peter Howard (Aldershot: Ashgate, 2008), 2, where they also explicitly define their approach as "constructionist."
25 See Graham and Howard, "Heritage and Identity," 2.
26 David C. Harvey, "The History of Heritage," in *The Ashgate Research Companion to Heritage and Identity*, ed. Brian Graham and Peter Howard (Aldershot: Ashgate, 2008), 19.
27 Emma Waterton and Steve Watson, "Heritage as a Focus of Research: Past, Present and New Directions," in *The Palgrave Handbook of Contemporary Heritage Research*, ed. Emma Waterton and Steve Watson (New York: Palgrave, 2015), 1.
28 See David C. Harvey, "Heritage Pasts and Heritage Presents: Temporality, Meaning and the Scope of Heritage Studies," *International Journal of Heritage Studies* 7, no. 4 (2001): 319–38.
29 Harvey, "Heritage Pasts," 320.
30 Harvey, "Heritage Pasts," 326.
31 Harvey, "Heritage Pasts," 338.
32 Jessica Moody, "Heritage and History," in *The Palgrave Handbook of Contemporary Heritage Research*, ed. Emma Waterton and Steve Watson (New York: Palgrave, 2015), 113–29.
33 Moody, "Heritage and History," 113.
34 For a more extensive discussion of the "uses" of the past in pedagogical contexts overlap with the larger debates of the nature of historical consciousness and history at large, see my "The Claim of the Past—Historical Consciousness as Memory, Haunting, and Responsibility in Nietzsche and Beyond," *Journal of Curriculum Studies* 51, no. 6 (2019): 798–813.
35 Cornelius Holtorf and Anders Högberg, "What Lies Ahead? Nuclear Waste as Cultural Heritage of the Future," in *Cultural Heritage and the Future*, ed. Cornelius Holtorf and Anders Högberg (London: Routledge, 2021), 144–58.
36 See Jan Assmann, *Cultural Memory and Early Civilization: Writing, Remembrance and Political Imagination* (Cambridge: Cambridge University Press, 2011), 2. For a longer discussion of Assmann's work, see the last chapter of my *Being with the Dead*.
37 Assmann, *Cultural Memory and Early Civilization*, 45.
38 Aleida Assmann, *Cultural Memory and Western Civilization: Arts of Memory* (Cambridge: Cambridge University Press, 2011), 170.

Traditional Sources

Plato, *Laws*.

Bibliography

Assmann, Aleida and Jan Assmann. *Cultural Memory and Western Civilization: Arts of Memory*. Cambridge: Cambridge University Press, 2011.

Assmann, Jan. *Cultural Memory and Early Civilization: Writing, Remembrance and Political Imagination.* Cambridge: Cambridge University Press, 2011.

Bennington, Jeffrey. *Interrupting Derrida.* New York: Routledge, 2000.

Derrida, Jacques. *For Strasbourg: Conversations of Friendship and Philosophy.* Edited and translated by Pascale-Anne Brault and Michael Naas. New York: Fordham University Press, 2014.

Derrida, Jacques. *Of Grammatology.* Translated by Gayatri Chacravorty Spivak. Baltimore: Johns Hopkins University Press, 1998.

Derrida, Jacques. *Specters of Marx: The State of the Debt, the Work of Mourning, and the New International,* Translated by P. Kamuff. New York: Routledge, 1994.

Fritsch, Matthias. *The Promise of Memory: History and Politics in Marx, Benjamin, and Derrida.* Albany: State University of New York Press, 2005.

Graham, Brian and Peter Howard. "Heritage and Identity." In *The Ashgate Research Companion to Heritage and Identity*, edited by Brian Graham and Peter Howard, 1–15. Aldershot: Ashgate, 2008.

Haddad, Samir. *Derrida and the Inheritance of Democracy.* Stanford: Stanford University Press, 2013.

Hartog, François. *Regimes of Historicity: Presentism and Experiences of Time.* Translated by Saskia Brown. New York: Columbia University Press, 2015.

Harvey, David C. "Heritage Pasts and Heritage Presents: Temporality, Meaning and the Scope of Heritage Studies." *The International Journal of Heritage Studies* 7, no. 4 (2001): 319–38.

Harvey, David C. "The History of Heritage." In *The Ashgate Research Companion to Heritage and Identity*, edited by Brian Graham and Peter Howard, 19–36. Aldershot: Ashgate, 2008.

Heidegger, Martin. *Sein und Zeit.* Tübingen: Niemeyer, 2001.

Holtorf, Cornelius and Anders Högberg. "What Lies Ahead? Nuclear Waste as Cultural Heritage of the Future." In *Cultural Heritage and the Future*, edited by Cornelius Holtorf and Anders Högberg, 144–58. London: Routledge, 2021.

Lowenthal, David. *The Heritage Crusade and the Spoils of History.* Cambridge: Cambridge University Press, 1998.

Moody, Jessica. "Heritage and History." In *The Palgrave Handbook of Contemporary Heritage Research*, edited by Emma Waterton and Steve Watson, 113–29. New York: Palgrave, 2015.

Naas, Michael. *Taking on the Tradition: Jacques Derrida and the Legacies of Deconstruction.* Stanford: Stanford University Press, 2003.

Ruin, Hans. *Being with the Dead: Burial, Ancestral Politics, and the Roots of Historical Consciousness.* Stanford: Stanford University Press, 2019.

Ruin, Hans. "The Claim of the Past—Historical Consciousness as Memory, Haunting, and Responsibility in Nietzsche and Beyond." *Journal of Curriculum Studies* 51, no. 6 (2019): 798–813.

Waterton, Emma and Steve Watson. "Heritage as a Focus of Research: Past, Present and New Directions." In *The Palgrave Handbook of Contemporary Heritage Research*, edited by Emma Waterton and Steve Watson, 1–17. New York: Palgrave, 2015.

4

Multilayered Temporalities Underlying Transitional Justice

Rethinking Resentment and Melancholia from Jean Améry and Walter Benjamin

Rafael Pérez Baquero

Introduction: Dilemmas and Temporalities Underlying Transitional Process

After the collective violence of the twentieth century, political debates on how to deal with historical debts stemming from such dreadful events have become the ground upon which ethical categories engage with sociohistorical processes. Due to events such as the Holocaust, the Soviet Gulag, the Apartheid, or colonial warfare, notions of collective guilt, historical responsibility, and political forgiveness were brought to the fore in public discourse and ethical debates. Owing to the legacies of such violence within post-conflict societies, there is a growing sense that the unsettling past persists in the present demanding recognition and accountability. Obviously, the victims who had suffered systematic and state-sponsored violence have become a prism through which unsettling historical debts haunt the present. Dealing with the voices of victims demanding justice and reparation is considered the most important goal of the juridical and political processes defined as "transitional justice,"[1] which provides priceless resources for ensuring both stability and legitimacy of new democracies, after violent political transformations. At the end of the twentieth century, in different parts of the world—South America, Eastern and Southern Europe, South Africa—new democratic regimes emerged from authoritarian dictatorships. The new democracies not only had to deal with the tasks of reconstructing and modernizing their societies to avoid falling back into struggles but they also had to prosecute the crimes committed by those who had previously held power.

Such endeavors, however, are not devoid of difficulties. After all, due to political instability and social unrest, transitional justice needs to deal with and account for new democracies' flaws when punishing perpetrators and restituting victims' rights. In different historical instances, after transition to democracy, criminals still held enough power and influence within society to hinder the extent to which transitional justice restituted the rights of their victims. Thus, transitional justice is caught between seeking moral reparation and seeking social and political stability, between doing justice to the historical debts stemming from the crimes of the past and not feeding social unrest in post-conflict contexts. As Ruti Teitel claims, within transitional justice, "the law is caught between the past and the future; between backwards looking and forward-looking," between meeting and forsaking the unsettling demands of victims.[2]

But what underlies transitional justice dilemmas does not concern only experts on politics or ethics. What this paper aims to shed light on is that behind each of these alternatives lies a different view of historical time and a particular way of framing the experience of temporality. Consequently, the choice between justice and forgetfulness or between past and present, could be reshaped as the "temporal antagonism between justice and history."[3] Whereas the time of justice focuses on the haunting nature of the past that refuses to go away, the time of history tends to erode its historical debts. In this regard, the feature that defines the time of history is irreversibility. It is a linear temporality according to which the past always automatically disappears.[4] This conception of time forms the basis for a particular way of dealing with historical debts. After all, if the past unavoidably fades and disappears because of the passing of time, there is no sense in reopening old debates and juridical records, which could only bring about social unrest and political instability. Irreversible and linear time are thus identified with the practical consequences of clock time, which can be summarized as follows:

> This means-ends clock time; its mantras are: get over it, forget about the past, time marches on; progress is coming, the *future* will bring it—so just go with the flow.[5]

The ethical and political project of bringing victims' rights to the fore goes against the tide of such linear and irreversible conception of time. According to this temporality, administering justice in relation to a criminal event that happened in the past seems less urgent as time goes by. In contrast, when seeking restitution for the victims of past crimes, "chronological time is set aside in favor of a moral and juridical regulation of time."[6] To this view of temporality, debts stemming from collectives' crimes that happened decades ago are not considered simply part of the past. On the contrary, they are framed as fully contemporary as they challenge the ethical foundations of present societies. Within this temporality, "the past is reclaimed as an ethical space where past, present, and future coincide."[7]

On balance, underlying the application of transitional justice are not only an ethical decision between justice or political and social stability but also a confrontation between different and multilayered temporalities that frame how the past is conceived. Despite the fact that seeking justice strives to counteract linear temporality, one should not overlook the fact that the political project of transitional justice also engages with such a linear and irreversible form of temporality. Even though it seeks to judge perpetrators of mass crimes and to safeguard the rights of their victims, transitional justice also tries to overcome an unsettling and burdensome past. As Jill Stauffer claims, transitional justice revisits the wrongdoings of the past "with the hope of opening up a future not fully determined by the past."[8] This is why transitional justice needs to rely on linear and irreversible temporality. Despite the fact that transitional justice seeks to restore victims' rights, its ultimate objective is to achieve reconciliation and definitively end the unsettling past.

In this regard it is worth highlighting the extent to which the recent literature on transitional justice has revolved around the notion of reconciliation and closure. Margaret Walker points out that

> Interwoven with political movements and social consciousness come the theories and research programs explaining, justifying, comparing, and contesting specific practices of moral and social repair. The questions range over legal remedies, political and institutional processes, moral order, and social cohesion, tolerance, and reconciliation.[9]

Within the contemporary trends on transitional justice, forgiveness and reconciliation are often considered the only way for overcoming both individual negative emotions and social conflicts and for promoting peace after violence. Andrew Rigby's *Justice and Reconciliation*,[10] Mark Amstuzt's *The Healing of Nations*,[11] Desmond Tutu's *No Future Without Forgiveness*,[12] and Villa-Vicencio's "Getting on With Life,"[13] to name a few, are examples of the focus on social reconciliation when dealing with transitional processes. The common assumptions of their approach are highlighted by Thomas Brudholm as "the rhetoric of moving on, the all too easy denouncements of negative emotional responses, the appeal to surviving victims not to turn into 'mirror images.'"[14] Thus, underlying their perspective is a linear conception of time, which compels one to leave the past hurts behind so as to look toward the future.

These multilayered temporalities explain why transitional justice coexists with pleas to move on and overcome the anger, resentment, and other emotions stemming from the experience of systematic violence. Regardless of the extent to which transitional justice deals with the rights of victims, its projection is always subordinate to the complex task of overcoming the past and of striving to live in a social context not determined by its past. Transitional justice is thus built upon shaky grounds: between justice and stability, between past and present, between the irreversible time of history and the temporality of justice. These ethical and temporal entanglements account for the role that victims play within such processes, especially the victims who strongly refuse to leave behind this past with the harm they suffered. Since transitional justice seeks to help a society overcome its traumatic past, victims who are still resentful, even after the passage of time and even after receiving different compensations, undoubtedly hinder the fulfillment of transitional justice aims. Due to the temporality underlying transitional justice, those victims who forgive achieve mourning, whereas those who refuse to offer forgiveness continue to relive their traumatic past. As a consequence, the victims of extreme violence who, after the passage of time, still feel resentment are framed as melancholic subjects unable to move beyond the past. In different historical contexts, such as South Africa, Argentina, or Chile's transition to democracy, some victims of state-sponsored violence refused to join the process of social reconciliation and let go of their resentment. By doing so, they prevented transitional justice from fulfilling its goals. That is how Thomas Brudholm explains it within the analysis of the South African process of social reconciliation: "To encourage forgiveness, commissioners thus represented the emotions that the forgiving had overcome or were willing to abandon in a negative way. What happened when commissioners came to face real resistance to, or dissent from, the rhetoric of forgiveness from victims who refuse to forgive?"[15]

Against the backdrop of assumptions underlying the understanding of victims' refusal to let bygones be bygones, this paper aims at shedding new light onto this reluctance by reframing two notions that the contemporary theory on transitional justice has used to label victims: melancholia and resentment. This interpretation is inspired by and echoes Walter Benjamin's and Jean Améry's ideas about these notions. In contrast to the seeking of reconciliation and closure after collective trauma, which underlies recent literature on transitional justice, the arguments in this paper open new paths for reframing the ethical and temporal grounds for dealing with the past as an endless task that keeps haunting contemporary societies and bringing about forthcoming ethical challenges.

Dealing with Uncooperative and Unforgiving Victims

The previous section has highlighted the extent to which ethical decisions concerning transnational justice depend on the way in which temporality is conceived. "How one deals with ethical questions is deeply influenced by how one conceives the past."[16] Thus, how the passing of time is framed constitutes the deepest layer underpinning some of the most important ethical decision-making within transitional contexts. Such complex interplay between temporality and ethical priorities frames the way in which resentful victims of violence are conceived by transitional justice projects. As long as it aims to promote the collective overcoming of traumatic and contested pasts, transitional justice needs to engage with linear temporality, which seeks to leave unsettling memories behind. This is why victims who, years after being harmed, refuse to forgive, forget, or move on, hinder the fulfillment of transitional justice goals. As a result, from the perspective of the specific temporality and ethical values underlying transitional justice, the uncooperative victims have been viewed in a negative way, as stranded in the traumatic past and unable to move on. The ethical and psychological characterization of these victims also stems from this perspective.

Transitional justice is based on the premise that after a period of time has passed since the painful experience, victims, and societies should be able to move on. As it is not possible to go back in time and reverse the harm that has been done, looking forward seems to be the only available path. This perspective is based upon the assumption that time heals the deepest wounds, which is premised on linear and irreversible temporality. From this point of view, "humans should be expected to simply move on as if we were a piece of unaffected nature."[17] As a result, victims who refuse to let their anger and resentment pass despite the passage of time are considered to instance an unnatural temporality. As Berber Bevernage outlines, "living anachronism" has become a popular metaphor to describe resentful, embittered, and vengeful victims.[18] Due to their inability to look forward, their temporality is disrupted "as if the distance between the past and the present has been obliterated."[19] Instead of mourning their losses, they are driven by a senseless desire for "undoing the past." This backward temporal orientation highlights the extent to which linear temporality—which underlies the overcoming of traumatic past—has no hold on them. Rather than healing their wounds, they strive to "subvert the progressive and linear imaginary of time."[20]

This particular relation between the victims and their haunting past accounts for their being negatively labeled as moral agents. Because of their own actions, desires, and feelings, they hamper the process through which an entire collective is expected to break free from a contested and controversial past. According to this perspective, despite the fact that anger and bitterness after serious suffering are understandable, those feelings are expected to end, after which the victims are able to accept loss and move forward. One could say that "the unforgiving victims are represented as consumed by bitterness."[21] Their emotional attachment to a painful past is considered a kind of moral failure for not allowing the beneficial effects of forgiveness and reconciliation to take place. The victims' resentment hampers not only their recovery from the harm suffered but also the social process of working through the traumatic past. This is why, after a long time and after the application of transitional justice, societies become tired of survivors who remain stuck in the past. Ultimately, the behavior of resentful and embittered victims tends to be seen as pathological, and they are considered to be unable to overcome their most compulsive passions and most painful traumas. What testifies to this includes the many clinical and ethical categories by which discourses within transitional justice depict backward-looking victims: traumatized, melancholic, and so on.

On balance, the temporality in which different social and political projects of transitional justice are embedded explains why victims who refuse to join the process of reconciliation are labeled negatively. With regard to the underlying temporality, they are considered to be prisoners of the past. From a moral point of view, for instance, their abilities as moral agents are considered to be consumed by their resentment. From a psychological perspective, the trauma they suffered is deemed to have turned them into melancholic subjects unable to overcome the aftermath of such experiences. "The refusal of mourning comes to be seen as a regrettable offense against one's own psychological recovery and autonomy."[22] Thereby melancholia and resentment have become two of the most common labels to describe the victims' failure to heal their wounds and contribute to the social process of transitional justice. Those are precisely the categories that the following sections aim to shed light onto. Against the backdrop of this understanding of melancholia and resentment, this paper delves further into different readings of these notions to pave the way toward questioning these critical readings.

In this section, three different layers have been highlighted when framing the behavior of backward-looking victims. The first layer is the temporality underlying the overcoming of the past which compels one to let bygones be bygones as time is irreversible. The second layer is the moral perspective that emphasizes the victims' incapacity to behave as moral agents. The final layer is the psychoanalytic view that regards victims as addictively stranded in the past. In this regard, resentment is the notion related to the moral level, and melancholia is related to the psychoanalytical one. In the following sections, both notions are reframed to allow for critical rethinking of the temporalities underlying transitional justice projects and for shedding light onto different and heterogeneous ways of dealing with the contested and traumatic past. In this regard, Benjamin's melancholia and Améry's resentment offer the grounds upon which to contest forward-looking temporalities underlying some approaches to transitional justice and to restore the ethico-political value of such attachments to the past.

Holding onto Bitterness: Rethinking Resentment from Jean Améry

Few would dispute that Améry's *At the Mind's Limits* is a priceless historical and philosophical essay for contemplating the temporalities underlying ethical responses to hurtful experiences. Written by a survivor of the Holocaust, it provides theoretical tools for analyzing the connections between the temporalities and ethical decisions related to dealing with the burden of the past. As Brudholm outlines in *Resentment's Virtues*,[23] Améry's analysis paves the way for critically questioning the assumptions underlying transitional justice, and more specifically, for undermining the assumptions of the recent trends within the transitional justice literature that prioritize social reconciliation over anything else. As described previously, the linear and irreversible temporality is aligned with the ethical assumptions that the past should be dealt with by forgiving and reconciliation.

Améry's critique of the way Germany dealt with its past offers useful insights for questioning the moral and temporal assumptions underlying the overcoming of a traumatic past that could shed light on different contexts beyond the German one. Améry's analysis of temporality revolves around a German term that is worth presenting in the original: *Vergangenheitsbewältigung*. This notion refers to the critical engagement with a painful and contested past with the aim of overcoming it. Nonetheless, it must be noted that the notion of *bewältigung*—which can be identified as *working through*—has been negatively labeled by Améry. When dealing with the traces of national socialism within German society, *bewältigung* holds negative connotations. It is viewed as disguised forgetting or it is seen as downgrading Germany's criminal past into a discourse of grief and sorrow. Thus, from Améry's perspective, transitional justice risks assuming a temporality according to which the past should be forgotten and left behind so as to avoid its aftermath in the future. Transitional justice thus incorporates a temporality according to which the "future," as Améry puts it, "is obviously a value concept. What will be tomorrow is more valuable than what was yesterday. That is how the natural feeling for time will have it."[24]

From Améry's perspective, this temporality "tends to create an irrevocable experience of time" from which there is no sense in trying to reverse and redeem the past.[25] These temporal assumptions in the transitional justice discourse lead to an ethical imperative on how to deal with the past. Providing that historical time is irreversible, the best possible course of action is to leave it behind and overcome its aftermath. In contrast, Améry's concept of resentment strives to block such *working-through* the past. He says:

> Absurdly, it demands that the irreversible be turned around, that the event be undone. Resentment blocks the exit to the genuine human dimension, the future. I know that the time-sense of the person trapped in resentment is twisted around, dis-ordered, if you wish, for it desires two impossible things: regression into the past and nullification of what happened.[26]

Despite the fact that these aims seem impossible to fulfill, Améry's critique paved the way toward rethinking the ethos of memory underlying transitional justice. According to Améry, linear temporality is based upon the irreversibility of time. It is not possible to change the past, and the wisest thing to do is to let bygones be bygones. But Améry argues that there is no moral sense to such a view as it only proves the inexorability of the passing of time. Consequently it was not possible for Améry to accede to linear temporality and join the social process of *Vergangenheitsbewältigung* in which a part of the German society engaged. This impossibility was grounded in the fact that he continued to suffer through the aftermath of the traumatic experiences decades after the end of the Holocaust.

As Jean-Marie Vivaldi claims, the tactile memory inherent to the tortured body makes victims reluctant to move on.[27] The traumatic effects of the torture one has suffered account for the collapse of the past and present within a victim's consciousness. This is why Améry's disrupted temporality sheds new light on the criticism of the linear conception of time upon which the overcoming of a traumatic past is based. And his stubborn resentment should not be tied to traumatic self-preoccupation or senseless longing for redemption.[28] On the contrary, resentment works as an engine of resistance against the irreversible time of history, as a moral reminder that persists despite the passing of time. Despite the fact that its demands are impossible to fulfill, the ethical refusal to let bygones be bygones is an engine for the moralization of history. Améry writes:

> Man has the right and the privilege to declare himself to be in disagreement with every natural occurrence, including the biological healing that time brings about. What happened, happened. This sentence is just as true as it is hostile to moral and intellect. The moral power to resist contains the protest, the revolt against reality, which is rational only as long as it is moral. The moral person demands annulment of time.[29]

As long as historical justice can be achieved only when history is moralized, Améry's resentment compels us to rethink the grounds of transitional justice. According to him, dealing with the past should always counteract the tendency to move on and forget the historical debts as a consequence of assuming the impossibility of reversing the past. Améry as a resentful person actually instances a living anachronism.[30] But that does not mean that this resentment lacks practical and historical consequences as it is essential for undermining the temporality underlying the social processes of *Vergangenheitsbewältigung*. "I hope that my resentment—which is my personal protest against the antimoral natural process of healing that time brings about, and by which I make the genuinely humane and absurd demand that time be turned back—will also perform a historical function."[31] In this regard, as Brudholm suggests, the desire of Améry's resentful persona highly resembles Benjamin's Angel of History.[32] Benjamin's *Angelus Novus* aims at stopping the progression of historical time, which compels the victims and rubble of the past to be forgotten and left behind. Despite being anachronistic, such endeavor is nonetheless critical as it radically questions the moral foundations of different processes that deal with the past by *working through* it.

This contemporary reading of Améry's resentment does not view the victims' persistent refusal to let go of their anger or grief as a source of self-pity and hopelessness, which are hindrances for the overcoming of traumatic pasts. Instead, their resentment could present an ethical demand which may open new critical avenues for rethinking the temporal and moral basis of transitional justice. Most importantly, Améry's ideas compel us not to pathologize the behavior of backward-looking victims in the context of collective violence. In this sense, the analysis of resentment needs to be complemented by a critical study of another notion that has traditionally been used to pathologize the state of being stuck in the past: melancholia.

Stranded in the Past: Rethinking Melancholia from Walter Benjamin

It is impossible to summarize in a single statement all the features that have been associated with melancholia throughout centuries. The philosophical and scientific discourse about melancholia goes from ancient times to contemporary psychoanalysis and postmodern philosophy, from the writings of Aristotle and Galen to Klein and Kristeva, including Kant and Baudelaire. The list of features that have been ascribed to melancholia is endless. Among others, its symptoms have included self-loathing, feelings of shame, suicidal tendencies, and hopelessness. In ancient times, the source of this unusual mood state was thought to be located in the human body rather than in the mind. Specifically, melancholia was thought to be caused by an excess of black bile in the body, with the most visible manifestations being the states of sadness and passivity. However, in the Middle Ages, melancholia was dematerialized and became a malaise of the soul and mind and was often described as *acedia*.

Regardless of how melancholia has been depicted in different contexts, there are some features that underlie its behavioral effects that cannot be overlooked. First of all, melancholia refers to the emergence of the feelings of sadness, fear, and grievance, which cannot be justified by the events the melancholic subject is facing. The lack of equilibrium between reality and reaction reveals the subject's tendency to overreact and inability to overcome obstacles. As Jennifer Radden describes it, "melancholia is characterized by a feeling of misery which is in excess of what is justified by the circumstances."[33] Additionally, melancholia is also associated with idleness. As Robert Burton asserts in *The Anatomy of Melancholy*, "there is no greater cause of melancholy than idleness, no better cure than business."[34] This idea takes on an ironic twist when he claims, "I write of melancholy, by being busy to avoid melancholy."[35] This description of melancholia focuses on the melancholic's inability to be a successful member of society and to live in the present. In this regard, it is worth quoting Wolf Lepenies' historical analysis in *Melancholy and Society*, in which he described melancholy as an unfitting phenomenon as it does not play any functional role within the organization of society. "Melancholy as a form . . . retreatism . . . can thus be understood, in terms of a more dynamic description . . . as a loss of order, and, in terms of a static description, as non order, nonconformity, dis-order."[36] Projecting this idea onto the context of this discussion, a melancholic subject might hinder the success of transitional justice in post-violence periods. Moreover, to appreciate the temporality underlying a melancholic's behavior and to grasp the tendency to pathologize this mood state in victims of serious violence, it is necessary to look into the twentieth-century discussion on melancholia by Sigmund Freud. After all, the different features that have enriched melancholia's physiognomy took on a new meaning with the psychoanalytic insight into this malaise.

In the aftermath of the First World War, Freud wrote a short essay titled "Mourning and Melancholia" in which he outlined his position regarding both of these moral emotions or psychological states.[37] According to him, mourning and melancholia could be considered as different ways of dealing with a loss stemming from past experiences. Nevertheless, whereas mourning is viewed as a step in the process of *working through* the trauma that precedes the overcoming of the past and allows for forward-looking recovery, melancholia is described as a painful dejection in which the subject refuses to accept the loss and cannot thus overcome it. Freud thus reshaped their relationship into a hard dichotomy according to which melancholia stems from the "inability to mourn."[38] It is based in "the presumption that mourning might follow melancholia" and in the imperative that mourning must follow melancholia.[39]

Engaging with the ideas on temporality described at the beginning of this chapter, it is possible to reframe mourning as a look-forward elaboration of the past and melancholia as a permanent backward-looking practice that blocks the overcoming of trauma. As Bernstein indicates, "the strong dualism between mourning and melancholy has become a way of exposing the personal and social idea that we are entitled to a new beginning."[40] It needs to be remarked that Freud's insights on melancholia are more heterogeneous than presented in "Mourning and Melancholia," and he actually changed them several times over the years. Evidence of this is that Freud's *The Ego and the Id* deeply questioned the dichotomy between mourning and melancholia as their boundaries tend to get blurred.[41] Nevertheless, "Mourning and Melancholia" was so influential as to become a benchmark for rethinking personal relationships with loss, which is why it is used as a reference in this text as well. After all, Freud's groundbreaking insights on melancholia as a backward-looking pathology have pervaded different disciplines and theoretical spaces.[42] This is why it has become a prism through which to define victims of massive violence who, after the passage of time and the application of transitional justice, remain melancholically bound to a painful past that they refuse to leave behind. The following paragraph from Julia Kristeva's *Black Sun* perfectly captures the understanding of temporality underlying melancholia:

> As the time in which we live is the time of our discourse, the alien, retarded, or vanishing speech of melancholy people leads them to live within a skewed time sense. It does not pass by, the before/after notion does not rule it, does not direct it from a past towards a goal. . . . a *moment* blocks the horizon of depressive temporality or rather removes any horizon, any perspective. . . . everything has gone by, they seem to stay, but I am faithful to those bygone days, I am nailed down to them, no revolution is possible, there is no future . . . . An overinflated, hyperbolic past fills all the dimensions of psychic continuity.[43]

Through the Freudian psychoanalytic discourse on melancholia, victims' backward-looking behavior has become pathologized. They are depicted as pillars of salt whose depressive engagement with deceitful memories accounts for the disruption of their underlying temporality. It is possible to find examples of victims not willing to mourn their losses within different transitional processes: Madres de la Plaza de Mayo in Argentina, descendants of the Francoism victims in Spain, victims of the dictatorship in Chile, among others, "refuse to fulfill the traditional task of mourning."[44] According to the psychoanalytic readings outlined so far, these victims might be regarded as stranded in a pathological and hurtful emotional attachment to their memories of a painful past, which hampers social closure after the end of violence.

Nevertheless, based on our reading of Améry's resentment resistance to forgiveness and reconciliation, such blocked temporality might play a critical role within transitional justice. For this reason, it is necessary to reframe the categories and labels used to describe melancholia. Going beyond the psychoanalytical framework and echoing Benjamin's insights into melancholia, the rest of this section aims at shedding light onto a different understanding of melancholia which, instead of endorsing a linear historical time, opens a path for rethinking multifarious temporalities which contest traditional ways of dealing with the past.

As Roger Bartra suggests, Freud's interpretation of melancholia is in opposition to the way in which it has been framed within the European tradition.[45] This is the same tradition that Benjamin recovered and actualized by rethinking the grounds of melancholic attachments toward the past.[46] There are different works in which Benjamin delves into mourning and melancholia. From "Left-Wing Melancholia" to the *Origin of the German Trauerspiel*,[47] Benjamin's insights are so diverse that it is hard to systematize his remarks into a coherent theory.[48] Nevertheless, with a view to highlighting the critical potentialities Benjamin ascribed to melancholia, it is worth considering his essay "On the Concept of History."[49]

In this unfinished text, Benjamin resorts to different metaphors to capture the haunting and revolutionary nature of recovering memory and stubbornly refusing to leave the past behind. The nourishing "image of enslaved ancestors,"[50] the angel who "would like to stay, awaken the dead and make whole what have been smashed,"[51] the "weak messianic power . . . on which the past has a claim," "the tiger's leap into the past"—all these expressions reveal a conception of time that refuses to let bygones be bygones, or (to use the previously mentioned terms) that refuses to fulfill the traditional task of mourning.[52] From the perspective obtained from Benjamin's critical reading, it is possible to appreciate the extent to which the assumption that melancholia must be followed by mourning relies on a linear and irreversible temporality. Nevertheless, the melancholic historical materialism he defended strives to make "the continuum of history explode."[53] In this regard, the temporality underlying Benjamin's approach does not lead him to assume that the past must be overcome by the future. On the contrary, the past, present, and future are entangled within a "historical constellation."[54] Owing to these connections, it is possible to use marginal and forgotten memories to criticize the society that has been based upon systematic violence and airbrushing of unsettling and contested memory. As a consequence, his insistence on not letting the dead rest in peace is intended to question the grounds on which societies have been rebuilt after violence without confronting properly the memory of the past and the fate of the victims.[55]

Benjamin does not deny the negative and pathological symptoms ascribed to melancholia: the loss of the ability to love, the emergence of feelings of shame, or the lack of interest toward the world. Nevertheless, such reactions do not bring about self-complacency and narcissistic self-pity. For the melancholic the devaluation of the world is already critical insofar as it brings to the fore the flaws of social processes of dealing with the past when restituting victims' memories.[56] Benjamin's groundbreaking analysis thus reversed previous ideas on melancholia. As Jonnathan Flatley suggests, "for Benjamin, melancholia is not a problem to be cured; loss is not something to get over with and leave behind."[57] Instead it is something to engage with critically so as to change the ways in which traumatic collective pasts have been confronted. Rather than remaining a prisoner of the past, Benjamin makes a virtue of the failure to overcome it, and as a result the relation between mourning and melancholia is viewed in a different way.[58] Instead of blocking the process of working through the past, melancholic attachment to painful memories could become a new step for a more inclusive and critical process of mourning. As Enzo Traverso claims while echoing Benjamin's insights, "if we abandon the Freudian model and depathologize melancholy, we could see it as a necessary premise of a mourning process; a step that precedes and allows mourning instead of paralyzing it and thus helps the subject to become active again."[59] It comes as no surprise that contemporary authors such as Enzo Traverso, Dominick LaCapra,[60] Douglas Crimp,[61] or Judith Butler,[62] echo Benjamin's understanding of melancholia by reframing it as resistance to techniques of power and social standards. Such problematic relationships with a loss that is not fully abandoned goes against the grain of the social process by means of which public losses are mourned collectively. Thus, Benjamin's analysis of melancholia provides fruitful resources to problematize and delve further into the polemics and complex processes of implementing transitional justice when reconciling and mourning.

Conclusions: Reconsidering Transitional Justice from Resentment and Melancholia

At the beginning of his work *Justice and Reconciliation*, Andrew Rigby echoes recent trends within the contemporary transitional justice theory by defending the following idea:

> Individuals, like collectives, for the sake of peace must somehow become capable of accepting loss and moving on. This ability to let go of the pain of the past is at the heart of what many understand to be forgiveness. Hatred and the quest for revenge can consume people, turning them into mirror image of those whom they hate.... At the core of any reconciliation process is the preparedness of people to anticipate a shared future.[63]

It is clear that Rigby's thesis on transitional justice is inclined to promote reconciliation over resentment, forgiveness over embittered anger, and future over past. Rigby's passage is an example of recent trends within the literature on transitional processes for dealing with legacies of traumatic pasts.

Within the last decades, discourse and politics surrounding transitional justice have been subordinated to the broad aim of promoting and achieving social reconciliation after violence. By expecting the overcoming of contested legacies and collective traumas, projects of transitional justice tend to be embedded in a linear and irreversible temporality according to which the past should be left behind in order to look enthusiastically to a bright new future. As outlined in the introduction of this chapter, some recent literature on transitional justice and post-violence reconciliation has uncritically engaged with that view of temporality, thereby assuming its ethical implications.[64] As a consequence, forgiveness and forgetting are highly esteemed, whereas resentment and remembering tend to be viewed as obstacles to the overcoming of such traumatic legacies. The concepts of mourning, working through, reconciliation, healing process, and forgiveness, all constitute the theoretical framework of contemporary trends on transitional justice, which tend to gloss over the victims' ongoing resentment.

By revealing the assumptions underpinning such approaches, this chapter has attempted to bring to the fore the multilayered temporalities underlying transitional justice. These differing views of time account for different ethical perspectives of the behavior of the victims and alternative perspectives on the multifarious processes underlying the overcoming of traumatic and contested legacies. My reading of Améry's resentment and Benjamin's melancholia presents both authors' painful experiences and groundbreaking ideas as paving the way for a different conception of temporality, morality, and psychology underlying victims' refusal to leave the past behind. After projecting their ideas onto contemporary debates, it is possible to appreciate the extent to which traumatized victims of systematic and state-sponsored violence might become the kernel from which to moralize history and contest the flaws of transitional justice and social reconciliation. Against the backdrop of different contemporary trends that dismiss resentful and melancholic victims, this chapter attempted to present different theoretical paths for questioning discourses on reconciliation and transitional justice and highlighting the critical and moral potentialities stemming from victims' insistence on keeping their wounds open and refusing definitive closure despite the passing of time. The lasting effects of these wounds are undoubtedly multifarious. On the one hand, they testify to refusal to forgive and look forward. On the other hand, they refer to traumatized victims' inability to overcome the aftermath of such hurtful experiences.

Acknowledgments

This research has been produced thanks to support from: "Memoria y experiencia de las víctimas del terrorismo – para una mayor visibilidad en Europa" (620406-EPP-1-2020-1-ES-EPPJMO-SUPPA) (Erasmus+Program Jean Monnet activities).

Notes

1. Jon Elster, *Rendición de cuentas: La justicia transicional en perspectiva histórica* (Buenos Aires: Katz, 2002). Sandrine Lefranc, *Políticas del perdón* (Valencia: PUV, 2004); Ruti Teitel, *Transitional Justice* (Oxford: Oxford University Press, 2000).
2. Ruti Teitel, "Transitional Historical Justice," in *Justice in Time: Responding to Historical Injustice*, ed. Lukas H. Meyer (Baden-Baden: Nomos Verlagsgesellschaft, 2014), 210.
3. Berber Bevernage, *History, Memory, and State-Sponsored Violence: Time and Justice* (New York: Routledge, 2012), 45.
4. Victoria Fareld, "History, Justice, and the Time of the Imprescriptible," in *The Ethos of History: Time and Responsibility*, ed. Stefan Helgesson and Jayne Svenungsson (New York: Berghahn Books, 2017), 60.
5. Jonathan Flatley, *Affective Mapping: Melancholia and the Politics of Modernism* (Cambridge, MA and London: Harvard University Press, 2008), 71.
6. Fareld, "History, Justice," 55.
7. Bevernage, *History, Memory*, 19.
8. Jill Stauffer, *Ethical Loneliness: The Injustice of Not Being Heard* (New York: Columbia University Press, 2015), 113.
9. Margaret Walker, *Moral Repair: Reconstructing Moral Relations after Wrongdoing* (New York: Cambridge University Press, 2006), 12.
10. Andrew Rigby, *Justice and Reconciliation: After the Violence* (London: Lynne Rieneer, 2001).
11. Mark Amstutz, *The Healing of Nations: The Promise and Limits of Political Forgiveness* (Lanham: Rowham and Littlefield, 2005).
12. Desmond Tutu, *No Future Without Forgiveness* (New York: Doubleday, 1999).
13. Charles Villa-Vicencio, "Getting on With Life: A Move Towards Reconciliation," in *Looking Back Reaching Forward: Reflections on the Truth and Reconciliation Commission of South Africa*, ed. Charles Villa-Vicencio and Wilhelm Verwoerd (Cape Town: University of Cape Town Press, 2000).

14 Thomas Brudholm, *Resentment's Virtue: Jean Améry and the Refusal to Forgive* (Philadelphia: Temple University Press, 2008), 171.
15 Brudholm, *Resentment's Virtue*, 30.
16 Bevernage, *History, Memory*, 84.
17 Brudholm, *Resentment's Virtue*, 83.
18 Bevernage, *History, Memory*, 15.
19 Bevernage, *History, Memory*, 15.
20 Magdalena Zolkos, *Reconciling Community and Subjective Life: Trauma Testimony as Political Theorizing in the Work of Jean Améry and Imre Kertész* (New York: Continuum, 2010), 23.
21 Brudholm, *Resentment's Virtue*, 5.
22 Bevernage, *History, Memory*, 157.
23 Brudholm, *Resentment's Virtue*; Thomas Brudholm, "A Confiscated Past: Jean Améry on Home and Exile," *The Hedgehog Review* 5, no. 3 (2005): 7–19; and Thomas Brudholm, "Revisiting Resentments: Jean Améry and the Dark Side of Forgiveness and Reconciliation," *Journal of Human Rights* 5, no. 1 (2006): 7–26.
24 Jean Améry, *At the Mind's Limits: Contemplations by a Survivor on Auschwitz and its Realities*, trans. Sidney and Stella Rosenfeld (Bloomington: Indiana University Press, 1980), 76.
25 Bevernage, *History, Memory*, 64.
26 Améry, *At the Mind's Limits*, 68.
27 Jean-Marie Vivaldi, *Reflections on Jean Améry: Torture, Resentment, and Homelessness as the Mind's Limits* (New York: Palgrave Macmillan, 2018), 30.
28 Brudholm, *Resentment's Virtue*, 36.
29 Améry, *At the Mind's Limits*, 72.
30 Carlos Thiebaut and Antonio Ramos Gómez, *Las razones de la amargura* (Barcelona: Herder, 2018), 74.
31 Thiebaut and Gómez, *Las razones*, 77.
32 Brudholm, *Resenment's Virtue*, 109.
33 Jennifer Radden, *The Nature of Melancholy: From Aristotle to Kristeva* (New York: Oxford University Press, 2000), 12.
34 Robert Burton, *The Anatomy of Melancholy* (London: NYRB Classics, 2001), 145.
35 Burton, *The Anatomy*, 145.
36 Wolf Lepenies, *Melancholy and Society* (Cambridge, MA and London: Harvard University Press, 1992), 8.
37 Sigmund Freud, "Mourning and Melancholia," in *On Murder, Mourning an Melancholia*, ed. Maud Ellmann, trans. Shaun Whiteside (London: Penguin, 2005).
38 Freud, "Mourning and Melancholia," 205.
39 Judith Butler, "After Loss, What?" in *Loss: The Politics of Mourning*, ed. David L. Eng and David Kazanjian (Berkeley, Los Angeles, London: University of California Press, 2003), 472.
40 Jeffrey Bernstein, "Améry's Devastation and Resentment: An Ethnographic Transcendental Deduction," *Tijdschrift voor Filosofie* 76, no. 1 (2014): 23.
41 Sigmund Freud, "The Ego and the Id," in *Beyond the Pleasure Principle and Other Writings*, trans. John Reddick (London: Penguin, 2003), 101–50.
42 Wendy Brown, "Resisting Left Melancholia," in *Loss: The Politics of Mourning*, ed. David L. Eng and David Kazanjian (Berkeley and Los Angeles: University of California Press, 2003); Charles Maier, "A Surfeit of Memory? Reflections on History, Melancholy and Denial," *History and Memory* 5, no. 2 (1993): 136–52.

43 Julia Kristeva, *Black Sun: Depression and Melancholia* (New York: Columbia University Press, 1989), 60.
44 Bevernage, *History, Memory*, 42.
45 Roger Bartra, *El duelo de los ángeles* (Valencia: Pre-textos, 2004), 141; Roger Bartra, *La melancolía moderna* (Valencia: Pre-textos, 2019), 37.
46 Peter Fritzsche, *Stranded in the Present: Modern Time and the Melancholy of History* (Cambridge, MA: Harvard University Press, 2004).
47 Walter Benjamin, *Origin of the German Trauerspiel* (Cambridge, MA: Harvard University Press, 2019).
48 See Max Pensky, *Melancholy Dialectics: Walter Benjamin and the Play of Mourning* (Amherst: Massachusetts University Press, 2001).
49 Walter Benjamin, "On the Concept of History," in *Selected Writings: Vol 4*, ed. Howard Eiland and Michael Jennings (Cambridge, MA: Harvard University Press, 2006).
50 Benjamin, "On the Concept of History," 391.
51 Benjamin, "On the Concept of History," 392.
52 Benjamin, "On the Concept of History," 395.
53 Benjamin, "On the Concept of History," 395.
54 Benjamin, "On the Concept of History," 397.
55 Martin Jay, "Against Consolation: Walter Benjamin and the Refusal to Mourn," in *War and Remembrance in the Twentieth Century*, ed. Jay Winter and Emmanuel Silvan (Cambridge: Cambridge University Press, 1999), 230.
56 Pensky, *Melancholy Dialectics*, 220.
57 Flatley, *Affective Mapping*, 64.
58 Jay, "Against Consolation," 229.
59 Enzo Traverso, *Left-Wing Melancholia* (New York: Columbia University Press, 2017), 45.
60 Dominick LaCapra, *History and Its Limits* (Ithaca and London: Cornell University Press, 2009).
61 Douglas Crimp, *Melancholia and Moralism* (Cambridge, MA: MIT Press, 2002); Douglas Crimp, "Melancholia and Moralism," in *Loss: The Politics of Mourning*, ed. David L. Eng and David Kazanjian (Berkeley, Los Angeles, London: University of California Press, 2003), 188–204.
62 Judith Butler, *Precarious Life: The Powers of Mourning and Violence* (London and New York: Verso, 2006).
63 Rigby, *Justice and Reconciliation*, 12.
64 Tutu, *No Future*; Rigby, *Justice and Reconciliation*.

Bibliography

Améry, Jean. *At the Mind's Limits: Contemplations by a survivor on Auschwitz and its realities*. Translated by Sidney and Stella Rosenfeld. Bloomington: Indiana University Press, 1980.

Bartra, Roger. *El duelo de los ángeles*. Valencia: Pretextos, 2004.

Bartra, Roger. *La melancholia moderna*. Valencia: Pretextos, 2019.

Benjamin, Walter. "On the Concept of History." In *Selected Writings: Vol 4*, edited by Howard Eiland and Michael Jennings, 389–400. Cambridge: Harvard University Press, 2006.

Benjamin, Walter. *Writing of the German Trauerspiel.* Massachusetts, London: Harvard University Press, 2019.
Bernstein, Jeffrey. "Amery's Devastation and Resentment: An Ethnographic Transcendental Deduction." *Tijdschrift voor Filosofie* 76, no. 1 (2006): 5–30.
Bevernage, Berber. *History, Memory, and State-Sponsored Violence: Time and Justice.* New York: Routledge, 2012.
Brown, Wendy. "Resisting Left Melancholia." In *Loss: The Politics of Mourning*, edited by David L. Eng and David Kazanjian, 458–66. Berkeley and Los Angeles: University of California Press, 2003.
Brudholm, Thomas. "A Confiscated Past: Jean Améry on Home and Exile." *The Hedgehog Review* 5, no. 3 (2005): 7–19.
Brudholm, Thomas. *Resentment's Virtue: Jean Améry and the Refusal to Forgive.* Philadelphia: Temple University Press, 2008.
Brudholm, Thomas. "Revisiting Resentments: Jean Améry and the Dark Side of Forgiveness and Reconciliation." *Journal of Human Rights* 5, no. 1 (2006): 7–26.
Burton, Robert. *The Anatomy of Melancholy.* London: NYRB Classics, 2001.
Butler, Judith. "After Loss, What?" In *Loss: The Politics of Mourning*, edited by David L. Eng and David Kazanjian, 467–74. Berkeley and Los Angeles: University of California Press, 2003.
Butler, Judith. *Precarious Life: The Powers of Mourning and Violence.* London and New York: Verso, 2006.
Crimp, Douglas. *Melancholia and Moralism.* Cambridge: MIT Press, 2002.
Crimp, Douglas. "Melancholia and Moralism." In *Loss: The Politics of Mourning*, edited by David L. Eng and David Kazanjian, 188–204. Berkeley and Los Angeles: University of California Press, 2003.
Elster, Jon. *Rendición de cuentas: La justicia transicional en perspectiva histórica.* Buenos Aires: Katz, 2002.
Fareld, Victoria. "History, Justice, and the Time of the Imprescriptible." In *The Ethos of History: Time and Responsibility*, edited by Stefan Helgesson and Jayne Svenungsson, 54–69. New York: Berghahn Books, 2017.
Flatley, Jonathan. *Affective Mapping: Melancholia and the Politics of Modernism.* Cambridge, Massachusetts and London: Harvard University Press, 2008.
Freud, Sigmund. "The Ego and the Id." In *Beyond the Pleasure Principle and Other Writings*, translated by John Reddick, 101–50. London: Penguin, 2003.
Freud, Sigmund. "Mourning and Melancholia." In *On Murder, Mourning and Melancholia*, edited by Maud Ellman and translated by Shaun Whiteside, 201–18. London: Penguin, 2005.
Fritzsche, Peter. *Stranded in the Present: Modern Time and the Melancholy of History.* Cambridge, Massachusetts and London: Harvard University Press, 2004.
Hermann, Judith. *Trauma and Recovery: The Aftermath of Violence.* New York. Basic Books, 2015.
Jay, Martin. "Against Consolation: Walter Benjamin and the Refusal to Mourn." In *War and Remembrance in the Twentieth Century*, edited by Jay Winter and Emmanuel Silvan, 221–30. Cambridge, MA: Harvard University Press, 1999.
Kristeva, Julia. *Black Sun: Depression and Melancholia.* New York: Columbia University Press, 1989.
LaCapra, Dominick. *History and Its Limits.* Ithaca and London: Cornell University Press, 2009.
Lefranc, Sandrine. *Políticas del perdón.* Valencia: PUV, 2004.

Lepenies, Wolf. *Melancholy and Society*. Cambridge, MA: Harvard University Press, 1992.
Maier, Charles. "A Surfeit of Memory? Reflections on History, Melancholy and Denial." *History and Memory* 5, no. 2 (1993): 136–52.
Pensky, Max. *Melancholy Dialectics: Walter Benjamin and the Play of Mourning*. Amherst: Massachusetts University Press, 2001.
Radden, Jennifer. *The Nature of Melancholy: From Aristotle to Kristeva*. New York: Oxford University Press, 2000.
Rigby, Andrew. *Justice and Reconciliation: After the Violence*. London: Lynne Rienner, 2001.
Stauffer, Jill. *Ethical Loneliness: The Injustice of not Being Heard*. New York: Columbia University Press, 2015.
Teitel, Ruti. *Transitional Justice*. Oxford: Oxford University Press, 2000.
Teitel, Ruti. "Transitional Historical Justice." In *Justice in Time: Responding to Historical Injustice*, edited by Lukas H. Meyer, 209–22. Baden-Baden: Nomos Verlagsgesellschaft, 2014.
Thiebaut, Carlos and Antonio Ramos Gómez. *Las razones de la amargura*. Barcelona: Herder, 2018.
Traverso, Enzo. *Left-Wing Melancholia*. New York: Columbia University Press, 2017.
Tutu, Desmond. *No Future without Forgiveness*. New York: Image Books, 2000.
Villa-Vicencio, Charles. "Getting on With Life: A Move Towards Reconciliation." In *Looking Back Reaching Forward: Reflections on the Truth and Reconciliation Commission of South Africa*, edited by Charles Villa-Vicencio and Wilhelm Verwoerd, 199–209. Cape Town: University of Cape Town Press, 2000.
Vivaldi, Jean-Marie. *Reflections of Jean Améry: Torture, Resentment, and Homelessness as the Mind's Limits*. New York: Palgrave Macmillan, 2018.
Walkter, Margaret. *Moral Repair: Reconstructing Moral Relations after Wrongdoing*. New York: Cambridge University Press, 2006.
Zolkos, Magdalena. *Reconciling Community and Subjective Life: Trauma Testimony as Political Theorizing in the Work of Jean Améry and Imre Kertész*. New York: Continuum, 2010.

Section II

Agency, Relativity, and Affect

5

The Relativism of Historical Distance and the Contextual Constitution of Agency

Nora Hämäläinen

Introduction

In her 1997 book *Fieldwork in Familiar Places*, Michele Moody-Adams criticizes what she calls the "relativism of historical distance," by which she means the inclination not to judge people of the past by the same standards that we use to judge our contemporaries.[1] One of her central motivations for this criticism is the conviction that a consistently applied universalism enhances our commitment to central (universal) moral values. Applying different standards to people of the past encourages, in her view, a lax rather than appropriately committed and self-critical attitude to moral issues in our own time.

This argument is of interest because it represents something of a pure case of the quite common view that "relativism" is harmful for a self-reflective realization of "the good." But it also has bearing on contemporary movements toward critical and political reconsiderations of the recent and more distant past: the removal of statues, rethinking of literary canons, the posthumous reconsideration of people's contributions to society. Should we think of people of the past as our peers, in a moral respect, or is it better to think of them as in some sense fundamentally different? People of the past—their works and their conceptions—are usually not considered exempt from our critical moral reflection. But how should this critical reflection be understood, how does it affect our relation to the past and its heroes, and how does it impinge on our relation to our own present moral commitments? These are of course large and multidimensional issues. I will here address them by focusing on the role of universalizing moral judgment in moral engagements with the past.

I argue here, in contrast to Moody-Adams, that withholding moral judgment in relation to people who have lived under different social conditions may be an essential prerequisite for navigating our own moral challenges in a responsible and responsive way.[2] Rather than thinking about past moralities and people of the past in terms of moral judgment, we are often morally better served by investigating the complex conditions under which morally relevant moves are made in the lives of individuals and communities. This may also involve passing moral judgments, though these are more likely to be contextual and conditional ones, adjusted to the lives we are seeking to understand and thus "relative" to historical context.

This chapter is structured as follows: In the first section of this chapter I provide a few words about the context of Moody-Adam's critique of varieties of "relativism of historical distance." In the second section I provide some reflections on the vicissitudes in applying moral judgment to the past in the context of historical fiction, and what might be gained from not doing so. In the third section I move on to anthropologist Veena Das's "ordinary ethics" by engaging cases from her early fieldwork on post-partition India and later work in low-income neighborhoods in Delhi. I highlight how they do a distinctive kind of moral philosophical work by purposively deflecting from the register of (universalizing) moral judgment and delving into the complex moral worlds that can be made available to us through ethnography and historiography, for example. In the last section I offer some reflections on the embeddedness of moral thought and action in a life of day-to-day necessities and tasks.

I conclude that a variety of a relativism of historical distance is methodologically helpful for making philosophical sense of the complexities, tensions, and dynamics of past as well as present moral lives.

The Relativism of Historical Distance

In a wide array of contemporary intellectual debate, thinkers often extend relativist hypotheses about moral diversity to the understanding of historical reflection, defending a relativism of "historical distance"—in Bernard Williams' phrase—which seeks to shield past practices from contemporary moral reflection and criticism. In a familiar example, some historians have claimed that contemporary readers cannot fault Thomas Jefferson for being a slave-holder—in spite of his defense of equality—because to do so is to judge him according to standards that do not apply to the past.[3]

In contrast to these relativists of historical distance who demand different standards of judgement for people of the past, Moody-Adams asks us to apply the very same kind of critical moral reflection to the past that we apply to the present. This does not, for her, imply only that we may judge past people by the same moral standards we would apply to our contemporaries but also that we must do so and that we must hold people of the past accountable in a way analogous to how we hold our contemporaries accountable. "Significant moral criticism" is, by her lights, "an effort to encourage reinterpretation of the structure of moral experience as a way of bringing about change in practice."[4] But such criticism "never involves the invention or application of radically new ideas."[5] Our inclination toward a "relativism of historical distance" is, she thinks, an important issue to take a stand on because the past may play a trick on our judgment. Many people who would eschew relativism and apply universalist forms of moral judgment in a contemporary world are likely to relax their requirements in relation to people of the past. We may judge that slave owners were not necessarily bad people, though willingly participating in a practice that today is universally condemned. But this, in her view, is something we should not do. People of the past should be held accountable to universal standards (as we know them) even if this, of course, can no longer affect them. It is, in her view, important for us, because it helps us sort among our own judgments and be vigilant about the residues in our thinking of views that we now recognize as immoral.[6] But this is also prompted by her understanding of what morality essentially is. If morality is about objective, universal values, then we are obfuscating this fact for reasons of convenience in applying relativizing clauses to people of the past.

The critique of relativisms of historical distance is part of Moody-Adams's wider argument against moral relativism. We need to take a brief look at these arguments in order to see what she is up to. She thinks moral relativism depends on a range of mistaken ideas about culture. Moral relativism, she believes, is premised on the false idea that moral cultures are clearly bounded, fully integrated, and unchanging wholes. A relativist, in her view, believes that such self-enclosed wholes are the source of culturally relative moral truths. But given that any cultural setting has fuzzy boundaries, contains internal conflicts and tensions, and undergoes significant changes also in its moral beliefs and practices, moral relativism cannot, in her view, be right. Morally significant conversations and critique are possible and indeed ordinary between people of different cultures: oppressed groups fighting for their rights make meaningful alliances with oppressed groups from other cultural locations; moral ideas travel across boundaries and are appropriated in new contexts.

And because moral conversations are possible and relevant, relativism is wrong. We are all, as moral creatures, engaged in the same, shared quest for the good (recognized, for example, in twentieth-century movements for social justice), and all forms of relativism run the risk of leading us astray from it.

Part of the problems with Moody-Adams's account is due to her description of relativism, which is too narrow to capture the views of many people who sympathize with relativist modes of thought.[7] The relativity of right and wrong to context (cultural or situational) does not require a picture of moral cultures as homogeneous, self-enclosed, and unchanging. Quite to the contrary, many thinkers who by Mood-Adams' criteria would easily be filed as relativists are well aware of the complex, dynamic, and potentially antagonistic nature of moral communities; they know that moral cultures are not clearly bounded, but that they are internally heterogeneous and mutable.[8] This knowledge adds complexity to the picture but does not remove the profound differences between the moral worlds of different times and places: norms, duties, orderings of values, conceptions of self, moral practices. For these thinkers, taking this variety seriously undermines claims to normative *sameness* between distant times and places, of a kind that should or even could be pinned down by philosophical or other theoretical means.

I will not here further seek to challenge Moody-Adams's understanding of the nature of relativism but focus on discussing how forms of relativized reflection and judgment are a benign and fruitful feature of moral thought. Applied in relation to people of the past, a relativism of historical distance displays, in my view, not necessarily the laxity of our moral commitments but instead a capacity to engage and reflect upon different moral life-worlds—a capacity that is conductive to sensitive moral appraisals and quite necessary for sustaining a working morality in complex and changing circumstances. Relativity, understood not as a doctrine (relativism) but as an aspect of lived morality, is not antithetical to confidence in making moral claims with universalizing appeal in relation to concrete moral issues or more generally. But it is antithetical to attempts at fixating the supposedly universal nature of morality and our moral obligations by philosophical means, either by seeking to codify them in normative moral theory, or like Moody-Adams seek to prove through a meta-ethical argument that morality is always and everywhere the same.

Typically, people are neither full-blown relativists nor full-blown universalists when it comes to thinking about people of the past. We judge slavery, Nazism, racial segregation, and the systematic subordination of women bad or evil, but we do not necessarily think that everyone who has contributed to an oppressive social order as morally blameworthy. We do not think, for instance, that patriarchal men making decisions for their wives, grown daughters, and unmarried sisters in past generations of our families were necessarily bad people, even when their decisions strike us as unfair, selfish, and ill-considered. We may think of slavery as an abominable practice but still find morally significant differences between slave owners and deem some of them good, or good enough, people. We tend to think of Nazis as bad people, but in the vast array of Nazi collaborators we are willing to see people whose actions are morally understandable and even excusable because of the strange and unhappy historical circumstances of their lives that we may call vicissitudes of moral luck. Perhaps there is a range of moral "crimes" for which we find ourselves unable to take differences of conditions as assuaging circumstances, but the range of what we count as such crimes is also historically variable. It also often makes a certain difference to our judgments if people were aware of standards different from the ones they were living. Collective descents into violence and oppression (e.g., in war or political conflict) may affect our posthumous judgment differently than long-term structural features of past moral orders.

Yet, there are meaningful conversations to be had about these things, and a significant part of our imaginary moral engagement with historical figures revolves around moral complexities related to historical difference. Moody-Adams is not exactly saying that we should not engage in these conversations; only that we should not consider insight into historical circumstances as a reason for judging people differently because "morally speaking, there is never anything fundamentally 'new' in a new historical epoch."[9] But by demanding sameness in our judgments of people of the past she is eclipsing much of the potential for imaginary moral engagement with these people and the realities they inhabited.

Lessons from Fiction?

Applying the moral standards of our time to past worlds can be quite disturbing in ways that we do not need to be philosophers to recognize. *Anne with an E*, a three-season Netflix television series adaptation of L. M. Montgomery's *Anne of Green Gables* released between 2017 and 2020, is a case in point. Its makers, like generations of readers, seem to have been impressed and inspired by Anne's spirit but find the late nineteenth-century world she inhabits too depressing. Thus, one by one the series engages issues of social justice, significantly modifying the contents and moral world of the book. In the series Anne's newly invented artistic, sensitive gay schoolmate Cole finds a new home and a world where he is accepted as a protegee of the elderly "aunt" Josephine Berry, who is recast as a lesbian socialite. Gilbert Blythe (the schoolmate whom Anne of the books later marries) leaves Avonlea to work on a steam ship and returns with his new friend, a black man from Trinidad who becomes his partner on the farm. The new schoolteacher, a young woman, drives a motorbike, wears trousers, refuses the corset, and practices learning by doing in the classroom, much to the dismay of the local dignitaries. Anne befriends (in spite of the prejudice of the adults around her) a native American girl who ends up locked into an oppressive boarding school where the children are forced to speak English.

The result is a tour of moral judgments that a contemporary liberal Western person is likely to want their children to share on a range of questions of social justice. Watching the series with my eleven-year-old, I find myself having no quarrel with the (contemporary, largely social liberal) values expressed, but I do find myself at odds with the way they are glued onto a world where the compassion they mobilize would have come to expression in very different ways, if at all. This kind of revisionism is more usual in children's fiction, given a quite widely shared expectation that such fiction should be at least modestly educative. But it also raises questions concerning what may mean to be morally educated through fiction.

Growing up in the 1980s, reading Montgomery's *Anne* and *Emily*, Ingalls Wilder's *Little House* on the Prairie, Alcott's *Little Women*, Blyton's *Adventure-* and *Five* series, and Frances Hodgson Burnett's *The Secret Garden*, along with Swedish classic *Kulla-Gulla*, set in late nineteenth-century rural Sweden and written in the late 1940s and 1950s, I was, like most of my contemporary avid child readers immersed in complex layered worlds of moral historicity: my own world, the world of the author and the fictionalized historical worlds where the stories were set. Most of these books are still reissued as children's classics. All of them represented moral worlds quite different from the one in which my friends and I grew up and still more different than the world in which our children grow up.

When reading such books, children intuitively practice a kind of relativism of historical distance. They learn upon reading what does and does not make sense, morally speaking, within the worlds of the novels, knowing, for the most part, how to tell the difference between a fantasy world, and something that purports to describe an actual past. They are immersed in worlds in which girls are brought up to marry well and barred from substantial careers; in which race, class, and gender are represented in ways that strike a contemporary child as foreign and potentially immoral; and in which they certainly would feel confined. Yet they are able to pick up the moral energies of those worlds and follow the child protagonists in quests that make moral sense: the conquering of prejudice, the care of siblings, the discovery of friendships or new parents, the building of trust, the catching of criminals, the challenges of growing up and leaving home. Forms of rebellion against or reinterpretations of social and moral conventions have their place in much of the youth fiction that has survived to our day, but the reader is required to accept many things as integral parts of the worlds of the narratives that they would not accept as part of their own.

We may reflect a bit on what is going on in such reading. It is not that readers abandon the moral orientation of their present. Neither do they cling to that orientation, to navigate the fictive "historical" world. It is something else or something in-between, an immersive learning of difference, an exercise in imaginative moral world-making. A moral world is put together from what is familiar and what is strange: new patterns of recognition emerge, applicable to new narratives set in the same or similar historical or fictional settings.[10] This may be as simple or as complex as the reader can muster or the work demands. I may compare my own immersive reading of *Little House on the Prairie*, aged eight or nine, with my equally immersive but at the same time more complexly analytic reading of Hilary Mantel's *The Mirror and The Light* at age forty-two. In the latter a number of layers are added: the historical distance between Mantel and the Tudor world; her craft of both keeping that world real and translating it to the moral sensibilities of the implied reader; my own grown up and relatively trained eye on the results of this craft; an avid readers' appreciation of the textual and structural aspects of the novel; and a running reflection on how, potentially, to use this novel for more academic (moral philosophical) purposes. Yet in both cases the energy of the texts is dependent on the readers' capacity to inhabit its world of fundamental hierarchies while at the same time remaining in their own world.

Both the pleasure and the intellectual challenge of such reading are premised on a recalibration of moral judgment for the purposes of navigating the moral world of the work. An integral part of the artistic success of historical fiction depends on the crafting of a credible moral world, no matter how hypothetical. Mantel's world is ambitious in this respect, playing complexly with closeness and distance. *Anne with an E* is an exercise in moral anachronism, which effectively makes the moral world of L. M. Montgomery's novels, premised on a moral world of turn of the century Canada, unavailable, not only in the sense that the past always is unavailable but in the way that it steers away from imaginative immersion in difference.

There is surely a difference between applying the same moral judgement to past and present (as Moody-Adams demands that we do) and recreating a fictive past to accord with current moral sentiments (as in *Anne with an E*). The latter could be thought of as merely using the historical setting of the fiction as a starting point to tell a story, and thus not an engagement with the historical world at all. But it is premised on a very definite revisionary rejection of that world, which thwarts such interpretation. Its way of actively *engaging* that historical world is much like Moody-Adams's recipe for engaging history. They share a common core conception of what it means to be critical and morally discerning in relation to the past: it means applying our contemporary supposedly universal terms of normative judgment to it, uncut.

I have discussed this at some length because I think there is something recognizably tedious about morally motivated anachronisms in historical fiction. Most readers and viewers can recognize instances of when they have reacted in a way similar to my reaction to *Anne with an E*. It is not just an aesthetic matter; it often has a moral aspect. Seeking to improve on a past world instead of exploring it hides from us the distinctive moral dynamics of the past depicted. The exercise of seeking to engage a different world is eclipsed, because of a keenness to hunt down injustice. The only moral capacity exercised is that of applying one's vigilance for injustice to unfamiliar situations. I am not saying that this is unimportant. It is just a very thin slice of the morally valuable activity engendered by confrontations with difference.

Everyday Negotiations of the Good

Moral thought is many things, and not all of them can be cashed out as moral judgment (in terms of good and bad, good and evil, or some thicker moral concepts). This is an important insight present in much contemporary virtue ethics and phenomenological ethics, but it finds some of its most insistent defenders in a tradition of ethics after Wittgenstein, represented by Cora Diamond, Alice Crary, and Anne-Marie Søndergaard Christensen, among others.[11] Surely Moody-Adams would agree to this in general terms, but it is not always easy, when engaged in moral philosophy, to resist the pull of moral judgment, in order to let other aspects of moral life come to the fore.

If we think of overt moral judgment as the tip of the iceberg, we should want to know what the remaining 90% is made of. The anthropologist Veena Das, also inspired by Ludwig Wittgenstein and Stanley Cavell, as well as by Cora Diamond, is one of the contemporary thinkers who is helpful here. Her ethnographic work has been focused on India, from her early work with survivors of post-partition violence to work in low-income neighborhoods in Delhi; and many of the lives she has followed have been fraught with readily nameable major moral challenges: violence, poverty, social injustice. Yet her anthropological attention, rather than focusing on such wrongs, traces in these lives a varied and complex activity of practical moral world-making: the careful crafting and maintenance of relationships, the negotiation of values, the upholding of normality, the negotiation of gifts, the solving of practical problems, as well as day-to-day efforts to live with loss, fraught social relations, deficient infrastructures and precarity. There are great differences between the stories from different periods and places of work, but they all contribute to a way of viewing moral life that I think is instructive here: one where "every single second has a moral tag."[12] This, however, does *not* mean that every single second opens up for moral judgment, but rather that every moment forms part of a continuous moral activity that we need to familiarize ourselves with, not least because much of it is routinely neglected in moral philosophy.

In one of the stories from her fieldwork Das follows her relatively well-to-do friend Manjit to visit a cousin, Manpreet, who lives in confined and dependent circumstances with her son and daughter in law.[13] The friend knows that her cousin is not faring well and wants to help her. But giving money openly would be showing off her wealth in relation to the relatives and would be improper especially since Manjit is younger than her cousin. As the winter is approaching, she would like to give her cousin a warm shawl, but the gesture could be taken as a criticism directed toward the daughter in law for not providing the elder woman with the comfort she needs. An option would be to give shawls to both her cousin and the daughter in law, but there seems to be no relevant occasion to warrant such a gift. When they arrive at the house the cousin sends a grandchild to get Coca-Cola and *pakoras* from the market. A quick negotiation ensues; Coca-Cola (outrageously expensive) is averted with reference to the guest's diabetes, but the *pakoras* must be accepted. Finally, Manjit manages to tuck some money into the clothes of her cousin, without catching the attention of her family. Help is given, without raising attention that could disturb a fragile social balance among the woman, her cousin, and the daughter in law. Conventions, conceptions of responsibility, care and propriety, pride, dependency, and the complex social economy of gift giving are in this simple act managed to a working result. Is she also contributing to maintaining a social situation that is harmful for her cousin? In the best of worlds help would not be needed, or it could be given and taken openly. Perhaps in a different world the latent reproach toward the family could be voiced, and a more long-term solution could be negotiated. But in all the human worlds we know, social interaction is complex and much damage can be done, especially in difficult situations, by careless moves.

In such scenes the textures of human togetherness, along with some of its mediating objects (money, shawls, Coca-Cola) are made visible to the reader. Moral life may indeed be the acting on principles and goods that transcend such situations, but it is also the maintenance of togetherness by one's best lights. It would be misleading to speak of this work as the situated application of principles and ideals. Although these women could certainly verbalize some of the principles and values that accompany and guide their own and other's action, such verbalizations are often ex post facto, not descriptions of what was "applied" but a continuation of the weaving of the fabric of moral life by connecting reflections on what people are doing in morally challenging situations to familiar ideas and ideals.

Another story comes from Das's early engagement with survivors of the violence of the partition of Pakistan from India in 1947. During the period of unrest many women were raped, and some were abducted: Muslims by Hindus, Hindus by Muslims. Some were forcibly married and yet made a home and a life for themselves. Some escaped and returned, stigmatized as unmarriageable "spoiled goods," and had to settle into circumstances that were far from optimal. Experiences were covered in silence. Family members disappeared and sometimes returned, unable to speak of what had passed.

In this context Das relates the story of Asha, an upper-caste Hindu woman who, after losing her husband in 1941, at the age of twenty stays to live with his brother's family and receives much care and affection from his sisters.[14] One of them even "gives" the childless Asha her infant son, a gesture of generosity not unheard of between women of an extended family in this setting where childrearing is construed as a collective endeavor. But the family is dislocated and loses everything in the turbulence of the partition, and she ends up staying for a while with her natal family, where she is welcomed by her parents but not by her brother and his wife, who see her as future burden. Also in her conjugal family, to which she returns, she finds herself increasingly treated as an outsider and a target of psychological abuse. For some time, she moves between these two families, working hard with childcare and domestic chores to make herself useful, maintaining the humble and selfless demeanor expected of the widow. When a brother-in-law (widower after her late husband's dead sister) starts making sexual advances on her, she is pushed to make a change in her situation. A friend of her late husband promises to arrange her marriage to a rich somewhat older man with two children, whose wife has left him. This new arrangement, considered a breach against propriety, results in serious reproach from her natal family and a complete break with her late husband's family (including her "adopted" son). Asha has two daughters with her new husband and her conjugal relationship is peaceful and constructive. Yet, rather than severing ties with her past, she works hard to regain contact with her late husband's family. Only after eight years she succeeds, thanks to his younger sister with whom she was particularly close, in many ways closer than with her husband who died so early.

The narrative and Asha's perception of her situation are communicated to Das in bits and pieces. While never providing a full "account" of her life, the pieces put together by Das evoke the image of a new life perpetually lived in the ruins of an old one: her true family is the family of her first husband, but her relations to it were broken down in the hardships suffered during and after the partition. She has made her way out, but also severed her already fraught relationships on the way. In her new family she seems to see herself, in Das words, "more like a concubine than a wife," the husband's previous wife being still alive and visiting them occasionally. On her own part, she wants to be a good wife to him "in this life" while her relation to her late husband and his family has a transcendent quality, which prevails over the destruction of relationships.

Das describes Asha's situation as living in a "gesture of mourning," a gesture she also finds in other women in her fieldwork who endured hardships, violence, and the severing of familial ties in the partition. Mourning here is not to be seen in contemporary psychological and normative terms, as being *stuck* in the past. It is, rather, a quality to the way in which these women manage to reinhabit a moral and filial world that has once been broken. It is a way of containing the "inordinate" knowledge of the abyss—the unraveling of the social fabric that makes life possible—and yet to go on living and striving to do one's due.

In Cavell's vocabulary inordinate knowledge is excessive knowledge, knowledge that overwhelms us,[15] in contrast to "mere or bare or pale or intellectualized, uninsistent, inattentive, distracted, filed or archived."[16] For Das it becomes a word qualifying the knowledge of evils that cannot be spoken and woven into the narratives of one's life. For many of the women, harder hit than Asha, this knowledge includes experiences of rape, abduction, forced marriage that cannot be acknowledged in the communities where they need to go on living. These women's work to reinstall themselves as members of the community in which they live is a feat of moral courage, in ways that can only be made visible if we attend to rather than abstract from the complexities of their situations. Precariously incorporating the inordinate knowledge in a new everyday, while both unable and unwilling to eradicate it, shows itself here as a form of moral fortitude.

By attending to the women's moral courage in rebuilding a livable world, containing the inordinate knowledge, Das should not be seen as neglecting issues of social justice, (as we would construe them today in largely Western academic contexts), but rather as accompanying the women as well as her reader through another entrance into moral life and moral thought. Deflecting the issue of universal moral idealities, she focuses on how the people she follows make a moral life possible, by their own best lights, in a world not just imperfect but severely damaged. Asha's persistence in following her own sense of moral possibility and crafting her relations to her families enables her not only to escape the abyss of her fraught situation but also to follow a path of her own, regaining (as a small token of success) the relation to her sister-in-law and adopted son, whom she lost when remarrying.

It comes naturally to read Asha's story as a case of Cavellian moral perfectionism, parallel to the studies of the perfectionist register that he explores in his essays on Hollywood golden age cinema. Perfectionism here means not the achievement of a predetermined goal but the unfolding of a life under the auspices of a determination to do what is best, what comes forth as morally necessary for a person inhabiting a particular place in the world, even when it may to the external gaze seem incomprehensible (as such striving easily does in fraught conditions). A case of such fraught perfectionism is the heroine of the Hollywood movie Stella Dallas, where the factory girl Stella marries an executive, fails to fit into her new social role, and divorces, but gives, through significant sacrifice and complex ingenuity of her own, her daughter the gift of the more privileged and easier life. It is distinctive to Cavell's readings of his perfectionist theme in films and literature that he finds worth in the way characters negotiate the confinements of their situation and in doing so open up something new for themselves.

Cavell frames this as a register of moral thought different from the one in standard moral philosophy.[17] But is it merely complementary, perhaps broadening our sense of what moral philosophy might attend to and what moral life may include? Seeing the registers of personal striving described by Cavell and Das as an additional area of moral concerns offers an easy and non-confrontative way forward. But they also carry the potential for a more ambitious challenge to the moral theories of abstract ideals and principles.

Das's emphasis in the stories is on people's capacity to navigate worlds that are far from perfect in a moral respect: worlds where people are encumbered by circumstances that thwart their capacity to flourish in any ordinary sense, or that require ingenuity in the realization of moral demands. Moral life in these stories is not a quest for universal justice, the application of ready principles, but rather the day-to-day weaving of the fabric of an everyday life amidst constraints, also as victims or perpetrators of different forms of ills.

The nature of everyday life and everyday morality is highlighted by the way many of these lives are lived close to some abyss, close to the unraveling of the textures of livable life. Constraints and vulnerability do not make them fringe cases of moral life, from a philosophical point of view. Rather, it helps us to see certain features that characterize also more sheltered lives: the complexity of interdependencies; the reproduction of the material, as well as social necessities of day-to-day life; the continuous activity of maintenance of and care for relations; the social embeddedness of action in structures of kinship, hierarchy, social roles; the deep connection between moral strivings and more personal, idiosyncratic quests; the vulnerability of desired outcomes to chance circumstances; the connection between vision and action.

As Iris Murdoch noted, we can only act in a world we can see.[18] Her emphasis, when picking up this theme, is usually the necessity to work on our vision, to see more and see better in order to act better in a complex world of other people. But this thought has another side too, which she is well aware of: that visions of our world and the possibilities in it are situated, lived, subject to historical conditions and chance, as well as full of idiosyncrasies. Thus, every extension to our vision, every deepening, development, clarification of it, is also subject to such situatedness. Limitations give shape, encumbrances are also enabling: they bring something distinctive to the world, and we must lend an ear to it.

We could think of this situatedness in terms of limitations or encumbrances, and in such forms it goes well together with an idea of universal values and goods: an idea of the good and the right as always the same. There is something right in this picture: a kind of reaching, at the core of moral experience, toward a good which transcends the temporal and the local. But we should beware of translating this dynamic into a picture of a fallen, limited, encumbered world in the process of reaching toward objective, universal goods of which we know the names. The lived world is full of moral potentialities, the names of which we do not know, and affordances that are not well captured in terms of familiar universal values. Neither the potentialities nor the affordances are always the same.

Practicing a relativism of historical distance in this way is about seeing difference and taking it seriously. It offers a route away from moral simplicity to appreciation of the complexities of lived morality. This requires that we are genuinely interested in these complexities and differences and do not merely use references to some differences as excuses for making general moral normative proclamations of what was "right for them" or is "right for us" or, alternatively, for ruling out evaluative reflection on past or otherwise distant places.

Taking differences seriously routinely raises the worry of thinkers who, like Moody-Adams, want to secure the objectivity of our commitments and values by argumentative means, as if they would otherwise crumble. But this gesture of securing adds little to our commitments, although it may sometimes function as a refreshing rehearsal of them. There is hardly any reason to think that a relativism of historical distance, conceived as a philosophical, non-judgmental inquiry into the embeddedness of moral lives, leads to weakened commitment to the values we hold dear. Why? Precisely because the *differences* between our own predicament and those of people of other times and places are brought to the center of attention. I dedicate the final part to exploring what such inquiry involves.

The Embeddedness of Moral Life: Material, Social, Historical

Matters of moral concern are not pre-given as a host of commands or principles but arise in the midst of things and are negotiated with regard to a plurality of considerations, relations, needs, and shared knowledge of a common world. Great insight into the lives concerned is necessary for a fair assessment of the nature and worth of a real-life course of action. Any such assessment may and most often will include reflections of an abstract, general, and universalizing kind: that violence is bad, that many ills in the lives of women or of the poor could be avoided through more equitable social forms of organization, that slavery is a crime against the dignity of human beings, that the forced assimilation of native peoples is wrong, and so on. But these form just a slice of what it means to engage in moral reflection over one's situation as well as over events, people, and conceptions of a historical or fictionalized past.

To know the worlds we are contemplating we need to pay attention at least to the following three dimensions:

1. Material conditions: what is required for daily and yearly sustenance and how do people's roles in the reproduction of the material conditions of life shape their understanding and possibilities for action, collectively and as differently placed individuals?
2. Social relations: what are the networks of social ties like in a given community—relationships of care and responsibility, hierarchies, alliances, friendships, loyalties, modes of association, forms of influence, forms of formal and informal power, social sanctions, self-conceptions, ambitions, and so on— and how do they shape differently placed individuals moral understanding and possibilities for action, again collectively and as differently placed individuals?
3. Historical trajectories: communities have a past and a future and undergo change, but change is premised on the affordances of the past. The moral understanding of people at any point in time draws on past experiences and on past and emergent problematizations, linguistic resources that reflect past as well as present needs and affordances. Everyday conceptions of the nature of things are shot through with traces of what has been. Thus in order to understand people's moral world we need to understand the historical fibers (of ideas, practices, linguistic resources, distributions of wealth and power, among other things) that run through it and how they may affect differently placed people in different ways.

What, then, does it mean to say that people's agency, including their moral agency, is historically, socially, materially constituted? It does not mean that people are, alas, mostly unable to see and act beyond the requirements of their (historical) situation and thus fall short of higher, universal ideals. It rather means that any ideals construed as higher come to existence and are realized in and through the affordances of the situations people find themselves in, the material conditions that enable and give meaning to action, the conceptual spaces shared with one's interlocutors, in worlds of worth. Morality is only possible in a complex human form of life, the practical necessities, moral intensities, and ideological tensions of which overflow any universalizable conception of the good and the right. You cannot teach a child to live a morally responsible life by teaching them a moral code and its theoretical motivation. You teach a child by living with it, working with it in institutional settings such as kindergarten and school, doing things and solving problems together. The things done in different locations and times are not identical and thus the outcomes in terms of what we would call moral orientation are not identical. The pieces of explicit moral code that get taught as the child grows make (or fail to make) sense against this shared life and the often much more complex rules and practices that get taught in more tacit ways, through example and interaction.[19]

One could perhaps say that my disagreement with Moody-Adams involves a clash of philosophical and ontological priorities. For her morality is essentially in the higher principles that are imperfectly realized in lived lives; from the philosophical point of view that I have been laying out here, it is essentially in the complex evaluative searchings and negotiations of togetherness of everyday life, some of which condense into—and are carried forward in the form of—abstract, prioritized principles.

Das draws our attention to the labor of maintenance of a human form of life in its contextual specificities. She points at the way in which matters of moral concern arise in the day-to-day interactions between people and at how care and concern are circulated through such interactions to maintain a livable world, a world where there is a place for the good, for meaningful strivings, for hopes. Principles and overt judgments have a place in such a world but they are not, if one may say so, what a moral world is essentially made of. The necessities, which come to be construed as the moral necessities of life, are responsive to an environment out of which human beings need to draw their material and social sustenance.

If asked about moral principles people may produce varieties of generic phrases about duty, kindness, and truthfulness. But most of us face the moral challenges of our days through quite material tasks of different kinds, in a more or less timely, more or less expedient, more or less beneficial manner. The farmer follows the seasons, the sun and rains, the frost, to secure the season's crops. The academic raises at dawn to write a page before a day of faculty meetings and lectures. Even in repetitive manual labor, offering little freedom, human beings resist alienation in their experience of their tasks. The rhythms of physically monotonous labor, the cycles of effort, fatigue, and well-deserved rest are imbued with purpose but also with moral meaning. There is moral satisfaction and pleasure in doing things well. The most part of people's moral energies go into maintaining and upholding the normality and the sufficient standards of their daily tasks. Among those tasks, things occur that are overtly marked as moral and that may spur explicit moral reasoning and reproach. A student has filed a complaint over discriminatory treatment by a professor. A company's overseas subcontractor is targeted as using child labor. A bureaucrat is revealed to have taken bribes for overlooking the environmental consequences of a lucrative local business. Such issues get their meaning and what we could call their moral energy from the circumstances that surround them and that make them issues of a given kind. Which behaviors are readily recognized as bad, evil, or morally fraught depends on shared expectations, values, conceptions of normality, and linguistic resources, which change as societies change.[20]

Does immersion in the complexities of a given historical present condone people's harmful actions, individual, or collective? I think this is the wrong question here, because it co-opts too much of Moody-Adams's understanding of what it means to engage in moral thought over past events, people, and worlds. Situatedness is a constitutive part of people's actions, and in order to judge those actions we need to try to understand them. Sometimes this makes the passing of moral judgment harder. Sometimes judgment seems easy but philosophically unsatisfactory: little in terms of new understanding seems to be gained by stating that slavery is and was wrong, because everyone in the seminar room already thinks that. The claim that the normative truths about morality are always and everywhere the same appears, from this perspective, more than anything like a way of saying that *we* will, no matter what, always stand by a given set of values and require everyone, no matter where or when, to do so as well. This can be politically and morally admirable, but is often philosophically unhelpful.

Suspending or tempering moral judgment in the face of lives differently constituted than our own, we exercise moral sensibilities that are easily silenced by universalizing judgment. We are invited to imagine living in a world where daily chores and tasks are different and differently distributed, where different things make sense, different things are taken for granted, and different things arouse moral concern and engender moral activity. Often enough, as readers of historiography, biography, and historical fiction, we accept these invitations and return from our visit, not with a weakened commitment to our own moral precepts, but a complicated understanding of human predicaments.

As I quoted before, Moody-Adams suggests that a relativism of historical distance "seeks to shield past practices from contemporary moral reflection and criticism."[21] But it seems that the contrary is the case, at least if this relativization is conceived in the way I have outlined it here, as attention to the ground-up practical making and sustenance of moral worlds that differ from each other. A certain relativism here opens up the past for reflection and enables a more fine-grained and perceptive criticism of actions, people, and conditions, both past and present. Moral criticism of the past comes forth as an interpretive effort, where judgment in terms of right and wrong is not the primary form of engagement, and the grounding and application of supposedly universal values play subsidiary or more flexible roles.

The skills of interpretive engagement practiced in relation to the past provide a great asset also in thinking about such contemporary issues where normative judgments, without relativizing clauses, have immediate practical import for our lives together. These skills help us to interpret the complex interplay between conditions of life and the values and norms they uphold, and thus to better negotiate areas of changing circumstances and emerging moral insight.

Notes

1 Michele Moody-Adams, *Fieldwork in Familiar Places: Morality, Culture, and Philosophy* (Cambridge, MA: Harvard University Press, 1997).
2 By "withholding moral judgment" I do not here suggest that it would be possible or even desirable to obtain morally neutral accounts of human lives, given that any choice of wording, perspective, narrative plotting reveal evaluative commitments. Historian Donald Bloxham has recently argued in *History and Morality* (Oxford: Oxford University Press, 2020) it is important for historians to acknowledge such evaluative aspects of historiography in order to gain control over them. The same goes for philosophers engaging history, but such awareness and control does not entail a markedly normative approach.
3 Moody-Adams, *Fieldwork in Familiar Places*, 8.
4 Moody-Adams, *Fieldwork in Familiar Places*, 191.
5 Moody-Adams, *Fieldwork in Familiar Places*, 191
6 See especially the chapter "The Use and Abuse of History," in *Fieldwork in Familiar Places*, ed. Moody-Adams, 61–106.

7 A certain narrowness of this kind is quite typical for critiques of relativism. We find it in closely related form, for example, in John Cook, *Morality and Cultural Difference* (Oxford: Oxford University Press, 1999).
8 See for example David B. Wong, *Natural Moralities: A Defense of Pluralistic Relativism* (Oxford: Oxford University Press, 2006); Clifford Geertz, "Distinguished Lecture: Anti Anti-Relativism," *American Anthropologist* 86, no. 2 (1984): 263–78; Bernard Williams, *Ethics and the Limits of Philosophy* (Cambridge, MA: Harvard University Press, 1985).
9 Moody-Adams, *Fieldwork in Familiar Places*, 8.
10 For further discussion on the capacity to inhabit alternative moral orders through fiction see Edmund Dain, "Sympathy for the Devil: The Puzzle of Imaginative Resistance, the Role of Fiction in Moral Thought, and the Limits of the Imagination," *Philosophy* 96, no. 2 (2021): 253–75.
11 Alice Crary, *Beyond Moral Judgment* (Cambridge, MA: Harvard University Press, 2007); Alice Crary, *Inside Ethics: On the Demands of Moral Thought* (Cambridge, MA: Harvard University Press, 2016); Cora Diamond, *Reading Wittgenstein with Anscombe, Going On to Ethics* (Cambridge, MA: Harvard University Press, 2019); Cora Diamond, *The Realistic Spirit* (Cambridge, MA: The MIT Press, 1991); and Anne-Marie Søndergaard Christensen, *Moral Philosophy and Moral Life* (Oxford: Oxford University Press, 2021).
12 Iris Murdoch, *Metaphysics as a Guide to Morals* (London: Chatto & Windus, 1992), 495.
13 Veena Das, *Textures of the Ordinary: Doing Anthropology After Wittgenstein* (New York: Fordham University Press, 2020), 103–4.
14 Veena Das, *Life and Words: Violence and the Descent into the Ordinary* (Berkeley: University of California Press, 2007), 77–94.
15 Das, *Textures of the Ordinary*, 310.
16 Stanley Cavell, "The Touch of Words," in *Seeing Wittgenstein Anew*, ed. William Day and Viktor J. Krebs (Cambridge: Cambridge University Press, 2010), 84.
17 Stanley Cavell, *Cities of Words: Pedagogical Letters on a Register of the Moral Life* (Cambridge, MA: Harvard University Press, 2004).
18 Iris Murdoch, *Existentialists and Mystics* (London: Chatto & Windus, 1997), 329.
19 This can be compared to the account of language learning as an introduction to a form of life that we find in Ludwig Wittgenstein, *Philosophical Investigations* (Oxford: Blackwell, 1998).
20 For recent and growing important discussions on moral changes and their dynamics see, for example, Kwame Anthony Appiah, *The Honor Code: How Moral Revolutions Happen* (New York: W. W. Norton & Co., 2010); Robert Baker, *The Structure of Moral Revolutions: Studies of Changes in the Morality of Abortion, Death, and the Bioethics Revolution* (Cambridge, MA: The MIT Press, 2019); Cecilie Eriksen, *Moral Change: Dynamics, Structure, and Normativity* (New York: Palgrave Macmillan, 2020); and Jonathan Lear, *Radical Hope: Ethics in the Face of Cultural Devastation* (Cambridge, MA: Harvard University Press, 2008).
21 Moody-Adams, *Fieldwork in Familiar Places*, 8.

Bibliography

Appiah, Kwame Anthony. *The Honor Code: How Moral Revolutions Happen*. New York: W. W. Norton & Co., 2010.

Baker, Robert. *The Structure of Moral Revolutions: Studies of Changes in the Morality of Abortion, Death, and the Bioethics Revolution*. Cambridge, MA: The MIT Press, 2019.

Bloxham, Donald. *History and Morality*. Oxford: Oxford University Press, 2020.

Cavell, Stanley. *Cities of Words: Pedagogical Letters on a Register of the Moral Life*. Cambridge, MA: Harvard University Press, 2004.

Cavell, Stanley. "The Touch of Words." In *Seeing Wittgenstein Anew*, edited by William Day and Viktor J. Krebs, 81–98. Cambridge: Cambridge University Press, 2010.

Christensen, Anne-Marie Søndergaard. *Moral Philosophy and Moral Life*. Oxford: Oxford University Press, 2021.

Crary, Alice. *Inside Ethics: On the Demands of Moral Thought*. Cambridge, MA: Harvard University Press, 2016.

Crary, Alice. *Beyond Moral Judgment*. Cambridge, MA: Harvard University Press, 2007.

Diamond, Cora. *The Realistic Spirit*. Cambridge, MA: The MIT Press, 1991.

Diamond, Cora. *Reading Wittgenstein with Anscombe, Going On to Ethics*. Cambridge, MA: Harvard University Press, 2019.

Dain, Edmund. "Sympathy for the Devil: The Puzzle of Imaginative Resistance, the Role of Fiction in Moral Thought, and the Limits of the Imagination." *Philosophy* 96, no. 2 (2021): 253–75.

Das, Veena. *Life and Words: Violence and the Descent into the Ordinary*. Berkeley: University of California Press, 2007.

Das, Veena. *Textures of the Ordinary: Doing Anthropology After Wittgenstein*. New York: Fordham University Press, 2020.

Eriksen, Cecilie. *Moral Change: Dynamics, Structure, and Normativity*. New York: Palgrave Macmillan, 2020.

Geertz, Clifford. "Distinguished Lecture: Anti Anti-Relativism." *American Anthropologist* 86, no. 2 (1984): 263–78.

Lear, Jonathan. *Radical Hope: Ethics in the Face of Cultural Devastation*. Cambridge, MA: Harvard University Press, 2008.

Moody-Adams, Michele. *Fieldwork in Familiar Places: Morality, Culture, and Philosophy*. Cambridge, MA: Harvard University Press, 1997.

Murdoch, Iris. *Existentialists and Mystics*. London: Chatto & Windus, 1997.

Murdoch, Iris. *Metaphysics as a Guide to Morals*. London: Chatto & Windus, 1992.

Wong, David B. *Natural Moralities: A Defense of Pluralistic Relativism*. Oxford: Oxford University Press, 2006.

Williams, Bernard. *Ethics and the Limits of Philosophy*. Cambridge, MA: Harvard University Press, 1985.

Wittgenstein, Ludwig. *Philosophical Investigations*. Oxford: Blackwell, 1998.

6

Heroism, Self-determination, and Magnanimity

Hegel and Brandom on Self-conscious Agency

Chiel van den Akker

Introduction

It is central to our conception of agency that we are responsible for the actions we perform intentionally and the consequences we know will follow from them. Hegel formulates this basic conception of agency thus in his *Philosophy of Right*.

> It is . . . the right of the will to recognize as its *action*, and to accept *responsibility* [*Schuld*] for, only those aspects of its *deed* which it knew to be presupposed within its end, and which were present in its *purpose*. I can be made *accountable* for a deed only if *my will was responsible* for it—*the right of knowledge*.[1]

Note the distinction between deed (*Tat*) and action (*Handlung*) and how the latter requires intent and knowledge of its consequences. Note also that Hegel does not exclude being responsible for *unintended* consequences of actions. I might unwillingly and unknowingly hurt someone with my action, and may be held and feel responsible for the hurt, but I am not responsible for *intentionally* hurting that person. Therefore I do not *have* to accept the responsibility for the action under a description that does not include my intention—this Hegel calls the *right of intention*. He adds that children, imbeciles, and lunatics are not to be held fully responsible for their actions, for they are not expected to know in full what they are doing and what the consequences are of their actions.[2]

Although we have the *right* to accept responsibility—blame (*Schuld*)—only for what we did intentionally, we know that other, true descriptions of our doings are possible, including descriptions under which our actions are *not* done intentionally and have consequences we did *not* foresee. Take a simple example. I am responsible for the essay I am writing at this very moment and to a certain extent I am responsible for consequences that I know might follow from it. But if someone describes this essay in terms of scholarship during COVID-19, or in terms of Hegel's legacy in the 2020s, or in terms of someone realizing she has made a mistake in one of her articles or I in mine, the descriptions may be true and accurate, but not ones I intended. I might be held or feel responsible for the consequences of my action under those descriptions, but, given my rights of intention and knowledge, I do not *have* to accept that responsibility. For the action to be truly mine, I must have willingly and knowingly performed it.

This conception of agency Hegel contrasts with the sense of agency found in ancient tragedy, where its heroes typically *do* accept responsibility for actions they did not do intentionally and for consequences they did not know would follow from them. Hegel writes:

> The *heroic* self-consciousness (as in ancient tragedies like that of Oedipus) has not yet progressed from its unalloyed simplicity to reflect on the distinction between *deed* and *action*, between the external event and the purpose and knowledge of the circumstances ... but accepts responsibility [*Schuld*] for the deed in its entirety.[3]

Note once again the distinction between deed and action: only the latter requires intent and purpose.[4] In Greek tragedy, the action performed is a *deed* for which the hero accepts responsibility, regardless of his intent. In Sophocles' *The Oedipus Trilogy* and in Euripides' *The Phoenician Women*, Oedipus heroically accepts responsibility (*Schuld*) for patricide, for marrying his mother Iocaste, for the death of their two sons who each mortally wounded the other in battle, and for her suicide because of it, even though Oedipus did not intentionally kill his father, which set the unfortunate course of events into motion. The deed as an external event, as Hegel calls it, means that the description of the deed does not take into account its purpose seen from the point of view of the agent—its internal description so to speak. A deed is heroic when the agent accepts responsibility for the consequences of her action, even though she was not aware of those consequences or intended those consequences to happen. It has nothing to do with heroic and great deeds on the battlefield or in the stadium, or with actions in the face of grave danger.

In this essay I am interested in the distinction between heroic deeds and intentional actions as Hegel draws it in his *Philosophy of Right* and as the present-day reader of Hegel, Robert Brandom, interprets it in his recent *A Spirit of Trust*.[5] I am particularly interested in how this distinction relates to the distinction between premodern and modern conceptions of self-conscious agency. I will argue that the one distinction is not to be conflated with the other: the heroic conception of agency is not a premodern conception and the intentional conception of agency is not a modern conception.[6]

To Hegel becoming modern is the most important event in human history.[7] Distinguishing between the premodern and modern conceptions of agency allows us to understand this pivotal moment in the history of *Geist*, of what we are to ourselves as social, self-conscious, thinking, normative creatures. "The axis around which modernity resolves, for Hegel," Brandom notes, "is the idea that we make the norms that make us what we are. The dawn of the modern is accordingly the rise of a new kind of self-conscious subjectivity."[8] Hegel, in Brandom's reading of him, is a social pragmatist about norms: it is up to us to institute the norms that we live by through our practices. New about modernity is the self-conscious realization of this fact about us. Brandom also extensively discusses Hegel's distinction between the heroic deed and the intentional action. On the heroic self-conscious agent he writes: "Tragedy is the unavoidable submission of the heroic agent to *fate* . . . . This is the intimate relation of mutual presupposition between *tragedy*, *fate*, and *heroism*."[9] The heroes in tragedy are at the mercy of forces—fate—outside their control and knowledge. And those forces determine the content of what the heroes do and heroically take responsibility for. "The tragic side," Brandom observes, "is that one actually has authority only over what one intends and can foresee."[10] Or, more precisely, I might add, what makes an action tragic, is that the agent *suffers* from the unintended and unforeseen consequences of her own actions. In what follows I will say more about suffering in relation to agency and justice as vital for a proper understanding of tragedy. Hegel is interested in tragedy precisely because of this relation. The core features of tragedy I will identify will resonate in the remainder of this essay and help us grasp both the distinctions between heroic deeds and intentional actions, and between premodern and modern self-conscious agency.

The modern sense of agency crystallized at the end of the eighteenth century in the Enlightened Western world. Its contrast in this essay is—as it is in Hegel and Brandom—with the ancient Greek sense of agency. As Bernard Williams aptly puts it: "the Greek past is specially the past of modernity."[11] Brandom's interpretation of Hegel also anticipates a postmodern sense of agency. I will conclude this essay with this third phase of Spirit. It will bring to light a sense of agency that arguably our day and age are in need of.

The Justice of Suffering

Let us start with a famous passage from Sophocles' *Antigone*, where Antigone, one of Oedipus' two daughters, after having buried her brother Polynices against the will of the king, Creon, who had branded Polynices a traitor for his attack on Thebe, exclaims the following:

> What law of the mighty gods have I transgressed? . . .
> Very well: if this is the pleasure of the gods,
> once I suffer I will know that I was wrong.
> But if these men are wrong, let them suffer
> nothing worse than they mete out to me—
> these masters of injustice![12]

Several key features of tragedy come to the fore here. One is the *topos* that we learn through suffering (*pathei mathos*)[13]—"once I suffer I will know that I was wrong."[14] Antigone knew that what she did was forbidden by her uncle Creon, who was upholding the *human* law as Hegel calls it. Whether she truly *is* guilty of an offense depends not on Creon's edict, but on whether she transgressed a *divine* law: "What law of the mighty gods have I transgressed?" she asks. Suffering, caused by future consequences of her action, will be proof that she in fact did commit an offense. Justice is in the hands of the gods (fate), not Creon's.

If a law is transgressed, retribution will follow. Either by fate, or, if one suffers from an injustice committed by another person, one is justified (or so one thinks) in retributing the offence in equal measure. Retribution points to the reciprocal conception of agency that was built into the world of the Greeks.[15] An eye for an eye, as some of us still say, or, as Creon has it, "pay back blood with blood."[16] The distinction between the agent's transgression of a divine law and an injustice being done to the agent (human law) becomes clear in the next verse, as the chorus comments that "Fate will never punish a man / for returning harm first done to him."[17] Fate befalls a person only when he transgresses a divine law, even if he did so unknowingly and unwillingly, as was the case with Oedipus, as Antigone emphasizes in response to the comment just quoted. And after having unwittingly committed his deeds, he cannot but accept his fate. At the start of *Oedipus at Colonus*, Oedipus resignedly states: "Acceptance—that is the great lesson suffering teaches."[18]

Tragedy is concerned with morality, with justice, and with retribution—and, of course, with fate, which functions as punishment for the transgression of divine law. This conception of fate informs the sense of justice that is at stake in Greek tragedy. Oedipus is punished for transgressing the law through the unintended and fateful consequence of his actions, for which he heroically accepts the responsibility (*Schuld*). Antigone argues that the judgment of burying her brother is in the hands of the gods. Only when she suffers will she know that she was wrong. This divine justice overrides any justifications that individuals may give for their action. The consequences of an action, which are evidence of divine justice, determine its appropriate description. Because the tragic agent suffers from the unintended and unforeseen consequences of his actions, his actions cause both pity (*eleos*) and fear (*phobos*). Pity and fear are not to be understood as inner states of the mind only. *Phobos* is a bodily manifestation and its awareness is a cold shudder, as Aristotle has it.[19] Hegel has very precise ideas about how to understand both pity and fear:

> What a man has really to fear is not an external power and oppression by it, but the might of the ethical order which is one determinant of his own free reason and is at the same time that eternal and inviolable something which he summons up against himself if once he turns against it.

The might of the ethical order in tragedy *is* fate and the suffering it causes. Its violation by the tragic heroes inspires fear in the public, and, Hegel continues, "true pity," that is, sympathy "with the sufferer's moral justification."[20] We know that Oedipus did not willingly and knowingly kill his father in order to set the fateful course of events into motion but instead acted in self-defense. But we also know that he did violate the ethical order.

Pity and fear in turn awaken a higher feeling in the spectator, the feeling of *catharsis*, or reconciliation, which is made possible by the justice being delivered, according to Hegel:

> A truly tragic suffering... is only inflicted on the individual agents as a consequence of their own deed which is both legitimate and, owing to the resulting collision,

blame-worthy, and for which their whole self is answerable. Above mere fear and tragic sympathy there therefore stands that sense of reconciliation which the tragedy affords by the glimpse of eternal justice.[21]

The tragic agent cannot escape his fate. Justice will be done. This justice has not to do with the actions for which the tragic agent is held accountable by his fellow citizens. It is the gods that disapprove of the transgression of their eternal laws. They make the hero suffer for having committed a wrongful act. In this sense, his suffering is the consequence of his own action.

A final feature of tragedy, and one observed by Hegel, is that in tragedy there is no moral bond, no *sittliche Verbindung* between its heroic characters and the members of the community, who form the chorus in tragedies. The members of the community are passive, deedless; they cannot intervene but can only comment on what happens and appeal to the gods.[22] As a result, the heroes and heroines are not held accountable for their actions by the community, nor do heroes and heroines accept responsibility (blame) for their actions in relation to members of their community. "Their conduct and their ruin," Hegel observes, "are individual"; and they do and undergo them alone.[23]

Heroic Deeds and Intentional Actions

The distinction I am interested in is the distinction between the premodern and the modern conception of agency as it is drawn by Hegel and its relation to the distinction between heroic deeds and intentional actions. For a proper understanding of this, two considerations are crucial.

First, and this is rather obvious, in antiquity individuals too performed intentional actions, pursued private goals, and were held responsible for what they knowingly and willingly did. It is not that in antiquity all actions were heroic deeds. The ancient Greek conception of agency and responsibility is not that different from our own. Take the following somewhat famous example (Protagoras and Pericles are said to have discussed this incident for a whole day long). A boy was throwing a javelin in a gymnasium and accidentally killed another boy who, going on some errand, rushed across the field, not paying attention to the sportsman. We know that the sportsman is responsible for throwing the javelin, but is he responsible for killing the boy: Is he to blame for the killing? The discussion was eventually settled, and it was decided that the boy throwing the javelin could not be held accountable for the other boy's death, since he was just practicing his sport and did not throw the javelin at the boy with the intention of killing him. The boy who foolishly crossed the field should have known about the danger involved and should have been more careful and attentive. He is to blame, so it is argued, for his own death.[24] The point is that the Greek sense of agency and responsibility is very much our own, despite there being a conception of heroic self-conscious agency which is found in Greek tragedy, and despite the many differences in beliefs and societal structures between the Greeks and us.[25] We should also note that tragedy is full of intentional actions. Recall for instance Antigone pursuing the goal of properly burying her brother. Or think of Oedipus who at times takes responsibility only for what he did intentionally. Thus, in Sophocles' *Oedipus the King*, after he finds his mother and wife having hanged herself, Oedipus intentionally sticks out his eyes with golden pins from her robes. Sophocles has Oedipus say:

> Apollo, friends, Apollo—
> he ordained my agonies—these, my pains on pains!
> But the hand that struck my eyes was mine,
> mine alone—no one else—
> I did it all myself![26]

Oedipus decides to blind himself, even though his fateful suffering was ordained by the gods. Elsewhere Oedipus points out that he cannot be blamed for killing his father because he struck the man in self-defense and did not know that he was killing his father.[27]

> I fell to blows with my father, cut him down in blood—
> blind to what I was doing, blind to whom I killed—
> how could you condemn that involuntary act
> with any sense of justice?[28]

The tension between voluntary action and fate is typical of tragedy. The hero always decides to perform an action; he does not do something because of fate telling him so. Only afterward, when the full extent of the action becomes clear, does the hero realize that his deed in fact was fated under a description not available to him at the time of its performance. As he realizes that his knowledge at the time of the action fell short, he takes full responsibility for the action and its consequences. In tragedies, the hero's will *must* be free. This makes him not only responsible (blameworthy) for his actions but also for their fateful consequences he did not intend nor foresee. His fate is the consequence of his own action, for which he alone is to be blamed. That makes the action tragic. "The pains we inflict upon ourselves hurt most of all."[29] Voluntarily, Oedipus solved the riddle of the Sphinx, liberating Thebes from this beast. As a consequence he was given the hand of Iocaste in marriage—not knowing, of course, that she was his mother. Oedipus is also responsible for finding out the truth about being married to his mother through a quest he pursued voluntarily, but this knowledge did make Iocaste hang herself in *Oedipus the King*, for which death Oedipus heroically too takes responsibility in Sophocles' tragedy. This is the reason he struck out his eyes.

The main points here are that we find heroic deeds and intentional actions in tragedies, and the heroic self-conscious agent performs intentional actions. The latter is simply part of the concept of agency. To count as a deed (*Tat*), there *has* to be a description under which the deed is intentional, that is, an action (*Handlung*), despite there being other descriptions available under which it is not intentional.[30] The tragic agent's heroism consists of accepting responsibility (blame) for all the deed's consequences, rather than only those he purposefully wanted to bring about with his action. Since we find intentional actions in tragedies, and since heroic self-conscious agents perform intentional actions, the distinction between premodern and modern conceptions of agency is not to be modeled on the distinction between heroic deeds and intentional actions. It appears that there is something else at stake in distinguishing the premodern and modern conceptions of self-conscious agency, something which does somehow relate to tragedy.

The second consideration is as follows. The heroic self-conscious agent did not disappear with modernity, and she can still be found in our present-day dramas. Consider for instance the movie *Manchester by the Sea* from 2016, in which the main character of the story, Lee Chandler, played by Casey Affleck, takes up the responsibility (blame) for the death of his children, who died in a fire. Lee Chandler had lit the fireplace because it was cold, especially for his children, and because he knew the central heating was giving his wife headaches. As he went to a night-shop—it was already in the middle of the night, so his wife and children were asleep—a piece of firewood must have fallen out, which started the fire, burning down the house and killing his children. His wife was saved. Presumably, Lee had forgotten to put the fire-screen in front of the fireplace, which would have prevented the piece of wood from falling out. We know that he did not intentionally kill his children, nor did he foresee the consequences of his actions—he was heating the house, going to a night-shop, not placing a fire-screen. He was, however, drunk; and there is a moment as he walks to the night-shop when he asks himself whether he had placed the fire-screen in front of the fireplace. In another scene Lee is questioned by the local police about the fire, and they immediately decide not to prosecute him, since not placing a fire-screen is not a criminal offence. In another scene, several years later, his wife forgives him. But Lee Chandler heroically keeps on holding himself alone accountable for the death of his children. He is responsible for his deed and its consequences, and incapable of taking the deed for the intentional action it also was.

So not only do we find heroic self-conscious agents (and intentional actions) in ancient tragedies, we also find heroic self-conscious agents (and intentional actions) in our current dramas. Again, the distinction between the premodern and modern conceptions of agency is not to be modeled on the distinction between heroic deeds and intentional actions. Perhaps we should simply conclude that in tragedy and drama there are both heroic deeds and intentional actions, whereas in real life, there is intentional action and, occasionally, heroic deeds. This is the case both in antiquity and in modernity. This conclusion is, I think, warranted; however, it does leave open the question of whether there is a distinction between premodern and modern conceptions of agency. And we want to make this distinction if we are to understand why according to Hegel becoming modern is the most important event in human history. There is a history of what Spirit is to itself.[31]

Conscience

So let us turn to crucial parts of Hegel's *Philosophy of Right*. We start with the following:

> [My] will is responsible for a deed only in so far as I have knowledge of it. Oedipus, who unwittingly killed his father, cannot be accused of parricide, although the

legal codes of antiquity attached less importance to the subjective element, to responsibility [*Zurechnung*], than is the case today.[32]

Interestingly, this passage shows that Hegel agrees with the observation we made earlier that the Greek sense of agency and responsibility is very much like our own, albeit that the "legal codes of antiquity attached less importance to the subjective element."[33] In the passages that follow, Hegel emphasizes the many consequences a deed can have, some foreseen, but many not. But, he claims, "The will . . . has the right to accept responsibility only for the . . . consequences . . . [that] were part of its purpose."[34] And this is true for all actions, in antiquity and modernity, even though tragic agents accept responsibility for consequences they did not intend or foresee. Although we are only responsible for consequences we intended and knew would follow from our actions, we should admit that when we have acted, the consequences are to a certain extent out of our hands. Hegel uses an old proverb to underline this point:

"The stone belongs to the devil when it leaves the hand that threw it." By acting, I expose myself to misfortune, which accordingly has a right over me and is an existence of my own volition.[35]

This is also the wisdom we find in ancient Greek tragedy. Doings have contingent consequences, outside of the knowledge of the thinking agent and over which she has no control.[36] It is a mark of agency to ask what effects of an action can be attributed to the agent.[37] And where the heroic self-conscious agent accepts responsibility (blame) for contingent consequences of actions she did not intend and had no knowledge of, the intentional conception of agency states that the agent has the right to accept responsibility only for those consequences she intended and could have foreseen. Still, as we said, the agent might be held accountable (and punished) for what she did not do intentionally. So much is clear, but we want to know what makes us modern, and heroic self-consciousness is not helpful in this regard.

In the following passage Hegel *does* draw a distinction between the premodern and modern conceptions of self-conscious agency:

The right of the subject's *particularity* to find satisfaction, or—to put it differently—the right of *subjective freedom*, is the pivotal and focal point in the difference between *antiquity* and the *modern* age.[38]

Subjective freedom is expressed in all of modern life, but it is best understood in terms of *conscience* (*Gewissen*), which I define as the capacity to self-consciously *approve* of the communal norms that bind one's actions.[39] This idea, a variant of what is usually referred to as self-determination or self-legislation and central to the German idealists, qualifies modern agency. It is in opposition to the premodern conception of agency, where the norms one was bound by were *not* self-consciously approved of. In antiquity, one too had intentions, pursued private interests, had hopes, wishes, and so on. One's inner life and convictions too lead to particular intentions. But whether these intentions and interests were rightfully to be pursued depended, in Hegel's view, on some given norm or rule external to oneself, regardless of whether those laws were conceived to be natural, divine, or man-made, for the latter too did not require self-conscious approval to be binding. On this premodern sense of agency Hegel writes:

> This is the point of view of thought which does not yet comprehend the will in its freedom, but *reflects* on its content as something natural and given—as, for example, in the days of Croesus and Solon [in the sixth century B.C.].[40]

In antiquity, what one ought to do was objectively given.[41] Habit and custom determined the norms binding the actions.[42] There was no such thing as the self-conscious approval of the communal norms that bound one's action. To be sure, one could convince oneself to pursue private interest in disregard of objectively given norms, but that, Hegel observes, leads to corruption and disorder.[43] It requires conscience to prevent such corruption and disorder when norms are no longer objectively given.

To act, Hegel emphasizes, is to acknowledge what counts as or validates an action in the world.[44] In antiquity, such validity was determined in relation to the *ethos*, the *Sittlichkeit* or ethical life of one's community. Here, in Brandom's terms, the given norms had *authority* over one's (subjective) attitudes.[45] By contrast, the modern's subjective freedom, according to Hegel, brought *morality* into being, that is, the determination of individuals as to what norms their actions are bound by.[46] In modernity, Brandom summarizes, "the rise of subjectivity is the realization that the communal norms whose acknowledgment makes us cultural, and not just natural creatures, depend in turn on our attitudes and activities to actualize them."[47] No longer are actions bound by objective norms existing antecedently to and outside of the agent's doings; instead they are bound by objectified norms that are self-consciously recognized to be communally instituted. By acting, one affirms the communal norm (if one breaks the norm one affirms it by breaking it). Without affirmation, communal norms lose their force. The relation between self-conscious approval and communal norm is a living one in that the latter has to be constantly instituted by the former by acting and constantly self-consciously approved of.

Conscience, according to Hegel, is a *modern* phenomenon: "conscience represents an exalted point of view, a point of view of the modern world, which has for the first time attained this consciousness, this descent into the self."[48] He continues:

> Earlier and more sensuous ages have before them something external and given, whether this be religion or right; but [my] conscience knows itself as thought, and that this thought of mine is my sole source of obligation.[49]

It is the subjective right of any self-conscious individual to know for herself what is good and right, that is, what her moral obligation is.[50] And this form of consciousness is not mere subjective opinion, as if the appeal of conscience solely to itself would make something good or right. It is not that my conscience allows me to determine what is right or wrong, good or bad, as Hegel underlines: "its appeal solely to itself is directly opposed to what it seeks to be—that is, the rule for a rational and universal mode of action which is valid in and for itself."[51] A conscientious agent knows in itself and from itself what is right, and that means that the agent has the capacity to self-consciously approve ("from itself") of the communal norms that bind her action, norms which are ("in itself") acknowledged to be right by the light of the community she is a member of.[52] I might add that what is taken to be right in itself is to be understood as resulting from the community's history.

This understanding of the modern sense of agency in contrast to its premodern sense has hardly anything to do with the heroic self-conscious agent we already said so much about. I will conclude this section by relating the one to the other.

In premodern times what one ought to do was something natural and given. In tragedy, as our discussion showed, this is so in the rather specific sense that the consequences of actions make evident what one should have done. Antigone knew that she transgressed Creon's edict and the norm to which she bound her action was set by her obligation toward her brother. But the focus in the tragedy is on her realizing that the *approval* of her action is in the hands of the gods. It is not up to the community to judge and (dis)approve of her action, nor is it up to herself, but it is up to the gods. The consequences of her action will show whether what she did was right or not—"once I suffer I will know that I was wrong." It implies that (future) *reality* exercises *authority* over the moral judgment of the action. Agents know that the consequences of their actions are to a certain extent out of their hands. This Antigone admits. But there is more to this: the judgment whether the action is right or wrong first becomes evident from those consequences. This explains why heroic agents take up the responsibility (*Schuld*) for the consequences of their actions. Their actions are re-described in terms of consequences they did not intend nor foresee, but those consequences do make evident whether what they did was something they *should* have done or not. The consequences of an action tell the agent what it is she in fact did, what its true description is.

In the second part of his *Philosophy of Right* on morality, Hegel refers to the heroic sense of agency to distinguish between deed (*Tat*) and action (*Handlung*). At the start of the Spirit chapters in his *Phenomenology of Spirit*, Hegel discusses the *Antigone* to distinguish between divine and human law. These are two rather different discussions: the latter has hardly anything to do with the theory of action. In antiquity, in tragedy, and in social and political life, agents have the right to accept responsibility for their action and its consequences inasmuch as they intended the action and knew what would follow from it.[53] The difference between the premodern and modern sense of agency, Hegel emphasizes, has to do with subjective freedom, which is typically modern, and is best understood in terms of conscience.

What is crucial about agency in tragedy, is that the agent suffers from the unintended and unknown consequences of her own deed, consequences which make evident *that* the agent transgressed a divine law, which is why she is punished. If Oedipus lived in modern times, he would accept responsibility for the killing of the man who turned out to be his father, as he did in antiquity, in terms of the particular purpose he had for his action. His anger at having been about to be brutally thrust off the road led to the fight in which he killed his father.[54] In today's world, Oedipus would know that killing is wrong, as he did know in antiquity. The difference is that as a modern person, in this reading of Hegel, he would disapprove of his action because his action defied what he self-consciously would approve of as a member of society. This self-conscious approval *is* the subjective freedom typical of modernity.[55] Another difference is that the suffering his actions caused would not be proof of transgression of a divine law and the punishment for it. Such meaning modern suffering no longer allows. In *Manchester by the Sea*, Lee Chandler accepts responsibility for consequences he did *not* intend or foresee. As in ancient tragedy, the consequences of his actions did make evident to him what he in fact did, what its true description is. Chandler cannot live with himself, just like Oedipus after having found out the truth in *Oedipus the King* could not live with himself. But to Lee, as a typical modern character, this means that he cannot self-consciously approve of his action as a member of a community. This is why—and this is what the movie is about—he constantly withdraws himself from participating in the community, even though the circumstances allow and motivate him to re-enter the community. His brother, who made Chandler in his testament responsible for his son, died. Chandler thereafter is incapable of taking this task upon himself. Also his wife forgives him, but this too does not persuade him to re-enter the community.

Oedipus too decides to withdraw from the community at the end of *Oedipus the King*; first by striking out his eyes and then by leaving the city. But he did not do so because he could not self-consciously approve of his action as a member of the community, but instead because he realized that he is responsible for the suffering he caused. He alone had set the fateful course of events into motion. His ruin is his own. This is true of Chandler as well. The suffering both endure is justified in the eyes of both men. For Oedipus, his suffering is punishment for transgressing a divine law. For Chandler, there are no longer any gods doing the punishing. He alone can punish himself, and self-consciously justify that punishment, by going to a bar and starting a fight to get beaten, and by isolating himself from his community. Only in the third, postmodern phase of Spirit, one's ruin is no longer one's own. Such a phase, Brandom argues, was already envisioned by Hegel.

A Spirit of Trust

Brandom is very interested in the distinction between the premodern and modern conceptions of agency, and he offers a rich reading of it in his vast and fascinating book on Hegel. He at times associates the distinction between heroic deeds and intentional actions with the distinction between premodern and modern agency, although we should not do this for the reasons given in the section titled Heroic Deeds and Intentional Actions. Brandom erroneously suggests that the ancient Greeks had no conception of the right to restrict responsibility to what is intended and reasonably foreseeable by the agent.[56] There is plenty of evidence that they did. In antiquity, one obviously performed actions intentionally,[57] in tragedy and in real life, as we saw. There is a heroic sense of agency to be found in tragedies, but, as we said, such agency can also be found in modern dramas. It is simply not true that the premodern conception of agency is a heroic conception, where agents "take responsibility for their doings under all the descriptions true of those doings."[58] The Greek sense of agency and responsibility is very much our own, as we saw in the section titled Heroic Deeds and Intentional Actions. But we also saw in the section titled Conscience that what distinguishes the premodern from the modern conception of agency is that according to the latter agency is understood in relation to subjective freedom. In modernity, it becomes possible for agents to self-consciously approve of the communal norms that bind their actions. And we in part relied on Brandom's reading of Hegel to understand this typically modern form of self-conscious agency.

Brandom emphasizes that, next to a premodern and modern stage, Hegel envisaged a third, postmodern stage of self-conscious Spirit, where "individuals acknowledge and are attributed responsibility for their whole deed, under all its specifications."[59] On this third stage he writes:

> [The] deed is understood as not done by the agent alone, but as also done in a different, although equally constitutive sense by the agent's community. All are responsible for the doings of each, and each for the doings of all. Appreciating this is the fundamental practical, agentive aspect of the self-understanding of *Geist* that is fully self-conscious.[60]

Thus "The agent and the community together are responsible for the action under all its specifications."[61] This is how agency in the age of trust, as Brandom calls it, re-achieves its heroic character.[62] It is no longer up to fate to approve of one's action, nor up to oneself, but up to the community in that the unknown and unintended consequences of an action are the responsibility of the community at large. In his reading of Hegel, Brandom describes this third stage of Spirit and its associated conception of agency in terms of confessing and forgiving.[63] I *trust* that if I do something unknowingly and unwillingly, and thereby transgress some communal norm, I will be forgiven by other members of the community, who share the responsibility for my action and its consequences, and who recognize me as a member of that community by forgiving me. For such forgiveness, I first must confess that what I did is a transgression of some norm, even though I had unknowingly and unwillingly transgressed that norm, and by confessing I recognize those I confess to as members of my community. The conception of agency in the third stage of Spirit therefore is called magnanimous (*edelmütige*) agency. Brandom writes:

> Trusting is both acknowledging authority of those trusted to forgive and invoking their responsibility to do so. Prospective trust that one will be forgiven for what one confesses is the recognitive attitude complementary to forgiveness. Together these reciprocal practical attitudes produce a community with a symmetrical, *edelmütig[e]* recognitive structure.[64]

A simple example of what Brandom has in mind is that of a person stealing a loaf of bread. We can simply hold that person responsible for her action; but we can also, as magnanimous creatures, admit that our society apparently brought that person to such a position that she had no choice but to steal the bread. Such a postmodern view of shared responsibility may include understanding (and forgiving) the agent's fallibility and shortcomings. What she did then is brought into agreement not with her own character, as in tragedy, but, we might say, in agreement with the magnanimous character of the community at large.

What I have done in the age of trust is not settled after the deed has been concluded. Brandom writes that future actions by others may affect its consequences, allowing for a re-description of my action, retroactively changing what I did.[65] This *historical* sense of agency does not discharge the agent from her responsibility for her action, as this basic element in the sense of responsibility is part of our concept of (intentional) agency and found in each stage of Spirit. What makes the magnanimous sense of agency a historical sense of agency is that we understand that the attribution of responsibility depends on the action's relations to subsequent actions, an understanding that becomes apparent only afterward and that requires retroactive alignment of those actions and events, the sort of which we typically associate with *narrative*. Heroism is re-achieved in that the right to accept responsibility for an action depends not on what the agent intended and knew would follow from her action, but on the action's future consequences and the actions of others, which together allow for its assessment as to whether it was right or wrong.

Conclusion

The most important lesson that the ancient Greeks taught us, and a lesson that is drawn by Williams, is that "the responsibilities we have to recognize extend in many ways beyond our normal purposes and what we intentionally do."[66] In Brandom's reading of Hegel we only fully internalize this lesson when blessed with the spirit of trust. It is a lesson we should take to heart in response to climate change, economic inequality, discrimination, immigration, the loss of biodiversity, the pandemic, and animal suffering. We should reflect on our responsibility (*Schuld*) for these phenomena beyond what we intend to bring about with our actions. Especially when future reality reclaims its normative authority over our actions.

Notes

1. Hegel, *Elements of the Philosophy of Right*, ed. Allen W. Wood, trans. H. B. Nisbet (Cambridge: Cambridge University Press, 2003), §117.
2. Hegel, *Philosophy of Right*, §120.
3. Hegel, *Philosophy of Right*, §118.
4. Purpose [*Vorsatz*] issuing from a thinker comprises intent [*Absicht*]. Hegel, *Philosophy of Right*, §119. The commonly used term "intentional action" will mean "purposeful action" in this essay.
5. Robert Brandom, *A Spirit of Trust: A Reading of Hegel's Phenomenology* (Cambridge, MA: Harvard University Press, 2019).
6. Both distinctions are central to Brandom, but sometimes he erroneously conflates the two. The relation between the distinctions is hardly addressed in the literature. Here my discussion of the literature is limited to Brandom's book.

7   Brandom, *Spirit*, 643.
8   Brandom, *Spirit*, 30.
9   Brandom, *Spirit*, 728.
10 Brandom, *Spirit*, 491–2.
11 Williams, *Shame and Necessity* (Berkeley: University of California Press, 2008), 3.
12 Sophocles, *Antigone*, lines 921–7. References are to verse lines in the Greek text and to Sophocles, *The Three Theban Plays: Antigone, Oedipus the King, Oedipus at Colonus*, trans. Robert Fagles (Penguin Books, 1984).
13 See also the conclusion of the *Antigone*, 1351–2. Aeschylus introduced this *topos* in his *Agamemnon*, 176–7. Aeschylus, *Oresteia*, trans. and intro. Christopher Collard, (Oxford: Oxford UP 2008).
14 Hegel translates this line in his *Phenomenology of Spirit*, trans. A. V. Miller (Oxford: Oxford UP, 1977), §470. The distinction between human and divine law is introduced by Hegel in his discussion of *Antigone* in the *Phenomenology* §448ff. Hegel relegates the divine law to the family, the household, which is the (private) sphere of women, and human law to the (public) sphere of the state, which is the sphere of men. He returns to it in the Religion chapter of his *Phenomenology*. The distinction between human and divine law is not typical of antiquity but still common in the early modern world. It became unfashionable in the Enlightenment. For Hegel's view on Greek tragedy, see also Miguel de Beistegui, "Hegel: Or the Tragedy of Thinking," in *Philosophy and Tragedy*, ed. Miguel de Beistegui and Simon Sparks (London and New York: Routledge, 2000), 11–37.
15 This conception is for example also central to the work of Herodotus, who was a friend of Sophocles. See John Gould, *Herodotus* (London: Weidenfeld and Nicholson, 1989), 82–6. Sophocles' *Electra*, ed. Edith Hall and trans. H. D. F. Kitto, (Oxford: Oxford UP 2008), as a whole is a prime example of the reciprocal conception of action. Interesting too are Electra's words to her mother, lines 566–83.
16 Sophocles, *Oedipus the King*, 100.
17 Sophocles, *Oedipus at Colonus*, 228–30.
18 Sophocles, *Oedipus at Colonus*, 6.
19 Aristotle, *Poëtica*, trans. N. van der Ben and J. M. Bremer (Amsterdam: Athenaeum, 1995), 53b4–13.
20 Hegel, *Aesthetics: Lectures on Fine Art: Volume II*, trans. T. M. Knox (Oxford: Clarendon Press, 1975), 1198.
21 Hegel, *Aesthetics*, 1198.
22 Hegel, *The Philosophy of History*, trans. J. Sibree, (Mineola, NY: Dover Publications, 2004), 231.
23 Hegel, *Philosophy of History*, 232.
24 The example is found in Antiphon and is discussed in Williams, *Shame*, 60–3.
25 That the Greek concept is our own is a central claim of Williams in his *Shame*. Williams does of course not deny the many differences between the ancient Greeks and us, but he argues against those who deny the ancient—and archaic—Greeks a sense of agency and responsibility we hold to be ours.
26 Sophocles, *Oedipus the King*, 1329–31.
27 Sophocles, *Oedipus at Colonus*, 270–8. See also 543–8.
28 Sophocles, *Oedipus at Colonus*, 975–7. Oedipus continues that he cannot be blamed for marrying his mother, at lines 980–90.
29 Sophocles, *Oedipus the King*, 1230–1.

30 Davidson, "Agency," in his *Essays on Actions and Events*, 2nd ed. (Oxford: Clarendon Press, 2013), 50. This reference to Davidson should not surprise. A central claim of Michael Quante's important *Hegel's Concept of Action* (Cambridge: Cambridge University Press, 2004) and Brandom's *Spirit* is that Hegel's views on agency agree with Davidson's. I might add that in one of his other essays, Davidson, who studied ancient Greek and had read all of Greek drama, uses the same example as Hegel when he writes "Oedipus struck the rude old man intentionally, but he did not strike his father intentionally. But on my theory, these strikings were one [and the same action, albeit one described in one way, and one in another], since the rude old man was Oedipus' father." Davidson, "Criticism, Comment, and Defence," in *Essays on Actions and Events*, 147.
31 It is not that in the modern age agents are *necessarily* self-consciously modern. But the modern age has put particular social and political structures in place that allow agents to become self-consciously modern and be recognized as such.
32 Hegel, *Philosophy of Right*, §117.
33 Williams seems to agree. See his, *Shame*, 64–5.
34 Hegel, *Philosophy of Right*, §118. To be sure, one is withheld from exercising one's will when being enslaved or when otherwise limited by societal structures.
35 Hegel, *Philosophy of Right*, §119.
36 In his *Philosophy of Right*, §120, Hegel distinguishes between contingent consequences that agents cannot be held fully accountable for—this is the case when the agent is not a fully self-conscious *thinking* agent, as in the case of children and lunatics—and contingent consequences of actions in their external existence, that is, outside of the knowledge of the thinking agent.
37 Davidson, "Agency," 54.
38 Hegel, *Philosophy of Right*, §124.
39 Hegel puts it thus: "*Conscience* expresses the absolute entitlement of subjective self-consciousness to know *in itself* and *from itself* what right and duty are, and to recognize only what it thus knows as the good." *Philosophy of Right*, §137. Brandom puts it thus: conscience is a practical attitude "towards the constitution of communal norms and their determination of appropriateness of individual performances" (*Spirit*, 539). And: "The normative status of *being* responsible is instituted by the attitude of the subject who acknowledges it *as* binding" (*Spirit*, 540). The capacity referred to is what agents need to develop while growing up. The social conditions that *make* this capacity to develop *possible* are the result of a long historical process culminating in the French Revolution. Dean Moyar, *Hegel's Conscience* (Oxford: Oxford University Press, 2014), 12n11, lists the relevant literature on conscience in Hegel. He too emphasizes that "conscience" is a concept of action rather than of moral reflection (22–3) and discusses self-conscious approval of communal norms in terms of rational authority and answerability to others (16–18).
40 Hegel, *Philosophy of Right*, §123.
41 The ancient Greeks did however debate the nature of laws, and the fifth-century sophists opposed the belief in the existence of divine laws upheld by the gods.
42 Hegel, *Philosophy of History*, 255, 267.
43 Hegel, *Philosophy of History*, 253–4, 265. See also the Preface to the *Philosophy of Right*. This lesson Hegel no doubt learned from Thucydides and Plato. With regard to Socrates who "turned inwards" to decide what is good and right, Hegel notes that he did so because the community no longer supplied guidance as to what was good and

right (*Philosophy of Right*, §138). So here too there is no self-conscious approval of the communal norms that bind one's action.
44 Hegel, *Philosophy of Right*, §132. This I take to be the most crucial datum of Hegel's concept of action. Cf. Hegel, *Phenomenology*, §640. Cf. Quante, *Hegel's Concept of Action*, 94–5, where this point would have been of help to him to explain why according to Hegel actions involve "the will of others." Hegel, *Philosophy of Right*, §113.
45 Brandom, *Spirit*, 647.
46 Hegel, *Philosophy of Right*, §124.
47 Brandom, *Spirit*, 498.
48 Hegel, *Philosophy of Right*, §136.
49 Hegel, *Philosophy of Right*, §136 [Add.].
50 Hegel, *Philosophy of Right*, §140.
51 Hegel, *Philosophy of Right*, §137.
52 This agrees with Robert Stern's argument that Hegel presents a social command account of moral obligation. Stern, *Understanding Moral Obligation. Kant, Hegel, Kierkegaard* (Cambridge: Cambridge University Press, 2012), 150–61.
53 As Hegel puts it later in another context (*Phenomenology*, §733): "The hero [in tragedies] is himself the speaker, and the performance displays to the audience—who are also spectators—*self-conscious* human beings who *know* their rights and purposes, the power and the will of their specific nature and know how to *assert* them."
54 Sophocles, *Oedipus The King*, 800–13.
55 This subjective freedom thus also affects self-conscious agency in modern tragedy, for instance as theorized by Friedrich Schiller. On the latter, see Frederick Beiser, *Schiller as Philosopher: A Re-Examination* (Oxford: Oxford University Press, 2005), 238ff.
56 For example Brandom, *Spirit*, 476–7: "[T]he modern idea of restricting responsibility to what is intended and reasonably foreseeable by the agent producing a performance was a decisive advance in our practical and theoretical understanding of normativity and agency." See also *Spirit*, 453, 491, 626, and 728.
57 This Brandom accepts (*Spirit*, 489).
58 Brandom, *Spirit*, 727.
59 Brandom, *Spirit*, 476.
60 Brandom, *Spirit*, 734.
61 Brandom, *Spirit*, 627.
62 Brandom, *Spirit*, 754.
63 He notes the centrality of these terms in Christian religion.
64 Brandom, *Spirit*, 621. We should note that "community" for Brandom is any community instituted by its each other recognizing members. The question vital to Hegel how communities relate to the state and civil society is not one pondered by Brandom.
65 Brandom, *Spirit*, 625.
66 Williams, *Shame*, 74.

Traditional Sources

Aeschylus. *Oresteia*. Translated and introduction by Christopher Collard. Oxford: Oxford University Press, 2008.

Aristotle. *Poëtica*. Translated by Nicolaas van der Ben and Jan-Martin Bremer. Amsterdam: Athenaeum, 1995.
Sophocles. *The Three Theban Plays: Antigone, Oedipus the King, Oedipus at Colonus*. Translated by Robert Fagles. Harmondsworth: Penguin Books, 1984.
Sophocles. *Antigone, Oedipus the King, and Electra*. Edited by Edith Hall. Translated by H. D. F. Kitto. Oxford: Oxford University Press, 2008.

Bibliography

Beiser, Frederick. *Schiller as Philosopher: A Re-Examination*. Oxford: Oxford University Press, 2005.
Brandom, Robert. *A Spirit of Trust: A Reading of Hegel's Phenomenology*. Cambridge, MA: Harvard University Press, 2019.
Davidson, Donald. *Essays on Actions and Events*. 2nd ed. Oxford: Clarendon Press, 2013.
de Beistegui, Miguel. "Hegel: Or the Tragedy of Thinking." In *Philosophy and Tragedy*, edited by Miguel de Beistegui and Simon Sparks, 11–37. London and New York: Routledge, 2000.
Gould, John. *Herodotus*. London: Weidenfeld and Nicholson, 1989.
Hegel, G. F. W. *Aesthetics: Lectures on Fine Art: Volume II*. Translated by Thomas Malcolm Knox. Oxford: Clarendon Press, 1975.
Hegel, G. F. W. *Phenomenology of Spirit*. Translated by Arnold V. Miller and John N. Findlay. Oxford: Oxford University Press, 1977.
Hegel, G. F. W. *Elements of the Philosophy of Right*. Edited by Allen W. Wood and translated by Hugh Barr Nisbet. Cambridge: Cambridge University Press, 2003.
Hegel, G. F. W. *The Philosophy of History*. Translated by J. Sibree. Mineola, NY: Dover Publications, 2004.
Moyar, Dean. *Hegel's Conscience*. Oxford: Oxford University Press, 2014.
Quante, Michael. *Hegel's Concept of Action*. Cambridge: Cambridge University Press, 2004.
Stern, Robert. *Understanding Moral Obligation: Kant, Hegel, Kierkegaard*. Cambridge: Cambridge University Press, 2012.
Williams, Bernard. *Shame and Necessity*. Berkeley: University of California Press, 2008.

7

Farness and Immemorial Time

An Ontology of Vestiges

Roberto Wu

Introduction

What kind of being is a vestige? What can one expect from a temporal approach to vestiges? What are the distinguished traits of this approach and which advantages and difficulties does it involve? These guiding questions help us to formulate an ontology of vestiges, to inquire into the peculiarity of its temporal existence, and to investigate what kind of meaning it may present. Instead of conceiving vestiges as mere indications of an absent being that are able to provide nothing but secondary contents to complement current narratives, I propose considering them as phenomena capable of engendering a different temporality.

In this chapter, I seek to develop the thesis that vestiges necessarily entail some dimension of immemorial time, one that eludes any sort of presentification. An understanding of these phenomena demands a reconfiguration of one's perception of temporality. It relates to, but it is not determined by, the thought of Jacques Derrida, Emmanuel Levinas, and others, which has developed ways of approaching the past through discussing the existence of phenomena that refuse direct apprehension, such as traces, vestiges, and remnants, as an alternative to ontologies centered on presence. I begin by explaining that (1) events, in contrast to mere occurrences of nature, convey expressions of alterities as vestiges and that (2) the investigation of a vestige does not lead us to some presence of the past but to an understanding of beings from the perspective of an immemorial time. Contrary to Levinas, who has exclusively an ethical interest in the immemorial time, I also explore the importance of this temporality in the constitution of meanings, by connecting it with vestiges and their evocation of alterity.

I conclude by suggesting that (3) an adequate account of the dynamics of vestiges involves an openness to farness, here understood as a hermeneutic condition to open up the dimension of the immemorial.

Expressive Events

The starting point of my analysis is that meanings do not primarily concern present-at-hand beings but rather concern events.[1] As this chapter strongly relies on the correspondence between understanding of being and historicity[2]—prior to the distinction between natural and human sciences—it leaves aside the naturalized conception of events that philosophers such as R. G. Collingwood and Donald Davidson discuss in their works.[3] Contrary to their views, my study considers events in their connection with alterity in several layers of constitution of meaning, particularly in the pre-predicative level. By alterity, I mostly assume Levinas's conception of the other as a face, to whom I am ethically responsible and who, accordingly, cannot be equated to something previously known—that is, to the same.[4]

Phenomenologists such as Martin Heidegger, Hans-Georg Gadamer, Hannah Arendt, Jacques Derrida, and Emmanuel Levinas employ the term *event* in a historical sense, or, at least, assume a form of temporality that refuses its naturalization. Because they criticize the vulgar concept of time, namely that which conceives it as a flow of sequential moments, their conception of event brings forth notions as origin, rupture, encounter, language, and otherness, which are of interest in this chapter.[5] Nevertheless, the many affinities with their theories should not overshadow the differences between our goals, as I am not interested, for example, in discussing the event in its epochal meaning, as one reads in Arendt's works or Heidegger's later writings, but rather in developing an account of event that helps us to understand how inscriptions of alterity are conveyed in time.

On the one hand, this concept of event belongs to a level that stands prior to historiographic interest, which methodologically narrows the way something appears as a historical object. On the other hand, it may contribute to historical studies, as it leads to a consideration of neglected aspects of the ontology of history. Henceforth in this chapter I will consistently employ *event* as the inscription of the other in time, an historical account that rejects metaphysical commitments of the subject-object scheme and the ontology of the present-at-hand.

Schemes of meaning based on the distinction between subject and object, as formulated by modern epistemology, fail in properly discussing events. The linguistic and historical turns suggest that subjectivity is derived from a manifold of effects that pervades us historically and is bequeathed by means of language and institutions. By the same token, a version of pure objective meaning in terms of history is also misleading. Meanings are not limited to present-at-hand features that beings bear, but, rather, they are referred to as involving intertwining connections that are historically constituted. Because the scheme of knowledge as constituted by subject and object is a theoretical construction rather than an original state of meaning, it reveals itself to be ineffective for apprehending temporal phenomena. In what follows, I discuss some disadvantages of this theoretical schema based on the present-at-hand as an approach to history.

Conceptions based on a metaphysics of the present-at-hand have the drawback of offering a limited account of historicity, as they generally impose the present onto other dimensions of time. Conversely, when beings are interpreted in their relation to multiple historical events, which generate a myriad of interconnected effects, one may relate to them as bearing a wider meaning of vestiges. In this broader scope, vestiges are not simply the fragments present-at-hand that result from finished events but beings that bear the potentiality of evoking events and enacting a peculiar openness to history. In turn, events presuppose a relation to human beings, whose interference, to a greater or a lesser degree, is conveyed by them. Events transmit a manifold of expressions, which does not derive directly from subjectivity reflected action but from our being-in-the-world, which is from the outset open to our belonging to a historical community. As conjoining different forms of expression, vestiges linger through time and signal both to the events in which they partook and to the alterity of those who were involved or evoked in such events.

A Preliminary Overview of Vestiges

Although surrounded by vestiges, our experience of these phenomena is far from satisfactory. This situation is mainly due to our incapacity for apprehending vestiges in their temporal peculiarity, because one often sees them as a secondary phenomenon, as mere indicative signs that have no significance of their own, allegedly because of their ontological dependence on beings that have once existed. Therefore, they are mostly considered parts of a totality that does not exist anymore, in the sense that some vestiges are taken as fragments of a previous whole being, like the head of a broken statue—but also in the sense of being part of a historical and cultural totality that did not completely survive, as a spear is a fragment of the Roman Empire. Either if we take vestiges as pieces of an entire being that existed before or consider them as an indication of the culture of other epochs, it is clear that they are consistently taken as matters present-at-hand or as signs that lead to a previous presence.

Vestiges are often mistaken, either because we normally overlook their peculiarity and regard them in terms of their presence or because we take them as a mediator to another being. In this latter case, vestiges may appear as dislocated presences remaining from the past. This way of describing vestiges may be deceptive, for it refers to past phenomena in terms of the present and, accordingly, circumscribes the former into the latter. Or, to put it another way, because such an account of vestiges extends the realm of presence into other realms of temporality, it muffles different forms of expression that may arise from distinct strata of time.

In historical research, traces are usually taken as physical evidence of what past people have left in the world.[6] To this extent, they work as indexes to a past being or context. In this regard, two points require further explanation. Firstly, as I conceive them, vestiges do not indicate a former presence but evoke receding alterities. They exceed an indexical function as they transcend every recollective attempt of reconstitution. Secondly, vestiges are not reducible to their eventual physicality, which does not mean a dismissal of the latter. It is rather a matter of ontological priority. Unfortunately, even Levinas, as providing a discussion of traces, exemplifies them through physical marks, a procedure that yields some confusion.[7] Conversely, Derrida declares from the outset that his concept of trace is not to be conflated with a form of being present.

Coined as the *différance* itself and "the absolute origin of sense in general," in Derrida's account, "the trace is not more ideal than real, not more intelligible than sensible, not more a transparent signification than an opaque energy and *no concept of metaphysics can describe it*."[8] My account of vestiges enacts a similar methodological gesture, as it does not implicate a rejection of physicality but rather claims a leeway that exceeds it. In this respect, vestiges are addressed here in the context of meaning formation and not immediately as physical evidence. A chain of vestigial evocations may relate to a physical being, but not necessarily. As an example, the activity of remembering may be awakened by physical remains that evoke a bygone alterity, but it may also be triggered off by the occurrence of a remembrance, whose prominence sets a pathway of evocations alongside other vestigial thoughts that remain in the background.

A question that may naturally arise is: how can this view of vestiges be of some interest in historical research if it does not lead to positive knowledge of the past? As I see this matter, it presents the advantage of calling attention to certain aspects that prevent dogmatism regarding our engagement with the past. It does not reject the importance of knowing and reaching accord about the past by means of diverse methodologies. It just reminds us that historical research cannot capture the past as a present-at-hand, for any knowledge of it only conducts us to an even more remote past due to inscriptions of alterity in events.

Considering difficulties that result from the hegemony of an ontology of presence in our relations with beings and history, I suggest an approach to the vestige that is based on an ontology of the immemorial past. It avoids the path that leads to a privilege of presence, insofar as it conceives different articulations of meaning in history. It acknowledges a dual production of effects in history: one that corresponds to more stable threads in history, as generated by present-at-hand categories; and another one that does not form an articulated totality, as it consists in dispersion and withdrawal. Historical research is inclined to consider every phenomenon uniquely from the first perspective, even the absent ones. By relying in processes of making matters present, such an approach fails to acknowledge and elaborate dimensions of history that stand outside a metaphysics of presence, as it exclusively produces the characteristic knowledge of a presentist ontology. Without denying the possibility of elaborating meanings with account to making matters present, this chapter focuses on how vestiges yield historical significance that recede from being captured as presences. In order to access such phenomena, we must elaborate an account of the immemorial past, as well as how this dimension of time is sheltered in vestiges.

The Temporality of Vestiges

Vestiges are not presences. In fact, when they are forced to become such a thing, they vanish. Their particular ontology brings into consideration the possibility of an absence being meaningful in its farness, as a receding phenomenon in time. In this light, the analysis will henceforth focus on the irreducibility of vestigial phenomena to presence as a basis to analyze the temporal tension between past and present.

Levinas's usage of the term *le trace* (vestige, trace), as a concept that he employs in his critique against Heidegger's fundamental ontology, is pivotal for my proposal.[9] Despite Heidegger's contempt for metaphysics, with which Levinas agrees to some extent, the German philosopher's work is mainly interpreted by the latter as a sophisticated form of thinking that merely confirms the privilege of the same. In opposition to the perpetual confirmation of one's horizon of understanding (as he reads the hermeneutical circle in Heidegger), which merely assimilates strangeness and transforms it into familiar meanings, Levinas develops a conceptuality that preserves alterity from being possessed by understanding.[10] Considering that the other consists of a face (*Visage*) that does not count as a sheer being among other beings, or as an object, for it means absolute transcendence, one cannot apprehend this alterity by means of her actual properties, insofar as the other refuses being captured as a presence.[11]

In Levinas's account, the other does not consist of presence, with the distinctive trait of merely being someone else except me, but is instead a face that does not belong to the economy of presence. Alternatively, vestiges retain in themselves inscriptions of the alterities that become their bearers. Vestiges transcend the function of being a mark of something or someone that exists, as an index that points to its presence; on the contrary, vestiges evoke forms of alterity that, as such, recede from being captured in present-at-hand reconstitution. Therefore, meanings opened up by vestiges differ from those based on an ontology of the present-at-hand, which determine most of one's interpretation in the world. Connections among vestiges cannot be retraced to a notion of original presence, because vestiges express alterities involved in a chain of historical events.

Vestiges bear these inscriptions of alterity, although one ordinarily fails to notice them while approaching them in terms of something present-at-hand. The prevalence of a metaphysical interpretation of being reflects an account of temporality that merely connects events in a linear pattern. In order to avoid this conception of temporality, as it prevents an access to historicity, an understanding of receding meanings is needed. As it is proposed here, the uses of vestiges in historical research are far from being mere reconstitutions of presences, as they disrupt our horizon putting us in contact with a bygone past.

In everyday affairs the past does not appear as such, but, rather, as an extension of the present. It is readily taken as part of the major horizon of the present, without any need of mediation because it is already assimilated as a presence, even if a fragmented one. The idea of a fragment conserving a part of the past shares, in a certain sense, this premise. Underlying this attitude, there is the assumption that what counts as meaningful is only that which meets present-at-hand standards. The ubiquity of this attitude blocks a proper access to past phenomena as such, because it levels the past to the present. As temporal phenomena, past and present necessarily conflict, for they engender contrary movements: the former moves away from the present and tends to fade out while the latter tends to incorporate the past as presence. There are plenty of categories designed to capture the past into the present, although it is rare to find concepts compatible with the withdrawal of the past, which does not consist of the retreat of something present-at-hand but of an openness to a bygone alterity.[12] As one is usually unprepared to deal with receding phenomena, the ordinary understanding of vestiges is far from reaching its full potential.

Vestiges are essentially disruptive, for they engender insurmountable intervals between the present and the past. They elicit a discord between the past and the present and, as such, provide an experience of time, instead of simply displaying the past. Rather than reconstituting a bygone world, vestiges evoke the vastness of what has been, which always surpasses any attempt to represent it as a presence. Meanings evoked by vestiges bring forth the tension of the disruption of an elusive past in the present. These meanings do not consist of a plain combination of past and present, but rather they express the mode in which these dimensions of time compete among themselves.

As vestiges do not belong to the present, it would be natural that scholars identify them as diachronic phenomena. However, I avoid discussing temporality in terms of diachrony and synchrony, as they still echo linear metaphors. Undoubtedly each scholar adapts and discusses this opposition in different ways since Ferdinand de Saussure's original program. Levinas, for example, understands synchrony, with which he identifies philosophers such as Descartes, Kant, Husserl, and Heidegger as egological and reserves the term "diachrony" to describe the temporal responsibility for the other. This diachrony expresses the temporality of the immemorial past and its potentiality of disrupting our present horizon. To be sure, this is primordially an ethical claim, in which diachrony corresponds to the responsibility for the other that is prior to any experience. Although I agree with Levinas on the main lines of his proposal, I would rather discuss history in hermeneutical terms, for they enable a broader discussion on historical meaning. While Levinas's interest in temporality is restricted to alterity, my aim is to provide a comprehensive account of meaning that explores the relevance of expressions in history and provides an adequate conceptuality that welcomes the other that is evoked by them.[13]

Regarding Levinas's rejection of hermeneutics, one may dispute his characterization of this subject as one-sided, as he expects a theory of the responsibility for the other that is lacking, according to his reading, in the works of Husserl and Heidegger. However, hermeneutics as developed by Hans-Georg Gadamer, Paul Ricoeur, and Gianni Vattimo, to name a few, places the subject of alterity in the heart of their proposals.[14] My account, which is indebted to this tradition as much as it acknowledges the relevance of Levinas's and Derrida's critiques, indicates the possibility of understanding historical meaning by means of vestiges, as the interpreter does not do violence to the alterity they convey but instead perceives a significance that constitutes itself in the farness.

Challenges of Elusive Phenomena

Inasmuch as the hegemonic ontology that works as the basis for every comportment in the world relies on presence, one is inclined to interpret elusive phenomena as secondary or imperfect ones, in comparison with presence. This results in a general difficulty in recognizing the importance of vestiges themselves because they are often overshadowed by a correspondent presence. However, the hermeneutic orientation toward vestiges differs from methodologies that examine them as something present-at-hand. The metaphysical standpoint uses a methodology based on a stable set of categories that may be applied to a cluster of phenomena. Conversely, the hermeneutic orientation depends on an entirely different attitude, which must correspond to the peculiar way in which vestiges evoke the past in a series of dispersive references.

While the impermanence of present-at-hand phenomena is linked to an alteration coming from a stable configuration or stabilizing tendency, the dispersive dynamic of vestiges belongs to a distinct sphere, namely to that of alterity. Here I draw on Levinas's conception of the other as infinite. The primary character of vestiges is not that of the announcement of presence but the double feature of evoking an infinity and realizing that this act can never be achieved by anything present-at-hand. Vestiges are not simple impermanent phenomena, although they resemble other transient beings in some respects, but, rather, primarily phenomena that channel alterity. Vestiges point out not only to a bygone past but also to the very impossibility of our coincidence with that past.

An interpretation of vestiges does not bring us back to a present-at-hand origin, but, rather, it sends us to a polyphony of voices or a multiplicity of expressions, to a complex, intertwined, and never-ending production of effects. Vestiges are bearers of a manifold of inscriptions produced by alterity that successively direct us to other events.

As elusive phenomena, vestiges transcend the present in their evocations. The present takes place within a broader horizon of time that it cannot encompass, although its cognitive tools create the illusion that it can extend to other epochs. Despite the fact that some past beings persist in our present, they never fit perfectly to it, as they also refer to a time that differs from ours. A vestige produces a gap that cannot be completely fulfilled, for while it persists in the present, it also bears inscriptions of a remote time that refuse presence. Every vestige is itself the bearer of multiple inscriptions, which redirect our understanding to orientations of meanings in nonlinear patterns. This vastness of inscriptions does not form a figure; rather, it is properly the refusal of any encompassing picture. Threads opened up for inscriptions lead to paths that conflict our horizon, instead of merely extending it.

If one attempts to follow the chain of vestiges, then one is always conducted to something prior, without being able to deploy entirely this chain of meanings. In other words, the experience of vestiges brings up the experience of an immemorial time. The other leaves her mark in the world of vestiges by engrafting a different temporality in them. In Levinas's account, the immemorial time refers to the infinite responsibility toward the other, which has no beginning as it is always prior to any behavior in the world. As a modification of the Levinasian proposal of immemorial time, I propose the experience of farness as the phenomenological counterpart for the ethical proximity with the other. I establish or realize a relation of proximity with the other every time her face leads me to an infinite responsible engagement with them. Nevertheless, this proximity also entails a sense of farness, inasmuch as in order to meet the call of the other I am required to consider the inevitable distance between me and a transcendence, a remoteness that is hinted at in each vestige.

Vestiges, Farness, and Immemorial Time

An ontology of vestiges requires a completely different attitude concerning being and history. On the one hand, it challenges the predominant interpretation of beings in their character of presence; on the other hand, it opens up the possibility of considering other ways of relating to temporality. Although vestiges may eventually incorporate some features of indexes, they distinguish themselves from the latter as they do not limit themselves to indicating something present in the world. The connection between an index and what it indicates is generally based on the present-at-hand ontology, which simply links a being to another. Conversely, vestiges do not aim to present-at-hand beings but to the otherness of bygone beings. They evoke them in order to maintain their otherness in comparison with anything present. This interval, which simultaneously links us with the past and preserves it as such, is that of *farness*.

An experience of vestiges as such entails necessarily an emergence of farness. Most of the conceptual tools derived from a theory of signs are insensible to such a dimension of meaning, as they involve a version of ontology based on present-at-hand assumptions. Phenomenological reconsiderations of fundamental categories of understanding, including time and space, are usual since Husserl's critique of the so-called "natural attitude." According to Husserl, this attitude takes naively our behavior toward beings as grounded in, among other assumptions, a given world constituted by means of the mathematization of the world. Conversely, Husserl shows the interdependence of world and consciousness, for any content of meaning is intentionally co-constituted.[15] A similar methodology is employed in Heidegger's critique of vulgar conceptions of space and time in *Being and Time*, which states that any concept taken in its metaphysical sense is derivative from Being-there's (Dasein's) existential structure. In particular, §22–24 analyze how the metaphysical account of space is possible only assuming the existential spatiality of Dasein that takes place in his "there" (*Da*), in his openness to being.[16] Without assuming Husserl's and Heidegger's theoretical backgrounds or purposes, I draw on their phenomenological gestures in order to propose a notion of farness distinct from that which is conceived in mathematical-spatial terms.[17]

As belonging to our existential structure, the understanding of something from the perspective of its farness differs from the mere measurement of the distance between two present-at-hand coordinates. In general, our involvement with beings considers them uniquely in their presence, both in temporal and spatial sense. Our connections with beings are presently oriented, whether performing tasks employing tools, or talking to another person that lives in a distant country by means of some device, or remembering someone seeing her or his photograph. Most of the time, activities such as these focus on present features; and when they deal with dimensions of past and future, they tend to presentify them. Present-centered operations disregard other forms of relating with spatiality and temporality, as they tend to absorb and transform past beings into present-at-hand objects. The presentification of vestiges does not only mean a consideration of them from the viewpoint of the present, while ascribing values and conception of our time, but also an interpretation of their significance in terms of present-at-hand data, either as quantitative information, while converting them into numbers or physical properties, or qualitative indexes, as confirming or discrediting historical beliefs. In dealings with vestiges, one usually takes them as remaining forms of the past, in the sense that they *present* a piece of the past. Considering its ontological naivety and its commitment with metaphysical assumptions, I propose we abandon this interpretation of vestiges.

The in-between character of vestiges, which often allows them to be taken as present beings and disregarded in their past dimension, also contains the possibility of relating properly to their pastness. The past is experienced only through farness, as it communicates to us from a bygone time. Experiencing something as a vestige, and not as a present-at-hand, means to be exposed to an expression that has not completely ceased and which has developed other significance throughout time. Vestiges do not belong entirely to the present, but they are not vanished phenomena either. Describing them as having an in-between character may be deceptive, as one may interpret them as simple connections between two domains of time that are present-at-hand. However, the privilege of the present threatens the very possibility of a proper openness to the past. Considering that the present tends to overshadow other dimensions of time, interpretations of historical meanings must take into account the asymmetry in temporal relations. In order to avoid the submission of the past (and the future) to the present, an attitude that favors an experience of other forms of temporality without limiting them to the latter is needed.

Farness cannot be quantified as a present-at-hand distance. It does not emerge from numbers but from events in which alterity is involved. Time embodies the infinity of the other as a farness and therefore configures the way beings appear to us. This infinity manifests itself in time as a farness of a world of alterities that cannot be fully reconstituted and yet expresses itself to us. Farness is not an obstacle to understanding, as something that blocks our access to beings and events coming from the past, but rather it is the primary perspective through which the past may be experienced as such. Any fixation of the past exclusively by means of categories grounded in the present is an illusory experience of the past, whereas it shuts down the driving forces coming from unfamiliar historical contexts. The subordination of the past to an interpretation centered in the present fails to experience temporality, because *it disregards the irreducibility of the past to the present as a condition of possibility of historical meaning*. Time temporalizes the gap between past and present engendering an experience of the depth of a farness, toward which our actual understanding realizes its inability at apprehending phenomena that are not contained in its habitual horizon. The experience of this gap reflects in our expressions, as it pushes our language to its boundaries in order to render unfamiliar phenomena. Vestiges direct the interpreter interested in rendering their meaning from her immanent horizon toward paths that do not form a totality. While the past reaches us as multiple paths that do not plainly converge, its experience leads us to interpret beings and events that reveal themselves as unfamiliar. Paths evoked by inscriptions in vestiges appear from a farness, which simultaneously constrains the validity of our interpretations based on the present and demands an enlargement of our understanding toward elusive phenomena.

A brief example may be useful. In Latin America, many countries had their democratic regimes overthrown by coups d'état in the 1960–1970s and replaced by military dictatorships. In Brazil, this took place between 1964 and 1985 resulting in the murder and disappearance of roughly 421 people, a situation that was even more violent in countries such as Chile (3,065 deaths and disappearances) and Argentina (more than 30,000 cases).[18] The 1979 Amnesty Law, at the final phase of the dictatorship in Brazil, freed more than twenty-five thousand political prisoners, but numbers and documents are deceptive, as much documentation was lost and other evidence was adulterated.

A facility used in 1964 as headquarters of military police in the city of Teresina-PI and reformed after the end of the dictatorship to be a mall of handmade commodities (Central de Artesanato Mestre Dezinho) is helpful to understand the dynamic of vestiges. In one of the stores (box. 34), the owner, Antonio Carlos de Oliveira, invites people to go to the basement to see the place where many political prisoners were tortured and perhaps killed. On the walls of this basement, one notices not only stains of blood and scratches of the victims but also two screws that served to tie people for torture.[19] Physical remains such as these may have an indexical function: one might take a sample of blood and proceed to a DNA exam in order to discover someone's identity. Considering them as indexes is not the same as taking them as vestiges, for the latter do not conduct us to present-at-hand information. The torture room does not solely evoke the people who were tortured there, even if we had complete information about them, but also their family and friends who cared for them, other people who have lived a similar situation, their offenders, and so on. As a palimpsest with countless layers, each investigation finds more and more expressions of past others.

Vestiges evoke a farness of a field of significance that confronts our previous understanding. In this case, the engagement with the dimension of the past does not result in a possession of a being or a meaning present-at-hand, as any meaning that shows up connects with other significances that cannot be entirely apprehended, since they belong to a remote time that refuses complete reconstitution. Therefore, vestiges are a form of pastness that disrupts the present, in order to announce a time that never returns. Because this pastness is not convertible into something present-at-hand, actual concepts and schemes fail to grasp it. Vestiges bring forth an absence that is impossible to fulfill, for it does not belong exclusively to my horizon of understanding, as it contains several inscriptions of alterity.

The source of the significance of the past is immemorial time, which is not to be confused with a point present-at-hand in the past, prior to an event; rather, it consists in the untraceable background of actual involvements. In this sense, it seems to be only a negative limit regarding the horizon of the present, which merely indicates the existence of phenomena that are not encompassed in such a horizon. However, the immemorial does refer to some phenomena, although not in the mode of something present-at-hand. A historical relation with immemorial phenomena requires an openness to the farness they involve.

Vestiges relate to an immemorial time in a nonlinear way. Each path evoked by a vestige leads to perspectives that are not represented in our horizon, inasmuch as they are inscribed by others. Yet horizons related to others do not form a unity, because they evoke successively endless realms of the past. The interpretation of vestiges relates to alterity, but only to the extent they are evoked. The immemorial time safeguards the other, while preserving her infinity. By experiencing the farness of this bygone time, we also experience the inapprehensible character of the other, which can only be welcomed but never dominated.

The evocation of the other does not take her to be something present-at-hand that may be used, but rather as someone who addresses us from a farness. If one accepts this premise, then one should also extend this principle of alterity to past people and reject an approach of them in terms of mere presence. Past people communicate to us on a deeper level, that is, not only by leaving a legacy through material bearers but also by addressing us as others. Following Gadamer, a proper relation with the past is always a dialogue, which cannot occur if I do not concede to the other the possibility of saying or doing something unexpected. To put it another way, a relation with the past entails the engagement with a multitude of expressions coming from other people, a "variety of voices" that can only be adequately corresponded if one does not take them as present-at-hand material but vestiges of other people that transcend my horizon of understanding.[20]

Vestiges evoke a manifold of inscriptions, that is, of events of alterity, which are sent in history. These events intertwine themselves in their sendings and in the reinscription of these sendings.[21] Every reinscription produces both a fracture on meanings and new instances of sendings. Therefore, every reinscription scatters the direction of transmission, because it hands over previous events as well as it generates new threads of meaning. This perpetual division in sendings shows that history, as heritage, is nothing uniform.

Final Remarks

These considerations about vestiges reveal that they are crucial to inquiring into historical meaning because they open up a realm of temporality that exceeds present-at-hand features. One often relates to the past as a dimension of the present, as a previous present. This dependence on the present flattens the sense of history, as one does not properly relate to the past but only to a rendered version of the past in the present. I suggest that our openness to history increases when we become aware that its meaning involves the alterity of past people and its irreducibility to present-at-hand phenomena. Because of their proper ontology, vestiges refuse direct apprehension as they redirect the interpreter to a bygone horizon. When they are taken exclusively in their present-at-hand traits, they offer themselves in a way that they are limited to the temporal boundaries of these traits, while withdrawing in their pastness. However, when one relates to them in order to explore what they open up, namely meanings that recede onto events that cannot be totally apprehend today for they belong to an immemorial time, one may experience a neglected dimension of time that the present overshadows.

Immemorial time is not a type of temporality in which we are in control of beings. Rather, it confronts our certainties showing that the horizon of the present is incapable of rendering the diversity of phenomena that are connected to our time coming from countless events. The experience of the immemorial time is also the openness to a diverse and infinite realm of expressions, which recede in their presence, in order to announce forms of alterity that have generated them. The human being has a tendency of extending his power over other beings, locations, and time; nevertheless, the other is not a being that she may dominate. Alterity can only be encountered in a form of openness, which rejects any kind of violence. As vestiges evoke types of alterities that are sheltered in the immemorial time, they do not present phenomena suitable to dominion but open up a dialogue with voices that express forgotten worlds. Vestiges signal to these distant horizons, not in order to absorb them but to experience their farness, through expressions that, despite their potentiality of being reduced to a present-at-hand, evoke an infinite distance.

Notes

1 Despite their differences, I assume Heidegger's and Derrida's critiques on the ontology of presence as a scheme to develop temporal and ontological issues. Regarding Greek ontology, Heidegger explains in *Being and Time* that "*legein* itself—or rather *noein*," as referring to "that simple awareness of something present-at-hand in its sheer presence-at-hand [*Vorhandenheit*]," "has the Temporal structure of a pure 'making-present' [*Gegenwärtigens*] of something." Consequently, Greek metaphysics provided a model by which beings "get interpreted with regard to the Present [*Gegen-wart*]; that is, they are conceived as presence [*Anwesenheit*] (*ousia*)." Martin Heidegger, *Being and Time*, trans. John Macquarrie and Edward Robinson (Oxford: Blackwell, 2001), 48. In turn, while discussing the history of metaphysics, Derrida states that "Its Matrix ... is the determination of Being as *presence* in all senses of this word. It could be shown that all the names related to fundamentals, to principles, or to the center have always designated an invariable presence—*eidos*, *archē*, *telos*, *energeia*, *ousia* (essence, existence, substance, subject) *alētheia*, transcendentality, consciousness, God, man, and so forth." Jacques Derrida, *Writing and Difference*, trans. Alan Bass (London: Routledge, 2005), 353.
2 In this chapter, historicity designates the fact that our understanding of the world, other people, and ourselves involves, each time, a temporal synthesis of meanings based on the facticity of having-been in such-and-such way, and on the anticipation of possibilities related to the situation we belong. It may as well be described as a temporal dialogue, a communitarian interchange with a tradition that has historically prefigured our world, to which we continuously respond, while generating other effects in history.
3 Donald Davidson employs events as an overarching concept upon which actions are to be distinguished as a particular class. See Donald Davidson, *Essays on Actions and Events* (Oxford: Oxford University Press, 2001). R. G. Collingwood distinguishes between events and actions from a methodological vantage point—the former supporting nomological explanation, the latter responding to cultural norms—reassuring, consequently, the great divide between natural science and history. See R. G. Collingwood, *The Principles of History*, ed. W. H. Dray and Jan van der Dussen (Oxford: Oxford University Press, 1999).

4 The same designates the realm in which there is no acknowledgment of alterity, as the other is systematically levelled to familiar terms. Levinas explicitly charges ontology as the foundation of the ambit in which violent assimilations of the other take place, whereas he names ethics the attitude that interrupts the reign of the same. See Emmanuel Levinas, *Totality and Infinity: An Essay on Exteriority*, trans. Alphonso Lingis (The Hague: Martinus Nijhoff Publishers, 1979), 33–52.

5 Derrida explains his account of hauntology in history in the following terms: "Repetition *and* first time, but also repetition *and* last time, since the Singularity of any *first time*, makes of it also a *last time*. Each time it is the event itself, a first time is a last time." Jacques Derrida, *Specters of Marx: The State of the Debt, the Work of Mourning, and the New International*, trans. Peggy Kamuf (New York: Routledge, 1994), 10. In Levinas's project of the deformalization of time, the responsibility for the other is expressed as "traumatizing blow," which breaks up synchronic time in favor of the diachrony that characterizes my encounter with the other. See Emmanuel Levinas, *Otherwise than Being or Beyond Essence*, trans. Alphonso Lingis (Dordrecht: Kluwer Academic Publishers, 1991), 53. Hannah Arendt reads the invention of the telescope, the Reformation, and the discovery of America as events that have shaped modern age, although not in a naturalist causal sense. Hannah Arendt, *The Human Condition* (Chicago: University of Chicago Press, 1998), 248. In *Being and Time*, Heidegger states, "Dasein does not exist as the sum of the momentary actualities of Experiences which come along successively and disappear" (426). Rather, Dasein is constituted as a stretching-along, a specific movement (*Bewegtheit*) of existence, which differs from mere motion (*Bewegung*) of something present-at-hand, and which is properly called "historizing" or event (*Geschehen*) (427). In his later writings, Heidegger employs the term *Ereignis*, which may be rendered as "event" or "enowning" (as suggested by Parvis Emad and Kenneth Maly), a concept that designates the event of being that appropriates itself in history. See Martin Heidegger, *Contributions to Philosophy (From enowning)*, trans. Parvis Emad and Kenneth Maly (Bloomington and Indianapolis: Indiana University Press, 1991). The tripartite division of Gadamer's *Truth and Method* reflects the "event of understanding" (467) or "event of being" (138) as "event of art" (138), "event of tradition" (290), and "event of language" (466). "Understanding proves to be an event, and the task of hermeneutics, seen philosophically, consists in asking what kind of understanding, what kind of science it is, that is itself advanced by historical change" (308). See Hans-Georg Gadamer, *Truth and Method*, trans. Joel Weinsheimer and Donald G. Marshall (London: Continuum, 2006).

6 As I conceive vestiges in a nonmetaphysical way, they fall outside the opposition between traces and tellings that is assumed in historical research. Regarding this contraposition, see Jonas Ahlskog, "The Evidential Paradigm in Modern History," *Storia della Storiografia* 71, no. 1 (2017): 111–28.

7 See Emmanuel Levinas, *Basic Philosophical Writings*, ed. Adriaan T. Peperzak, Simon Critchley, and Roberto Bernasconi (Bloomington and Indianapolis: Indiana University Press, 1996), 4: "In putting out my hand to approach a chair, I have creased the sleeve of my jacket. I have scratched the floor, I have dropped the ash from my cigarette. In doing that which I wanted to do, I have done so many things I did not want. The act has not been pure, for I have left some traces. In wiping out these traces, I have left others."

8 Jacques Derrida, *Of Grammatology*, trans. Gayatri Chakravorty Spivak (Baltimore: John Hopkins University Press, 1997), 65.

9 See Levinas's analysis of trace in Levinas, *Basic Philosophical Writings*, 33–64; and Derrida's incorporation of that notion in Derrida, *Of Grammatology*, 62–73. As it will be clear along this chapter, despite their description of the dynamics of the trace, neither Levinas's nor Derrida's account of it fits perfectly in my hermeneutical proposal.
10 As it would constitute a great detour to our goals, I left aside the debate between Heidegger and Levinas and consequently arguments that justify their views. Some interesting material may be found in Michael Fagenblat, "Levinas and Heidegger: The Elemental Confrontation," in *The Oxford Handbook of Levinas*, ed. Michael L. Morgan (Oxford: Oxford University Press, 2019), 103–33; and Jean Greish, "Ethics and Ontology: Some Hypocritical Reflections," in *Emmanuel Levinas: Critical Assessments of Leading Philosophers: Vol. 1*, ed. Claire Katz and Lara Trout (New York: Routledge, 2005), 215–26.
11 See Levinas, *Totality and Infinity*, 194.
12 This is not to say that only the past person can be considered a bygone alterity. Rather, the other, whether addressing me from the past or in the present, is someone who conveys the immemorial time in which I have contracted a responsibility to her. From the phenomenological viewpoint, however, the other in the present enacts intentional embodied courses of actions, whereas I can only engage with the other that is no longer alive by means of her vestiges.
13 See Ferdinand de Saussure, *Course in General Linguistics*, ed. Charles Bally and Albert Sechehaye, trans. Roy Harris (Illinois: Open Court, 1983); Emmanuel Levinas, *Time and The Other (and Other Essays)*, trans. Richard A. Cohen (Pittsburg, PA: Duquesne University Press, 1987), 97–120. See also footnote 5 about the traumatic encounter with the other in *Otherwise than Being*.
14 Gadamer's notion of fusion of horizons is the basis for his project of practical philosophy, in which the dimension of alterity is pivotal. See Gadamer, *Truth and Method*, 277–382; and Darren R. Walhof, "Friendship, Otherness, and Gadamer's Politics of Solidarity," *Political Theory* 34, no. 5 (2006): 569–93. See Ricoeur's engagement with Levinas's philosophy in Paul Ricoeur, "A Reading of Emmanuel Levinas's 'Otherwise than Being or beyond Essence'," trans. Matthew Escobar, *Yale French Studies* 104 (2004): 82–99. About Ricoeur's discussion of alterity, see Paul Ricoeur, *Oneself as Another*, trans. Kathleen Blamey (Chicago: University of Chicago Press, 1992). Regarding Vattimo's interest in otherness, see Matthew E. Harris, "Vattimo and Otherness: Hermeneutics, Charity, and Conversation," *Otherness: Essays and Studies* 4, no. 1 (2013): 1–21.
15 See Edmund Husserl, *Ideas for a Pure Phenomenology and Phenomenological Philosophy. First Book: General Introduction to Pure Phenomenology*, trans. Daniel O. Dahlstrom (Indianapolis: Hackett, 2014), 90. See Dermot Moran, "Husserl's Transcendental Philosophy and the Critique of Naturalism," *Continental Philosophy Review* 41, no. 4 (2008): 401–25.
16 See Heidegger, *Being and Time*, 147.
17 Many phenomenologists perform the same methodological gesture with different results, as one may read in Levinas's and Derrida's works. See, for instance, Emmanuel Levinas, *Existence and Existents*, trans. Alphonso Lingis (The Hague: Martinus Nijhoff, 1978), 65–96, where he presents conceptions such as here, place, body, and time; and Jacques Derrida, "Khôra," in *On the Name*, trans. Ian McLeod (Stanford: Stanford University Press, 1993), 89–130, which offers a discussion of the many senses of "Khôra," among them, its meaning as place.

18 See Afonso Benites, "Report says Brazil's Dictatorship was Responsible for 421 Deaths," *El País*, November 14, 2014. https://english.elpais.com/elpais/2014/11/14/inenglish/1415985145_550698.html.
19 See Patrícia Andrade, "Porão usado durante ditadura military no Piauí ainda tem manchas de sangue," *G1—Piauí*, April 2, 2014. http://g1.globo.com/pi/piauí/noticia/2014/03/porao-usado-durante-ditadura-militar-no-pi-ainda-tem-manchas-de-sangue.html.
20 Gadamer, *Truth and Method*, 285.
21 Although I partially share some of Derrida's ideas, our proposals disagree on many levels, as in our understanding of the role of events and their connection with expressions.

Bibliography

Ahlskog, Jonas. "The Evidential Paradigm in Modern History." *Storia della Storiografia* 71, no. 1 (2017): 111–28.

Andrade, Patrícia. "Porão usado durante ditadura military no Piauí ainda tem manchas de sangue." *G1 – Piauí*, April 02, 2014. http://g1.globo.com/pi/piauí/noticia/2014/03/porao-usado-durante-ditadura-militar-no-pi-ainda-tem-manchas-de-sangue.html.

Arendt, Hannah. *The Human Condition*. Chicago: University of Chicago Press, 1998.

Benites, Afonso. "Report Says Brazil's Dictatorship was Responsible for 421 Deaths." *El País*, November 14, 2014. https://english.elpais.com/elpais/2014/11/14/inenglish/1415985145_550698.html.

Collingwood, R. G. *The Principles of History*. Edited by W. H. Dray and Jan van der Dussen. Oxford: Oxford University Press, 1999.

Davidson, Donald. *Essays on Actions and Events*. Oxford: Oxford University Press, 2001.

Derrida, Jacques. "Khôra." In *On the Name*, translated by Ian McLeod, 89–130. Stanford: Stanford University Press, 1993.

Derrida, Jacques. *Of Grammatology*. Translated by Gayatri Chakravorty Spivak. Baltimore: John Hopkins University Press, 1997.

Derrida, Jacques. *Specters of Marx: The State of the Debt, the Work of Mourning, and the New International*. Translated by Peggy Kamuf. New York: Routledge, 1994.

Derrida, Jacques. *Writing and Difference*. Translated by Alan Bass. London: Routledge, 2005.

Fagenblat, Michael. "Levinas and Heidegger: The Elemental Confrontation." In *The Oxford Handbook of Levinas*, edited by Michael L. Morgan, 103–34. Oxford: Oxford University Press, 2019.

Gadamer, Hans-Georg. *Truth and Method*. Translated by Joel Weinsheimer and Donald G. Marshall. London: Continuum, 2006.

Greish, Jean. "Ethics and Ontology: Some Hypocritical Reflections." In *Emmanuel Levinas: Critical Assessments of Leading Philosophers: Vol. 1*, edited by Claire Katz and Lara Trout, 215–26. New York: Routledge, 2005.

Harris, Matthew E. "Vattimo and Otherness: Hermeneutics, Charity, and Conversation." *Otherness: Essays and Studies* 4 (2013): 1–21.

Heidegger, Martin. *Being and Time*. Translated by John Macquarrie and Edward Robinson. Oxford: Blackwell, 2001.

Heidegger, Martin. *Contributions to Philosophy (From enowning)*. Translated by Parvis Emad and Kenneth Maly. Bloomington and Indianapolis: Indiana University Press, 1991.

Husserl, Edmund. *Ideas for a Pure Phenomenology and Phenomenological Philosophy. First Book: General Introduction to Pure Phenomenology*. Translated by Daniel O. Dahlstrom. Indianapolis: Hackett, 2014.

Levinas, Emmanuel. *Basic Philosophical Writings*. Edited by Adriaan T. Peperzak, Simon Critchley, and Roberto Bernasconi. Bloomington and Indianapolis: Indiana University Press, 1996.

Levinas, Emmanuel. *Existence and Existents*. Translated by Alphonso Lingis. The Hague: Martinus Nijhoff, 1978.

Levinas, Emmanuel. *Otherwise than Being or Beyond Essence*. Translated by Alphonso Lingis. Dordrecht: Kluwer Academic Publishers, 1991.

Levinas, Emmanuel. *Time and the Other (and Other Essays)*. Translated by Richard A. Cohen. Pittsburg, PA: Duquesne University Press, 1987.

Levinas, Emmanuel. *Totality and Infinity: An Essay on Exteriority*. Translated by Alphonso Lingis. The Hague: Martinus Nijhoff Publishers, 1979.

Moran, Dermot. "Husserl's Transcendental Philosophy and the Critique of Naturalism." *Continental Philosophy Review* 41, no. 4 (2008): 401–25.

Ricoeur, Paul. "A Reading of Emmanuel Levinas's 'Otherwise than Being or beyond Essence,'" translated by Matthew Escobar, *Yale French Studies* 104 (2004): 82–99.

Ricoeur, Paul. *Oneself as Another*. Translated by Kathleen Blamey. Chicago: University of Chicago Press, 1992.

Walhof, Darren R. "Friendship, Otherness, and Gadamer's Politics of Solidarity." *Political Theory* 34, no. 5 (2006): 569–93.

Section III

Mortality and Personal Identity

8

Neither to Be, Nor Not to Be

The Interrelation of Life and Death in Tanabe's Later Philosophy of Death

Takeshi Morisato

Overture

Philosophical discussions on the notion of the ethical or any analysis of spatiotemporal existence in the context of philosophy tend to focus on the reality of living. Aristotle, for instance, entertains the possibility of the interaction between the living and the dead when in *Nicomachean Ethics* he briefly asks the question whether or not the fortune of the latter would be affected by the deeds of the former. But he quickly dismisses this question since the notion of the dead is to be at rest, whereas what determines the ethical value of our existence is our laborious habituation that determines our ontological values in accord with virtues that are inherent in our dynamic nature. Thus, at least for Aristotle among many others, to be is to make an active choice of living ethically while not to be means to be at rest—that is, to be dead like any other inanimate objects.

The ghost of King Hamlet is an outright rejection of this binary division between life and death. But modern and contemporary European philosophy has a tremendous difficulty in making the ghost speak, thus failing to reveal its purgatorial secret in the daylight of the ethical. Modern Japanese philosophy, contrariwise, seems to have no problem with facing the dead. In fact, its process of understanding the true nature of the world and self as nothingness (or as the self-negating act of no-self) seems to require the constitutive presence of the dead in the living. The most notable formulation of this interrelation between the living and the dead can be found in Tanabe Hajime's later "philosophy of death" (死の哲学), consisting of essays such as "Memento Mori" (1957), "Ontology of Life or Dialectic of Death" (1958), "My Interpretation of the Zen Foundation" (1959), and *A Memorandum on Mallarmé* (1961).[1]

This chapter will examine how Tanabe's conception of "existential communion" (実存共同), developed in his postwar philosophy of religion (1946–8), comes to include "death" as an indispensable moment of its temporal establishment and further illustrates how the texts mentioned above that represent Tanabean philosophy of the dead portray the constitutive interrelation of "to be" and "not to be" as the essence of human existence in immanence.

The Kyoto School and Philosophy of Death

The most controversial element in the works of the Kyoto School philosophers is the historical context in which they were written. Many of these thinkers are known to have studied mainstream philosophy under renowned thinkers in Germany and France in the 1920s–30s; and upon their return home, they critically reappropriated European philosophical ideas in reference to the intellectual resources available in their native historical and cultural backgrounds of Japan (and East Asia). As far as the content of their ideas and methodologies are concerned, most comparative philosophers and world philosophies scholars would not hesitate to acknowledge their original contributions to the history of philosophy either as a pioneer of comparative philosophy or as a trailblazer of modern Japanese philosophy. But what some of these scholars, and especially the major critics of the Kyoto School, find troubling about their philosophical contributions is the fact that they were made both before and after the Sino-Japanese and the Pacific War.

What is problematic about the Kyoto School philosophy, in other words, is not necessarily any of the specific concepts that they have left us but the seeming continuity in the development of their ideas when Japanese society itself went through a massive paradigm shift at the end of the Second World War. How could they function as good, authentic philosophers under the right-wing nationalism and do so without getting caught by government censorship or suffering from imprisonment by the regime (as a celebrated few like Tosaka Jun, Miki Kiyoshi, and Nakai Masakazu did)? Were they supporting Japanese colonialism in East Asia and in favor of the Pacific War against Western democracy? How could they possibly keep philosophizing after the war without scrapping everything they said before the rise of the new democratic government? There are certainly some historians and cultural theorists who categorically regard the works of the Kyoto School as being guilty of conceptually aiding and abetting the ideology of Japanese imperialism.[2] Most scholars of the Kyoto School, however, have made many very good scholarly contributions to show how their conceptual frameworks are in fact capable of promoting ideas that are against such military expansionism or an antidote to violent Japanism. Many of them even go so far as to say that they demonstrate positive political and ethical implications if they are to be put under a comprehensive textual critique and to be rigorously applied to our everyday life.

Still, the gap between these two camps seems to remain open, and I cannot see how it would close anytime in the future. This is probably because we can never get rid of an indeterminate malaise regarding the philosophical texts approved by the problematic censorship in the darkest times of twentieth-century Japan. Tanabe's reflection on the notion of death to some degree inherits this disconnection between philosophy and historical life. His philosophy of death, developed in the late 1940s and the 1950s, does not talk about three million Japanese war casualties during the war in any concrete terms. He was so invested in his students that he could not hold down his emotions of despair and helplessness when they were sent to the battlefields in 1943 onward. These students, or anyone who lost their lives during the war, never show up in his reflections on death.

We must also keep in mind that Tanabe delivered his magnum opus, *Philosophy as Metanoetics*, in 1946, based on his retirement lecture, which signaled a turning point in his method of philosophy. He called for transformative penance both from each individual and the collective in Japan and beyond as the only way to continue a philosophic life. It is remarkable to think that he made this point at the end of his career as a professor of philosophy at the Imperial University of Kyoto in 1945. This text also functioned as the foundation for developing his later philosophy of religion (which includes his theory of the dead). But his metanoesis, at least at the literal level, does not specifically call for our penance over the astronomical number of casualties that the Japanese military generated between 1937 and 1945. The voices of the war dead had to be lingering vividly in the back of any Japanese thinker's mind at that time, but they did not clearly surface in Tanabe's texts. We may certainly argue that, upon a systematic analysis, the framework of his philosophy of death must also include these voices but their unusual absence undeniably serves as the source of our intellectual malaise. How far could philosophy be removed from historical reality (or an ordinary sense of life for that matter) when the texts on death do not refer to a massive pile of dead bodies in their immediate surroundings? It is certainly a task for contemporary Japanese philosophers to think about the application of Tanabean philosophy of death to the reality of the dead in postwar and twenty-first-century Japan.[3]

Tanabe and the Age of Death after the Second World War

There are three types of death that are integral to the formation of Tanabe's philosophical understanding of it: (1) the presence of "nuclear power" in modern society; (2) Mahayana Buddhist notion of death interpreted in relation to the Zen and the Pure Land tradition; and (3) the loss of his wife, Tanabe Chiyo.

Tanabe Hajime emphasizes the present age as the "age of nuclear energy" and further describes it as evidence that we are living in the "age of death."[4] In "Memento Mori" he reflects on the importance of recognizing our own mortality by citing Ps. 90:12: "So teach us to count our days / that we may gain a wise heart." Our default position of life is that we always naively expect to live a long life or at least focus on what we can do today and leave the rest for tomorrow (and the day after that too). None of us in ordinary circumstances would think that the days of our life are numbered. Yet the religious teaching tells us to know our place as finite beings and refrain from wasting our days as if we had access to an infinite number of them.

The presence of nuclear energy in our society, Tanabe argues, plays a double role. On the one hand, it is capable of destroying a whole city (as it did to Hiroshima and Nagasaki in his time) or wiping out any signs of life for a long period of time (as it did to communities near Chernobyl or the Fukushima First Nuclear Plant in our time). It represents an extreme case where our life can be completely extinguished immediately, and because of that, it incarnates a real threat to a great number of individuals. Despite the fact that the number of nuclear warheads has significantly decreased since the end of the Cold War, each one of them is far more powerful than the ones dropped in Japan during the Second World War, and the number of nuclear power plants is steadily increasing worldwide. As far as all the several nuclear destructions in modern Japan are concerned, whether it is a weapon or a power plant, nuclear energy is literally holding everyone at a gunpoint.

On the other hand, the age of death due to radioactive elements does not lead us to face the reality of death and dying. Instead, we are driven to focus on the positive, life-affirming images even in the life-threatening power of the nuclear technologies: for instance, low-carbon power source, space exploration, research reactors, medical and industrial isotopes, and so on. We do not have any technology to neutralize nuclear wastes within our lifetime but most of us assume that we will develop one sometime in the future; and in order for us to have absolute control over nuclear power, it is necessary to build more power plants. Your Tokyo Electronic Power Company informed you (especially if you are living near them) that they are "absolutely safe" and "good for everyone."

Why has it been so easy for politicians in Japan to persuade the average citizen of the country to believe in the brighter future with the problem of the melted-down nuclear power plant and then to agree on turning on other nuclear power plants (despite their newly discovered safety issues)? That, according to Tanabe, is because nuclear energy represents the pinnacle of life-affirming science and technology, which, in principle, suffers from a profound contradiction that its excessive, one-sided affirmation of life ends up negating.[5]

This contradictory movement of life affirmation in science goes back to its advent in European modernity. Tanabe argues that the "liberation of life" during the Renaissance period provided a basis for the modern advancement of science and technology. Their primary "mission was undoubtedly to serve life in the beginning."[6] Anglo-European philosophers then reflected on the relation between life and science from the perspective of life, which gave rise to "pragmatic epistemology as self-awareness of science."[7] Also, Tanabe continues, "this philosophy did not stop at a critique of science but further developed itself into the universal self-consciousness of life by treating culture in general as the object of its critique." Tanabe identifies this type of thinking as "philosophy of life."[8]

Interestingly, Tanabe is not referring here only to the historical "philosophy of life" that has played an important role in contemporary continental philosophy since the nineteenth century but also, under the single label of *Lebensphilosophie*, including "German idealism," neo-Kantian (and Nishidian) philosophy of culture, and Heidegger's phenomenology. This point is clear from his characterization of the "philosophy of life" as an idealistic philosophy:

> So long as what we generally call "philosophy of idealism" regards a realization of ideal essence, which is peculiar to human beings, as the fulfillment of life, and claims that a service to something that is beyond life and death is done for the sake of life, it is nothing but "philosophy of life." Even if that "something" is thought

as that which transcends life towards "over there," so long as it is pointed by and demanded from life's "over here," it remains to be a postulated idea that is still based on the demand of life; there is no concrete proof that it is truly transcendent.[9]

The consequence of pursuing this philosophy of life, that is to hold the worldview that focuses on the importance of life only from the side of life, Tanabe thinks, can drive us to the "predicament of its unavoidable self-contradiction."[10] Science and technology are the leading cultural products of modernity that hold this perspective, and they are designed to enrich our life in every possible way. If there is a disease, we have invented cures. If there is any economic or social problem, we have created every conceivable device or system to overcome the limitations it imposes. That is because nothing is more sacred than life.

However, regardless of that, we cannot deny the fact that many instances of scientific/technological advancement have also made possible a greater destruction of the world and ourselves to an unprecedented magnitude.

The "crisis of modernity" or what existentialists have called *angst* is precisely the consequence of looking at this contradictory situation. Tanabe follows the same line of argument: life in immanence has served as the "principle of values" as we made an advancement in science and technology but because this whole process has driven us to its opposite, namely death, we are left with no choice but to say that life cannot be the self-sufficient ground for the fulfillment of itself. If we try to hold life as the foundation of what we do with it, our ground has no choice but to crumble. Thus, life, as it is considered in and of itself, ultimately falls victim to nihilism. Nuclear power as the pinnacle of modern science and technology, which assumes the principle of life, is the best instance of this serious problem. In this sense, Tanabe argues that "modern humans have faced the bankruptcy of 'philosophy of life,' and they are now facing the destiny where they have to think about 'philosophy of death' as the problem."[11] Given that life will push us to its edge and force us to stare at the abyss, we must grapple with the negative if we are to fully understand the significance of our self-contradictory life.

Zen *Koan* and the Death-and-Resurrection

Tanabe's later philosophy of religion in the second half of the 1940s is saturated with his insightful references to the inseparable relation between life and death. Then, in the 1950s, he explicitly discusses the fact that the only ways in which we can meaningfully conduct any philosophical investigations in the age of death are to face the self-contradictory nature of life and to reconsider the significance of death in life. This is when he starts using the language of the "dialectic of death" in contrast with the "ontology of life" (which includes phenomenology and all the other philosophies that he categorized under "philosophy of life"). It is important to keep in mind, however, that there are not so much structural differences between his trilogy in his later philosophy of religion from the 1940s (including *Philosophy as Metanoetics, Existence, Love and Practice,* and *Dialectic of Christianity*) and the abovementioned texts on death from the 1950s.[12] But his thematic focus shifts from the significance of religious faith in the process of grounding philosophical reason to the reality of death in his life, which was coming to an end.

We can also observe an interesting shift in his perspective on Japanese religions during the seventeen years between his retirement from his academic position in 1945 and his death in 1962—namely, his view of Zen Buddhism. It slowly moved from an outright rejection of Zen in favor of Shinran's Pure Land in *Philosophy as Metanoetics* to an ambivalent appreciation of it in *Existence, Love and Practice*, and then to a critical appraisal of it in *Dialectic of Christianity* onward.[13] As James Heisig rightly points out, "Tanabe acknowledged Zen as the best guide to a 'philosophy of death' near the end of his life."[14]

The most outstanding reference that Tanabe makes when explaining how Zen Buddhism could be the guide for his philosophy of death is the following *koan* from *The Blue Cliff Record*, the 55th case, "Tao Wu's Condolence Call" (道吾一家弔慰). Thomas Cleary's translation gives this passage as the following:

> Tao Wu (Jp. Dōgo) and Chien Yuan (漸源, Jp. Zengen) went to a house to make a condolence call. Yuan hit the coffin and said, "Alive or dead?" Wu said, "I won't say alive, and I won't say dead." Yuan said, "Why won't you say?" Wu said, "I won't say." Halfway back, as they were returning, Yuan said, "Tell me right away, teacher; if you don't tell me, I'll hit you." Wu said, "You may hit me, but I won't say." Yuan then hit him.
>
> Later Tao Wu passed on. Yuan went to Shih Shuang (石霜, JP. Sekisō) and brought up the foregoing story. Shuang said, "I won't say alive, and I won't say dead." Yuan said, "Why won't you say?" Shuang said, "I won't say, I won't say." At these words Yuan had an insight.[15]

The term *chōi* 弔慰 means not only to show a sympathy to the living for their loss but also to mourn for the dead by providing a memorial service to them. The first few lines, in this sense, should be read as a scene where the passionate student is asking his teacher about the whole point of commemorating the dead and giving their condolences to the family left behind. Tanabe argues that Zengen in this paragraph is initially suffering from an "antinomy" of either/or: that is, *either* life *or* death. If the answer to the question is "to be alive," then there is no need to commemorate the content of the coffin. (If this were the case, it would be a very strange situation!) If death, there is no way for their condolences to reach the dead person because she has passed to the other side of life.[16] The master monk refused to give any clear answer to the question by saying, "生也不道。死也不道." As we have seen above, Cleary translates this passage as "I won't say alive, and I won't say dead." This is certainly one possible way of reading this but an average reader in Chinese should immediately be reminded of the famous line in the opening of *Daodejing*: "Ways may be spoken of as dao, but they are not the eternal Dao; Names may be cited as names, but they are not the eternal name" (道可道, 非常道; 名可名, 非常名). In light of this passage, we should be able to see that the phrase, 生也不道, 死也不道, in *The Blue Cliff Record* literally means "not to be spoken as (it is) life, and not to be spoken as (it is) death." This translation shows that Dōgo is not only expressing his personal take on the issue of life and death as the "I" but also stating the fact that it cannot be answered either as life or death. If the teacher is taking a blow to his head for his inability to articulate his personal perspective, then this story is a terrible joke. But the teacher takes the risk of undermining his socioethical relation with the student, which structurally defines them as the teacher and his student, as he embraces the student's violent frustration over the truth that his question cannot be answered.

The brother disciple, Sekisō, serves as a mediator of the teaching when he highlights the essence of their master's statements by sayings, "*iwaji iwaji*" (Chinese: *budao budao*, 不道不道; "I won't say, I won't say"), which literally means, "not to be said, not to be said." Zengen then has a breakthrough. On the one hand, life and death should be distinguished as the opposite, and they cannot be established at the same time. But, on the other hand, "it is impossible for him to make a judgment about them in accord with a principle of contradiction."[17] The teacher had to know that only to those who were aware of the inseparable relation between life and death in their own self, this question about the nature of life (and its inseparable relation with death) would become meaningful. So long as the student is intellectually trying to make sense of them in terms of either/or, his question only reveals that he is far from looking in the right place for finding the truth about life and death.

The reason why the master did not respond to the question with this insight is because it cannot be transmitted from one person to another like information concerning external phenomena. Nor can it be extracted from him through individual or social coercion. Instead, the student must examine his life for himself and become aware of the interrelation between life and death within himself. What is required for shedding some light on the proper significance of life and death, then, is to achieve this self-awareness existentially instead of asking for an intellectual account of it from another person. This should remind us of Scrooge with the Ghost of Christmas Yet to Come. When we tap someone else's coffin to ask the meaning of life, we must first see ourselves as the dead therein. Otherwise, the question will be neither transformative nor meaningful to the person asking the question.

Sekisō's retelling of master's nay-saying makes Zengen realize the paradoxical truth: although the master said nothing during his life and continues to say nothing after his death, he has been guiding him all along to become aware of the truth of life and death in his own self. Dōgo's silence, mediated through Sekisō's repetition, is a self-negating act of compassion that allows Zengen to achieve his self-awareness. What we witness here, according to Tanabe, is the resurrection of the dead in the transformed heart of the living. In this case, Tanabe continues, a human being must give up its own self before the deadlock of "either life or death" and by doing so, "she can preserve the tension and interrelation [of life and death] when she lives her life as the dead, and thereby, convert death into life."[18] This is because "life and death are not originally separate from each other in self-awareness but they correspond with each other as the front and the back, and they must be mutually related to each other in a circular fashion through the act of dying."[19] This is the flipside of the self-contradiction in our obsession with life: just as our unconditional pursuit of life for its fulfillment has ended up inciting the threat of death, our self-abandonment can help us escape life's self-contradiction. Thus, a life of self-awareness in Zen Buddhism demonstrates the truth of death and resurrection, overcoming the binary and the disjunctive division of life and death.

Absolute Nothingness

Tanabe certainly assumes the metaphysical framework that he worked out and termed as "absolute dialectic" in the late forties when he talks about the conversion of self from the self-centered self that is obsessed with its own (self-contradictory) life into the selfless self that becomes aware of life's inseparability from (both threatening and supportive) death within itself in his fifties. What conceptually sustains this movement from the standpoint of "philosophy of life" to that of "philosophy of death," then, is twofold: (1) nothingness as the absolute negation (i.e., great death) that makes this circular and self-reflective movement of life's self-awareness possible and (2) the "existential communion" (実存共同, *jitsuzon kyōdō*) as its intersubjective manifestation of transcendent nothingness in immanence.

Tanabe clearly indicates that "nothingness" or "dialectical nothingness" corresponds to the notion of "nihility in Zen's '*iwaji iwaji*'."[20] The relation of human existence/life/being to its foundation as nothingness is described as the interrelation of the absolute to the relative, of eternity to time. Just like the dialogue between the student and his master in *Hekiganroku*, the way in which we recognize this relation between human existence and absolute nothingness is through our philosophical self-reflection on life/being. If a task of philosophy is to question where life comes from, where it goes, and how we should treat it in ourselves and others, that is to cultivate our "self-awareness of life," Tanabe argues that life has to be "contrasted to death as its opposite."[21] Otherwise, these philosophical questions will not make sense. Nor can they turn life into the "content of self-awareness." However, when we ask any questions regarding the "origin of life," we "presuppose life of [ourselves as] the ones asking them"; and, since "the origin of life cannot be recognized from the standpoint of life," we suffer from the problem of raising questions from the viewpoint that blocks us from answering them for ourselves.[22] Or more precisely, we ourselves become the questions (to borrow Nishitani's expression).[23]

At this point, we are tempted to think as do many metaphysicians in the history of European philosophy. We think about configuring the foundation of life as that which is neither born nor dying but "the determination of being that transcends life and death."[24] However, this often leads to the ontic problem of misconceiving the metaphysical ultimate or the absolute as unmediated being or static transcendence that stands over against our spatiotemporal existence as the relative in immanence.[25] In this case, we fall victim to the contradiction of placing the absolute transcendence as that which can stand opposite to relative immanence as another immanent and relative being. But this would certainly be to miss the sign of true transcendence in immanence. Tanabe argues that nothingness in his metaphysical thinking is a dialectical absolute, which gives a negative mediation irreducible to any sense of being in immanence. In that sense, it is a kind of transcendence, which we cannot understand in any immanent or ontic terms: hence, it is absolute. But at the same time, since it cannot be any relative thing that stands in opposition to all that is either as a part or the whole of it, for the absolute negation can serve as the enabling medium for everything to be what it is. It is empty transcendence when it is conceived in and of itself, and in fact there is nothing to be known about it conceptually or speculatively through our reason alone. But when it is understood properly in relation to the relative, that is for us to become aware of it through a certain way of being, we can witness the self-negating absolute as the boundless origin of all things in historical reality.

Tanabe's later philosophy of religion repeatedly describes this self-negating mediation of the absolute as "nothingness-qua-love" (無即愛). His philosophy of death further articulates this nothingness as "absolute mediation" or great compassion that grounds both inseparable togetherness and irreducible difference between life and death. When we concretely realize this point, we are experiencing "self-awareness of life as death-and-resurrection":

> We must say that the absolute that transcends life and death is the compassion that trans-formatively unifies antinomy, lets us witness life in death, and leads us to become aware that death-and-resurrection is nothing but the true life that is not threatened by death. It is the principle that negatively converts being of immediate life and turns it into life of death-and-resurrection, and makes possible the pursuit of essential life, it is called absolute nothingness-qua-love.[26]

The proper way to understand this dialectical relation between two opposing metaphysical terms of absolute nothingness and relative being, according to Tanabe, is to see on the one hand the absolute as that which is mediated through the interaction of the relative beings and on the other the whole of such relative beings as that which is made possible through the mediation of the absolute. Nothingness, in other words, is always already manifested through the intersubjective networks of those who give witness to its great significance and live their life in accordance with this notion of nothingness-qua-love.

Tanabe describes this self-sacrificial love of nothingness by both the Judeo-Christian term of *agape* and also the Mahayana Buddhist term of "the way of Boddhisattva" (Japanese *bosatsudō*, 菩薩道) on the other. It is interesting that his philosophy of death moves away from the distinction of self-power and other-power, which was quite prominent in the trilogy of 1940s. As it was derived from the Pure Land/Shin Buddhism, this distinction has a critical undertone over against the Zen tradition as the standpoint of self-power and regardless of nuanced reading of Zen Buddhism in *Existence, Love and Practice* or *Dialectic of Christianity* such that it could not help but bring up the contrast between Zen and Pure Land schools. The clear division between Christianity, Zen, and Pure Land Buddhism, which is quite visible in his essays compiled into the *Dialectic of Christianity*, is also less visible in the surface of these texts. It seems that Tanabe, facing his own death, cared less about the distinction between these religious traditions. With a profound conviction he wrote about the great compassion of Boddhisattva and self-emptying *agape* of Christ under the single heading of love.

To witness this *absolute nothingness as self-negation of love* means that a single individual as a relative being cannot hold love as the ideal end toward which the individual shapes her life and navigates through it. Love is not about the direct communication between the absolute and the single individual (as Kierkegaard's teleological suspension of the ethical suggests). But because the absolute is absolute self-negation, self cannot move toward its affirmation unless, paradoxically, the absolute status of the absolute is denied while relative self follows the same motion of self-emptiness by refraining from its immediate self-affirmation. Love of nothingness in this sense must mean to "die to self's egoity" and to practice "self-negation."[27]

We have seen that our unconditional pursuit of life has led us to the crisis of self-destruction and self-contradiction in modernity. Tanabe has called it "the age of death." The flip side of this contradiction is that if we give up our self for the sake of others and risk our life in our self-sacrificial/self-denying act of love as their affirmation, we can truly preserve the genuine sense of our self.[28] This is what Tanabe means by "death-and-resurrection." It is to live up to the sense of self ultimately as "empty being" and mirrors the movement of absolute nothingness. This infinite absolute embodies this movement without limit and the relative being cannot match its stature. However, this means that the absolute for Tanabe cannot be a self-enclosed being but the self-emptying act of creation, the act that continuously makes infinite room for all sentient beings and all existence to be and to be for themselves. Though relative beings in their selfless act of dedicating themselves for the other cannot exhaustively demonstrate the boundlessness of the absolute nothingness, they are the rightful symbol and concrete manifestation of it.

The Existential Communion of Love

What functions as the "symbol of nothingness" includes something more than a selfless act of a single individual in its process of dying to itself, namely the intersubjective networks of such compassionate acts that form a constitutive relationship between multiple individuals. Because a human being is both finite and mortal, she cannot autonomously achieve the realization of nothingness but always falls short of its ideal. In other words, we cannot bring ourselves to the level of the absolute through ourselves alone, and we will always remain far from "living in absolute joy beyond life and death through dwelling in eternal sanctitude," since "to live is already bound by anxiety and the struggle of death."[29] How can we escape this problem? Tanabe answers,

> We must actively sacrifice self for the other and put self's salvation on hold for that of the other; as the expedient means for that purpose of leading masses to enlightenment (衆生済度), we must take on this task and not avoid committing evil (which could immediately be an obstacle for turning self into Buddha) when it is necessary (for the other). Even then, so long as standing on the side of innocence (that is to have a clean and empty mind-and-heart), it transcends the realm of good and evil. . . . Life is necessarily suffering. But self-sacrifice that accepts that suffering and refrains from turning self into Buddha for the sake of others' effort

to do the same progresses the realization of Buddhahood as the practical exercise of nothingness, and thereby, suffering is backed up by joy. . . . The suffering of self-negation enters the relation of mutual correspondence with joy of self-affirmation where they are the same and different. . . . Instead of directly realizing the potential ability to become the Buddha as the faculty of a single individual, willingly sacrificing self for the other's ability to become Buddha, bearing the suffering, lamenting the irrationality of the fundamental evil lurks in the bottom of reality, collaborating with others as we are turned to evil, believing in the promise of realizing the Buddha nature, and being grateful for it: this is the Boddhisattva as the highest existence that human beings can reach.[30]

Putting others ahead of oneself is a genuine self-affirmation of ourselves as empty being. This means that an authentic self in the act of symbolizing nothingness calls for an intersubjective act of constituting the community of selfless individuals, which even enables self-centered individuals to engage in their inauthentic self-affirmation. Tanabe sees this as the communal manifestation of nothingness and calls it the "existential communion." In his mind, this is comparable to the *communio sanctorum* in Christianity or the "way of Boddhisattva" in Mahayana Buddhism. However, this community of agapeic individuals, which empowers all participants to be and be for themselves beyond their reciprocity based on an egocentric calculation, is free of any eschatological or mythological elements. It should strictly take place on earth as historical reality; and according to these essays on philosophy of death, its constituents must include both the living and the dead.

The vertical transcendence of the relative being to the infinite absolute in Tanabean metaphysics, therefore, is hardly a private communication between a human subject and a divine transcendence. It is not a leap of faith from the daylight of temporality to the darkness of eternity through death as a single individual. Nor can it be a vertical movement since there is not any "over there" but "over there" is only materialized in and through the faces of "over here." The interrelation of the relative and the absolute, in other words, takes place as an open communication of selfless individuals that exceeds the binary distinction of life and death in immanence, the communion of relative beings that die to themselves and choose to live their lives as the dead. This existential community consists of self-emptying self that recognizes its own life as that which is made possible by the dead, and this is precisely what Tanabe means by living life with a full awareness of it as "death-and-resurrection." This agapeic community, in which the dead serves as the ground of the living and the living becomes aware of it (by dying to itself), represents the concrete manifestation of nothingness as the divine absolute.

The Kōan from *The Blue Cliff Record* demonstrates this image perfectly: the teacher, Dōgo, realizes that the only way in which he could teach the secret of life as grounded in nothingness is to empty his self-centeredness and give a space for his student to figure out the meaning of life (and its constitutive relation with death) for himself. The student, Zengen, suffers from his propensity toward his egoity, a kind of self-obsession where he dwells in the side of life for achieving the knowledge of the absolute. Because of that, he cannot see the full significance of his life beyond its limited, oppositional relation to death. He even ends up committing the unethical act of disrespecting his teacher. Dōgo as the master of no-self goes along with this evil for the sake of his student. Sekisō's repetition of teacher's self-negating silence, then, guides the younger peer, Zengen, to break down his self-centeredness and break through to self-awareness where he can truly appreciate the genuine significance of his life—the life that is always already sustained, nurtured, and guided by the dead. What we witness here is a community of compassionate individuals where the unspoken presence of the dead continues to empower the living to achieve their self-awareness beyond the binary division of life and death.

The absolute nothingness-qua-love, in this sense, is realized through the act of compassion by the teacher toward his students. However, for the students to understand this point—that is for them to know the truth of their world and self through their teacher's self-negation—they must in turn dedicate themselves to others for the others' self-awareness. Stated differently, they must turn themselves into the same kind of selfless intellectuals who, out of their compassion, give a space for their fellow travelers to know the truth about the world and self through themselves, thereby serving as a mediator of the absolute nothingness. If we are to give witness to the fact that our life is sustained and nurtured by selflessness of the dead in the same way as these Zen monks do, then we must die to ourselves and dedicate our life to the life of others. A liberation from the self-contradiction of life is only possible when we become aware of ourselves as the participants of this existential community, thereby actively embodying its manifestation of absolute nothingness as the death-and-resurrection.

Concluding Historical Reflection: Unspoken Love of a Dying Philosopher

The resurrection of the dead is felt in the transforming hearts and minds (*kokoro* 心) of the living, which continuously dies to itself and dedicate its life for the life of others. If that is the case, then what makes us who we are is not just the community of sentient beings but also the network of undying love shared among both "to be" and "not to be" in the present. This is a powerful image of individual and communal self that transcends the limitation of self-obsessed life felt in the "age of death." Given that self's life is always already grounded in death of the other and that a complete picture of one's "self" must always require a depiction of the other, we are still left with a personal and concrete question about Tanabe's philosophy of death: who was the dead that sustained his life as a philosopher? As Dostoyevsky wisely said in *The Brothers Karamazov*, it is one thing to talk about "love of humanity" and another to actually love a single individual. If the existential community requires a practice of no-self and if a philosopher must become aware of her life as the death-and-resurrection, the content of her practical self-awareness must include an image of a specific individual as the dead. Just as Dōgo's death was indispensable for describing the life of his students, there had to be also an incognito otherness indispensable for describing Tanabe's life as a philosopher.

Once again, Tanabe hardly ever talked about this. Unlike Nishida's dairy, which is filled with his personal memoirs and reflections on historical events, Tanabe's notebooks are full of reflections over philosophy books; and even though he lived in the historical city of Kyoto over twenty years, he hardly visited any famous sites that would attract tourism or left any thoughts on artworks that would be exhibited at renown museums. He was much more interested in talking about theoretical physics and math as a metaphysician rather than a single individual living his everyday life at a specific point in human history. As impersonal and secretive about personal life as he could be, Tanabe occasionally showed his profound humanity through his books, personal notes, and interaction with his students. These passages implicitly show that the death of his wife, Tanabe Chiyo, was the source of his philosophical reflection on death and he was envisioning her as resurrected in their existential community.[31]

The story behind Tanabe Hajime's marriage with Chiyo, which took place when he was teaching in Sendai, is not well documented. It was probably an arranged one (like most marriages during the Meiji period); and just as Hajime was from an intellectual class in Tokyo, Chiyo was from a well-to-do family that had a strong tie with aristocrats in the Morioka region of north Japan. Their age difference was more than ten years, and it was most likely that the husband made most of the important decisions in their family matters. They did not have any children probably because neither of them was fit to conceive or bear a child of their own. Hajime was generally in poor health, and it was simply remarkable that he lived until his late seventies especially for someone who had gone through the open-stomach surgeries twice in his life in the early twentieth century. Chiyo suffered from tuberculosis in her early age in the late 1910s and died at the age of fifty-five in 1951. According to a novelist, Amino Kiku (1900–1978), Chiyo was fond of children and always wanted to have her own while Hajime was quite the opposite in this regard.

"Since they did not have any children," Amino reports, "they celebrated each and every one of Tanabe's publications"[32] as if it were a birth of their own child, and their care toward Tanabe's students was perhaps much more intimate and involved than those who had their own children to take care of. The scene of the farewell party for the youth going to the war clearly shows this point. Certainly, it is not difficult to imagine that Chiyo was subservient to Tanabe throughout her life and also that she mostly did what she was told to do mainly to support her husband's work as an academic. This was the time in which women were told to serve men in Japan, and many women did not have any means to enjoy an equal treatment with men. But several episodes confirm that Chiyo's dedication to Tanabe was far too extraordinary to be dealt with as a typical husband–wife relationship based on the male-dominant family values of Meiji Japan.

When Tanabe became seriously ill toward the end of his academic career, Chiyo took care of almost everything that he needed for living as a decent human being. Toward the end of the Second World War, they were both weak and suffering from a lack of proper nutrition. It is questionable whether Chiyo was doing any better than Hajime, but the older husband was far too weak and sick to be able to take care of himself after pushing himself to give retirement lectures on metanoetics. Abe Yoshishige once described Tanabe as "a kind of a natural child who was messy and chaotic for things that are not academic," while according to Amino et al., Chiyo was excellent at crafting things and often made small gifts for her friends or toys for their children.[33]

When they prepared for the move from Kyoto to Kita-Karuizawa, Tanabe hardly ever came out of his study while Chiyo was the one who pushed her thin and frail body forward, led the helpers, and made the whole transition possible. A student remembers her going straight to the third-class car while Tanabe, Nishitani, and Ōshima Yasumasa went to the second class when they took the train from Kyoto to Nagoya. When Ueda Yasuharu and others were invited to Tanabe's public lectures in Kita-Karuizawa in fall 1948 (which was later compiled as the *Introduction to Philosophy*), Chiyo was too sick to work on her own but gave orders to her helpers and prepared the dinner party for the visitors. I truly believe that this Japanese philosopher would not have lasted a day unless his wife (or someone like her) was there to look after him. Without her dedication, he would not have been able to live through his sickness or complete his later works on philosophy of religion. This is precisely the reason why he, who generally refrained from saying anything personal or emotional in his writings, thanked her support in his preface to *Philosophy as Metanoetics*.

According to Ōshima, Hajime and Chiyo went to the second-class car with Nishitani when they took the train from Kyoto to Kita-Karuizawa in 1945. Most of the passengers were young and low-ranked soldiers and because of that, they made a room for the older couple. Since Ōshima was the youngest of the four, he had to stand. But because Tanabe would like to talk about philosophy, which would occupy him throughout the journey, Chiyo quietly moved to the third class and gave a seat to Ōshima to be a conversation partner of Tanabe with Nishitani. This image of giving a room to others so that the others can freely intermediate with each other is precisely the kind of movement that Tanabe describes as the act of love or *gensō* movement of absolute nothingness. It is not an exaggeration to say that in supporting Tanabe in his everyday life and following his passion and will for his moral idealism, Chiyo sacrificed her life for him and that she exemplified the highest ideal in his philosophy of religion.

After the war, many people were too poor to feed themselves and had no choice but to resort to the black market for their daily supplies. Bernd Eversmeyer tells us, however,

> Tanabe felt that it would be irresponsible for someone like him, who worked for the imperial university as a philosopher and was receiving income from the state, to resort to the black market. As a result, he and his wife had to live only with the official and poor rationing, which really meant nothing but starvation. Tanabe's health was quite poor but since he had to work for his small family as well as for his philosophy, his wife gave him her portion of rice. Thanks to the lack of food and nutrition, his wife suffered from tuberculosis and after a long period of sickness, she passed away.[34]

Chiyo literally died for Tanabe. In dedicating her life to him, she let him keep the moral principle that he felt necessary to keep his integrity as a citizen and philosopher even at the cost of his life. For two years after the death of his wife, Tanabe could not think of anything but her; and he never buried her ashes in the ground as the proper ritual for the dead in Buddhism requires but always kept her close to him in his study until his death. Tanabe hardly wrote a poem but left one for the love of his life: "Wife, who sacrificed her life for me and passed away, is resurrected and lives in me."[35]

Tanabe once told Eversmeyer that his wife's death was "paradoxically the highest grace to his life" and that it enabled him to reach the state of religious belief. His theory of death was born in this unceasing gratitude toward his late wife, and her sacrifice exemplified the existential ideal of death-and-resurrection.

"My wife saved me," Tanabe often said to his visitors in his old age.[36] But after saying it, he looked up toward the ceiling, trying not to sob in front of his guests. Shimomura Tarataro recalls that Tanabe occasionally confessed in his letters that "he occasionally called out Chiyo's name and cried out loud."[37] Ueda Yasuji beautifully puts it: "for Tanabe, philosophy was his life," while "for Chiyo, dedication and love were her life." If love is the foundation of philosophizing and a self-sacrificial act of one toward another can save us from our egoity and self-obsession of self-contradictory life, Tanabe's wife showed the best example of what Tanabe was trying to articulate through his later works as a dying philosopher. Without her life and death, we can understand neither Tanabe's life nor the significance of his thought. The mutual relation of love with the dead, established beyond the boundary of life and death, cannot be merely a conceptual framework that helps us make sense of the significance of our life in the present age; instead, each of us must think about the specific dead who have silently dedicated their lives for us by following their footsteps with gratitude so that we may recognize their living presence at every step of our life and death. This was the death-and-resurrection that Tanabe was sensing, and encouraging others to recognize, when he wrote about the interrelation of life and death in his philosophy of death.

Notes

1 All these essays are compiled into a volume, entitled *Philosophy of Death* (Tokyo: Iwanami Shoten, 2010), in the Iwanami Bunko series. This series is equivalent to the most reputable pocket editions like Loeb Classical library at Harvard University Press or Oxford World's Classics. I will refer to this volume for citing passages from these essays instead of the first (and out of print) edition of the *Complete Works* of Tanabe (Tokyo: Chikuma Shobō, 1963–4), except when referring to the *Supplementary Volume*, as below in fn. 32.

2 Their name is legion but the representative voice is given by Sakai Naoki. See Sakai and Isomae Jun'ichi, ed., *Overcoming Modernity and the Kyoto School: Modernity, Empire, and Universality* (「近代の超克」と京都学派:近代性、帝国、普遍性) (Tokyo: Ibunsha, 2010), 67–8.

3 There are several contemporary Japanese philosophers working on this angle. Sueki Fumihiko, for instance, approaches this issue from the angle of the philosophy of religion, and Morioka Masahiro recently works on this issue in relation to the victims of the East Japan Great Earthquake and Tsunami victims in the context of ethics.

4 Tanabe, *Philosophy of Death*, 13, 224, and 300.

5. For the widespread problem of duality, see Natan Elgabsi, "Is There a Problem of Writing in Historiography: Plato and the *pharmakon* of the Written Word," *Metodo: International Studies in Phenomenology and Philosophy* 7, no. 2 (2019): 225–64.
6. Tanabe, *Philosophy of Death*, 14.
7. Tanabe, *Philosophy of Death*, 14.
8. Tanabe, *Philosophy of Death*, 14–15.
9. Tanabe, *Philosophy of Death*, 15.
10. Tanabe, *Philosophy of Death*, 15. Notice also that this is the logic of metanoesis that Tanabe deploys in *Philosophy as Metanoetics*. Instead of talking about the powerlessness of himself as a philosopher, Tanabe is applying the logic to his understanding of the "present age," thus expanding the framework of metanoetic philosophy to his understanding of the era.
11. Tanabe, *Philosophy of Death*, 16–17.
12. I refer to these three texts published between 1946 and 1948 as the "trilogy" of Tanabe's later philosophy of religion.
13. For this shift in his trilogy, see my analysis of it in *Faith and Reason in Continental and Japanese Philosophy: Reading Tanabe Hajime and William Desmond* (London: Bloomsbury, 2019), 150–64.
14. James Heisig, *Much Ado about Nothingness* (Nagoya, Japan and Brussels: Chisokudō Publications, 2016), 424, n64. See also Tanabe, *Philosophy of Death*, 17.
15. *The Blue Cliff Record*, trans. Thomas Cleary and J. C. Cleary (Boston: Shambhala Publications, 1977), 729–30.
16. This is often prominent in the case of secular funerals. We focus on giving condolences to the living while the significance of death remains a mystery to all participants. In a way, Chien Yuan's question is the type of questions that we ask as philosophers of religion or existentialists in the Anglo-European secular age.
17. Tanabe, *Philosophy of Death*, 19.
18. Tanabe, *Philosophy of Death*, 19–20.
19. Tanabe, *Philosophy of Death*, 20.
20. Tanabe, *Philosophy of Death*, 193; see also 290.
21. Tanabe, *Philosophy of Death*, 297.
22. Tanabe, *Philosophy of Death*, 297.
23. Nishitani Keiji, *Religion and Nothingness* (Berkeley: University of California Press, 1982), 3.
24. Tanabe, *Philosophy of Death*, 292.
25. Tanabe, *Philosophy of Death*, 292.
26. Tanabe, *Philosophy of Death*, 20.
27. Tanabe, *Philosophy of Death*, 204.
28. Tanabe, *Philosophy of Death*, 204.
29. Tanabe, *Philosophy of Death*, 248.
30. Tanabe, *Philosophy of Death*, 248–9.
31. A more detailed account of the relationship between Tanabe Hajime and his wife relative to Tanabe's students and Chiyo's friends can be found in Appendix to the Heisig translation of *Philosophy as Metanoetics* (Nagoya, Japan and Brussels: Chisokudō Publications, 2016). I have extracted some parts from this intellectual biography that focus on the husband and wife relationship in order to emphasize what is implicitly meant by the philosopher when he talks about the dead or the philosophy of death.
32. Every copy of the *Complete Works* comes with a small complementary pamphlet, called *bekkan* 別巻. Scholars and intellectuals who knew Tanabe personally wrote

their recollections and observations in addition to philosophical reflections there. I will call this the *Supplementary Volume* to the *Complete Works*. See *Supplementary Volume* 1:2 for this biographical note.
33   *Supplementary Volume* 1:3.
34   *Supplementary Volume* 4:6.
35   Tanabe, *Philosophy of Death*, 439.
36   Takeuchi Yoshinori, Mutō Kazuo, and Tsujimura Kōichi, ed., 田辺元：思想と回想 [*Tanabe Hajime: Thoughts and Recollections*] (Tokyo: Chikuma Shobō, 1991), 325.
37   Tanabe, *Philosophy of Death*, 425.

Traditional Sources

The Blue Cliff Record. Translated by Thomas Cleary and J. C. Cleary. Boston: Shambhala Publications, 1977.

Bibliography

Elgabsi, Natan. "Is There a Problem of Writing in Historiography: Plato and the *pharmakon* of the Written Word." *Metodo: International Studies in Phenomenology and Philosophy* 7, no. 2 (2019): 225–64.
Heisig, James. *Much Ado about Nothingness*. Nagoya, Japan and Brussels: Chisokudō Publications, 2016.
Keiji, Nishitani. *Religion and Nothingness*. Berkeley: University of California Press, 1982.
Morisato, Takeshi. *Faith and Reason in Continental and Japanese Philosophy: Reading Tanabe Hajime and William Desmond*. London: Bloomsbury, 2019.
Naoki, Sakai and Isomae Jun'ichi, ed. *Overcoming Modernity and the Kyoto School: Modernity, Empire, and Universality* (「近代の超克」と京都学派:近代性、帝国、普遍性). Tokyo: Ibunsha, 2010.
Tanabe, Hajime. *Complete Works*. Tokyo: Chikuma Shobō, 1963–4.
Tanabe, Hajime. *Philosophy as Metanoetics*. Translated by James Heisig. Nagoya, Japan and Brussels: Chisokudō Publications, 2016.
Tanabe, Hajime. *Philosophy of Death*. Tokyo: Iwanami Shoten, 2010.
Yoshinori, Takeuchi, Mutō Kazuo, and Tsujimura Kōichi, ed. 田辺元：思想と回想 [*Tanabe Hajime: Thoughts and Recollections*]. Tokyo: Chikuma Shobō, 1991.

Arresting Time's Arrow

Death, Loss, and the Preservation of Real Union

Megan Fritts

I shall lie down
With him in death, and I shall be as dear
To him as he to me.
It is the dead
Not the living, who make the longest demands[.]

—Antigone[1]

Introduction

After the early death of his wife ("H"), in a small book called *A Grief Observed*, the English writer and theologian C. S. Lewis wrote, "I was greatly concerned about my memory of H. and how false it might become."[2] Such a feeling is likely familiar to anyone who has lost someone with whom they had a close relationship. However, this concern did not occur to Lewis until after his wife's demise. Even though many memories of her must have constantly been drifting further into his past, his concern over forgetting—over false memories—only arose once she was no longer living.

In this chapter, I argue that the loss of loved ones requires a revised vision of our relationship to past persons. In particular, I argue that relating to deceased loved ones as points on an ordered, forward-moving timeline—on which they grow more distant from us by the moment—has a distorting and damaging effect on our own identity. When a loved one dies and is relegated to the realm of past historical events, the forward progression of time's arrow means that we may either detach our identity from the deceased individual or else be dragged into the past with them. Sometimes this is a choice we make—often, we have no choice. Both options, I argue, will result in the destruction of our individual selves. Detaching ourselves completely from those who sustain important aspects of our identity will change us deeply, causing a jagged break in our narrative where a new self must be constructed (whether by us or our circumstances) *ex nihilo*. On the other hand, in allowing ourselves to drift into the past with the dead—resigning ourselves to existence as an historical object—we find, as Lewis did, that we begin to fade. Either way, I will argue, both the self *and* the beloved are ultimately lost, since both depend on the lost union.

To reject both options is a tremendously difficult task that will require rethinking time and our relationship to the past. I argue that we can look to Søren Kierkegaard's work on maintaining contemporaneity with the historical past, particularly his warnings about how we must *not* respond to the loss of a beloved. In the last section of the chapter, I offer some suggestions for how we might, in a Kierkegaardian spirit, strive to maintain real union with deceased loved ones, thereby rising above the destructive current of time.

Loss

"I just wish Calvin were here," my grandmother murmurs wistfully, as is typical, for the second time today. It is 2021. Her husband, my grandfather Calvin, to whom she was married for fifty-nine years, died in 2015. The effects of time on her memory of her husband have been, in some ways, sweet. Missing someone leads us to recall many memories of them we had assumed were lost to time, when circumstance draws forth the unexpected prickly pain of tender recollection. In other ways, the effects of time have been cruel and destructive. Views of my grandfather that were once emotionally complex have flattened, softened with a warm haze into the confidence that he was the "best husband/father/grandfather," ever gentle, considerate to a fault (or nearly, since he had no faults). We cannot hold such idyllic views of anyone we are currently in a close relationship with. The tipsy adore of new lovers meets a daunting enemy in the first shared case of food poisoning or flush of jealousy. It is a particular cruelty of death that it tends to send the living back into the "honeymoon" phase but without the bittersweet promise of the eventual replacement of this feeling with complex and concrete intimacy. This is how my grandmother now exists, and it increases her sadness over her husband's absence even as it pulls her further and further away from *him* and closer to a hollow simulacrum.

While there is much philosophical debate over whether death is bad for the dead,[3] there is less philosophical work analyzing the effects of death on those who remain living. Partially, I imagine, this is because it seems quite obvious that it is bad for them, in virtue of all the suffering it causes. I will not depart from the obvious, but I will attempt to add to it. I want to argue here that this effect of death and the passing of time is *more* dangerous for the living lovers than is often assumed. That is, I believe the death of loved ones is probably much worse for us than most believe that it is, for reasons unrelated to pain and suffering. And I want to suggest further that there remains at least the possibility of avoiding this fate when death claims a loved one. To what extent this possibility is feasible and, therefore comforting, I will leave up to the reader.

Our Selves and the Dead

In Lewis's work on grief, there is a deep worry about bearing false memories of his beloved. Why? Surely Lewis was aware that he must have many false memories about many people, both living and dead. Why does the prospect of false memories of H worry him more than the near-certain fact of his false memories of countless others?

It seems unlikely that false memories of his wife would be harmful to his wife. Regardless of one's beliefs about what happens after we die—we cease to exist, we enter the afterlife, we are reincarnated, we become united with the world consciousness—nearly all potential views will rule out the possibility of the living exacting pain or injury to the dead.[4] Of course, a more expansive understanding of "harm" may allow some unjust or unfair memories of the beloved to count as a kind of "harm." Still, Lewis's memories of his late wife were never offensive or uncharitable—to the contrary, they were falsely *generous*, if anything. Additionally, false memories do not often tend to harm the living, either. If my husband retains some false memories of me, I am generally not offended or hurt by that fact unless the false memories are especially negative or humiliating. Again, in Lewis's case, the opposite was true: his memories of his wife were warping in a positive, warm direction, idealizing her in his mind.

It seems equally unlikely that, in Lewis's case, his false memories of his wife violated a duty he held, either in general or to her specifically. He had, we are told, done everything in his power to prevent losing his true memories of her. If "ought" implies "can," it certainly seems that he had done all he *could* do. Such a presumably inevitable effect of the passage of time, when the truth is dutifully attended to as far as possible, cannot amount to a moral wrongdoing on any plausible view of moral duties.

The obvious answer is that Lewis is especially worried about losing his memories of H because he wants his memories to accurately depict her. But the problem is not merely one of experience—that is, Lewis is not worried that he will *feel* the loss of true memories of H, and therefore suffer as a result—but he is worried about the objective fact of the matter, whether or not he notices that his memories are becoming less and less veridical. But if Lewis himself would not suffer or commit a wrong by having false memories of his wife, and if H likewise would not be harmed in any way, whence the badness of Lewis's idealizations?

It is natural to respond to the above question by saying, "because he loved her." Indeed, it is intuitive that loving someone entails that there is something good about seeing the beloved for who they truly are, which would in turn entail that having a falsely idealized image of them would be a bad thing. But what is it about love that would entail that such false memories were a bad thing?

While many theoretical aspects of love continue to be debated in the relevant literature, "it is a matter of widespread (but not universal) agreement among philosophers that love must involve union of some sort."[5] I will refer to a strong version of this idea as the Union Theory. Union Theory holds that love is the unified "we" that two people form when they are in a deep relationship with one another.

The first instance of this theory likely appears in Plato's *Symposium* and is described via myth by the character of Aristophanes. The myth goes as follows: in the early days of humanity, people existed as pairs of soul mates, with two individuals sharing one (round-shaped) body. Humans in this form were very powerful and often sought to overtake the gods. Zeus, wanting to quell human ambition in this regard, decided to have each pair cut in half. Aristophanes continues,

> This, then, is the source of our desire to love each other. Love is born into every human being; it calls back the halves of our original nature together; it tries to make one out of two and heal the wound of human nature. Each of us, then, is a "matching half" of a human whole, because each was sliced like a flatfish, two out of one, and each of us is always seeking the half that matches him.[6]

This allegory is an extreme version of this view that loving someone involves forming an existential unified "we" with them. This was likely not ever taken literally, and the meaning of the (presumed) allegory might seem opaque. Contemporary union views of love take seriously the task of uncovering what it means to form a "we" with another person such that the two people are, in some sense, one being. Roger Scruton, writing specifically about romantic love, writes that this "we" is formed "just so soon as reciprocity becomes community: that is, just so soon as all distinction between my interests and your interests is overcome."[7] Scruton here argues for a literal fusing together of the interests of the lover and the beloved.[8] That is, it is not merely that I happen to care and therefore am affected when bad things happen to the one I love; rather, when something bad happens to my love, it *constitutes* something bad happening to *me*.

The union view of love involves a literal union, a literal fusion, of two people who love one another, although there is disagreement on the nature of this union. Some, particularly those in the Christian philosophical tradition, argue that it is a mystical or spiritual union that forms between two immaterial souls. Robert Solomon adopts a much different, less mystical version of the unified soul picture, arguing that love is the mutual redefinition of each party in the relationship, such that each party understands themselves as fundamentally part of a unified single whole.[9] But no matter the nature of the union, the love-as-union view requires that each party in the relationship is no longer *their own*, but rather it is inextricably part of a larger whole such that, on a deep level, there is less of a meaningful distinction between the two individuals than there was when they were on their own.

Unlike other popular theories of love, the love-as-union picture can make perfect sense of the deep intrinsic badness of Lewis's warped memories of his late wife. This should be straightforward: if two people in a relationship of love form (in whatever sense we accept) a real unified "we," then to the extent that I lose the one I love I also lose myself. That it is bad for someone to lose oneself should be relatively uncontroversial. So, Lewis's loss of accurate memories of his wife is bad because (among perhaps many other reasons) it entails the loss of himself.

One of the many mysterious aspects of Union Theory is that it seems to say we can have multiple real unions with multiple people and yet each of these unions is totalizing. Parents may have one child or they may have twelve children, and each new child born to them initiates another totalizing union with a brand new loved one. Each new child born to them constitutes a point of the parents' utter vulnerability—if that child perishes, so will the parent, in every way but the physical sense. This is why others cannot provide true help after the loss of a loved one; the loss is the loss of the particular individual, the particular relationship of union. At the loss of a child, no parent is comforted by the prospect of simply having another child.

All this is not to say that the presence of others is unimportant. Having people to lament with is one of the great gifts of a human life and is crucial to moving forward in life in the midst of grief. But while others can lament with us, sit with us, and even distract us from the immediate pain, they cannot make loss *better*. Something we learn with the death of a loved one is that the existence of our world—what the world is, for us—depends on the continued presence of each person we love. Attempts to bring comfort by relaying a positive or hopeful message can often backfire, as though the well-wisher were utterly unaware of the level of destruction the griever has experienced.

In a famous section of Viktor Frankl's monumental *Man's Search for Meaning*, he recounts a former patient:

> Once, an elderly general practitioner consulted me because of his severe depression. He could not overcome the loss of his wife who had died two years before and whom he had loved above all else. Now, how can I help him? What should I tell him? Well, I refrained from telling him anything but instead confronted him with the question, "What would have happened, Doctor, if you had died first, and your wife would have had to survive you?" "Oh," he said, "for her this would have been terrible; how she would have suffered!" Whereupon I replied, "You see, Doctor, such a suffering has been spared her, and it was you who have spared her this suffering—to be sure, at the price that now you have to survive and mourn her." He said no word but shook my hand and calmly left my office. In some way, suffering ceases to be suffering at the moment it finds a meaning, such as the meaning of a sacrifice.[10]

This passage is well-known because it in many ways encapsulates the upshot of Frankl's entire book: suffering becomes bearable and in that way ceases (to some extent) to be suffering when it finds a purpose. Yet I cannot help but think that Frankl's analysis misses part of the source of strength this man took away from their meeting. Imagine that Frankl had suggested a different source of meaning for the widower's suffering. For example, suppose that the widower's wife would have been fine had she outlived her husband but that outliving his wife allowed the widower to use her life insurance policy to fund a new wing of the local hospital (for the sake of argument, assume such funding would have not been possible had the husband died first). In this revised version of the story, it is less obvious that the widower would have been able to take comfort in the "meaning" of his suffering, even though his outliving his wife had positive benefits for many others. Perhaps this fact may have brought some happiness to the widower—most of us take pleasure in being able to help others, regardless of the circumstances—but it is not clear that it would make the suffering of loneliness more bearable or meaningful for him.

I believe this discrepancy between cases makes perfect sense. In our revised version of the case, the widower's suffering had purpose, but that purpose was only incidentally connected to his wife. In the original case—the case in which the widower did actually find meaning and reprieve in the midst of his suffering—the suffering is reimagined by Frankl as an act of service *for the widower's wife*. It is not, I suggest, just any meaning that can make suffering bearable. In this case, the widower bore his loneliness for his wife; he bore it in her stead. It is hard to think of instances where we can act in love toward a person who is already deceased, and because of this the kind of love we hold toward those who are dead shifts from something active to a kind of passive warmth of remembrance. Frankl here shows us a case where a man found a way to actively love someone who had passed on before him. Here, the widower was able to relate to his wife in an active, present sense, rather than as a feature of the historical past.

Given the love-as-union picture, it makes sense that Frankl's widower was able to withstand the weight of loss and grief only after the circumstances of his grief became his means of actively relating to his wife. Namely, the ability to continue actively relating to her—and therefore actively engaging in the unified "we" of their loving relationship—allowed the widower to retain himself. And in returning this solidity, this selfhood, to his life, the widower found himself able to bear up under the pain of missing his wife.

The natural question is: can the unified "we" exist after one half of the union has died? Does death annihilate this union, leaving the still living to rebuild themselves from scratch (if they can) or else remain half a self (if they cannot)? Without a true persisting union, the mere illusion of a union would be of little use to us. On the love-as-union picture, self-deception will not cut it. If there is not a real sense in which I may continue to relate to those I am unified with in love after they are deceased, then I should expect that the loss of a loved one will bring with it a loss of my self. If this is true, then the death of loved ones is very much worse for people than we typically assume. Rather than being merely the source of severe emotional distress, the loss of a loved one can constitute a genuine existential threat to the person who remains living. Søren Kierkegaard's work was largely concerned with just such an existential threat in the realm of the religious life and had much to say on the topic of retaining such unions.

Kierkegaard on Contemporaneity

In *Fear and Trembling*, Kierkegaard, writing under the pseudonym Johannes de Silentio, spins this tale "[A] young lad falls in love with a princess, and this love is the entire substance of his life; and yet the relation is such that it cannot possibly be realized, that is, it cannot possibly be translated from ideality into reality."[11] In this brief passage we are shown a union-creating love: the knight's love was the "entire substance of his life," making the impossibility of a physical, personal union presumably all the more awful. We are not given specific details but are told simply that there was no way for the relationship to be instantiated in "reality"—that is to say, in the world we live in.[12] Silentio acknowledges that many may respond to such a situation by abandoning their love for the princess, writing off any continuation of the love as foolishness, and trying to move on to a relationship with someone they can be with. These people,

Silentio says, are "the slaves of the finite, the frogs in the swamp of life."[13] With these harsh words, Silentio wants to distinguish the aesthete's response from another infinite option. That is to say, the person who finds it foolish to continue loving the princess is stuck irremediably in the "finite," unable to understand the situation from the perspective of eternity. Silentio sees such a response as foolishness given the nature of the love—a totalizing union in which the knight's entire being is inextricably wrapped up in the princess' being and in his love for her. If we take this description seriously, we might think of the knight as having certain continuity conditions that make the response of the "slaves of the finite" wholly inadequate.[14] Moving on from an impossible love may seem coolly rational and wise, but it ignores the true nature and import of the relationship. Silentio then describes two additional ways the knight may respond to this impasse—ways that indicate an eternal perspective—illustrating the choices in the form of two different knights, the knight of infinite resignation and the knight of faith.

The knight of infinite resignation is, as the label suggests, resigned to the reality of not being with the princess in this world. But the knight has an eternal perspective and is realistic about the necessity of this union for his own self-constitution. This knight has no desire to ignore his present realities by hoping ceaselessly, against all evidence, that the princess may one day be his. Yet, he also rejects the aesthetic response; the knight of infinite resignation refuses to relegate the princess to his past and move forward without her. While he is resigned to not being with the princess in this world, he turns his attention to another world—the spiritual realm, afterlife, eternity—in which he anticipates their union finally coming to fruition. The knight of infinite resignation not only gives up on the hope of being with the princess in this life, he also gives up his mental presence in this life and turns his attention fully to eternity. Because he is deprived of his self-making union with the princess in this world, his earthly life is of little concern to him, and his love for the princess becomes, Silentio says, as a religious object, the sole object of his devotion.

The knight of faith, like the knight of infinite resignation, accepts that his union of love with the princess is the deepest aspect of himself and also that attempts to move on from this love will involve the loss of his own self. Unlike the knight of infinite resignation, however, the knight of faith does not resign his love for the princess to the spiritual realm or the afterlife. The knight of faith knows that his very existence depends on real union with the princess in this life, and he knows equally well that this union is impossible. The knight of faith makes what is well-known (but little understood) as a "leap" into faith,[15] acting on his dual conviction both that he could never be with the princess in this life and that he *would* be with the princess in this life. The knight of faith succeeds.

This movement—or "leap"—to faith discussed by Silentio is mysterious.[16] Additionally, there is no need to attempt to explain Kierkegaard's objective in positing such an opaque concept to illustrate religious faith. Kierkegaard's esoteric style is in large part a result of his conviction that on such matters of subjective (meaning, essential for the individual self) existential import we are forced into silence due to the inexpressible nature of the required actions—hence Johannes de Silentio. Again, what is important for our purposes here is Kierkegaard's exhortation that, although the knight of infinite resignation appears to preserve the union, he only allows himself to be lost along with the princess. Regaining the impossible unions will require us to act, in a much more difficult fashion, on a much stranger hope.

Fear and Trembling is written pseudonymously and should therefore not be taken as a perfectly straightforward picture of how Kierkegaard sees the world. But the idea of totalizing unions that require epistemic and pragmatic leaps from commonsense ideas of the possible is an important aspect of his general idea of religious—specifically Christian—faith. What we should notice in his descriptions of the two knights is that, even though the knight of resignation loves the princess as an object of religious devotion, he is *not* the knight who has faith. Rather, the knight who has faith realizes that union with the princess is an existential necessity for him *in this life*, and he makes the paradoxical movement to faith by acting as though the (seemingly) impossible must be true.

We can see these themes taken up in his nonpseudonymous work on the practical ins and outs of Christian faith. Specifically, Kierkegaard is concerned with the question of how someone in the modern age can truly be a Christian when (as Kierkegaard argued) being a Christian requires responding to the person of Christ as the disciples did. This seems impossible, he points out, because we look from what was the future back on Christ's life—the modern Christian cannot relate to Christ as the disciples did, because the disciples were ignorant of the ultimate trajectory of his life. Stephen Backhouse writes, "[T]o have the faith of the disciples Jesus demanded cannot be to assent to the historical and intellectual data that comprises the Christian religion."[17] Christianity, Kierkegaard contends, requires relating to Christ as though the human himself was before us in the same way he stood before the disciples over two thousand years ago. Anything less than contemporaneity is merely a historical interest in Christ, and history is essentially other than us; it is a realm we know about only through investigation—the more we come to know it, the more we objectify it and distinguish it from ourselves. The Christian, Kierkegaard argues, if she is to be a Christian at all, must relate to Christ as an event presently happening. Kierkegaard writes of those who "cannot bear contemporaneity" and eventually give up trying.[18]

The import of this theme should become clear to the reader by now: the person who has lost a dearly beloved, with whom they had formed a totalizing union, is herself under a kind of existential threat. The identity of a Christian is dependent on relating to Christ as one relates to a living and breathing other, rather than as a mere historical figure, the narrative trajectory of which we know entirely. This is because, for Kierkegaard, to be a Christian is to be a union of one's finite and infinite self—that is, a union of my bare self with the part of my self that has been made "crossed over into infinity" through a relationship with an infinite God.[19] But if love of others forms a genuine unified we, where the beloved is an inextricable part of my identity, then I also depend on these relationships with *others* with whom I have formed such a union. And similarly, this relationship must be a presently happening relation, not a relationship as we have to things in the historical past.

Under these conditions, it is not enough to be merely a knight of infinite resignation. It is not enough that we get dragged out of this life along with the one we love, trying to hold on to the union in the realm of memory or future hope. This is inadequate because it does not actually preserve the union; it merely preserves the *appearance* of the union to us. And his appearance can itself be a distorting screen between us and our beloved, as Lewis discovered when his memories of H began to become distorted and idealized. Those who are separated but do not realize the separation are, in some ways, further apart than the partners who stare separately into the blackness of the infinitely deep dividing chasm. The knight of infinite resignation *believes* that he has not given up his relationship to the princess; but by relegating their union to the realm of the mystical and forsaking the possibility of their union in this life, his heart *replaces* the princess with memories and ideas of her. The knight of infinite resignation wants to be religiously devoted but ends up merely haunted.

There are, of course, important differences between Kierkegaard's idea of the need for the Christian to become contemporaneous with Christ and the existential necessity of retaining the totalizing unions we form with beloved others. For example, for Kierkegaard the self-making aspect of contemporaneity with Christ is necessary for the formation of a true self and is therefore of primary importance over and above the contingent unions we form with other people. But what is important here are the reasons why the responses of both the "slaves of the finite"[20] and the knight of infinite resignation fail as adequate responses to the impossibility of being with the princess. The knight of faith—the only knight who succeeds—does so by acting in such a way that he displays full confidence *both* in the impossibility of being with the princess *and* the absolute metaphysical necessity of the union with the princess for his existence. Kierkegaard is silent on how the knight of faith does this. In fact, the unspeakability of the act is central to his understanding of faith. Kierkegaard's pseudonym of choice for *Fear and Trembling*, Johannes de Silentio, is our first clue as readers that a key feature of the knight of faith (and Abraham, his primary representative of such a knight) is the inability to communicate his actions of faithfulness to anyone else. Elsewhere, Kierkegaard writes,

> The truth can neither be communicated nor be received without being, as it were, under the eyes of God, without the help of God, without God's being a participant, the middle term, since God is the truth that can be communicated by and received only by the single individual.[21]

By "single individual," he means the person who has taken the steps to form a true, infinitized self. Each person individually has this potential but can only receive truth *as* an individual, never through a means of mass communication. Thus, the knight of faith is unable to explain what he does to readers; thus, we are unable to understand Abraham's act of faithfulness on Mount Sinai. While the knight of resignation can show us an insufficient way of responding to the potential loss of union with the beloved, the knight of faith cannot directly tell us how to respond. Whatever response is necessary to retain the union, it is, for Kierkegaard, largely incommunicable.

But here the reader may point out another seeming difference between Kierkegaardian contemporaneity and our existential need to retain our union with the deceased: while Christians believe that Christ overcame death and can communicate with them through the Holy Spirit, the deceased are cut off from the living. Regardless of what one believes about an afterlife, the separation between the living and the dead is thick and impenetrable. I cannot hold a conversation with a deceased loved one, nor embrace her, nor hear about her day, nor watch her walk through a room. How can we retain real union with someone from behind such a thick curtain? One possible answer, of course, is that maybe we cannot. While we may accept our existential dependence on these unions, perhaps this entails only that the death of dearly beloveds is magnitudes worse for us than we imagined. So much the worse, then, for the living. In the following section, I want to explore another response to the question of how such unions with the dead could be possible. The picture of time that I will describe sounds strange to modern readers, but, I believe, not for want of an argument.

Time

Charles Taylor begins *A Secular Age*,[22] with a description of the ancient distinction between "higher" and "secular time," known perhaps more popularly as "sacred" and "profane" time.[23] Taylor admits this distinction can be understood better in our contemporary dialect as a distinction between "temporality" and "eternity" but argues that the perception of two distinct planes of time goes back much further than our modern notions of nature and spirituality. Profane time, which Taylor calls "secular" time, is the time of ordinary events, the regular goings-on of everyday life, which pass through the present in a familiar stream. It is time as a stream, running continuously forward. In secular time, we labor and live the ordinary bits of our lives. My trip to the grocery store takes place in secular time, where events are ordered as past, present, or future, and I must take them as they come.

The ancient conception of what Taylor calls "higher times," as he describes it, "gather and re-order secular time. They introduce 'warps' and seeming inconsistencies in profane time-ordering. Events which were far apart in profane time could nevertheless be closely linked."[24] Taylor illustrates the idea this way: when we, for example, participate in the liturgy of Good Friday, we are, in some ways, closer to the event of Christ's death on the Cross than we are to yesterday or tomorrow. Higher time scrunches up the timeline, raises us to a plane above temporality, and places us beside the sacred things we revere and celebrate, to dwell beside them for a little while. Taylor argues that what makes this eternity "higher" than secular time is the idea, rooted in the Platonism that was influentially taken up by Plotinus and Augustine, that "the really real, full being is outside of time, unchanging. Time is a moving image of eternity. It is imperfect, or tends to imperfection."[25] The time that "passes" then is an output of Being and, therefore, imperfect. We who exist within secular time must take special measures to access these higher times. Most often, Taylor writes, this was the domain and purpose of ritual.

The idea of a "higher" time, over and above regular "secular" time, is retained in every ceremony and ritual practiced in commemoration of a past event or to mark a holiday. When a woman dons a white dress and walks down an aisle, wearing her grandmother's veil and her mother's pearls, with the intention to become bound for life to her partner, these traditions are ways of entering into a kind of "higher time" where otherwise ordinary actions take on the weight and authority of a marriage ceremony—

the bride joins a long line of women who have individually chosen the same ritual acts, thereby joining her to this line during the wedding ceremony. But how do rituals propel us from the saeculum to the higher time? Taylor, describing Augustine's work on the topic, describes the process as a kind of "gathering" together of time:

> Unlike his Greek sources, who looked at objective time, the time of processes and movement, Augustine in his famous discussion in *Confessions* XI examines lived time. His instant is not the "nun" of Aristotle, which is a limit, like a point, an extensionless boundary of time periods. Rather it is the gathering together of past into present to project a future. The past, which "objectively" exists no more, is here in my present; it shapes this moment in which I turn to a future, which "objectively" is not yet, but which is here qua project.[26]

Augustine, then, sees time as essentially a description of order that arises through living, rather than as a thing lived through. Because of this, the past is not a thing that I have left but is something that gets gathered up in my actions and projects and gives rise to what I do and to what I will do. And it gives rise to these things, not merely by causing (for example) what I do but by making my actions what they are. Augustine illustrates this idea in book XI of his *Confessions* by comparing this "gathered" nature of time to a poem or song: "What occurs in the psalm as a whole occurs in its particular pieces and its individual syllables. The same is true of a longer action in which perhaps the psalm is a part. It is also valid of the entire life of an individual person, where all actions are parts of a whole."[27] Because eternal things exist in ordinary time, and are drawn out over uncountable instants, the eternal in the saeculum gathers the past into the present to create the future.[28] This is the very heart of ritual, where we intentionally take up a (kind of) dutiful work to gather the past together with the present. Rituals are, by nature, more intentional than ordinary actions extended over time, because we are not ordinarily in the process of, say, sitting down at a Passover dinner, or washing an infant of original sin, or joining two souls in matrimony. But on this (we may call it) Platonic understanding of "higher" time, ritual allows us to intentionally gather the past into the present. This in turn allows future actions that follow from the ritual to take on the character as a step out of the profane ordinary, the way that the beginning of a song can determine the nature of the ending.

So, on this ancient conception of higher and secular time, it is clear why ceremony and ritual held a place of such great importance. Rather than being merely tools for spurring memories of the past, they were literally our means of joining with historically past events in an act of shared presence. But this ancient conception of time has gone out of the intellectual mainstream (to put it mildly), and ceremonies are now often seen merely as a means of honoring someone or remembering an event. But if rituals can only serve to commemorate, rather than drawing up the past to meet us in the present, then the best we can hope for us to become knights of infinite resignation, clinging to the memory of our beloveds as spiritualized, idealized objects, and allowing ourselves to fade out of the present and into the past with the other parts of our unions of love.

It would be easy to think of the distinction between a higher and lower time as fanciful, a figment of ancient and medieval mysticism that should be understood purely allegorically in our present age. This question is important for our discussion here because, as I have previously argued, real union with the beloved involves a *two-way relationship* between us and them. If they no longer exist, then there is no way for them to really relate to us, and real union is impossible. However, philosophers have always taken seriously the idea that our perception of time as a flowing river—our intuition that the present is what is "really happening" and that there is an objective past and future—may be incorrect.

The view of time discussed by Taylor in the previous section—time as "less than real" in the deepest sense, as traversable, or gatherable, or able to be risen above—is also not at odds with any scientific or general empirical consensus on the nature of time. There is, in fact, no such consensus at all, and the scientific and philosophical communities have in recent decades found themselves divided on the question.

It is generally accepted that a view of the "arrow of time" as an illusion is far more compatible with general relativity than the "common sense" view of time. Albert Einstein once wrote, "For people like us who believe in physics, the separation between past, present and future has only the importance of an admittedly tenacious illusion."[29] Hermann Minkowski, a mathematician who worked on Einstein's theory of general relativity, concurred, arguing that a picture of space and time as "unified" was necessary to make sense of what we know about relativity. Complicating matters, however, those working on quantum mechanics argue that presentism—the view of time as a flowing river, with only the spotlight of the *present* as truly real and existing in reality—must be assumed to make sense of what we know about physics at the quantum level.[30]

John McTaggart was perhaps the first to bring the discussion of the nature of time into "contemporary" analytic philosophy, in his famous paper "The Unreality of Time."[31] Therein, McTaggart argues that the commonsense view of time as an objective and forward-moving arrow entail that tensed semantic expressions are full of contradictions. From this, he concludes that time must be, in a deep sense, "unreal." There have, of course, been responses to McTaggart's argument, and responses still to those in defense of the ultimate unreality of time. Still, McTaggart's argument has had "staying power"[32] and sparked a renewed interest in the topic of time in twentieth-century analytic philosophy. Suffice to say, on the topic of time, philosophers and scientists are at a collective loss with no clear consensus emerging. How, then, ought we live in the face of the loss of a beloved?

If time could, as Augustine thought, be gathered together in simultaneity through acts that stretch across it like a song, then perhaps those acts could preserve our real unions with those who have gone before us. The nature of those acts is, I worry, not something that one can theorize about in the abstract, because they are themselves continuations of the particular relationships in question. Frankl's widower patient gathered his wife to him through the act of carrying her would-be suffering for her, sparing her the pain. Other relationships may be continued through other forms of active relating: the continuation of shared projects, for example. What is important is that one is relating to the beloved herself, rather than to memories of her or an idealized picture of her. This is a difficult task under ordinary conditions—far more difficult, to be sure, when death separates you. We can only offer our best attempts, in what may fairly be called an act of faith.

Conclusion

In this chapter I have argued for a few things. First, that the Union Theory of love best explains why the distortion of our memories of deceased loved ones is a bad thing. Second, if the Union Theory is correct, then the death of a beloved with whom I have formed a unified "we" also entails the loss of that "we"—a loss of my self. Therefore, the death of our beloved is much worse for us than we think. I have further argued that our well-being depends upon our being able to retain our unions with the deceased. And finally, I argued that such a retention may be possible, especially given a rather plausible picture of time that has (in various versions) been accepted by philosophers for millennia.

In arguing that we may have, and should act in, hope, I am not arguing for something mystical. We should accept that, whatever may be true of life, death, and time, the living will be separated from the dead. The widower's loneliness was not soothed by the opportunity to continue serving his wife. The pain itself was his means of continuing to serve and relate to her. Rather, what we may hope for is the ability to retain a unified "we" consisting of both persons in a relationship of love with one another, even if in all sensory respects they are cut off from each other. Doing so would be difficult. The temptation would be strong to become like Kierkegaard's knight of infinite resignation, clinging relentlessly to the memory of the beloved, or to try to move on from the beloved entirely. Rather than either of these actions, we should understand time as Augustine did—gatherable, the present drawing the past to itself and into the future via diachronically extended activities. It is in this picture of higher time as an instant of simultaneity that our hope lies. And it is indeed only a hope—the success of our attempts to retain real union depends on there really being two beings relating to one another. I ended my paper on a discussion of time and argued that we have good reason to doubt that the present is all that truly exists and therefore good reason to hope that continued unions may be possible in theory. There is, therefore, equally good reason to *act in hope* that such real unions can be maintained even in the face of death. Genuine unions of love may, in fact, obligate us to do so.

Notes

1. *The Antigone of Sophocles*, trans. Dudley Fitts and Robert Fitzgerald (New York: Harcourt, Brace and Company Inc., 1939), 5.
2. C. S Lewis, *A Grief Observed* (New York: Harper, 2001), 50.
3. See Ben Bradley, "When is Death Bad for the One Who Dies?" *Noûs* 38, no. 1 (2004): 1–28; F. M. Kamm, "Why Is Death Bad and Worse Than Pre-Natal Non-Existence?" *Pacific Philosophical Quarterly* 69, no. 2 (1988): 161–4.
4. Some Catholics may contend that the living can harm the dead by omission by, for example, failing to pray for their souls in purgatory.
5. Alexander Jech, "The Twofold Task of Union," *Ethical Theory and Moral Practice* 17, no. 5 (2014): 988.

6 Plato, "Symposium," in *Plato: Complete Works*, ed. John M. Cooper (Indianapolis: Hackett, 1997), 191d.
7 Roger Scruton, *Sexual Desire: A Moral Philosophy of the Erotic* (New York: Free Press, 1968), 230.
8 See also Mark Fisher, *Personal Love* (London: Duckworth, 1990), who argues for a literal fusing of at least some interests.
9 Robert C. Solomon, *About Love: Reinventing Romance for Our Times* (Lanham: Madison Books, 2001), 63.
10 Victor E. Frankl, *Man's Search for Meaning: An Introduction to Logotherapy*, 4th ed., trans. I. Lasch (Boson: Beacon Press, 1992), 117.
11 Søren Kierkegaard, *Fear and Trembling/Repetition (Kierkegaard's Writings, Volume 6)*, trans. Howard Hong and Edna Hong (Princeton: Princeton University Press, 1983), 41.
12 Kierkegaard, *Fear and Trembling*, 41.
13 Kierkegaard, *Fear and Trembling*, 41.
14 Kierkegaard, *Fear and Trembling*, 41.
15 Kierkegaard, *Fear and Trembling*, 36.
16 This is called the movement of "repetition." See Kirkegaard, *Repetition*, 149.
17 Stephen Backhouse, *Kierkegaard: A Single Life* (Grand Rapids, MI: Zondervan Press, 2016), 275–76.
18 Søren Kierkegaard, *Practice in Christianity (Kierkegaard's Writings, Volume 20)*, trans. Howard Hong and Edna Hong (Princeton University Press, 1992), 88.
19 Kierkegaard, *Fear and Trembling*, 36.
20 Kierkegaard, *Fear and Trembling*, 41.
21 Søren Kierkegaard, *The Point of View (Kierkegaard's Writings, Volume 22)*, trans. Howard Hong and Edna Hong (Princeton University Press, 2009), 140.
22 Charles Taylor, *A Secular Age* (Cambridge: Belknap Press, 2007).
23 Mircea Eliade, *The Sacred and the Profane: The Nature of Religion*, trans. Willard R. Trask (San Diego: Harcourt Brace, 1957), 10.
24 Taylor, *A Secular Age*, 55.
25 Taylor, *A Secular Age*, 54–55.
26 Taylor, *A Secular Age*, 55.
27 Augustine of Hippo, *Confessions*, trans. H. Chadwick (Oxford: Oxford University Press, 2009), 40.
28 This idea bears some similarities, though also many differences, to what Henri Bergson called "lived time"—time as we experience it, as paused, gathered, and rushed, at various points—which for him was distinct from "objective time." Henri Bergson, *Time and Free Will: An Essay on the Immediate Data of Consciousness*, trans. F. L. Pogson (New York: Humanities Press, 1910), 100.
29 In a letter to the family of Michele Besso, discussed and quoted in: Thomas Venning, Christie's London, "Time's Arrow: Albert Einstein's Letters to Michele Besso," November 14, 2017. https://www.christies.com/features/Einstein-letters-to-Michele-Besso-8422-1.aspx.
30 F. M. Christensen, *Space-like Time: Consequences Of, Alternatives To, and Arguments Regarding the Theory That Time Is Like Space* (Toronto: University of Toronto Press, 1993), 283; Tim Maudlin, "Remarks on the Passing of Time," *Proceedings of the Aristotelian Society* 102, no. 1 (2002): 259–274.
31 John E. McTaggart, "The Unreality of Time," *Mind* 17, no. 68 (1908): 457–74.
32 Nina Emery, Ned Markosian, and Meghan Sullivan, "Time," in *The Stanford Encyclopedia of Philosophy* (Winter 2020 Edition), ed. Edward N. Zalta.

Traditional Sources

Augustine of Hippo. *Confessions*. Translated by H. Chadwick. Oxford: Oxford University Press. 2009.

Plato. "Symposium." In *Plato: Complete Works*, edited by John M. Cooper, 921–1273. Indianapolis: Hackett, 1997.

Bibliography

Backhouse, Stephen. *Kierkegaard: A Single Life*. Grand Rapids, MI: Zondervan Press, 2016.

Bergson, Henri. *Time and Free Will: An Essay on the Immediate Data of Consciousness*. Translated by F. L. Pogson. New York: Humanities Press, 1910.

Bradley, Ben. "When is Death Bad for the One Who Dies?" *Noûs* 38, no. 1 (2004): 1–28.

Christensen, F. M. *Space-like Time: Consequences Of, Alternatives To, and Arguments Regarding the Theory That Time Is Like Space*. Toronto: University of Toronto Press, 1993.

Eliade, Mircea. *The Sacred and the Profane: The Nature of Religion*. Translated by Willard R. Trask. San Diego: Harcourt Brace, 1957.

Emery, Nina, Ned Markosian, and Meghan Sullivan. "Time." In *The Stanford Encyclopedia of Philosophy* (Winter 2020 Edition), edited by Edward N. Zalta.

Fisher, Mark. *Personal Love*. London: Duckworth, 1990.

Frankl, Victor E. *Man's Search for Meaning: An Introduction to Logotherapy*. 4th ed. Translated by I. Lasch. Boson: Beacon Press, 1992.

Kamm, F. M. "Why Is Death Bad and Worse Than Pre-Natal Non-Existence?" *Pacific Philosophical Quarterly* 69, no. 2 (1988): 161–4.

Jech, Alexander. "The Twofold Task of Union." *Ethical Theory and Moral Practice* 17, no. 5 (2014): 987–1000.

Kierkegaard, Søren. *Fear and Trembling/Repetition. (Kierkegaard's Writings, Volume 6)*. Translated by Howard Hong and Edna Hong. Princeton: Princeton University Press, 1983.

Kierkegaard, Søren. *Practice in Christianity. (Kierkegaard's Writings, Volume 20)*. Translated by Howard Hong and Edna Hong. Princeton University Press, 1992.

Kierkegaard, Søren. *The Point of View. (Kierkegaard's Writings, Volume 22)*. Translated by Howard Hong and Edna Hong. Princeton University Press, 2009.

Lewis, C.S. *A Grief Observed*. New York: Harper, 2001.

Maudlin, Tim. "Remarks on the Passing of Time." *Proceedings of the Aristotelian Society* 102, no. 1 (2002): 259–74.

McTaggart, John E. "The Unreality of Time." *Mind* 17, no. 68 (1908): 457–74.

Scruton, Roger. *Sexual Desire: A Moral Philosophy of the Erotic*. New York: Free Press, 1968.

Solomon, Robert C. *About Love: Reinventing Romance for Our Times*. Lanham: Madison Books, 2001.

Venning, Thomas. "Time's Arrow: Albert Einstein's Letters to Michele Besso." Christie's London, Christies.com, 14 November 2017. https://www.christies.com/features/Einstein-letters-to-Michele-Besso-8422-1.aspx

Taylor, Charles. *A Secular Age*. Cambridge: Belknap Press, 2007.

10

Heidegger's Process Metaphysics of Personhood

Anne Sophie Meincke

Thinghood itself needs first to be elucidated with respect to its ontological origin so that it becomes possible to ask how the non-reified Being *of the subject, the soul, the consciousness, the spirit, the person is* positively *to be understood.*

—Martin Heidegger, *Sein und Zeit*

Introduction

Since John Locke raised the question of what it takes for a person to persist through time, metaphysicians have struggled to give a satisfactory answer. Adherents of the so-called Complex View, which can be traced back to David Hume, have offered a variety of reductionist analyses of personal identity in terms of empirical relations of continuity, psychological, biological, or both, none of which, however, captures the robust sense of mineness and self-identity commonly associated with the concept of personal identity. In contrast, proponents of the so-called Simple View, as first suggested by Joseph Butler and Thomas Reid, venture to save personal identity by insisting on its primitiveness. According to them, who is identical with whom in a given diachronic context cannot be read off from any empirical facts; there is nothing that constitutes a person's identity other than—possibly—the identity of that person's individual soul.[1]

In this chapter, I want to show that Martin Heidegger has something interesting to contribute to the debate on personal identity. More specifically, I want to convince both Heidegger scholars and contemporary analytic metaphysicians that Heidegger's early theory of Dasein offers resources for resolving the dilemma of personal identity. There is no need to either dismiss personal identity as a metaphysical illusion or, else, construe it as a deep further fact that evades informative, noncircular explanation, provided that we discard the traditional conception of persons as substances or things in favor of a new understanding of persons as processes.[2]

I should clarify the terminology here. A *thing*, as I define it, is an entity for whose identity change is not essential. A thing is what it is regardless of whether or not it changes—it need not change in order to exist. Its identity is a primitive given, preceding change and remaining unaffected by it. In contrast, a *process*, I suggest, is an entity for whose identity change *is* essential. A process must change in order to exist and be what it is; its identity is brought about by change.³ Accordingly, *thing ontology* is an ontology that gives the ontological priority to things, whereas *process ontology* regards reality as being fundamentally processual. For the process ontologist, change comes first, not second.

Heidegger is not usually considered a defender of process ontology, but he is well-known for his critical attacks against substance ontology, the historically most influential version of thing ontology.⁴ According to Heidegger, Western metaphysics is substance metaphysics as a result of its failure to ask what it means, for whatever there is, to be. What are we committing ourselves to when saying that something "exists" or is an "entity," a "being"? In *Being and Time*, Heidegger explains that answering this question requires first elucidating the Being of that being, which raises the question of what Being in general is: the Being of ourselves.⁵ Accordingly, *Being and Time* begins with a theory of ourselves—a theory of "Dasein" (Being-there).

While Heidegger scholars have frequently been interested in Heidegger's understanding of self and subjectivity entailed by his theory of Dasein, very little attention has been paid to Heidegger's thoughts on the diachronic dimension of selfhood specifically. The few existing studies on this topic mostly take a pragmatist or narrativist approach and do not (sufficiently) recognize Heidegger's profoundly ontological or metaphysical ambitions.⁶ It must not be overlooked that Heidegger, despite opposing "metaphysics" in the specific sense of Western substance metaphysics, remains a metaphysical thinker: by investigating the meaning of Being, Heidegger seeks to correct a failure of traditional metaphysics—its "oblivion of Being"—rather than doing away with metaphysics altogether. Similarly, it would be mistaken to infer from Heidegger's explicit refusal to use the term "person" because of its substance ontological connotations that he does not have anything to say about persons.⁷ On the contrary, Heidegger endeavors to deconstruct the customary substance ontological misconception of personhood through an investigation of the Being of "person," which he characterizes as "Dasein."⁸ Heidegger's theory of Dasein *is* a metaphysics of personhood, namely—as I am going to demonstrate—a *process* metaphysics of personhood that, as such, entails a process theory of personal identity.

I proceed as follows. First, I introduce Heidegger's theory of Dasein as the cornerstone of Heidegger's general attack against substance or thing ontology. According to Heidegger, a specific mode of self-realization causes Dasein to misunderstand itself as a thing and, in general, to mistake Being for thinghood. This "inauthentic" (*uneigentlich*) mode is characterized by concealment of processuality at various existential levels (section 2). I then reconstruct Dasein's identity through time as consisting in a threefold temporal process of interactive existential self-stabilization, which only in an "authentic" (*eigentlich*) mode of self-realization reveals Dasein's primordial temporal extendedness, the latter, however, in the sense not of a pre-given primitive fact but of an existential task, which Dasein continuously has to fulfill in order to exist (section 3). I conclude with some critical reflections on the contribution Heidegger's version of a process metaphysics of personhood makes to the contemporary debate on personal identity.

Dasein's Thing Ontological Self-Misunderstanding

Heidegger's critique of substance metaphysics is founded upon the diagnosis that Being in general is misinterpreted exactly to the extent that Dasein misunderstands its own Being. Because Dasein, failing to explicitly problematize its Being, mistakenly assumes itself to be a substance, "being a substance" or, more generally, "being a thing" becomes a model for Being as such. Only by correcting this misunderstanding can we hope to uncover the meaning of Being as such. To this end, Heidegger claims, we need both an understanding of what he identifies as the "existential" structure of Dasein and an account of how Dasein's self-misunderstanding arises from the very existential structure of Dasein.

This double task is taken up by the so-called "existential analytic" of Dasein, which derives its name from the central claim that "the essence of Dasein lies in its existence."[9] This is directed against the traditional view that one can grasp what an entity is—its "essence"—independently of its existence—"existence" in the sense of mere presence, primitive givenness, or, as Heidegger calls it, presence-at-hand (*Vorhandenheit*).[10] Such an approach fails in the case of Dasein, which is nothing beyond its existence—"existence" now being existentially reinterpreted as the activity of being its Being. "Existence," in the existential sense, is not something one *is* but something one *does*; and Dasein *consists* in this doing. This is programmatically marked by the German noun "Dasein": qua nominalization of the verb *dasein*—"to be there"—"Dasein" is, as Heidegger puts it, a "pure expression of Being" (*ein reiner Seinsausdruck*), meant to express the activity of Being-there rather than some real definition answering the question of "what" something is.

Dasein as the activity of existing or Being-there qualifies as a *process* in the sense previously specified. It is an entity for whose identity change is essential—change in the form of activity. Dasein is the active process of existing or Being-there. Asking about the origins of Dasein's substance ontological self-misunderstanding accordingly amounts to asking: how can a process misunderstand itself as a thing? To answer this question we need to get a better grasp on the processual constitution of Dasein: what exactly does the process of existing consist in? Heidegger discusses both in several rounds of interpretation of increasing complexity and specificity.

To start with, Heidegger characterizes Dasein as a being "that in its Being is concerned with this Being."[11] This implies two things. First, Dasein's concern with its own Being is hermeneutic; it involves (at least) some rudimentary understanding of Being, which is exactly why Heidegger hopes to unveil the meaning of Being by means of an investigation into Dasein's Being.[12] In contrast, a stone lacks a relation to and, hence, understanding of its Being. A stone does not "exist"; it is a being that is just given or "present-at-hand"—a thing. Second, being concerned with its Being, Dasein has this Being as in each case its own (*je meines*).[13] Dasein—Being-there—has a perspective on Being and, hence, is not a "what" but exists in the way of a "who."[14] It is a *person* as opposed to a thing.[15]

Against the common equation of persons and things, which remains in place even where a reification of the person is disclaimed,[16] Heidegger insists on their fundamental ontological difference: "The person is no thing, no substance, no object."[17] To be a person means to be Dasein, and it would amount to a category mistake to analyze the Being of persons in terms of notions denoting the Being of non-Dasein-like beings, such as things or substances. Dasein's ontological characteristics, rather than being "present-at-hand 'properties' of some present-at-hand being that 'looks' so and so," are "in each case possible modes for it to be, and only that."[18] Hence, whatever is revealed by the existential analytic are not "categories" but "existentialia," characteristics flowing from Dasein's basic existential structure.[19]

As Heidegger further explains, these two basic aspects of Dasein—existence and mineness (*Jemeinigkeit*)—must be interpreted on the basis of another ontological characteristic: the so-called Being-in-the-world.[20] By being concerned in its Being with this Being, Dasein is intrinsically related to the world. Dasein is "Being-in-the-world" in the sense that all possible and actual modes of its existence are modes of an interaction with the Being of other beings—including other Dasein[21]—encountered in the world and, that is, Dasein's modes of existence are modes of an understanding of world.[22] Even the understanding of its own Being is one Dasein gains through an understanding of world.[23]

The discovery of the existential status of "world," Heidegger believes, solves the traditional conundrum of intentionality. There is no question as to how Dasein, as a self-content "subject" encapsulated in an inner sphere, could manage to relate to "objects" outside in the world.[24] Instead, Dasein's selfhood is constituted by the very fact that Dasein, insofar as it exists, is always "outside" alongside entities, which it encounters and which belong to a world already discovered. Dasein is "beyond" or "ahead-of" itself; it exists in the sense of ek-sist, standing out, being-*there* (*Da-*sein). This primordially "ecstatic" or "transcendent" character of Dasein's Being sets Dasein dramatically apart from Being-present-at-hand.[25] While the latter is complete at any instant, Dasein "is constantly 'more' than it factually is"; "it *is* what it becomes or what it does not become."[26] Dasein *is* its possibilities.

However, exactly the fact that Dasein is always already "handed over" to, or "thrown into," the world in which it has to be its "there" brings it about that the ecstatic or transcendent nature of Dasein usually remains invisible.[27] In their inextricable conjunction, "existentiality"—Dasein's projecting itself into its possibilities—and "facticity"—Dasein's thrownness into its personal "there"—entail Dasein's "falling" into the world: a total immersion into worldly affairs at the expense of self-transparency (*Durchsichtigkeit*). Dasein's concern with its Being, initially and most commonly (*zunächst und zumeist*), takes the form of being caught up in the multifarious demands of everyday business, this tendency being reinforced through the impersonal narratives that typically accompany any actions and interactions in the social sphere. These narratives (*Gerede*) systematically draw Dasein's attention away from its respectively own, that is, personal possibilities, by implementing norms as to what "one" or "they" (*man*)—an anonymous, impersonal collective—ought to do. Falling means self-alienation.[28]

By failing to appreciate its possibilities, Dasein fails to appreciate its existential constitution as Being-toward-possibilities, mistaking itself for Being-present-at-hand. Note that this failure is not merely an intellectual shortcoming and in this sense a negligible surface phenomenon. Dasein tends to overlook its primordial existential character just as much as it tends to level out this character in practice. This tendency of practical and hermeneutical self-reification is a possibility built into the existential structure of Dasein, and this not as any possibility but as the most natural one. Qua Being-in-the-world, Dasein is *disposed toward* losing sight of the world, and thereby of itself as Being-in-the-world, in favor of the things it encounters in the world, comparable to the eye that cannot see itself.

Moreover, Dasein actively welcomes being distracted from seeing itself as what it truly is since this would confront Dasein with death. Heidegger argues that we most rudimentarily understand Being against the background of its negation, death—however, usually in the mode of turning away from it, fleeing it.[29] Rather than explicitly projecting ourselves into our possibilities in the face of the "ultimate possibility," death, we are prone to allowing for our possibilities to become determined externally by beings that themselves do not have any possibilities because they do not "exist": by the "ready-to-hand" things we deal with in practical everyday life and by beings that like us flee from their possibilities—the "They" of public life.[30]

Heidegger claims that taking this deficient, "inauthentic" mode of existence as the starting point for an ontological self-interpretation unavoidably leads to the illusion that the Being of Dasein is no different from the Being of a thing: "Because . . ., in being absorbed in the world, the phenomenon of world gets passed over (*übersprungen*), it is replaced by what is present-at-hand within the world, the things."[31] More precisely, readiness-to-hand is turned into presence-at-hand through an act of theoretical explication: as they become objects of assertions (*Aussagen*), the things we deal with in practical everyday life ("equipment," *Zeug*) get deprived of their embeddedness in a network of practical meanings and references (*Bewandtnisganzheit*), being exhibited instead by way of "pure looking there."[32] This transition from so-called circumspective interpretation (*umsichtige Auslegung*) of innerwordly beings toward their theoretical or logical exposition consolidates and reinforces the levelling of Dasein's primordial existential character, which as a tendency is manifest already in Dasein's inauthentic way of everyday life.

Dasein's thing ontological self-misunderstanding, we have seen so far, originates from a self-concealment inherent in Dasein's existential structure as Being-in-the-world. However, there is yet another—and, in fact, the most important—layer of this existential structure, to be uncovered in yet another round of fundamental-ontological interpretation. This is the primordially *temporal* nature of Dasein. The famous key thesis of *Being and Time* is that time is the meaning of Being. Dasein understands Being, including its own Being, ultimately in the "horizon" of time.[33] Why? Because Dasein's Being, according to Heidegger, is a characteristic manifestation of time itself. To be Dasein—"be there"—means to happen temporally in such-and-such ways.

Dasein's modes of interaction with the world, together with the corresponding interpretations of the Being of beings encountered in the course of these interactions, thus can be reinterpreted in temporal terms. The three core aspects of Dasein's Being—existentiality (projection into possibilities), facticity (thrownness into one's "there"), and falling (preoccupation with things encountered in the world), the unity of which Heidegger calls "care" (*Sorge*)[34]—correspond with the three so-called "ecstases" of primordial time or temporality: future, having-been, and present.³⁵ Dasein, formally analyzed as "ahead-of-itself-Being-already-in-(the-world) as Being-with (entities encountered within-the-world)," is the unified process of coming-toward-itself from a projected future possibility of itself, of thereby coming-back-to what it has been and of thus being-with other beings in the present situation.³⁶

The ultimate origin of Dasein's ecstatic or transcendent character as Being-in-the-world, hence, turns out to be its temporality: Dasein is carried away into the three directions of "toward," "back to," and "with" because temporality itself is carried away into its ecstases;³⁷ temporality is "the primordial 'outside-of-itself' in and for itself," the "paradigmatic ekstatikon."³⁸ As such, temporality is what grounds the processuality of Dasein. There is no unchanging, static essence in Dasein because Dasein—qua "existing"—is a flow of time, a temporal movement with a threefold dynamic structure. This dynamic structure may realize itself differently, which finally explains how it is possible that the process that is Dasein mistakes itself for a thing: realized inauthentically, processuality covers itself up.

Again, the latter happens in two steps, corresponding to the two steps of levelling out existentiality previously described. First, in everyday life, that is, in the mode of falling into the world, time is relocated from the Dasein into the world "in which" Dasein is assumed to be as in a container and accordingly is misunderstood as the "within-time-ness" (*Innerzeitigkeit*) of so-called "world-time" (*Weltzeit*).³⁹ Second, in the course of theoretical interpretation, world-time degenerates into the so-called "ordinary concept of time" (*vulgäre Zeit*) as an infinite sequence of now-points.⁴⁰ This latter concept of time, which guides the interpretation of nature, creates and solidifies the illusion that it be possible for Dasein to run away from the facticity of its finitude, a finitude that is evident in primordial ecstatic time but "forgotten" in ordinary time.⁴¹

Insofar as Dasein misunderstands and misinterprets time, it misunderstands and misinterprets its own Being—and Being in general. The present becomes the leading temporal horizon of the interpretation of Being, this distorting the primordial existential organization of the three ecstases in which future has the priority.⁴² Being, that is, becomes synonymous with "being present" in a way that obscures the present's ontological dependence on the primordial and indivisible movement of time constituted by the "ahead-of" and "back-toward" of future and having-been.⁴³ The hegemony of substance ontology in Western metaphysics, according to Heidegger, has its roots in this distortion: in the inauthentic self-realization of primordial time, that is, in an inauthentic self-realization of the process of Dasein in which the temporal processuality of Being becomes invisible to itself.

Personal Identity as the Temporal Process of Interactive Existential Self-Stabilization

Heidegger's provoking thesis about the origin of substance or thing ontology entails an interesting, though no less provoking stance on personal identity.

Heidegger notes that, when reflecting on its identity, all that Dasein appears to find is a multiplicity of discrete experiences, which occur in a sequence in time. How do these experiences hang together? In addition to their diversity, Dasein encounters the difficulty that each experience is "real" only insofar as it is present-at-hand in the respective "now," while past and future experiences are either not anymore or not yet "real." One, therefore, can never literally tie Dasein's experiences together; Dasein rather seems to "hop" from one "now" to the next.[44] As an attempt to address this problem, a "frame" or "track" filled up successively by these experiences may be stipulated. However, Heidegger asks, how could there be such a frame, given that its "boundaries, birth and death, being past and only yet-to-come, are not 'real'" in the supposed sense of being present-at-hand?[45]

Compare the debate on personal identity in contemporary analytic metaphysics. Complex Theories of personal identity fail exactly in the attempt to construct personal identity out of sequences of distinct experiences or distinct "mental events." Whatever kind of continuity relation is postulated to tie together these experiences or mental events, the resulting connection remains superficial and liable to branching scenarios, which can be prevented only by circularly presupposing the identity that ought to be explained.[46] Acknowledging that the binding relations are too weak to warrant strict numerical identity over time, defenders of a Complex View hasten to explain that identity actually is not what matters.[47] Thus, we are left with the discrete events that, themselves unchanging, are assumed to make up a person as an "aggregate" that, if any, "changes" only in the sense that it consists of these different events.[48] This analysis is typically combined with a denial of the passage of time so that what appears to us as fleeting "nows" are in fact fixed, nonchanging positions in four-dimensional space-time, each of these being equally real (so-called eternalism).[49] A person is conceived of as a "perduring" four-dimensional space-time worm, which, if time were to pass, would fill up a virtually predefined track just in the way indicated by Heidegger.[50]

In contrast, Simple Theories of personal identity endorse the idea that the self must be something pure and simple that underlies, as a nonchanging, self-identical subjectum, the change of experiences. This unchanging subjectum is, as Heidegger puts it, copresent (*Zusammenvorhandensein* or *Mitvorhandensein*) with its experiences.[51] However, while the experiences are located in time, this is not true for the subject that has them. The subject is considered an "enduring" three-dimensional substance that is related to time only indirectly via its time-indexed properties (or via its time-indexed having of properties).[52] The Simple View, as it were, equates the person with an alleged container or "frame" for experiences, whose presence is taken to be a primitive, atemporal fact.[53]

From Heidegger's point of view, both types of personal identity theory come too late in the sense that they aim to reconstruct personal identity after it has been lost. They follow the "natural horizon for questions" instead of deconstructing it.[54] According to Heidegger, a serious ontological investigation into personal identity that is sensitive to the existential status of Dasein in the first place has to be, and unavoidably is, an investigation into the personal *non*-identity of Dasein. Understanding that Dasein is the more obsessed with its identity the less it actually is itself helps us to put the question of personal identity in the right way:[55]

> The question is not: by means of what does Dasein achieve the unity of connectedness so as to ex post tie together the completed and ongoing sequence of "experiences"? It is rather: in which mode of its own Being *does Dasein lose itself such that it has to, as it were, ex post gather itself together from the dispersion and to think up a unity to embrace the "together"?*[56]

The traditional task of finding a way to unify a given multiplicity of experiences is to be replaced with the task of illuminating the mechanisms of self-loss that cause Dasein's fragmentation into a multiplicity of experiences. Heidegger's existential analytic addresses the latter by analyzing Dasein in its "average everydayness" (*durchschnittliche Alltäglichkeit*), revealing that the theoretical assumption of sequences of discrete experiences originates from Dasein's practical fragmentation in everyday life in the course of "falling into" the world: the daily absorption in practical concerns (*Besorgungen*) that involve engagements with ready-to-hand tools and facilities and with the "They."[57] "Everyday Dasein has been dispersed into the multiplicity of what daily 'happens'"—a dispersion that deepens as it is subjected to theoretical interpretation.[58] The same mechanisms that obscure processuality and lure Dasein into mistaking itself as a thing, as shown previously, are thus also detrimental to Dasein's identity.

For Heidegger, the very question of what it takes for a person to persist through time is a symptom of inauthenticity. Inauthentic Dasein loses sight of the ontological unity of the process it is—indeed, of being a process at all—exactly to the extent that it, qua inauthentic, is ontically flat and fragmented. This prompts the question of what Dasein's identity over time consists in. However, this is also to say that the loss of identity that Dasein suffers in everyday life is never total.[59] Just as little as inauthenticity wipes out processuality, does it wipe out identity. Instead, what we find here and there is self-concealment: a covering up, Dasein standing in its own way as it tries to understand its Being out of a deficient mode of self-realization.

The thought that personal identity is concealed in inauthenticity rather than literally lost needs to be defended against two misunderstandings.

First, this thought does not entail that personal identity is a pseudo-problem. Inauthenticity is a real, in fact the default, mode of existence and so is inauthentic personal nonidentity. We cannot dismiss as merely illusory the lack of unity of experiences that raises the question of how they hang together. Instead, there is a real fact of the matter to be revealed about both the usual nonidentity of Dasein, as an ontic reality, and the underlying ontological structure of identity.

Second, this, ontologically speaking, primordial identity is not a primitive "deep further fact" as presupposed by contemporary Simple theories of personal identity. Recall the key claim of the existential analytic that Dasein's essence lies in its existence. Accordingly, all questions as to a positive explication of our identity through time are exclusively answered by the way we perform our existence. There is no identity—as a "deep further fact"—beyond the process of constantly bringing this identity about by projecting oneself into possibilities and thereby taking oneself over as what one has become. Dasein *per*-sists insofar as it *ek*-sists. Nor is Dasein's identity "primitive" in the sense that it could not be further analyzed—Heidegger's existential analysis of Dasein in terms of Being-in-the-world qua threefold transcendence-generating temporal process is just such an analysis.[60]

Still, it might be objected that Heidegger's process view of personal identity, as outlined so far, is not so different after all from a Simple View: Dasein is with respect to its existential identity just as things are with respect to their present-at-hand identity; it simply has its identity insofar as it exists. The reply to this is that, indeed, persistence is entailed in the existence of Dasein but exactly not as something that is simply given; assuming so would amount to tacitly equating "existence" with "being-present-at-hand" once again. Qua existential, Dasein's identity through time does not come for free.

The opposite is true. To exist, in the existential sense, means in one's Being to be concerned with this very Being; it means the struggle to actively maintain one's existence through an ongoing interaction with the world, most authentically, according to Heidegger, in the mode of anticipating, or "forerunning into," death (*Vorlaufen zum Tode*). The only thing here that is, as it were, "given" is the fact that Dasein is "thrown" into this struggle, the fact that Dasein, if it is to exist, does not have a choice about whether or not to struggle. However, this "facticity" "is not the *factum brutum* of something present-at-hand, but a characteristic of Dasein's Being which has been taken up into existence, even if mostly thrust aside."[61] Identity through time is hard won. It is exactly a sign of a lack of authenticity, should existence feel easy: Dasein tries to steal away from the challenge of existence, thus slipping into the deficient mode of personal nonidentity.

Dasein is a self-maintaining process, a process whose existence/persistence is dependent on its own efforts to maintain itself as the very process it is. Hence, we cannot but acknowledge the radical difference between the diachronic identity of a thing and the diachronic identity of Dasein. Dasein persists through time not in the sense that it—in one way or the other—happens to be present-at-hand at more than one point "in" time; its identity is neither reassembled from experiences as static discrete existents, nor is it the static identity of a "self-thing, persistingly present-at-hand" in the function of a frame or track for experiences.[62] Instead

> Dasein stretches *itself* along, such that in advance its own Being is constituted as stretching-along. The "between" with respect to birth and death lies already in the Being of Dasein.[63]

The ultimate ground of this primordial "stretching-along" is, of course, temporality. Whereas ordinary time maps discrete experiences onto discrete points in time, existential time—temporality—lacks a sequential structure. The three ecstases, future, having-been, and present, in the unity of which Dasein "temporalizes" itself, do not occur in succession but are aspects of a structured whole, by being the "horizons" in which Dasein as Being-in-the-world unfolds.[64] Therefore, when speaking with respect to Dasein of an identity "through time," we must keep away any associations of multiple occurrences at multiple points "in" time.[65] What we must rather think is a *holistic and intrinsically temporal* identity. Dasein exists and persists as a unified threefold dynamic process of bringing itself about—either authentically, that is, explicitly as what, or rather *who*, Dasein is, or in a deficient, inauthentic mode that conceals Dasein's own existential origin. In this latter case, in the inauthentic mode of existence, Dasein does not actually lapse into being a "self-thing" present-at-hand at different times. It just looks as if that were the case, whenever Dasein undertakes to interpret its own Being in the state of inauthenticity.[66]

While it may be challenging to prevent inauthentic self-identity from being confused with thing identity, the fundamental ontological difference between personal identity and thing identity is obvious in the authentic mode of Dasein's self-realization.[67] Heidegger characterizes the latter as a process of gaining "self-stability" (*Selbst-ständigkeit*), that is, as a process of interactive existential self-stabilization.[68] By anticipating death in the way Dasein interacts with the world, Dasein gains a standing in the world; it manages to "stand on its own feet" rather than being the passive victim of both the "They's" resolutions and the demands of the things it is concerned with.[69] Authentic Dasein is stable or "has a standing" "in the double sense of stable steadfastness (*beständige Standfestigkeit*)."[70]

This character of identity as being something that has to be achieved, in a constant fight against the inner tendency to flee from death and to let the "They" and the things take over, reveals the "gap ontologically separating the selfsameness of the authentically existing self from the identity of the 'I' that is supposed to persevere throughout the plurality of its experiences."[71] The stability of Dasein results from a process of self-stabilization rather than either being pre-given, as a mysterious deep further fact, or, else, being composed through the "adjoining of 'moments' one to another"; instead, these moments (the experiences) are themselves products of the process of self-stabilization, that is, they "arise from the temporality of the futurally-having-been-repetition (*zukünftig gewesende Wiederholung*) which is already stretched along."[72]

According to Heidegger, a comprehensive and satisfactory explanation of personal identity ultimately requires an investigation into the so-called historicality (*Geschichtlichkeit*) of Dasein, which is rooted in Dasein's temporality.[73] Things do not have a history but Dasein has—namely because of the specific way Dasein realizes or manifests time: coming-toward-itself from projected future possibilities, Dasein comes back to what it has been, that is, to its history; and only through this unified bidirectional movement, a present moment, with affordances for action, emerges. Dasein thus exists in a way that carries along its past—it "historizes."

This process of historizing, Heidegger emphasizes, cannot be mapped onto a succession of discrete moments of existence. Dasein, rather, "moves" in the sense of a "stretched-stretching-itself-along."[74] It is a "stretched stability" (*erstreckte Ständigkeit*), which in the mode of authentic historicality explicitly "incorporates in its existence birth and death and their 'between'" so as to embrace and enact the "world-historical" dimension of its respective "situation."[75] The common belief that birth and death are not "real" thus is revealed to be mistaken—mistaken because this belief rests upon the mistaken assumption that both Dasein and time are present-at-hand, that is, can be analyzed in thing-ontological terms. To acknowledge the historicality of Dasein means to acknowledge the existential status of birth and death as existing through and in Dasein's existence and, hence, to acknowledge Dasein as their dynamic and indivisible "between."[76]

Conclusions

In this chapter, I have presented an approach to personal identity that radically breaks with the idea that persons are things—an idea that has predominated traditional discourses on personal identity and is still prevalent today. Whether we were to follow the Complex View in conceiving of a person as a bundle or aggregate of discrete mental states occurring in time or the Simple View of personal identity in equating a person with a primitively self-identical substance outside of time, in each case would we have to accept that a person is something that does not need to change in order to exist. Change is construed *ex post* on the basis of the given identity of either a multiplicity of things or one simple thing, out of fear that change may otherwise undermine the person's identity.[77]

Heidegger's process approach, in contrast, sees change and time as sitting at the heart of what it is to be a person. This is why Heidegger prefers referring to persons as "Dasein"—to emphasize the absence of anything static and unchanging within the activity of existence or "Being-there." Dasein exists *through* and *as* the temporal process of interactively stabilizing itself as Being-in-the-world. Dasein *is* time—time organized into a dynamic whole structured by the three ecstases or horizons of the future, having-been, and present. As such, Dasein is intrinsically temporally extended. Being a person entails being self-identical through time—either genuinely ("authentically") in the sense of an existential stability that one explicitly achieves and maintains or, else, deficiently ("inauthentically") when one fails to make such explicit efforts. It is in this latter mode of self-realization that Dasein mistakes itself for a thing.

Heidegger's process metaphysics of personhood appears to offer a way out of the dilemma faced by the contemporary debate on personal identity. It provides us with a notion of personal identity that does not suffer from the weakness of continuity relations as invoked by the Complex View to *ex post* tie together separate experiences. As a fundamental-ontological relation that Dasein—qua being who is concerned in its Being with this Being—has with itself and has to enact in one way or another, personal identity, as presented by Heidegger, is robust without thereby lapsing into the uninformative primitiveness characteristic of the Simple View. The existential analysis also gives us a clear sense of the distinctive character of mineness involved, by showing a personal perspective to emerge from the transcendent, relational structure of existence.

However, this is not to say that Heidegger has solved the problem of personal identity and that we should endorse every single element of Heidegger's account.

What is certainly hard to swallow is its link with the doctrine of authenticity and inauthenticity, including the claim that substance or thing ontology is the symptom of an inauthentic way of life. The somewhat dubious character of Heidegger's ideal of authenticity has been widely criticized.[78] But what is more, some sort of confusion appears to be involved. It is true that the phenomenon of personality ought not to be excluded from metaphysical discourses about personal identity.[79] Yet, Heidegger's particular way of discussing the selfhood of Dasein that evokes associations with personality psychology remains irritating and threatens to weaken the ontological ambitions of his project to deconstruct Western (substance) metaphysics.[80]

A crucial aspect of this problem is Heidegger's idealism. To be sure, the "interaction with the world" that is supposed to be constitutive of the process of existential self-stabilization is fully immanent insofar as "world" as such, including the beings encountered "in" the world, is a characteristic of Dasein as Being-in-the-world. There is no "outside" of Dasein apart from the "outside" that is built into Dasein, that is, apart from the ecstatic horizons of existential time. According to Heidegger, Dasein needs to maintain itself as the process it is, as opposed to being simply given like a thing. However, whether or not Dasein succeeds in maintaining itself seems to depend on nothing but on Dasein's own efforts; Dasein's "fate" (*Schicksal*), to use Heidegger's problematic term, lies in Dasein's hands alone, in Dasein's "anticipatory resoluteness" (*vorlaufende Entschlossenheit*) to choose itself as what it is in the face of death.[81]

I think there is no alternative to releasing Dasein from its idealist immanence in order to find a home for it in the real world.[82] Insofar as we are concerned with *human* persons, this will involve talking about biology. Human persons are organisms, and organisms must interact with their environment in order to survive, most fundamentally through exchanging matter and energy. Ontologically, we find here the same basic structure that Heidegger has described for Dasein: a coincidence of existence and persistence. Organisms exist *as* the persisting processes of interactive self-stabilization; and they exist/persist as long as interactive self-stabilization can be maintained. But there is one important difference: the success of interactive self-stabilization depends on conditions that are only partly under the organism's control. Biological identity is a truly *inter*-active process in that it depends on interacting with something other than just itself:[83] an environment that is as real as the possibility, and finally facticity, of death.[84] It contains an element of genuine transcendence.[85]

Appreciating the ontological constitution of organisms as interactively self-stabilizing processes can serve as a basis for a comprehensive process theory of human persons.[86] Such a theory—let's call it "processual animalism"—would interpret the specifically personal aspects of our identity through time in terms of a self-stabilization through social interactions with other persons, which is fundamentally enabled by our processual-interactive biological nature. Put on a biological footing, Heidegger's process metaphysics of personhood may very well make a valuable contribution toward a satisfactory metaphysical account of personal identity.

Acknowledgments

I gratefully acknowledge funding from the Austrian Science Fund (FWF) under the Elise Richter funding scheme, grant agreement number V 714-G30 (grant holder: Anne Sophie Meincke). I am also indebted to the editors, Natan Elgabsi and Bennett Gilbert, and to Mark Sinclair for helpful feedback on earlier versons of this chapter.

Notes

1 See Anne Sophie Meincke, *Auf dem Kampfplatz der Metaphysik: Kritische Studien zur transtemporalen Identität von Personen* (Münster: Mentis, 2015), for a systematic presentation of the debate.

2 With different arguments I have myself advocated such a move, see Anne Sophie Meincke, "Persons as Biological Processes: A Bio-Processual Way-Out of the Personal Identity Dilemma," in *Everything Flows: Towards a Processual Philosophy of Biology*, ed. Daniel J. Nicholson and John Dupré (Oxford: Oxford University Press, 2018), 357–78; Anne Sophie Meincke, "Human Persons – A Process View," in *Was sind und wie existieren Personen?*, ed. Jörg Noller (Münster: Mentis, 2019), 57–80; and Anne Sophie Meincke, "Processual Animalism: Towards a Scientifically Informed Theory of Personal Identity," in *Biological Identity. Perspectives from Metaphysics and Philosophy of Biology*, ed. Anne Sophie Meincke and John Dupré (London: Routledge, 2020), 251–78.

3 Note that these are generic definitions that can possibly be satisfied by different kinds of beings—there can be different types of both things and processes. For example, things may be material or immaterial and primitive or composed of other things. They might be so-called substances; but thinghood might apply also to ontological categories traditionally distinguished from objects, such as states or events, depending on how these are conceptualized. The same goes for processes. There can be different kinds of processes: material, immaterial, simple, complex, living, nonliving, mechanical, volitional and so on. The claim that persons are things or processes, respectively, does not by itself commit one to either of these particular interpretations. There are different versions of both thing ontological and process ontological theories of personhood, just as there are different versions of thing ontology and process ontology *tout court*.

4 As we will see, Heidegger's critique actually targets thing ontology as a whole. Johanna Seibt laudably mentions Heidegger as making "an analytic-interpretive contribution to process philosophy." Johanna Seibt "Process Philosophy," in *The Stanford Encyclopedia of Philosophy* (Winter 2016 Edition), ed. Edward N. Zalta. Heidegger is also included in *The Oxford Handbook of Process Philosophy and Organizational Studies*, ed. Jenny Helin, Tor Hernes, Daniel Hjort and Robin Holt (Oxford: Oxford University Press, 2014). But these are exceptions. The common neglect of Heidegger's process metaphysical leanings is partly due to the fact that *Being and Time* remained a fragment. As a result, we know far more about what Heidegger thought is wrong with substance metaphysics than about what he thought should take its place: a processual approach not only to understanding the Being of the person but also to understanding Being as such.

5 Martin Heidegger, *Being and Time*, trans. John Macquarrie and Edward Robinson (Malden: Blackwell, 1962), based on *Sein und Zeit*, 18th ed. (Tübingen: Niemeyer, 2001). English quotations from Heidegger's works are mostly my own translations. If not stated otherwise, emphases in quotations appear as in the original text. I follow the convention among (the majority of) English-speaking Heidegger scholars to capitalize the Being of beings as distinguished from these beings (according to what Heidegger calls the "ontological difference," see *Die Grundprobleme der Phänomenologie, Gesamtausgabe Volume 24* (Frankfurt on the Main: Vittorio Klostermann, 1975), 109; *The Basic Problems of Phenomenology*, trans. Albert Hofstadter (Bloomington and Indianapolis: Indiana University Press, 1988), 78).

6 See, for instance, Matthew Ratcliffe, "Heidegger, Analytic Metaphysics, and the Being of Beings," *Inquiry* 45, no. 1 (2002): 35–58; and Georg W. Bertram, "Die Einheit des Selbst nach Heidegger," *Deutsche Zeitschrift für Philosophie* 61, no. 2 (2013): 197–213. Exceptions are Stephan Käufer, "Heidegger on Existentiality, Constancy and the Self," *Inquiry* 55, no. 5 (2012): 454–72; and Tony Fisher, "Heidegger and the Narrativity Debate," *Continental Philosophy Review* 43, no. 2 (2010): 241–65.

7 Heidegger, *Sein und Zeit*, 46ff. and 114–5; *Being and Time*, 72ff. and 150.
8 John Haugeland interprets Heidegger's theory of Dasein as a theory of person, however, in pragmatist terms and without paying special attention to diachronic identity. John Haugeland, "Heidegger on Being a Person," *Noûs* 16, no. 1 (1982): 15–26.
9 Heidegger, *Sein und Zeit*, 50 and 43; *Being and Time*, 76 and 67.
10 Heidegger, *Sein und Zeit*, 42; *Being and Time*, 67.
11 Heidegger, *Sein und Zeit*, 12; *Being and Time*, 32.
12 Heidegger, *Sein und Zeit*, 12; *Being and Time*, 32.
13 Heidegger, *Sein und Zeit*, 42; *Being and Time*, 67–8.
14 Heidegger, *Sein und Zeit*, 45; *Being and Time*, 71.
15 "When addressing Dasein, because of its character of in-each-case-being-mine, one has to use the *personal* pronoun: 'I am', 'you are.'" Heidegger, *Sein und Zeit*, 42; *Being and Time*, 68.
16 Heidegger, *Sein und Zeit*, 46ff. and 114–5; *Being and Time*, 72ff. and 150.
17 Heidegger, *Sein und Zeit*, 47; *Being and Time*, 73.
18 Heidegger, *Sein und Zeit*, 42; *Being and Time*, 67.
19 Heidegger, *Sein und Zeit*, 44; *Being and Time*, 70. The term "categories" refers to Kant's concept of categories, developed in his *Critique of Pure Reason*. Heidegger's theory of Dasein emerges from a critical engagement with Kant, amounting to an ontological (re)interpretation of Kant's transcendental Ego. See Meincke, *Auf dem Kampfplatz*, chapter 3.3.2.
20 Heidegger, *Sein und Zeit*, 53; *Being and Time*, 78.
21 Heidegger, *Sein und Zeit*, §26.
22 "World is understood beforehand when objects encounter us," and understanding world as such a "horizon" for the understanding of the Being of beings other than Dasein belongs to Dasein's existential structure. Heidegger, *Grundprobleme*, 424; *Basic Problems*, 299.
23 Heidegger speaks of a "reflection (*Rückstrahlung*) of the understanding of world onto the interpretation of Dasein." Heidegger, *Sein und Zeit*, 16; *Being and Time*, 36–7; see also Heidegger, *Sein und Zeit*, 21; *Being and Time*, 42.
24 Heidegger, *Sein und Zeit*, 60; *Being and Time*, 87.
25 "The *selfhood* of Dasein *is founded on its transcendence*," thus turning upside down the traditional doctrine that the "objects" of knowledge are "transcendent" by lying outside the "subject" that perceives them. Heidegger, *Grundprobleme*, 425; *Basic Problems*, 300.
26 Heidegger, *Sein und Zeit*, 145; *Being and Time*, 185–6.
27 Heidegger, *Sein und Zeit*, 134–5; *Being and Time*, 173–4.
28 Heidegger, *Sein und Zeit*, 178; *Being and Time*, 22.
29 For an in-depth discussion of Heidegger's well-known concept of Being-toward-death, see my article Anne Sophie Spann, "Endlichkeit ohne Unendlichkeit? Heideggers 'Wegkreuzung' mit Hegel im 'Seinsproblem,'" *Philosophisches Jahrbuch* 119 (2012): 283–316.
30 Heidegger, *Sein und Zeit*, §53 and §27.
31 Heidegger, *Sein und Zeit*, 130; *Being and Time*, 168.
32 Heidegger, *Sein und Zeit*, 158; *Being and Time*, 201.
33 "... we shall show that time is that from where Dasein tacitly understands and interprets something like Being" (*Sein und Zeit*, 17; *Being and Time*, 39).
34 Heidegger, *Sein und Zeit*, Division 1, chapter 6.

35 Heidegger, *Sein und Zeit*, 327; *Being and Time*, 375. Heidegger on purpose does not call the second ecstasis the "past" because "'[a]s long as' Dasein factically exists, it is never past; instead it has always already been in the sense of 'I am-having-been.' And it *can* only *be*-having-*been* as long as it *is*" (*Sein und Zeit*, 328; *Being and Time*, 376).
36 Heidegger, *Sein und Zeit*, 192; *Being and Time*, 237, and § 65. For comprehensive analyses of Heidegger's early concept of temporality, see Marion Heinz, *Zeitlichkeit und Temporalität: Die Konstitution der Existenz und die Grundlegung einer temporalen Ontologie im Frühwerk Martin Heideggers* (Amsterdam: Rodopi, 1982); William D. Blattner, *Heidegger's Temporal Idealism* (Cambridge: Cambridge University Press, 1999); and Heath Massey, *The Origin of Time: Heidegger and Bergson* (Albany: State University of New York Press, 2015).
37 Heidegger, *Grundprobleme*, 377; *Basic Problems*, 266–7.
38 Heidegger, *Sein und Zeit*, 329; *Being and Time*, 377. See also *Grundprobleme*, 377; *Basic Problems*, 266–7: "Temporality as unity of future, having-been-ness and present does not carry Dasein away just at times and occasionally; instead, as *temporality*, it is itself *the original outside-itself*, the ekstatikon."
39 Heidegger, *Sein und Zeit*, 411ff.; *Being and Time*, 464ff.
40 Heidegger, *Sein und Zeit*, 420ff.; *Being and Time*, 472ff. See Spann, "Endlichkeit ohne Unendlichkeit?" for a more detailed discussion.
41 Heidegger, *Sein und Zeit*, 424ff.; *Being and Time*, 477–8. Nature is itself a privative derivative of world; see *Sein und Zeit*, 65; *Being and Time*, 93.
42 Heidegger, *Sein und Zeit*, 25; *Being and Time*, 47; see also §69, in particular b. In the function as a "horizontal schema" of "enpresenting" (*Sein und Zeit*, 365; *Being and Time*, 416) Heidegger calls the ecstasis of the present "praesens" (*Praesenz*); see *Grundprobleme*, §21 a. Future, with death being the ultimate future possibility, has the priority within the holistic threefold structure of Dasein's Being because it most fundamentally constitutes Dasein's existentiality. See *Sein und Zeit*, 329; *Being and Time*, 378.
43 This also explains the primacy of space or spatial categories in the theoretical articulation and interpretation of meaning; see Heidegger, *Sein und Zeit*, 369; *Being and Time*, 421.
44 Heidegger, *Sein und Zeit*, 323; *Being and Time*, 425.
45 Heidegger, *Sein und Zeit*, 374; *Being and Time*, 426.
46 Meincke, "Persons as Biological Processes" and "Processual Animalism."
47 Derek Parfit, *Reasons and Persons* (Oxford: Clarendon Press, 1987), for example, 215 and 279.
48 David K. Lewis, "Survival and Identity," and "Postscripts to 'Survival and Identity,'" in *Philosophical Papers: Volume I* (New York: Oxford University Press, 1983), 55–73 and 73–7. The components (also known as "temporal parts") of the person qua aggregate cannot themselves undergo change if the "problem of temporary intrinsics" (see note 50 below) is not to repeat itself for them.
49 Eternalism contrasts with so-called presentism, according to which only present things exist. Presentism is accused of rendering persistence impossible—a criticism reminiscent of Heidegger's abovementioned observation that experiences seem "real," in the presumed sense of being present-at-hand, only in the respective "now." See David K. Lewis, *On the Plurality of Worlds* (Oxford: Blackwell, 1986), 204.
50 According to Lewis, something "perdures" if it persists "by having different temporal parts, or stages, at different times, though no one part of it is wholly present at more than one time" (Lewis, *Plurality of Worlds*, 202). The perdurance theory of persistence

is meant to solve the so-called "problem of temporary intrinsics," that is, the apparent contradiction that numerical identity, according to Leibniz's Law, implies identity of intrinsic properties but change implies difference in intrinsic properties (*Plurality of Worlds*, 203–4). Attributing the different properties to the different temporal parts of a persisting thing, the perdurantist claims, avoids the contradiction. However, perdurantism *de facto* eliminates both change and identity through time. See Anne Sophie Meincke, "The Disappearance of Change: Towards a Process Account of Persistence," *International Journal of Philosophical Studies* 27, no. 1 (2019): 12–30.

51 Heidegger, *Sein und Zeit*, 204 and 321.
52 As Lewis (*Plurality of Worlds*, 202) defines, to persist by "enduring" is to persist "by being wholly present at more than one time." The two alternative ways of time-indexing constitute the difference between so-called relationalist and adverbialist versions of endurantism. See Meincke, "Disappearance of Change," for a critical discussion of endurantism.
53 This corresponds with Kant's conception of an "inner sense" of time, which, qua pure form of intuition, cannot itself be in time; see *Sein und Zeit*, 204; *Being and Time*, 248; and the discussion in Meincke, *Auf dem Kampfplatz*, 272ff.
54 Heidegger, *Sein und Zeit*, 390; *Being and Time*, 442.
55 "It is possible that Dasein, when addressing itself most closely, always says: It's me, and actually the loudest, when it is 'not' this being." Heidegger, *Sein und Zeit*, 115; *Being and Time*, 151.
56 Heidegger, *Sein und Zeit*, 390; *Being and Time*, 442.
57 Heidegger, *Sein und Zeit*, 44; *Being and Time*, 69.
58 Heidegger, *Sein und Zeit*, 389; *Being and Time*, 441.
59 See also Käufer, "Heidegger on Existentiality."
60 Key concepts of Heidegger's analysis apart from those I am able to discuss here are "mood" (*Befindlichkeit*), "understanding" (*Verstehen*), "care" (*Sorge*), "guilt" (*Schuld*), "call of conscience" (*Ruf des Gewissens*), "projection" (*Entwurf*), and "disclosedness" (*Erschlossenheit*).
61 Heidegger, *Sein und Zeit*, 135; *Being and Time*, 174.
62 Heidegger, *Sein und Zeit*, 374 and 323; *Being and Time*, 426 and 370. "Dasein does not exist as the sum of the momentary actualities of experiences which come along successively and disappear. Neither does this succession gradually fill up a framework." Dasein does not "fill . . . up a track or stretch 'of life'—one which is somehow present-at-hand—with the phases of its momentary actualities" (*Sein und Zeit*, 374; *Being and Time*, 426).
63 Heidegger, *Sein und Zeit*, 374; *Being and Time*, 426.
64 "Temporalizing does not signify that ecstases come in a 'succession'. The future is *not later* than having been, and having been is *not earlier* than the Present. Temporality temporalizes itself as a future which makes present in the process of having been" (*Sein und Zeit*, 350; *Being and Time*, 401).
65 Compare Lewis's supposedly neutral definition of persistence according to which something persists if it "exists at various times." Lewis, *Plurality of Worlds*, 202.
66 This includes the widely assumed simple and formal character of the self: "For the absorption in the everyday multiplicity and rapid succession of concerns, the Self of the self-forgetful 'I-am-concerned' shows itself as something simple, being constantly the same but indefinite-empty, given that one *is what* one is concerned with" (*Sein und Zeit*, 322; *Being and Time*, 368).

67 "If already the Being of everyday Being-with-one-another, which seems to come close ontologically to pure presence-at-hand, actually is different in principle from the latter, still less can the Being of the authentic self be conceived as presence-at-hand" (*Sein und Zeit*, 130; *Being and Time*, 168). For some doubts as to how radical the difference between Dasein's authentic self-stability and the self-identity of substances really is, see my article Anne Sophie Spann, "Substanz, Relation oder beides? Augustinus und Heidegger zur Frage 'Was sind Personen?,'" in *Crossing Borders, Grenzen (über) denken*, ed. Alfred Dunshirn, Elisabeth Nemeth and Gerhard Unterthurner (Vienna: Österreichische Gesellschaft für Philosophie, 2012), 839–55, and note 85 below.

68 The German term *Selbst-ständigkeit* is commonly translated as "self-constancy." However, this translation obscures the connotation of being something achieved through effort and activity. Macquarrie and Robinson suggest "stability" as a more accurate translation; see *Being and Time*, 369n1.

69 Heidegger refers to this deficient mode of identity through time as "Nonself-stability" (*Unselbst-ständigkeit*) or "in-stability" (*Un-ständigkeit*). Heidegger, *Sein und Zeit*, 322 and 390; *Being and Time*, 369 and 442.

70 Heidegger, *Sein und Zeit*, 322; *Being and Time*, 369.

71 Heidegger, *Sein und Zeit*, 130; *Being and Time*, 168.

72 Heidegger, *Sein und Zeit*, 391; *Being and Time*, 443.

73 "The question of Dasein's 'connectedness' is the ontological problem of its historizing" (*Sein und Zeit*, 391; *Being and Time*, 427).

74 Heidegger, *Sein und Zeit*, 374–5.; *Being and Time*, 447. Heidegger's idea of an indivisible intrinsic temporal extendedness bears strong resemblance to Henri Bergson's notion of duration (and so do Heidegger's concepts of "authenticity" and "inauthenticity" to Bergson's two aspects of the self, the "profound" and the "superficial" self). See Anne Sophie Meincke, "Bergson and Process Philosophy of Biology," in *The Bergsonian Mind*, ed. Mark Sinclair and Yaron Wolf (London: Routledge, 2021), 432–45, on Bergson's concept of duration; Meincke, *Auf dem Kampfplatz*, chapter 3.3.3, on Bergson's view of personal identity; and see Massey, *Origin of Time*, on the relation between Heidegger's and Bergson's concepts of time.

75 Heidegger, *Sein und Zeit*, 390; *Being and Time*, 442.

76 "Factical Dasein exists in the mode of being born, and in the mode of being born it is already dying in the sense of Being-towards-death. Both 'ends' and their 'between' *exist* as long Dasein factically exists, and they *exist* in the only way possible given the Being of Dasein as *care*. In the unity of thrownness and fleeing or forerunning Being-towards-death, birth and death 'hang together' in the characteristic Dasein-way. As care, Dasein *is* the 'between'" (*Sein und Zeit*, 374; *Being and Time*, 426–7).

77 The idea that change is logically incompatible with identity and, therefore, has to be constrained or eliminated altogether runs deep through the history of Western metaphysics; see Meincke, "Disappearance of Change," and Meincke, "Persons as Biological Processes."

78 For a paradigmatic and influential criticism, see Theodor W. Adorno, *The Jargon of Authenticity*, trans. Knut Tarnowski and Frederic Will (London: Routledge and Kegan Paul, 1973).

79 Anne Sophie Meincke, "Personale Identität ohne Persönlichkeit? Anmerkungen zu einem vernachlässigten Zusammenhang," *Philosophisches Jahrbuch* 123 (2016): 114–45, and Anne Sophie Spann, "Persönlichkeit und personale Identität: Zur Fragwürdigkeit eines substanztheoretischen Vorurteils," in *Persönlichkeit:*

Neurowissenschaftliche und neurophilosophische Fragestellungen, ed. Orsolya Friedrich and Michael Zichy (Münster: Mentis, 2014), 163–87.

80 Narrativist misreadings according to which Heidegger's theory of Dasein merely concerns the narrative organization of beliefs, values, and norms into a coherent life story testify to this. For a general critique of narrativist approaches to the problem of personal identity, see Anne Sophie Spann, "Ohne Metaphysik, bitte!? Transtemporale personale Identität als praktische Wirklichkeit," in *Personale Identität, Narrativität und praktische Rationalität*, ed. Georg Gasser and Martina Schmidhuber (Münster: Mentis, 2013), 241–65.

81 Heidegger, *Sein und Zeit*, 384ff.; *Being and Time*, 435ff.; and §62. Heidegger construes authenticity formally as explicating the implicit, that is, inauthentically concealed, existential structure of Dasein—a process that involves the meta-choice of choosing to choose oneself (*Sein und Zeit*, 268; *Being and Time*, 312–3).

82 In Adorno's words: There is no alternative to "break[ing] through the deception of constitutive subjectivity." Theodor W. Adorno, *Negative Dialectics*, trans. Ernst B. Ashton (New York: Seabury Press, 1973), xx.

83 Anne Sophie Meincke, "Autopoiesis, Biological Autonomy and the Process View of Life," *European Journal for Philosophy of Science* 9, article 5 (2019).

84 Contrary to its rhetoric, Heidegger's famous doctrine of the "Being-towards-death" neutralizes death to the extent that it fails to take death seriously as a biological fact; see Spann, "Endlichkeit ohne Unendlichkeit?"

85 In fact, Dasein's existential immanence that conceals Dasein's ontological dependence could appear as a remnant of the very idea of a substance that Heidegger intends to criticize; see Spann, "Substanz, Relation oder beides?"

86 Meincke, "Persons as Biological Processes"; Meincke, "Human Persons", Meincke, "Processual Animalism"; and Anne Sophie Meincke, "Biological Subjectivity. Processual Animalism as a Unified Account of Personal Identity," in *The Unity of a Person: Philosophical Perspectives*, ed. Jörg Noller (Routledge: London, 2021), 100–26.

Bibliography

Adorno, Theodor W. *The Jargon of Authenticity*. Translated by K. Tarnowski and F. Will. London: Routledge and Kegan Paul, 1973.

Adorno, Theodor W. *Negative Dialectics*. Translated by E. B. Ashton. New York: Seabury Press, 1973.

Bertram, Georg W. "Die Einheit des Selbst nach Heidegger." *Deutsche Zeitschrift für Philosophie* 61, no. 2 (2013): 197–213.

Blattner, William D. *Heidegger's Temporal Idealism*. Cambridge: Cambridge University Press, 1999.

Fisher, Tony. "Heidegger and the Narrativity Debate." *Continental Philosophy Review* 43, no. 2 (2010): 241–65.

Haugeland, John. "Heidegger on Being a Person." *Noûs* 16, no. 1 (1982): 15–26.

Heidegger, Martin. *The Basic Problems of Phenomenology*. Translated by Albert Hofstadter. Bloomington and Indianapolis: Indiana University Press, 1988.

Heidegger, Martin. *Being and Time*. Translated by John Macquarrie and Edward Robinson. Malden: Blackwell, 1962.

Heidegger, Martin. *Die Grundprobleme der Phänomenologie, Gesamtausgabe Volume 24.* Frankfurt on the Main: Vittorio Klostermann, 1975.
Heidegger, Martin. *Sein und Zeit.* 18th ed. Tübingen: Niemeyer, 2001.
Heinz, Marion. *Zeitlichkeit und Temporalität: Die Konstitution der Existenz und die Grundlegung einer temporalen Ontologie im Frühwerk Martin Heideggers.* Amsterdam: Rodopi, 1982.
Helin, Jenny, Tor Hernes, Daniel Hjort, and Robin Holt, ed. *The Oxford Handbook of Process Philosophy and Organizational Studies.* Oxford: Oxford University Press, 2014.
Käufer, Stephan. "Heidegger on Existentiality, Constancy and the Self." *Inquiry* 55, no. 5 (2012): 454–72.
Lewis, David K. *Philosophical Papers: Volume I.* New York: Oxford University Press, 1983.
Lewis, David K. *On the Plurality of Worlds.* Oxford: Blackwell, 1986.
Massey, Heath. *The Origin of Time: Heidegger and Bergson.* Albany: State University of New York Press, 2015.
Meincke, Anne Sophie. *Auf dem Kampfplatz der Metaphysik: Kritische Studien zur transtemporalen Identität von Personen.* Münster: Mentis, 2015.
Meincke, Anne Sophie. "Personale Identität ohne Persönlichkeit? Anmerkungen zu einem vernachlässigten Zusammenhang." *Philosophisches Jahrbuch* 123 (2016): 114–45.
Meincke, Anne Sophie. "Persons as Biological Processes: A Bio-Processual Way-Out of the Personal Identity Dilemma." In *Everything Flows: Towards a Processual Philosophy of Biology*, edited by Daniel Nicholson and John Dupré, 357–78. Oxford: Oxford University Press, 2018.
Meincke, Anne Sophie. "Autopoiesis, Biological Autonomy, and the Process View of Life". *European Journal for Philosophy of Science* 9, article 5 (2019), https://doi.org/10.1007/s13194-018-0228-2.
Meincke, Anne Sophie. "The Disappearance of Change: Towards a Process Account of Persistence." *International Journal of Philosophical Studies* 27, no. 1 (2019): 12–30.
Meincke, Anne Sophie. "Human Persons—A Process View." In *Was sind und wie existieren Personen? Probleme und Perspektiven der gegenwärtigen Forschung*, edited by Jörg Noller, 57–80. Münster: Mentis, 2019.
Meincke, Anne Sophie. "Processual Animalism: Towards a Scientifically Informed Theory of Personal Identity." In *Biological Identity: Perspectives from Metaphysics and the Philosophy of Biology*, edited by Anne Sophie Meincke and John Dupré, 251–78. London: Routledge, 2020.
Meincke, Anne Sophie. "Bergson and Process Philosophy of Biology." In *The Bergsonian Mind*, edited by Mark Sinclair and Yaron Wolf, 432–45. London: Routledge, 2021.
Meincke, Anne Sophie. "Biological Subjectivity: Processual Animalism as a Unified Theory of Personal Identity." In *The Unity of a Person: Philosophical Perspectives*, edited by Jörg Noller, 100–26. London: Routledge, 2021.
Parfit, Derek. *Reasons and Persons.* Oxford: Clarendon Press, 1987.
Ratcliffe, Matthew. "Heidegger, Analytic Metaphysics, and the Being of Beings." *Inquiry* 45, no. 1 (2002): 35–58.
Seibt, Johanna. "Process Philosophy." In *The Stanford Encyclopedia of Philosophy* (Winter 2016 Edition), edited by E. N. Zalta.
Spann (née Meincke), Anne Sophie. "Endlichkeit ohne Unendlichkeit? Heideggers 'Wegkreuzung' mit Hegel im 'Seinsproblem.'" *Philosophisches Jahrbuch* 119 (2012): 283–316.

Spann (née Meincke), Anne Sophie. "Substanz, Relation oder beides? Augustinus und Heidegger zur Frage "Was sind Personen?"" In *Crossing Borders, Grenzen (über) denken*, edited by Alfred Dunshirn, Elisabeth Nemeth and Gerhard Unterthurner, 839–55. Vienna: Österreichische Gesellschaft für Philosophie, 2012. https://fedora.phaidra.univie.ac.at/fedora/get/o:128384/bdef:Content/get

Spann (née Meincke), Anne Sophie. "Ohne Metaphysik, bitte!? Transtemporale personale Identität als praktische Wirklichkeit." In *Personale Identität, Narrativität und praktische Rationalität*, edited by Georg Gasser and Martina Schmidhuber, 241–65. Münster: Mentis, 2013.

Spann (née Meincke), Anne Sophie. "Persönlichkeit und personale Identität: Zur Fragwürdigkeit eines substanztheoretischen Vorurteils." In *Persönlichkeit: Neurowissenschaftliche und neurophilosophische Fragestellungen*, edited by Orsolya Friedrich and Michael Zichy, 163–87. Münster: Mentis, 2014.

Section IV

Reconsidering Ontology

11

"When the Time Is Right..." In the Māori World

Georgina Tuari Stewart

He Poroporoaki (In Memoriam)
I wish to acknowledge the contribution to this work made by the thinking of Charles W. Mills, who passed on 20 September 2021, while the chapter was in preparation.
—Haere rā, e te rangatira (Farewell, esteemed leader).

Introduction

"Ethics" and "time" are two powerful ideas to put in conversation with each other in any cultural context. Ethics and time are universal ideas in the sense of transcending ethnic cultures since all humans constantly experience the grinding inevitability of the passage of time over the span of a day, a year, a life; and everyone faces ethical dilemmas over the course of their lifetime—moments of agency in which their choices reflect their personal, ethical values, based on their particular subjectivity and sense of self in the world. I write this chapter as a person from a cultural group (Māori) that has been subjected to more than two hundred years of assimilatory political and economic power—a process that has involved the destruction and denial of Māori difference at material, linguistic, and philosophical levels. A central catalyst in my work is the Māori-Pākehā cultural binary represented by Te Tiriti o Waitangi (the Treaty of Waitangi in 1840), accepted as the founding document of the nation-state of Aotearoa New Zealand. The document literally represents the Māori-Pākehā cultural binary in that the two versions, English and Te Reo, vary in some details significant enough to support a claim that they are not translations of each other but two different documents. This cultural relationship warrants being called a "binary" from a Māori perspective to describe how things have been since the British invasion of Aotearoa and creation of New Zealand, as captured by the commonly reported Māori experience of "living in two worlds." Māori identity is a "real," that is, either-or binary, concept because fundamentally a person either has whakapapa (descent lines, see below for explanation) or not: one can either claim to be Māori or not. Being Māori is a group identity, not one based on personal choices.

Te reo Māori, the Māori language, forms a second "natural" linguistic binary with English as the two natural languages representing the founding national cultural binary. Te reo Māori has undergone revival since the 1980s as a result of (among other things) immersion language education, at early childhood, schools and tertiary levels, and is currently enjoying more support than ever among the general public, although a backlash is evident on talkback radio and social media. Māori words are not italicized but treated as normal text in this chapter, a writing practice that aligns with Kaupapa Māori principles, in which te reo Māori is considered to be normal. This approach is practical given the large number of Māori words in the text, some of which are considered part of New Zealand English, and in keeping with the status of te reo Māori as an official language of Aotearoa New Zealand. It also follows the central tenet of sociolinguistics "that the normalization of minority languages within the public domain is a legitimate and defensible sociological, political and linguistic activity."[1]

Māori have been subjected to hierarchical binaries for many generations, so from a Māori perspective there is much to be gained from reversing the yardstick of comparison as a kind of thought experiment, while remaining on guard against the traps of reification and simplistic thinking. This approach is part of decolonial thinking: inspecting the old Eurocentric notions, inverting them where useful, and/or discarding them altogether. Other apparent binaries can be rethought as two ends of a continuum of positions.

Māori philosophy is a result of identifying as Māori at basic fundamental levels dealing with philosophical questions. It is an assertion of Māori philosophical rights to think Māori, to think as a Māori, and to think with Māori cognitive resources. This work begins from seeing Indigenous/Māori knowledge as having educational potential for Western culture and philosophy and digs into Māori concepts of time and ethics in efforts to add substance to that thought and assist in furthering that potential. The "digging" involves careful conceptual unpacking and analysis of relevant ideas from both Māori and Western traditions, each in their own terms as much as possible.

I approach this work in the spirit of "working the hyphens" between Māori (Indigenous) and Pākehā (Western) thinking about how the world works.[2] By this I mean that in thinking about a particular concept or scenario, I will consider dominant ideas related to that concept in both Māori and Pākehā terms. This process inevitably involves oversimplifying, which I will mitigate by maintaining awareness that such comparisons are inevitably relative, not absolute. For example, a certain view may be stronger in a Māori worldview than in a Pākehā worldview, but this does not mean that the two views are mutually exclusive. My comparisons of the two worldviews pursued below are from the perspective of being Māori in Aotearoa New Zealand, writing about dominant Pākehā views and Māori-Pākehā comparisons, and seeing these as *partially* representative of more general Indigenous-Western patterns of difference but with awareness of the limited and partial nature of this comparison. A disclaimer is that I *am* more interested in differences than similarities, so my analyses may sound unbalanced, though I am actually trying to convey a Māori-centered point of view, not an anti-Pākehā/Western one. It is understandably difficult to avoid conveying a certain principled anger when writing as a Māori about the annihilation of Māori philosophy that has been a strong, though unnamed, force in the national history of New Zealand. It is a Māori naming of the process by which critical discourse analysis proceeds to deconstruct and work, from a Māori perspective, with the binaries of identity noted above.

This work aligns with Kaupapa Māori research and theory because it is Māori-centered or "Māori-centric" and engages as Māori with both the Māori world/content and the Pākehā or wider world/content. I aim to bring my Māori identity forward more strongly into my work, to contribute to Kaupapa Māori understood as an academic tradition of scholarship and research written from Indigenous/Māori perspectives. Generally speaking, the binary concept carries baggage and is outmoded in the social sciences, but (1) my focus on reading for difference against an overwhelming history of assimilation inevitably at times requires use of two complementary categories as a strategic essentialism for the purposes of comparison, and (2) many scientific studies of the Māori world characterize its nature as one of dualities, or complementary opposites.

Since a natural language encapsulates its cultural philosophy, te reo Māori is the best resource for understanding Māori knowledge and thinking. Leading contemporary New Zealand anthropologist Anne Salmond follows this logic to delineate te ao Māori using a semantic approach, in which "the Māori language itself is the main line of evidence, rather than reports by European observers as to how they viewed Māori custom."[3] The Māori world is profoundly metaphoric: in te reo Māori almost every lexical word can be used at many levels—literal, metaphorical, and philosophical. Salmond depicts a Māori cosmos structured by foundational oppositions or poles (pou), formed by pairs of attributes including ora/mate (life/death), tapu/noa (restricted/unrestricted), ao/pō (day/night), and many others.[4] These dualities are like dipoles in my original metaphor from chemistry, referring to the dynamic separation of electric charge (electron location) in an overall neutral molecule. The dipolar metaphor captures the sense of two complementary opposites that are separated yet joined and that neutralize each other's energies. The next section gives more detail about these pairs of attributes, but important to note here is the notion of "balance" or utu that relates to keeping all the dualities balanced and in equilibrium. Utu is a good example of the distorting effect of translating individualized Indigenous concepts into English, its meaning reduced and equated to the English-language concept of "revenge" at the expense of the more interesting and philosophically richer idea of "balance."

These ideas from te reo Māori (the language) about te ao Māori (the worldview) stand apart from standard science models of reality but are interesting in their difference, and in how they complicate and entangle notions that in the English language are seen as distinct. The point is that profound Māori concepts cannot adequately be explained within Pākehā/Western frameworks. All too often, Māori concepts are presented in academic literature in lists or in other ways that isolate them from each other, as if they are equivalent and separate, like marbles in a bag. These kinds of practices are visible in the current craze to include te reo Māori in a wide range of state and corporate discourses and policies.

All humans live in one physical world, on this one planet: we are all subject to the same natural and social forces that determine the context in which we live our lives. In contemporary Aotearoa New Zealand, "living in two worlds" means living in different segments of society—a brute economic fact reflecting the statistical division of wealth along ethnic lines. The feeling of living in two worlds is also a matter of living with two worldviews: living across the threshold between te ao Māori and te ao Pākehā. The concept of "worldview" is understood as a personal–cultural philosophical paradigm. The human world is in part a symbolic world, in which our direct experience of the world is mediated through language and the cultural narratives with which we identify. Te ao Māori, in addition to its manifestation in the lives of Māori people, is also a symbolic world that exists in te reo Māori, in Māori histories, and as represented in books and other written material and imagery, and understood as referring to a Māori worldview.

The Māori language reveals how Māori thinking is oriented to time and space: the phrase "i mua" means "before" in both senses: past time and in front of us. The paired phrase is "i muri," which means both after in time and behind us. In Māori thinking, the past is in front of us because we can see it; we walk backward into the future since we cannot look and see what it will bring. This orientation to the world encourages us to reflect on and learn from the past, including ancestor models of virtues and right action. Of course there is far more to comparing different cultural ideas of the past and future, but here I am interested in how this basic language for the orientation of a person (in front and behind of) maps differently to time in English (where one "faces the future" and the past is "behind us") and Māori, given the clues in language about worldview or cultural ontology, in the sense of a characteristic Māori model of reality.

Besides many linguistic differences in alphabets, verbal structures, and so forth, the incommensurate nature of the differences between Māori and Pākehā worldviews greatly contributes to the difficulties of Māori-English translations. Differences between worldviews are philosophical rather than strictly linguistic, which explains why word-for-word translations of central or "big" concepts fail, for example, the Māori value concepts of tika, pono, and aroha.[5] To adequately convey philosophical ideas when translating between incommensurate philosophies (carried by natural languages) requires the use of paragraphs rather than single word or phrase translations, which are truncated and partial at best.

Translations of Māori ideas are not only inadequate but also often deliberately and systematically distorted. Buried below the surface of "fair go" egalitarian New Zealand attitudes toward Māori language, culture and philosophies are the same racist ideas and "absences" (amnesias, blind spots) employed around the world in the White colonizing processes since the Age of Discovery began, over five centuries ago.[6] Translation is an inherently political activity, reflecting the particular social power dynamics of each context, but such considerations are swept aside in the current national craze for including te reo Māori in the public life of Aotearoa New Zealand (and the resultant racist backlash). The knowledge and language questions involved in these changes are complex and deserve close consideration. The work undertaken in this chapter has relevance to the current efforts to include Māori language and knowledge in the school curriculum and the role and possible effects of translating curriculum materials into Māori.

Salmond discusses these points: (1) the incommensurability between Māori and Western worldviews and (2) the tendency for Western scholarship to produce ideological distortions of Māori thought, with negative effects for Māori.[7] A natural language such as Māori encapsulates its cultural philosophy in its words and patterns; the example of Māori orientation to past and future shows how Indigenous thought can be radically different or opposite to today's dominant ideas.

Below, I sketch these two big ideas, ethics and time, as well as the links between them and how they operate in the life of a Māori person, within an overall framework of Māori thought and philosophy.[8] In my lifetime I have personally experienced the effects of assimilation: as an individual who could choose to "pass" as Pākehā or non-Māori, I have lived with the pressure to do so. These experiences fuel my interest in asserting and upholding the right of Māori to "be" different, including at the level of ruling narratives to live by, which connects to both psychology and philosophy. In the process, I will discuss interesting differences between Māori and Western worldviews, using the conceptual tools of chronopolitics applied to my local, Māori situation.[9] The next section sketches a model of the Māori symbolic world, or te ao Māori, which is then used as a context for describing ethics and time from a Māori-centric point of view. How does a fundamental idea, such as the "opposite" orientation to past and future, draw Māori philosophical thought and ethics in a particular direction?

To conclude this section I present below a brief original vignette, which inspires the title of this chapter and uses the short story genre to confront the reader with the depths of intercultural incommensurability experienced in everyday Māori life, in such banal details as the size of fish to eat for lunch. In simple terms such as "cuzzie," "the old house," and "Tangaroa," it paints a thumbnail sketch of Māori life and thought that recognizes, yet stands apart from, the dominant national norms.

"Come and Get It!"

As I slid into my seat and looked at my lunch, my heart gave a small lurch at the sight of the delicate little fried fish, not quite overlapping the sides of my plate from tip to tail. It was a mini version of the snapper I mostly see displayed on ice at the market. I was sure it was a very illegal catch.

"Where did these come from? They're way under."

"Cuzzie dropped them off—he had a good night out on the river last night, down below the old house—he gave everyone three or four. This is my favorite way to eat snapper—the sweetest."

"I feel complicit . . . guess I won't let it spoil my lunch though . . . would be a bigger crime to waste it now."

"Pāpā used to say the old Māori custom is to eat the little ones, but leave the big breeding fish alone—they are the ones that produce the future generations. When the time is right to eat these panfries, they come up the river in droves—one pass and the net is full. So enjoy—and feel good about working with Tangaroa, even if the Pākehā calls it a crime."

Te Ao Māori: The Māori Worldview

Te ao Māori has been a topic of great interest to Western scholars since its first contact with te ao Pākehā (the Pākehā world), and Māori are one of the most heavily researched peoples in the world. Books on all kinds of Māori topics have been and continue to be published, and a healthy academic literature intersects with te ao Māori. The "Māori" factor has a "holographic" nature in that it is placed like a lens or filter over almost any topic. Māori philosophy seeks to serve as a unifying category, to rehabilitate Eurocentric scholarship about Māori thinking and to articulate the undeniable difference of the Māori worldview, which is commonly expressed as "living in two worlds." This difference is routinely experienced by Māori people, including myself, despite being denied by most non-Māori scholars and commentators.

At the heart of the Māori world is Papatūānuku, the primordial mother earth deity. Above is Ranginui, the primordial father sky deity. Their many children are guardians of various domains, including: Tangaroa, god of the sea; Tāwhirimātea, god of winds; Haumiatiketike, god of wild foods; Rongomātāne, god of cultivated food, especially kūmara (a type of edible tuber or sweet potato, brought by Māori voyagers to Aotearoa from its tropical origins), hence "god of peace." Tūmatauenga is god of war, but the most important brother for humans is Tānemahuta (also known as Tāne, or sometimes Tāne-nui-a-Rangi), ancestor of mankind and all the trees, birds, insects, and other land animals and plants. It was Tāne who managed to separate their parents in the first place, to end their millennia-long tight embrace, with all their children crouched in the dark between them, and allow the light of day to enter the world. Tāne planted the trees of the forest and filled them with the birds and other living things. Tāne cloaked his father Ranginui with the night sky, adorned it with the stars, and begat humanity with Hineahuone, the primordial female ancestor god, who he fashioned from clay. Tāne ascended to the heavens and returned with the three baskets of knowledge for humankind. The rain is likened to the tears of love from Rangi to Papa and the mists her sorrowful sighs in return. The youngest unborn brother is Rūaumoko, god of earthquakes and volcanism. When he moves inside his mother's belly, the earth shakes and rumbles: perhaps in the twenty-first century his time draws near?

The above paraphrasing is just a taster of the Māori creation stories that continue down through many generations to result in the world around us, an idea that makes sense from a local Māori or (more correctly) iwi perspective, referring here to the world as the physical geography or natural environment making up the traditional homelands of one's people, connected through to the microlevel. The hills, valleys, and waterways of one's ancestral home area, known in Māori as one's tūrangawaewae (literally, place to stand), are part of the body of Papatūānuku, who is our ancestor. Plants and animals are the descendants of Tānemahuta, from whom people also descend, according to Māori ideas about the world.

These narratives describe the Māori genealogical model of the universe, which underpins any discussion of Māori knowledge, worldview, paradigm, or philosophy. Versions of these narratives have been published in English many times over since people first started writing books on Māori topics, which was soon after European contact with Māori, and which still shows no sign of stopping or slowing down. So these stories have long since passed into the public domain of social discourse in Aotearoa New Zealand. Down through the decades, numerous versions of these Māori creation stories have been published in books of all kinds, including children's reading books and educational materials, as well as on television, in plays, songs, artworks, exhibitions, and of course online.

Māori ideas about the world thus center on whakapapa, a word whose nearest English equivalent is "genealogy." But whakapapa has a wide range of meanings and allusions not applicable to the word "genealogy" and is also used as a verb. Whakapapa is a master or capstone concept of Māori philosophy, which encompasses culturally specific accounts of ontology, epistemology, and ethics. Whakapapa not only structures the content of knowledge about the world (beginning with the creation stories and continuing to include all the physical elements of the natural world) but also provides an ethical framework for right action, based on notions of kinship with/in the world. Whakapapa both explains the world and guides human behavior in the world. Whakapapa and the genealogical model of the universe provide a theoretical underpinning of the Māori values, based on ethical concepts of ecology and community. Whakapapa is how Māori people introduce themselves to each other and how they understand other people: a major topic of Māori conversation. Thus, usually within minutes of two Māori people meeting for the first time, they will ask each other "No hea koe?" usually translated as "Where are you from?" but literally meaning "where (which lands) do you belong (to)?"—a reference to whakapapa, in the sense that the Māori names for the different parts of the country are identical with the names of the iwi (larger kingroup) of that place, a simple but powerful example of how whakapapa is built into the Māori language and Māori thinking.

In short, Māori ideas about the world are captured in whakapapa in the Māori cosmogenic stories (I call them nature narratives rather than myths and legends), which act as both theories about reality and philosophies that give rise to ethics and values to guide behavior. There are two main types/levels of whakapapa narratives, one being the cosmogenic narratives and the other being the local ancestor stories and descent lines (tātai or whakaheke). The Māori nature narratives are not myths and legends as they are generally known in academic and lay terms, a prime example of how Māori knowledge has been disrupted and dismissed. At a philosophical level, the whakapapa kōrero of the genealogical universe serve as explanations of the world and natural phenomena, providing an underpinning theoretical framework for empirical Māori knowledge.[10] In these ways they play the same role in te ao Māori as the underpinning theories of reality in the standard account of science.

Whakapapa is graphically represented in Māori iconography for instance carvings "as a double spiral marked by chevrons to show successive epochs."[11] The spiral form of whakapapa is associated with the idea of growth and development over time, as in the unfurling fern frond or koru (spiral), which is a major motif in Māori iconography. The whakapapa concept is also a record of the passage of time, based on the imprecise unit of a generation. In a society organized along communal kinship lines, knowledge of whakapapa had both social/ethical value and economic/instrumental value. If whakapapa measures time, the spiral notation of whakapapa reflects a Māori notion of time as cyclic and circular, rather than the Western concept of linear time. Similar circular/spiral notions of time are found in many other Indigenous cultural knowledges, as, for example, in Aztec philosophy.[12] In this way, whakapapa connects together the concepts of ethics and time in Māori knowledge.

While the remnants of Māori knowledge bases are patchy, they have never been fully extinguished and are part of the ongoing cultural revival within Māori communities. An important Māori benefit of early adoption of literacy through missionary schools was the emergence of the category of taonga whānau (family heirlooms) of "pukapuka" or books, often accounting books or exercise books, containing handwritten records of family whakapapa, recorded by the first literate generations.

Almost all published comparisons between science and Indigenous knowledge suffer from simplistic or caricatural representations of *both* forms of knowledge, since even science experts often lack knowledge of the metalevel of science, that is, philosophy of science. Older Eurocentric scholars of Māori such as Elsdon Best and Raymond Firth disconnected the Māori genealogical model of the universe, contained in the cosmogenic narratives, from empirical Māori knowledge about the environment, calling the narratives "fireside tales" whence they have become known in dominant accounts as "Māori myths and legends."[13] Such practices, unsurprisingly, have led to gaps in understanding. Best, for example, made extensive studies of Māori forest lore but overlooked the theoretical significance of the cosmogenic narratives, leaving him famously puzzled about the *hau* of the forest and the hau of the gift.[14]

As well as being based on a genealogical or whakapapa model of reality, te ao Māori is a world of dualities or polarities that operate at many different levels, from cosmic through to the everyday physical dimensions, to psychological, spiritual, and philosophical levels. In classical anthropological analyses, these Māori dualities are characterized in terms of "complementarity" and "symmetry."[15] This dipolar nature of Māori reality is similar to concepts found in other Indigenous models, such as Yin Yang, the basic Taoist concept found across many dimensions from physical (for instance nutrition) to philosophical. Given the archeological suggestion of Taiwan as a jumping-off point for the ancient peopling of the Pacific, including eventually Aotearoa, it is unsurprising to find alignments between Indigenous Māori concepts and those of ancient Asian philosophical traditions.

I imagine these pou like the spokes of a spinning bicycle wheel, which is a metaphor for the spiral nature of time in Māori philosophy. The area in between the ends of the pou, represented by the hub of the wheel, is the pae—"the threshold, liminal zone that mediates the main oppositions."[16] The word "pae" or "paepae" has a range of literal meanings relating to "edge" ideas including horizon, circumference, and horizontal beam. In the dipolar model of the Māori cosmos, the pae is the zone of life, in which humans have moral agency to exercise will and act in the world. Salmond describes the central importance of the *pae* in Māori ideas about the world:

> The activity here [in the pae] is complex, indeed, for it encompasses all the major ritual genres of traditional Māori society—warfare, intergroup hospitality and magic—but it is orderly and the use of metaphor is systematic. It is this area that lends most conviction to a model based on intersecting opposites, because in the threshold zone the preoccupation is with balance, expressed in the terms *utu* "return, price, response, reply," *ea* "be requited, be paid, be performed (rite), come up (crop)," and *rite* "like, balanced, by equivalent, performed, completed."[17]

This model of the Māori world makes sense of Indigenous Māori concepts expressed by words that have no adequate English equivalent and do not fit within Western frameworks of knowledge. For example, the important word mana is usually translated as "prestige" or "power" but even in combination, these kinds of concepts fall short of its meaning, or more precisely, range of meanings, in the Māori world. In the dipolar Māori cosmos, mana exists in the ability to keep balanced or maintain utu—to stay in favor with the gods that personify the primal forces of the universe.

Salmond tested the "explanatory value of the model" by reconsidering the "hitherto unexplained and apparently eccentric ritual of biting the latrine beam."[18] Her analysis showed that the horizontal latrine beam, referred to as a paepae or a literal pae, was also a physical metaphor for the spiritual pae, this liminal zone called life that humans inhabit in between the oppositional cosmic forces. Thus the traditional village latrine area was strongly associated with spiritual forces and atua (gods): the area in front of the beam was designated as tapu and the area behind the beam as noa. "An informant called Tutaka says of the paepae [latrine beam]: 'koinei te kai patu i te tangata, koinei te kai whakaora i te tangata' ('it is the killer of man, it is the curer of man')."[19] Spiritual imbalance or imminent danger could be thwarted by certain rituals involving the latrine:

> The priest instructs him to bite the latrine beam, the head of the god, the seat of awesome power, to bite heaven and earth, above and below—in other words, to conquer orientational opposites and the threshold (paepae) that mediates them by the act of eating.[20]

In this work, Salmond shows that the dipolar, genealogical model of the Māori cosmos follows regular patterns, yet is complex enough to accommodate a wide range of concepts found in te ao Māori. This model of the Māori world as oriented by dynamic structuring binaries implies that Māori ideas are inherently concerned with boundaries, liminal zones, and movement between opposites: right action moves in the direction of life and light; wrong action moves toward the opposite. The next section considers how this framework of te ao Māori shapes Māori ideas of ethics and time.

Ethics, Time, and Whakapapa

In the Māori world, the principles of tapu (restricted) and noa (unrestricted) direct ethical thought and action in ways that are difficult to understand in non-Māori terms. The role of the tapu-noa dipole is strikingly demonstrated in the example above, given by Salmond. In combination with rituals and incantations, the spatial/literal/visible tapu-noa dipole of the latrine beam was used to intervene in the temporal/metaphorical/spiritual tapu-noa dipole created by the imminent danger or problem facing the person. This example illustrates how space and time are thought of together, and how degrees and states of tapu constantly change as time passes, in response to human actions and contextual circumstances. Tapu can be likened to an electric charge at atomic level, created by an imbalance of electrons, which puts the substance into a reactive state, ready to change.

The past ages of Māori history go on getting further away from us here in the present but retain importance for the generations of today and the future. Māori oral accounts of historical time are based on whakapapa and the imprecise unit of a generation, underscoring the importance of whakapapa knowledge in relation to history and larger overall schemata. Whakapapa is a "thick" historical narrative, an Indigenous version of what Eviatar Zerubavel calls the "time map" concept, which expands the linear notion of time from a one-dimensional (line or thread) to a two-dimensional (map or fabric) concept.[21] To expand the notion of time in this way creates space to include ethics, adding in the "qualitative" or "thick" dimension of human agency.

Whakapapa in its totality provides the ground or fabric of Māori philosophy, whereupon the basic principles of mana and tapu operate on the cosmic/spiritual polarities, and the ongoing work of maintaining them in balance. The next-level concepts are the key Māori values of tika, pono, and aroha.[22] This formidable conceptual triad provides a useful ethical framework by which Māori society judges and is judged by its people. Tika is the basis of tikanga, or doing what is right according to a Māori worldview. Pono is being honest and truthful and seeking after truth (i.e., the central mission of science and the university). Aroha superintends both tika and pono; it is described as a "supreme spiritual power" and the essence of a human/e response to reality/nature and the world/s in which we find ourselves as agentic ethical beings. Aroha is often translated by the single word "love" or even "compassion," but any one-word translation inevitably falls short of capturing such an expansive concept.

To understand the ethical thinking encapsulated in te reo Māori requires appreciating the overall worldview of te ao Māori and where each concept connects within the framework. The interconnected set of traditional Indigenous ideas—whakapapa, tapu, mana, aroha, and mauri—combine to provide a simple, flexible framework for right action, which consists in seeing all the nonhuman inhabitants of the planet as kin to humans, and therefore our responsibility—not ours to turn into monetary profit or use (up) as we see fit. Māori philosophy has been described in various ways, including as an environmental virtue ethics.[23] But one of the best comparisons is with the concept of Gaia (the Greek ancestral deity, the personified Earth mother), which proposes that the planet itself is a living organism, championed within science by James Lovelock.[24] The Māori worldview provides a powerful antithesis to the so-called "market" model of the individual person as a self-interested rational chooser, motivated to maximize their own personal accumulation of wealth (aka "homo economicus").

Time is notorious as one of the most difficult concepts to pin down, generating vast academic literatures across many disciplines including physics, biology, and psychology. Time is also studied in anthropology and sociology since all cultural groups plan and carry out actions according to time; find ways to measure time; and speak about time.[25] Time is a central concept to explore and expand on using a critical Māori philosophy approach.

When the old ones sat out overnight to watch the night sky, they saw the stories of their lives, the passing of time and people, reflected in the celestial dance: always different yet the same, every night a new show. Māori/Indigenous cultures use natural or astronomical time as "clock and calendar" to mark economic activities and social events. The diurnal, biological, seasonal, lunar, and astronomical cycles determine the rhythms of life in harmony with nature, which is one of the key features of the category of the "Indigenous." With the emergence of modernity in Western Europe, vast numbers of people underwent rapid wrenching changes in lifestyle that involved becoming disconnected from nature, both in terms of inhabiting natural spaces and also organizing daily life around natural time.

Clock and calendar time, or CCT, is "one of the West's most successful exports."[26] CCT is also known as "machine time" or Western time, while Māori/Indigenous time is found in the cycles of natural time. This dual nature of time is a both-and situation, not an either-or binary, since every person is aware of natural cycles. But CCT has been thoroughly overlaid across natural time within Western culture and rules the lives of most people in Westernized countries. Those individuals who do not adhere to CCT are not considered legally competent adults. The next section digs deeper into the political nature of time.

Māori Chronopolitics

Contemporary New Zealand society is one of the safest and most liberal in the world, where all cultural groups mix freely and overt racism is illegal and socially unaccepted, though talkback radio and social media attest to a racist undercurrent (which is tolerated in such a liberal democratic nation). Yet New Zealand is based on the same Eurocentric foundations as the rest of what was once the British Empire, even if expressed in milder terms than in most other ex-British colonies. The idea is embedded in White New Zealand that British colonization was beneficial for and even "saved" Māori people. It is still touted by politicians that colonization of Māori was peaceable and based on mutual agreement.[27] Other White national myths of New Zealand, promulgated through schools and books and based on evolutionist thought (e.g., social Darwinism), point to improved Māori conditions of living, gifting Māori the benefits of British citizenship, and so on.

The term "Māori time" is a racist joke of White New Zealand that refers to lack of punctuality, especially lateness that is habitual or for "no good reason." Equivalent forms are found (Island time, Indian time, etc.) in many other localities where local Indigenous people have been obliged to join the modern economy and time of the colonizers. The phrase "Māori time" is a language marker of the "gap" or hyphen between Pākehā and Māori; it is a reference to difference, that is, to the existence of te ao Māori. A Kaupapa Māori approach reclaims and rehabilitates the concept of "Māori time," turning it to a positive Māori claim to difference—of being relatively less enslaved by CCT, more in harmony with natural cycles.

John Postill draws attention to the hidden significance of CCT in social science, calling it a "missing anthropological problem,"[28] hence linking to Agnotology studies[29] and the role of structured ignorance (absence, amnesia, and propaganda) in maintaining the (White) status quo of power relations in social and intellectual systems at global levels. Postill lists shortcomings of typical anthropological studies of time, noting that they take Western thought as standard; romanticize non-Western cultures; and ignore the "irreversible global spread of CCT ever since the Industrial Revolution" and the role of mass media, especially television, in that colonizing spread.[30]

Caribbean philosopher Charles W. Mills defines "chronopolitics" as a recognition of, and response to, racialized accounts of the past. The time map concept draws attention to how unreflexive thinking about time becomes embedded in scientific concepts such as periodization, which support distinct (national/personal) identities, and historical ideologies including amnesias and myths. An example of how this works is the dominant Pākehā/White New Zealand national identity based on discontinuous views of Pākehā history, in ways that reinforce their feelings, even today, of security and superiority in relation to Māori.[31] The counter-history raised by Māori political protesters in every decade since the signing of Te Tiriti o Waitangi (1840) puts the lie to the dominant stories designed to reinforce Pākehā complacency. This continuous history of protest against colonial invasion and blatant treaty breaches is fitting to be called a "Māori chronopolitics" according to Mills's concept.

Conclusion

The notion of whakapapa extends from and interlaces with the natural cycles that mark the Māori clock and calendar, which binds the central idea of humans as part of nature together with everyday experience into a seamless whole, forming the worldview known as te ao Māori. Both space and time have gone unrecognized in social theory as being foundational in structures of social and personal power, and therefore in politics and systemic racism. Spatial justice is an emerging topic in domains like education, but temporal justice or chronopolitics still awaits attention. A delineation of whakapapa as a rich social record of the past, which links the measurement of time to an account of ethics as right action in the world, supports the claim made at the start of this chapter about the educational potential of studying Māori knowledge.

Considering the links between ethics and time from a Māori perspective leads to a Māori version of chronopolitics. Māori chronopolitics draws attention to the ways in which Pākehā/Western concepts of time are embedded in modern societies, specifically including New Zealand, and the continuous history of post-contact protest by Māori political activists, including Māori intellectuals, against the colonial suppression of Māori language, culture, and philosophy, in favor of Pākehā interests.

A more general outcome of researching the links between ethics and time from a Māori perspective is a greater personal appreciation of the extensive and productive nature of profound Indigenous concepts, such as whakapapa. I imagine thinking of myself as a "scholar of whakapapa" and the ramifications of such an academic identity. Only through writing this chapter does this "scholar of whakapapa" thought experiment even occur to me. This lesson is about what decolonization looks like in academic practice, and how it proceeds and deepens, even for a senior Māori scholar like me, living and working within a milieu in which the Māori concepts have been so thoroughly delimited and oversimplified. Not only is studying Māori knowledge productive and of ethical significance generally for regenerating a place to be with each other, it also counts as research done to support specifically Māori political aspirations.

Working with words on the page can still be of political significance for Māori causes: Māori philosophy acting as a scholarly form of Māori political protest and active resistance against intellectual colonization. Kia ora mai tātou katoa (Greetings to all).

Notes

1. Stephen May, *Language and Minority Rights: Ethnicity, Nationalism and the Politics of Language*, 2nd ed. (Essex, UK: Pearson Education, 2001), xiii.
2. See Alison Jones and Kuni Jenkins, "Rethinking Collaboration: Working the Indigene-Colonizer Hyphen," in *Handbook of Critical and Indigenous Methodologies*, ed. Norman K. Denzin, Yvonna S. Lincoln, and Linda T. Smith (Los Angeles: Sage, 2008); Georgina Tuari Stewart, "From Both Sides of the Indigenous-Settler Hyphen in Aotearoa New Zealand," *Educational Philosophy and Theory* 50, no. 8 (2018): 767–75.
3. Anne Salmond, "Te Ao Tawhito: A Semantic Approach to the Traditional Māori Cosmos," *Journal of the Polynesian Society* 87, no. 1 (1978): 5.
4. Salmond, "Te Ao Tawhito," 5–28.
5. Georgina Stewart, Valance Smith, Piki Diamond, Nova Paul, and Robert Hogg, "Ko Te Tika, Ko Te Pono, Ko Te Aroha: Exploring Māori Values in the University," *Te Kaharoa* 17, no. 1 (2021).
6. See Alan Moorehead, *The Fatal Impact* (Harmondsworth, UK: Penguin, 1968); Margaret Wetherell and Jonathan Potter, *Mapping the Language of Racism: Discourse and the Legitimation of Exploitation* (New York: Harvester Wheatsheaf, 1992).
7. See Anne Salmond, "Māori Epistemologies," in *Reason and Morality*, ed. Joanna Overing (London and New York: Tavistock Publications, 1985), 237–60, and her "Ontological Quarrels: Indigeneity, Exclusion and Citizenship in a Relational World," *Anthropological Theory* 12, no. 2 (2012): 115–41.
8. Georgina Tuari Stewart, *Māori Philosophy: Indigenous Thinking from Aotearoa* (London: Bloomsbury, 2020).
9. Charles W. Mills, "The Chronopolitics of Racial Time," *Time & Society* 29, no. 2 (2020): 297–317.
10. Takirirangi Smith, "Ngā Tini Āhuatanga O Whakapapa Kōrero," *Educational Philosophy and Theory* 32, no. 1 (2000): 53–60.
11. Salmond, "Māori Epistemologies," 247.
12. James Maffei, *Aztec Philosophy: Understanding a World in Motion* (Boulder: University Press of Colorado, 2014).
13. Raymond Firth, *Economics of the New Zealand Māori*, 2nd ed. (Wellington: Government Printer, 1972).
14. Elsdon Best, *Forest Lore of the Māori* (Wellington, New Zealand: Te Papa Press, 2005); Georgina Stewart, "The 'Hau' of Research: Mauss Meets Kaupapa Māori," *Journal of World Philosophies* 2, no. 1 (2017): 1–11.
15. F. Allan Hanson and Louise Hanson, *Counterpoint in Māori Culture* (London: Routledge & Kegan Paul, 1983).
16. Salmond, "Te Ao Tawhito," 15–16.
17. Salmond, "Te Ao Tawhito," 16.
18. Salmond, "Te Ao Tawhito," 25.
19. Salmond, "Te Ao Tawhito," 25.
20. Salmond, "Te Ao Tawhito," 25.

21 Eviatar Zerubavel, *Time Maps: Collective Memory and the Social Shape of the Past* (Chicago: University of Chicago Press, 2003).
22 Stewart et al., "Exploring the Use of Māori Values in the University."
23 John Patterson, "Māori Environmental Virtues," *Environmental Ethics* 16, no. 4 (1994): 397–409.
24 James E. Lovelock, *Gaia: A New Look at Life on Earth* (Oxford: Oxford University Press, 1987).
25 Barbara Adam, *Time and Social Theory* (London: Polity Press, 1990); Johannes Fabian, *Time and the Other: How Anthropology Makes Its Object*, foreword by Matti Bunzl (New York: Columbia University Press, 2014).
26 John Postill, "Clock and Calendar Time: A Missing Anthropological Problem," *Time & Society* 11, no. 2–3 (2002): 251.
27 Chris Bramwell, Radio New Zealand, "'Peaceful Settlement' View Challenged," November 25, 2014. https://www.rnz.co.nz/news/political/260174/%27peaceful-settlement%27-view-challenged
28 Postill, "Clock and Calendar Time," 251.
29 Robert Proctor and Londa L. Schiebinger, ed., *Agnotology: The Making and Unmaking of Ignorance* (Stanford, CA: Stanford University Press, 2008).
30 Postill, "Clock and Calendar Time," 253.
31 Avril Bell, *Relating Indigenous and Settler Identities: Beyond Domination* (New York: Palgrave Macmillan, 2014).

Bibliography

Adam, Barbara. *Time and Social Theory*. Oxford: Polity Press, 1990.
Bell, Avril. *Relating Indigenous and Settler Identities: Beyond Domination*. New York: Palgrave Macmillan, 2014.
Best, Elsdon. *Forest Lore of the Māori*. Wellington, New Zealand: Te Papa Press, 2005.
Bramwell, Chris. "'Peaceful Settlement' View Challenged." *Radio New Zealand*, 25 November 2014. https://www.rnz.co.nz/news/political/260174/%27peaceful-settlement%27-view-challenged.
Fabian, Johannes. *Time and the Other: How Anthropology Makes Its Object*. Foreword by Matti Bunzl. New York: Columbia University Press, 2014.
Firth, Raymond. *Economics of the New Zealand Māori*. 2nd ed. Wellington: Government Printer, 1972.
Hanson, F. Allan, and Louise Hanson. *Counterpoint in Māori Culture*. London: Routledge and Kegan Paul, 1983.
Jones, Alison, and Kuni Jenkins. "Rethinking Collaboration: Working the Indigene-Colonizer Hyphen." In *Handbook of Critical and Indigenous Methodologies*, edited by Norman K. Denzin, Yvonna S. Lincoln, and Linda T. Smith, 471–86. Los Angeles: Sage, 2008.
Lovelock, James E. *Gaia: A New Look at Life on Earth*. Oxford: Oxford University Press, 1987.
Maffei, James. *Aztec Philosophy: Understanding a World in Motion*. Boulder: University Press of Colorado, 2014.
May, Stephen. *Language and Minority Rights: Ethnicity, Nationalism and the Politics of Language*, 2nd ed. Essex, UK: Pearson Education, 2001.

Mills, Charles W. "The Chronopolitics of Racial Time." *Time & Society* 29, no. 2 (2020): 297–317.
Moorehead, Alan. *The Fatal Impact*. Harmondsworth, UK: Penguin, 1968.
Patterson, John. "Māori Environmental Virtues." *Environmental Ethics* 16, no. 4 (1994): 397–409.
Postill, John. "Clock and Calendar Time: A Missing Anthropological Problem." *Time & Society* 11, no. 2–3 (2002): 251–70.
Proctor, Robert, and Londa L. Schiebinger, ed. *Agnotology: The Making and Unmaking of Ignorance*. Stanford: Stanford University Press, 2008.
Salmond, Anne. "Māori Epistemologies." In *Reason and Morality*, edited by Joanna Overing, 237–60. London and New York: Tavistock Publications, 1985.
Salmond, Anne. "Ontological Quarrels: Indigeneity, Exclusion and Citizenship in a Relational World." *Anthropological Theory* 12, no. 2 (2012): 115–41.
Salmond, Anne. "Te Ao Tawhito: A Semantic Approach to the Traditional Māori Cosmos." *Journal of the Polynesian Society* 87, no. 1 (1978): 5–28.
Smith, Takirirangi. "Ngā Tini Āhuatanga O Whakapapa Kōrero." *Educational Philosophy and Theory* 32, no. 1 (2000): 53–60.
Stewart, Georgina. "Actual Minds of Two Halves: Measurement, Metaphor and the Message." *Educational Philosophy and Theory* 47, no. 11 (2015): 1227–33.
Stewart, Georgina Tuari. "From Both Sides of the Indigenous-Settler Hyphen in Aotearoa New Zealand." *Educational Philosophy and Theory* 50, no. 8 (2018): 767–75.
Stewart, Georgina Tuari. *Māori Philosophy: Indigenous Thinking from Aotearoa*. London: Bloomsbury, 2020.
Stewart, Georgina Tuari. "The 'Hau' of Research: Mauss Meets Kaupapa Māori." *Journal of World Philosophies* 2, no. 1 (2017): 1–11.
Stewart, Georgina, Valance Smith, Piki Diamond, Nova Paul, and Robert Hogg. "Ko Te Tika, Ko Te Pono, Ko Te Aroha: Exploring Māori Values in the University." *Te Kaharoa* 17, no. 1 (2021). https://doi.org/10.24135/tekaharoa.v17i1.344.
Wetherell, Margaret, and Jonathan Potter. *Mapping the Language of Racism: Discourse and the Legitimation of Exploitation*. New York: Harvester Wheatsheaf, 1992.
Zerubavel, Eviatar. *Time Maps: Collective Memory and the Social Shape of the Past*. Chicago: University of Chicago Press, 2003.

12

Levinas on Time

The Ethical Import of our Existential Chronological Inconsistency

Benda Hofmeyr

Introduction: An Existential Chronological Inconsistency?

The human condition is fundamentally temporal: everything comes to an end; time waits for no one. Although inherently diachronic (literally through time or broadly construed as a changing or evolving over time), the human condition is typified by a being "out of time," that is, it is never quite in sync, as if human experience is structured by a chronological inconsistency. The fundamental temporality of the human condition serves as a "transitory a priori," if you will, that is, as both a transcendental condition of being (we are all irremediably conditioned and structured by our temporality), yet for each of us it precisely remains *our* temporality. How I experience time is radically singularizing. I am in a unique relation to *my* past, present, and future, and as such what they signify and imply for me is different from—even incomparable to—what they mean for someone else. The unique way in which we undergo being fundamentally out of joint with time makes us who we are.

How may we understand this chronological inconsistency? Perhaps it has something to do with the fact that we are simultaneously beings conditioned by our past that never quite seems to pass into oblivion but has a recalcitrant way of usurping our present, pulling us backward by conditioning the possibilities at our disposal in the present and, as such, in the future. This operation of the past in the present is not teleological, however, and does not map out a fated outcome. At the same time, we are projected into a future that announces the radically unknown and thereby constantly disrupts any sense of equilibrium in the present. The human existential condition is therefore split: split between an "always-too-lateness" for recovering the past that inevitably slips away from the present but which nevertheless conditions the possibilities at our disposal in the present; and "an-always-too-earliness" for anticipating the future that cannot be evaded or predicted, a future that unsettles the present since it is somehow not capable of remaining the "wholly-still-to-come."

This chronological inconsistency might also relate to the fact that we can never know our beginning or our end. Our coming into existence is an event that necessarily happens without our being "there" or "present" in any proper sense of the word. Even more unbearable is the realization that in much the same way, we will disappear from existence; one's very being will cease. The inevitability and increasingly imminent fact of *my* end is different and far more unbearable than the knowledge that all people die. By its very nature, time is the radically unexpected, the coming of death, my inescapable demise. Time announces my mortality, the fact that my time will end.

In what follows, I attempt to come to a more precise and nuanced understanding of the fundamental chronological inconsistency of the human condition, which I propose is to be found in Emmanuel Levinas's preoccupation with time. As we shall see, Levinas is concerned with time not as time-consciousness but rather with the ethical significance of the elements of time that resist being comprehended by consciousness.

Levinas on Time

Levinas's ethical metaphysics provides an original perspective on the place of time in our being.[1] It is both concerned with our present life in-the-world *and* with the future beyond-this-world, with immanence and transcendence, with the self and the other person. His early phenomenological analyses, which proceed descriptively to uncover the essence of a matter, focus on the present, on our life in-the-world, and on immanence. Given his mature works' prioritization of the Other, the self's existential exploits in the world are more often than not interpreted by Levinas scholars as ontologically inferior or ethically inessential to the future, to transcendence. However, Levinas's thinking cannot be reduced to a binary opposition between immanence and transcendence. For him the promise of the future is a promise of resurrecting the past in such a way that it would begin anew. The happiness of a new beginning that the future can bring, a renewal of one's being, is the paradoxical happiness of the *felix culpa*. More than the loss of immanence and self, which could be interpreted as a fortunate fall because of the good that comes from it, it is the preservation of immanence in transcendence. For Levinas the "first" beginning in the now, the instant of immanence, is the very condition for the possibility of a second beginning, a "new birth."[2] Our life in-the-world is more than just a miserable series of events that will eventually lead to a happier outcome. The movement that leads an existent toward the Good is not a transcendence by which that existent raises itself up to a higher existence but is rather a departure from Being: an *ex-cendence*. As Levinas explains, this excedence and the Good necessarily have a foothold in being, and that is why Being is better than nonbeing.[3] A being is the very condition for the possibility of escaping Being. Levinas theorizes the chronological inconsistency of being as something that may only be resolved by means of the ethical encounter with the other person:

> The future that death gives, the future of the event, is not yet time. In order for the future, which is nobody's and which a human being cannot assume, to become an element of time, it must also enter into relationship with the present . . . the

encroachment of the present on the future is not the feat of the subject alone, but the intersubjective relationship.[4]

Levinas thus radically redefines the sense of time understood as an infinite succession of instants. According to his existential interpretation of time, an instant is indeed a commencement. This present is the awakening of consciousness, an *Augenblick*. The future is not to be understood as the recurrence of the now or its continuation. Rather, the future is the possibility of another instant or beginning, another chance for the now. The event that the future brings is a chance to recommence otherwise. This is the sense of time not as a determinate infinity of instants but rather of the *infinition*, the ever recommencing of the definitive.[5]

Death, the Future, and Time

In *Otherwise than Being or Beyond Essence* Levinas shifts the emphasis away from the present to an unfathomable and mysterious Other, which he equates with the future—a future that is inaugurated by an Other that is as enigmatic as death itself.[6] In the face of the Other/death, the existent is no longer actively self-transformative and transcending but reduced to a "bottomless" or "deathlike passivity."[7] Suffering and death announce the absolute strangeness of a future ever future. Death is always yet to come, and in its inevitable approach we are confronted with something that we cannot assimilate, not in life. Death is truly remaining in the beyond, since no one has returned from it. As such, it is an event that can be compared to the (ethical) encounter with the other person, the Other—that which will redeem us from our materiality and change our egoist nature never to wholly return to ourselves as we were. It is an event so mysterious that, for Levinas, nothing is more like it than death. In a certain sense, then, the encounter with the other person whose ethical appeal I respond to is a kind of death—the radical incapacitation of my egoism, which is a necessary condition for the possibility of ethical action. The moment of ethicality signals the "death" of my self-obsessed self and its resurrection as ethical self. To be sure, this "death" is not definitive, for as Levinas specifies, the difference between the future that the Other gives is time, whereas the future that death gives is not yet time.[8]

Levinas maintains that in physical pain one's engagement in existence is without equivocation and thereby it becomes impossible to detach oneself from being.[9] In suffering the existent finds herself "backed up to being," that is, to being without nothingness.[10] Along with the impossibility of nothingness, there is also in suffering the proximity of death—death that nevertheless belongs to the time of the future, as we shall see, although this future is not time. The unknown of death signifies that the subject finds itself in relationship with what is refractory to light, with mystery. In the face of death, the subject finds itself seized, overwhelmed, and utterly passive. For Heidegger, being-toward-death signals authentic existence, and hence, the very vitality of the subject. It is precisely *Dasein's* assumption of the uttermost possibilities of existence that makes possible all other possibilities. For Heidegger, death is an event of freedom, the "*possibility* of impossibility." For Levinas, on the other hand, death signals "the impossibility of possibility."[11] Death seizes us while stripping us of our ability to have powers—our power to be able (*nous ne 'pouvons plus pouvoir'*).[12] The other (*l'Autre*), announced in death, alienates not only my abilities and possibilities but also my very being.[13]

What is conjured in Levinas's lengthy descriptions of suffering and death is not only the alterity of death but also the alterity of the other person. What is common to death and social life is an encounter with radical alterity, with a Mystery. In fact, for Levinas, the encounter with the alterity of death is like nothing so much as the encounter with the alterity of the other person, "as though the approach of death remained one of the modalities of the relationship with the Other."[14] And if the Other is truly like death, it seems probable that the encounter with the Other will lead to the de-subjectivation or dissolution of the subject—the "end of mastery," the subject when stripped of all semblance of initiative or agency.[15]

Death is a mystery precisely because it is never present: "[if] you are, it is not; if it is, you are not."[16] According to Levinas, this ancient adage testifies to the eternal futurity of death. Our relationship with death is a unique relationship with the future. The fact that it deserts every present is not due to our evasion of death but to the fact that death is *ungraspable*, that it marks the end of the subject's vitality and heroism. The now is the fact that I am a master, master of grasping the possible. Death is never now.[17]

To die is to return to the state of irresponsibility, "the simple way out of all the little brick dead ends we scratch our nails against . . . where the burden, the terrifying hellish weight of self-responsibility . . . is lifted."[18] It marks a reversal of the subject's activity into passivity, like Macbeth's passivity when there is no longer hope, when he is finally confronted with Macduff, the man not of woman born, the one, according to the witches' prediction, who will bring him to his end: "I'll not fight with thee."[19] However, prior to death there is always a last chance; this is what heroes such as Macbeth seize: "yet I will try the last."[20] Death cannot be seized; it comes. Nothingness is impossible. Hamlet's line "to be or not to be" is not the question par excellence, Levinas insists, for in reality we have no choice but to be. Being is not accompanied by nothingness, as Jean-Paul Sartre thought; being is irremissible. It is nothingness that would have left humankind the possibility of assuming death and escaping from its material servitude.[21]

The relationship with the Other is thus a mystery that cannot be assumed but that alienates. But if death is the alienation of my existence, is it still my death? How can a being enter into relation with the Other without allowing its very self to be crushed by the Other? How can an existent as mortal persevere in its mastery? This is what Levinas calls the problem of the *preservation of the ego in transcendence* or that we might describe as the possibility of surviving one's future. What Levinas calls the possibility of vanquishing death is not conceived as a problem of eternal life. Rather, this possibility is to maintain, with the alterity of the event, a relationship that must still be personal. The existent is able to face up to the future/Other precisely because of the present, because of the independence and separation acquired through his/her economic exploits in the world. The generosity of the subject going toward the Other, breaking forth from the exclusive property of egoist enjoyment, is premised on that very independence, on the riches acquired. Because the subject has something to give, a personal relationship with the Other can be established.[22] "This is why," writes Levinas, "the life between birth and death is neither folly nor absurdity nor flight nor cowardice. It flows on in a dimension of its own where it has meaning, and where a triumph over death can have meaning."[23]

Because encountering death is also encountering the other person, death acquires another signification for Levinas. What death takes is time; what the Other gives is time. What then accounts for their equivocation in Levinas is the coming of a Mystery that cannot be assumed, the future. Death is not that which renders my "economic" earthly existence inferior to the hereafter, transcendence, or the ethical life. It is an encounter with the other person in need who not only appeals to me for aid but also relies on my ability to be able to help, to have something to give, a home to offer. This encounter, therefore, not only questions my egotistical selfish life and nature but also relies on the riches so accumulated. This structure renders this economic life a necessary condition for the ethical life. Giving is what gives meaning to having. What Levinas reiterates in *Totality and Infinity* is that when the egoist will is confronted with death, but a death ever future, it has time for the Other, and thus to recover meaning despite death.[24]

Fecundity

Another important temporal trope in Levinas is fecundity, which adds an additional dimension according to which the possibility of what Levinas calls the "victory over death" may be understood: "Before . . . a pure future, which is death, where the ego can in no way be able—that is, can no longer be an ego—it is [nevertheless] possible for it to remain an ego."[25] Through fecundity, the I can remain I in the alterity of another, without being absorbed or losing the self in the Other. In paternity, Levinas contends, the I returns to itself, but not unchanged: "Paternity is the relationship with a stranger who, entirely while being Other, is myself, the relationship of the ego with a myself who is nevertheless a stranger to me."[26] Levinas contends that I do not *have* my child; in some sense I *am* my child. Here, however, there is a multiplicity and a transcendence in the very "to exist." Eros opens the perspective of the future by way of the possibility of becoming a father. This possibility brings freedom about and "accomplishes" time, because fecundity as a relationship to the future other (the child), means that the existent therein receives the gift of the future, the gift of being temporal. The condition of possibility of the future is the feminine: "The encounter with the Other as feminine is required in order that the future of the child come to pass from beyond the possible, beyond projects."[27] Through the encounter with the feminine other, eros, and fecundity, the future can be thought of as carrying an unexpected newness. Between the past and the future, I have the present moment, which is the possibility of a new beginning. "Time," then, "constitutes not the fallen form of being, but its very event."[28]

Infinite Time and Completed Time

For Levinas, the present moment is not merely a succession from the previous instant but an interruption. Time itself is an experience of death-and-resurrection: "Time is discontinuous; one instant does not come out of another without interruption, by an ecstasy. In continuation the instant meets its death, and resuscitates."[29] According to Levinas, this possibility of resurrection presupposes the relation of the I with the Other, and fecundity across the discontinuous that constitutes time. Levinas continues by asking an age-old question: "Why is the beyond separated from the below? Why, to go onto the good, are evil, evolution, drama, separation necessary?"[30] Levinas does not answer this question directly but rather finds the rationale for the infinity of time, of infinite time in the possibility of judgment and justice that it brings therein that recommencement in discontinuous time brings youth, a possibility for the new through the possibility of truth that presides over the failure of goodness today. Infinite time is therefore necessary to convert the "particularism of the apology" into "efficacious goodness."[31] The experience of resurrection is realized by pardoning the past injustice. Pardon is not the effacement of the past but rather its purification so that a new beginning becomes possible. Levinas writes that the paradox of pardon may be found in its retroactive action, which inverts the natural order of things and implies the "reversibility of time."[32] The pardoned past is not the forgotten past; the pardoned being is not an innocent being but one whose past wrongdoings have been conserved in the form of a purified present. On the one hand, this purification reverses the order of time, treating the past instant as if it had not passed, so that it may be lived again. One the other hand, this preservation of the past instant is a transformation that allows the subject to live the same past differently. Therefore, the pardon constitutes an act of recreation so that a new future can freely begin. What a purified past makes possible is a future that can be absolutely other than what may be expected based on the past.[33] This suggests a nonteleological conception of time. Within this context, Levinas avers that truth requires an infinite time, but he argues in the same breath that what is also required is a completed time, which is not death but "messianic time."[34] Messianic time is a triumph since it secures us against the revenge of evil whose return infinite time does not prohibit. Levinas asks: "Is this eternity a new structure of time, or an extreme vigilance of the messianic consciousness?"[35] Here Levinas abruptly ends the discussion and simply concludes that this problem exceeds the bounds of the book. As readers, we are tempted to take this unanswered question as an indication of his line of reasoning on the matter that reasserts a nonteleological conception of time, and here specifically of messianic time. Levinas does, however, take up the notion of eschatology in the preface of *Totality and Infinity*.

Eschatological Time

What we have come to understand about Levinas's conceptualization of time prepares the ground for his thinking on eschatology. If time is discontinuity, capable of pardon, and if time renders possible a newness in which past is defined as immemorial, the future as openness to the unknowable, and the present instant as a new beginning, we have a conception of time that opens the way toward thinking the final events of history or the ultimate destiny of humanity. Does this general definition of eschatology coincide with Levinas's conceptualization of eschatology? For Levinas, eschatology is the domain of infinity:

> It does not introduce a teleological system into totality; it does not consist in teaching the orientation of history. Eschatology institutes a relation with being *beyond totality* or beyond history, and not with being beyond the past and the present. Not with the void that would surround the totality and where one could, arbitrarily, think what one likes, thus promote the claims of a subjectivity free as the wind. It is a relationship with a *surplus exterior to the totality*, as though the objective totality did not fill out the true measure of beings, as though another concept, the concept of *infinity*, were needed to express this transcendence with regard to totality, non-encompassable within a totality and as primordial as totality.[36]

To be "beyond" totality does not mean to deny history then but to be responsible vis-à-vis the other. As Levinas puts it, it "draws beings out of the jurisdiction of history and the future," calling them forth to their full responsibility.[37] Since history in itself is an endless chain of violence, eschatological time constitutes a judgment of history's violence. According to Levinas, this judgment is ultimately proper to God, the Absolute Other, and occurs in the moment. Importantly, to resort to God in Levinas's language does not always have a theophanic meaning. It is rather invoked, most of the time, to bring to light how I am bound to the other person.[38] "Salvation does not stand as an end to History, or act as its conclusion. It remains *at every moment* possible."[39] Judgment as a moment of interruption becomes the field of the manifestation of the invisible: "To be I . . . is precisely to be capable of seeing the offense of the offended, or the face."[40] In the moment of judgment, subjectivity is exalted, surpassing the limits of its being. "The judgement of God that judges me at the same time confirms me. But it confirms me precisely in my inferiority."[41] This interruption of time is goodness: "Goodness consists in taking up a position in being such that the Other counts more than myself. Goodness thus involves the possibility for the I that is exposed to the alienation of its powers by death to not be for death."[42] Thus, eschatology is not a matter of waiting for a better future; it is rather a matter of responsibility that principally concerns the present time. Eschatology is not beyond time, but in time, because time is envisaged from Levinas's perspective as discontinuity so that a radical novelty can always interrupt the chain of the homogeneity of totality.[43]

Diachronic Time

In *Otherwise than Being* Levinas deepens his conception of time. He maintains that the ethical obligation that the other places upon me is an affective infection that descends upon one from a past that has never been present, from the diachronic time of the Other. Diachrony, here understood from his earlier contentions regarding time, signifies an affective infection by the Other—death, the future—from an immemorial past that has never been present, or never present in the rational consciousness of the existent. In a past that evades recollection—the immemorial past—the I has been affectively infected with a vulnerability that sensitizes the I to the call of the Other. It is the taking up of the responsibility vis-à-vis the Other, that is the interruption of time in goodness, and the opening of the future that is not merely the continuation of the present into the future but also a radical departure from the present, a new beginning. It is this diachronic time that makes ethical action possible because ethical action is an acting for the Other first, before, or even at the expense of the self. We are therefore, according to Levinas's conceptualization of time, before our time, a time that cannot be recalled or be present but precisely through time— diachronically—susceptible to the ethical call of the Other. For Levinas, then, time is of supreme ethical import.

The ethical significance of time may be fleshed out by considering just how diachronic time makes ethical action possible, especially since diachronic time itself is impossible to grasp, opened as it is to the newness of the unknown.[44] Diachronic time of ethical philosophy is opposed to the time of synchrony, that is, the time of ontology, which, according to Levinas, operates by way of the violent reduction of otherness to sameness. Diachronic time disrupts or stalls this reductive tendency of the self by bringing to light the noncoincidence between the self and I. Levinas, then, thinks of time through the otherness that is irreducible to the same.[45] While Levinas mostly develops this notion of diachronic time in *Otherwise than Being*, it is already present in this earlier work. The aim of *Time and the Other*, Levinas contends, is to show that "time is not the achievement of an isolated and lone subject, but that it is the very relationship of the subject with the Other."[46] Here Levinas initially follows Edmund Husserl before departing from him. Husserl too establishes an analogy between the past and otherness:

> Similarly [in relation to the appresentation of the other Ego], within my ownness and moreover within the sphere of its living present, my past is given only by memory and is characterized in memory *as* my past, a past present—that is: an intentional modification.[47]

For Husserl the relation with the past has some similarity with the appresentation of the other Ego. This is due to the process of differentiation, principally realized by retentions and secondarily by memories. For Husserl, this process of differentiation signals an absence in the intimate life of consciousness. Insofar as the subject necessarily only apprehends itself afterward, it cannot totally be present to itself so that this relationship with itself is marked by some otherness.[48] Following Husserl, Levinas stresses the place of difference within sameness:

> This specific intentionality is time itself. There is consciousness insofar as the sensible impression differs from itself without differing: it . . . is other within identity . . . it undoes that coincidence of self with self in which the "same" is smothered under itself. . . . It is not in phase with itself; *just past, about to* come. But to differ within identity, to maintain the moment that is being altered, is "protaining" and "retaining"! Differing within identity, modifying itself without changing, consciousness glows in an impression inasmuch as it diverges from

itself, to *still* be expecting itself, or *already* recuperating itself. Still, already—are time, time in which nothing is lost. The past itself is modified without changing its identity, diverges from itself without letting go of itself, "becomes older," sinking into a deeper past: it remains identical with itself through retention of retention, and so on. Then memory recuperates in images what retention was not able to preserve, and historiography reconstructs that whose image is lost. To speak of consciousness is to speak of time. It is in any case to speak of a time that can be recuperated.[49]

However, Levinas departs from Husserl with the realization that in the latter's thought "the time structure of sensibility is a time of what can be recuperated."[50] Husserl's contention that the nonintentionality of the primal retention is not a loss of consciousness "excludes from time the irreducible diachrony . . . behind the *exhibiting* of being,"[51] which *Otherwise than Being* aims to bring to light. In Husserl's philosophy, then, the relationship with the past remains a relation of representation that mitigates the lived intensity of the difference. This past is not radically other than the present; rather it is a modified present, a result of representation.[52] Departing fundamentally from Husserl here, Levinas considers time as discontinuity, in which time is principally determined by *traces*. For Levinas, the notion of the trace introduces a past that cannot be a mere modified present that can be recovered through retentions or memories. The time of the trace is "a withdrawal of the Other and, consequently, nowise a degradation of duration, which, in memory, is still complete."[53] Unlike Husserl's represented past, the past to which the trace refers can nowise be recuperated. According to Levinas, "[t]o be qua leaving a trace, is to pass, to depart, to absolve oneself."[54] The trace signifies a radical immemorial past that cannot be known, which makes the otherness fundamentally irreducible to my representation. Herewith Levinas throws the ethical significance of his conceptualization of time into relief.

For Levinas, alterity occurs "as a divergency and a past which no memory could resurrect as a present."[55] This otherness of alterity is principally an experience of diachrony, which indicates that the Other is never present except through the lapse that interrupts the synchronization between the same and the other, the lapse that makes him/her other. The notion of the trace announces the self's radical passivity vis-à-vis the Other.[56] This means that the past is not what can be revived but the openness toward the Infinite: "[The] immemorial past is not an extrapolation from human duration, but the original anteriority or the original ultimacy of God in relation to a world."[57]

The instant when I am confronted with the fragility of the face of the Other revealed to me in its nakedness, is the saying, which belongs to a time of an immemorial past. It is fundamentally the time of the moral command:

> The neighbor strikes me before striking me, as though I had heard before he spoke. This anachronism attests to temporality different from that which scans consciousness. It takes apart the recuperable time of history and memory in which representation continues. For if, in every experience, the making of a fact precedes the present of experience, the memory, history or extratemporality of the a priori recuperates the divergence and creates a correlation between this past and this

present. In proximity is heard a command come as though from an immemorial past, which was never present, began in no freedom. This *way* of the neighbor is a face.[58]

Here Levinas theorizes what I have called the chronological inconsistency of the human condition as the inherent human capacity for ethical action, which is nevertheless not a power but an empowerment by way of the fundamental disempowerment of the egoist I by the Other. Richard Cohen describes this as a being "chosen before choosing."[59] In *Otherwise than Being*, this responsibility reveals the self's radical culpability: "A face is a trace of itself, given over to my responsibility, but to which I am wanting and faulty. It is as though I were responsible for his mortality, and guilty for surviving."[60] The "anachronous immediacy" of the face "is what puts into question the naive spontaneity of the ego."[61]

Recapitulation: Levinas on Our Existential Chronological Inconsistency

From my reading of Levinas, one might postulate that what I have described as the inherent chronological inconsistency of the human condition may be understood in Levinas's ethical metaphysics as the other (*autre*) within the self. This alterity within the self is an inherent Desire for time, time that can only be given by the other person, which for Levinas is the Other (*l'Autrui*). This means that the singular time of my being is not yet time, does not yet have time, but the singular I bears an inherent *Desire* for time within. This desire for time emanates from the inherent chronological inconsistency that typifies the existent being "out of sync" with itself, a diastasis or a "standing apart from itself." To be sure, this desire is not a need to be filled, but as desire, it is inherently insatiable. This desire conquers the ecstatic time of need and satisfaction and the inevitable return to the self, the collapse back upon oneself that follows when needs are satiated, and the return of the unbearable heaviness of being that it signals. The early Levinas (*On Escape*, 1935) was looking for an escape from this irremediable Being. Only four decades later in *Otherwise than Being* (1974) will Levinas come to fully plot out "a new path out of being," a temporal path that he started to chart in *Time and the Other* (1947), which forges a fundamental link between time and ethics. The time that the future brings is not merely the recurrence of the present instant or its continuation but the possibility of another instant or a new beginning. How can an existent in the instant recommence otherwise? The coming of the future announces another original instant that cannot be approached, but that comes; that cannot be assumed, since it appears as an epiphany. The existent is able to welcome the absolutely strangeness of the epiphany of the future because of the inherent susceptibility to fraternity and sociality, which is made possible by time. This, however, is not the time that the existent *has* like a possession but a capacity to welcome time that springs from an existential chronological inconsistency—a being temporally out of joint. To further specify, this "capacity" is not a power that the individual instant is endowed with. Quite to the contrary, faced with the radical strangeness of the future, with the alterity of the face of the Other, the existent is reduced to a "radical passivity." Passivity is the *radix* or root of ethical agency. The capacity that time gives is the capacity for generosity, the power to be able to give of the riches accumulated. This is not to turn away from one's egotistical selfish life once and for all but a being turned to be able to welcome the Other without being obliterated in the face of an absolute Mystery.

Levinas also theorizes this "survival" through time in terms of fecundity through which the I can remain I in the alterity of another without losing the self in the Other. The relationship with the child is a relationship with myself that is nevertheless a stranger to me. The child announces a multiplicity and a transcendence in existence by opening the perspective of the future. The child is not merely a continuation of the I but an interruption and resurrection across the discontinuous that constitutes time. The possibility that fecundity brings is the possibility of time and the ethical: the possibility for the new through the possibility of truth that presides over the failure of goodness today. This possibility of a new beginning is not the effacement of the past but the pardon that purifies the past and the injustices committed. Pardon consists in a retroactive action that inverts the natural temporal order of things and implies the "reversibility of time," as we have seen. Now, the past instant has not passed but can be lived again, differently.

In Levinas we find a nonteleological conception of time. Truth, Levinas contends, requires both an infinite time and a completed time conceived as "messianic time." Messianic time, more precisely, may be conceived as the "extreme vigilance of the messianic consciousness," since it is only such vigilant consciousness that can protect us against the revenge of evil—which infinite time cannot do. This notion of "messianic consciousness" is encapsulated in Levinas's conceptualization of eschatology, which is the infinity beyond totality or beyond history, without denying history. The eschatological is not realized at the end of time but rather in each instant in which our responsibility vis-à-vis the Other is realized. If this responsibility exempts us from the jurisdiction of history and the future, salvation is not to be found at the end of history but remains at each moment possible.

The mature Levinas develops the notion of diachronic time introduced in *Time and the Other*. Perhaps our existential chronological inconsistency might be best understood through the notion of diachronic time. Dia-chrony—through time—does not signal a teleological evolution over time but is an immemorial affective infection by the Other that exceeds rational recall by the existent. Before our time, before having time, we have been endowed with the capacity to welcome time. This "capacity," as we have seen, is the *Desire* for time. It is what makes possible my turning away from my selfish preoccupation with my present needs in the world to open to the infinite responsibility that I bear toward another. It is as if the egoist existent's *conatus essendi*—the self's very persistence in being—is momentarily stalled by an inherent susceptibility to hear and heed the call to responsibility. It is what awakens us to the necessity of a permanent messianic vigilance. This is how Levinas theorizes the possibility of time as "completed" in every instant of the present now. Hence it is the "discomfort" of an inherent chronological inconsistency that haunts our egoist existential exploits in the world that makes ethical action—a being first for-the-Other before being-for-oneself—possible.

Postscript: The Ethical Risk of Chronopathologies

Having considered the place and ethical significance of time in Levinas's ethical metaphysics, we might in the final instance consider the place of time in his thought from the vantage point of what Jack Reynolds calls "time-sicknesses" or "chronopathologies."[62] A salient feature of chronopathology is a metaphilosophical prioritization of one or two dimensions of time over another, or the privileging or exclusive reliance on one model of time at the expense of another. Examples of conceptualizations of time afflicted by such chronopathologies include the clock model of time, that is, a linear model of time where moments succeed one another—a model that analytic philosophy typically subscribes to—and the model of time based on the incalculable future, which, according to Reynolds, is the model utilized by post-structuralism. What Levinas's thoroughly "temporalized" ethical metaphysics throws into relief is the risk of ethical incapacitation that such afflicted "time-poor" philosophies are exposed to.

As we have seen, Levinas is explicitly concerned with the past, present and future. He conceives of the past as an "immemorial past." An immemorial past is not bygone events and experiences that have slipped into oblivion but a time at which the self has been infected by a trace of alterity that can in nowise be recuperated by way of representation. It is this fundamental elusiveness of the past that is of supreme ethical import since it makes otherness fundamentally irreducible to my other-reductive representation in the present. The operation of the past in the present, then, is the origination of an affective responsiveness in the self to the unknowable Other that approaches from a future as opaque as death. Whereas death is the end of my time, the impossibility of all my possibilities, the future gives me time, time to be otherwise than my egoist being. This is a time that stalls my self-enriching egoist economy and opens the possibility of generosity. The trace from an immemorial past makes me *able to hear and respond* to the call of the Other that comes to me in my present from an unknowable future. This is a call so foreign to the egology of the self that the self uninfected by the trace would remain deaf to it. This audibility makes possible the retroactive pardoning of my past injustices.

If time does in fact carry with it the risk of such disruptive self-indictment, it would account for much of the chronopathologies and indeed the chronophobia that time-averse, time-reductive, or time-selective philosophies are afflicted with. They attempt to reduce the extent to which the future and past affect us; they attempt to close the openness to the future that necessarily resists our calculative entreaties; and they attempt to reduce the immemorial past to a representable totality. Read from the perspective of Levinas's ethical metaphysics, philosophies that succumb to chronopathologies such as the prioritization of one dimension of time at the expense of others, or subscribing to a linear model of time, or temporal presentism are deprived of a temporality that opens the possibility of ethics. Yael Lin succinctly captures Levinas's conceptualization of the role of the various temporal dimensions in the possibility of an ethical existence:

> Levinas's turn to "the other" opens up "the pure, ungraspable future" beyond my finite time: "infinite" in the sense that desire for the good of the other is insatiable

and points beyond the life of any particular person towards a messianic future that would itself be open-ended. Furthermore, responsibility for the other is "always already" given with the face, not rooted in a choice by the subject or a contract between subjects; in this sense it attests to "an immemorial past." In responsibility, Levinas claims, "infinity" is revealed as involving "a future that cannot be fulfilled and a past that was never present."[63]

Notes

1. This section draws in part on Benda Hofmeyr, "Dying the Human Condition: Re-reading Ivan Ilyich with Levinas," *The International Journal of the Humanities* 5, no. 2 (2007): 126–36.
2. Emmanuel Levinas, *Time and the Other*, trans. Richard Cohen (Pittsburgh: Duquesne University Press, 1987), 81.
3. Emmanuel Levinas, *Existence and Existents*, trans. Alphonso Lingis (The Hague: Martinus Nijhoff, 1978), 15.
4. Levinas, *Time*, 79.
5. Levinas, *Time*, 14.
6. Emmanuel Levinas, *Totality and Infinity: An Essay on Exteriority*, trans. Alphonso Lingis (The Hague: Martinus Nijhoff, 1979), 234.
7. Emmanuel Levinas, *Otherwise than Being or Beyond Essence*, trans. Alphonso Lingis (Dordrecht/Boston/London: Kluwer Academic Publishers, 1991), 111, 124.
8. Levinas, *Time*, 79.
9. Levinas, *Time*, 69; Levinas, *Totality*, 238–9.
10. Levinas, *Totality*, 238.
11. Levinas, *Time*, 70–1; Levinas, *Totality*, 235.
12. Levinas, *Time*, 74.
13. Levinas, *Time*, 75.
14. Levinas, *Totality*, 234.
15. Levinas, *Time*, 74.
16. Epicurus, *Letter to Meneoceus* cited in Levinas, *Time*, 71.
17. Levinas *Time*, 71.
18. Sylvia Plath, *The Unabridged Journals of Sylvia Plath 1950–1962, Transcribed from the Original Manuscripts at Smith College*, ed. Karen V. Kukil (New York: Anchor Books, 2000), 149, 150.
19. Levinas, *Time*, 73.
20. "Spiro/spero," meaning "[if] I breathe, I hope" (Levinas, *Time*, 73).
21. Levinas, *Time*, 73.
22. Levinas, *Time*, 73.
23. Levinas, *Totality*, 56.
24. Levinas, *Totality*, 281.
25. Levinas, *Time*, 90.
26. Levinas, *Time*, 91.
27. Levinas, *Totality*, 267.
28. Levinas, *Time*, 92.
29. Levinas, *Totality*, 284.
30. Levinas, *Totality*, 284.

31 Levinas, *Totality*, 284.
32 Levinas, *Totality*, 283.
33 Nibras Chehayed, "Nietzsche and Levinas on Time," *Continental Philosophical Review* 52, no. 4 (2019): 52, 390.
34 Levinas, *Totality*, 285.
35 Levinas, *Totality*, 285.
36 Levinas, *Totality*, 22–3.
37 Levinas, *Totality*, 23.
38 Chehayed, "Nietzsche and Levinas," 391.
39 Emmanuel Levinas, *Difficult Freedom: Essays on Judaism*, trans. Sean Hand (Baltimore: The Johns Hopkins University Press, 1997), 84.
40 Levinas, *Totality*, 247.
41 Levinas, *Totality*, 246.
42 Levinas, *Totality*, 247.
43 Chehayed, "Nietzsche and Levinas," 391.
44 Chehayed, "Nietzsche and Levinas," 388.
45 Chehayed, "Nietzsche and Levinas," 388.
46 Levinas, *Time*, 39.
47 Edmund Husserl, *Cartesian Meditations: An Introduction to Phenomenology*, trans. Dorian Cairns (The Hague: Martinus Nijhoff, 1960), 115.
48 Chehayed, "Nietzsche and Levinas," 388.
49 Levinas, *Otherwise than Being*, 32.
50 Levinas, *Otherwise than Being*, 33.
51 Levinas, *Otherwise than Being*, 34.
52 Chehayed, "Nietzsche and Levinas," 388.
53 Emmanuel Levinas, *Basic Philosophical Writings*, ed. Robert Bernasconi, Simon Critchley and Adriaan Peperzak (Bloomington: Indiana University Press, 1996), 62.
54 Levinas, *Basic Philosophical*, 62.
55 Levinas, *Basic Philosophical*, 72.
56 Chehayed, "Nietzsche and Levinas," 389.
57 Emmanuel Levinas, *Entre Nous: Thinking-of-the-Other*, trans. Michael B. Smith and Barbara Harshav (New York: Columbia University Press, 1998), 57–8.
58 Levinas, *Otherwise than Being*, 88.
59 Richard Cohen, "Responsible Time," *Cahier d'études Lévinassiennes* 2 (2003): 51.
60 Levinas, *Otherwise than Being*, 91.
61 Levinas, *Otherwise than Being*, 91.
62 Jack Reynolds, "Time, Philosophy and Chronopathologies," *Parrhesia*, iss. 15 (2012): 77. Also see Jack Reynolds, *Chronopathologies: Time and Politics in Deleuze, Derrida, Analytic Philosophy, and Phenomenology* (Minneapolis, MN: Lexington Books, 2012).
63 Yael Lin, *The Intersubjectivity of Time: Levinas and Infinite Responsibility* (Pittsburgh: Duquesne University Press, 2013), 76.

Bibliography

Chehayed, Nibras. "Nietzsche and Levinas on Time." *Continental Philosophical Review* 52, no. 4 (2019): 381–95.
Cohen, Richard. "Responsible Time." *Cahier d'études Lévinassiennes* 2 (2003): 39–54.

Hofmeyr, Benda. "Dying the Human Condition: Re-reading Ivan Ilyich with Levinas." *The International Journal of the Humanities* 5, no. 2 (2007): 126–36.

Levinas, Emmanuel. *Basic Philosophical Writings*. Edited by Robert Bernasconi, Simon Critchley and Adriaan Peperzak. Bloomington: Indiana University Press, 1996.

Levinas, Emmanuel. *Difficult Freedom: Essays on Judaism*. Translated by Sean Hand. Baltimore: The Johns Hopkins University Press, 1997.

Levinas, Emmanuel. *Entre Nous: Thinking-of-the-Other*. Translated by Michael B. Smith and Barbara Harshav. New York: Columbia University Press, 1998.

Levinas, Emmanuel. *Existence and Existents*. Translated by Alphonso Lingis. The Hague: Martinus Nijhoff, 1978.

Levinas, Emmanuel. *On Escape*. Translated by Bettina Bergo. Stanford: Stanford University Press, 2003.

Levinas, Emmanuel. *Otherwise than Being or Beyond Essence*. Translated by Alphonso Lingis. Dordrecht/Boston/London: Kluwer Academic Publishers. 1991.

Levinas, Emmanuel. *Time and the Other*. Translated by Richard Cohen. Pittsburgh: Duquesne University Press, 1987.

Levinas, Emmanuel. *Totality and Infinity: An Essay on Exteriority*. Translated by Alphonso Lingis. The Hague: Martinus Nijhoff, 1979.

Lin, Yael. *The Intersubjectivity of Time: Levinas and Infinite Responsibility*, Pittsburgh: Duquesne University Press, 2013.

Plath, Sylvia. *The Unabridged Journals of Sylvia Plath 1950–1962, transcribed from the original manuscripts at Smith College*. Edited by Karen V. Kukil. New York: Anchor Books, 2000.

Reynolds, Jack. *Chronopathologies: Time and Politics in Deleuze, Derrida, Analytic Philosophy, and Phenomenology*. Minneapolis, MN: Lexington Books, 2012.

Reynolds, Jack. "Time, Philosophy and Chronopathologies." *Parrhesia* 15 (2012): 64–80.

13

Historical Time, Collective Memory, and the Finitude of Historical Understanding

Jeffrey Andrew Barash

Historical Understanding in the Contemporary Era

During recent decades, the magnitude, complexity, and unpredictability of changes that have transpired on an unprecedented scale have obliged us to reconsider the scope and the purpose of historical understanding. In the contemporary context, these changes have led us to question traditional political, social, and economic categories of historical interpretation and the grand narratives of national and world-historical development they promoted. In this contemporary situation, ushered in by the somber events of the Second World War, we can speak not only of meaning in history but, to employ Reinhart Koselleck's apt expression, also of an *absence* of meaning, of "nonsense" (*Unsinn*) that the contemporary period has made evident.[1]

As historical phenomena, mutation, disruption, and discontinuity bring about not only noticeable changes in the circumstances of human existence, they also make visible the relentless shifts in *perspective* through which these circumstances are apprehended and interpreted. They underscore both the ties that link language and other modes of symbolic comprehension to the context in which they emerge and the *limits* of understanding, on the basis of any one given context, of the concrete texture of a period that is foreign to it. Modifications in group perspective that accompany rapid change, dislocation, and discontinuity bring to light the contingency and finitude of historical understanding in its quest to comprehend the past in relation to the present.

In the pages that follow I will highlight this heightened sensitivity toward the finitude of historical understanding in view of examining a shift in its interpretation: a sharper focus on the mutability of group perspectives has brought to the fore underlying changes in the perception of the *temporal* structure that underlies historical thought and that orients conceptions of historical continuity and discontinuity it posits. In renouncing bold claims of the philosophy of history in its quest for the unity of history as an overall process, the problem of historical understanding takes as its more modest focus modifications in the perception of historical time. This phenomenon suggests the primary question I will address: in a period of dislocation and discontinuity with the past, how might we identify articulations of historical time through which group identities are configured? In view of the limits that shifts in group perspective impose on the possibility of historical understanding, how might we conceive of the cohesiveness of group identities and group histories over time in the sphere both of theory and of everyday practice?

I will begin by considering what I take to be three seminal interpretations of historical time in Western thought that have come to light over the course of the twentieth century. They have provided highly influential approaches to the question of the cohesion of history and of collective identities over time. This will lead in the second part of my analysis to a consideration of the heightened awareness of the contingency and variability of historical perspective as a source of the current critical appraisal of traditional ideas of historical time and of the subsequent emergence of the topic of collective memory to account for the phenomenon of group cohesion. I interpret collective memory to be not an overarching substantial entity encompassing human plurality but rather a group awareness of the past delimited within a specific horizon of human *temporality*. An understanding of the contours of this horizon, as I will argue, provides a fresh vantage point for a critical assessment of traditional historical theory permitting us to redefine historical awareness in contemporary perspective.

From the Bold Claims of the Philosophy of History to Reflection on Historical Time

At the moment of its emergence in the late nineteenth and early twentieth centuries, novel theoretical insight into the limits of comprehension of history as a total process focused investigation on changing perceptions of historical time. Wilhelm Dilthey, in his epoch-making work *Introduction to the Human Sciences*, elaborated the idea that each historical period is oriented by its own particular *Weltanschauung*, which, in anchoring its perspective in a given present, limits the possibility of divining, beyond the purview of this perspective, the sense of history as a whole. Dilthey thereby undermined the Hegelian claim to grasp history as a movement of the Absolute Spirit, while also refuting the assumptions of Auguste Comte's positivism that, on the basis of supposed natural laws of historical development, interpreted the meaning of history as a total process. In the framework of his celebrated "critique of historical reason," Dilthey deflected theoretical concern away from such grandiose historical constructs and turned toward epistemological investigation of the conditions of historical understanding. This investigation took as its focal point the anthropological significance of modifications in temporal perception through which historical understanding in Western culture came to the fore.

In *Einleitung in die Geisteswissenschaften* Dilthey traced the emergence of a novel historical consciousness in the West to the doctrines of the Christian religion. Christianity, in breaking away from Greco-Roman mythology and in nuancing metaphysical conceptions of fixed, unchanging truth, introduced the idea of an historical advent of truth in the successive revelations of the Divinity. After historical prefigurations of the coming of the Messiah in the Jewish Old Testament, Christ emerged in human history to embrace and supersede this earlier revelation. As Dilthey stipulated, this grasp of sacred truth as an historical advent conceived the unity of all human history in terms of a Providential plan, with a beginning, a middle, and an end. History, as Dilthey noted, far from taking on the temporal form of interacting causes, followed the temporal sequence of a unified teleology.²

It would be difficult to exaggerate the potency of this teleological doctrine for intellectual and public life, as for artistic imagination over the course of centuries. The theme of prefiguration, encompassing the narrative of the Old Testament in the temporal framework of the New, is graphically illustrated in the tradition of Western painting as, in the decades after Dilthey, art historians such as Erich Auerbach and Erwin Panofsky abundantly illustrated.³ The prophet Jonah, who spent three days and nights in the belly of a whale, was explicitly cited by Matthew (12:39-40) as a symbol prefiguring the resurrection of Christ. In similar fashion, the historical time of Christian eschatology provided a central motif for traditional Western culture. Consider, for example, the evocative Last Judgment altarpiece painting of Rogier Van der Weyden in the Hospices de Beaune in Burgundy, France (1443–52), on which the inscription underneath the lily of Christ who sits in judgment proclaims the unity of history, from the beginning to the end of time: "Come the blessed of my Father, receive as a legacy the Kingdom prepared for you since the foundation of the world."

Like Dilthey, the philosopher Karl Löwith, in his book *Meaning in History* from 1949, emphasized the originality of the Christian conception of history as the central paradigm for interpretation of historical time in the Western tradition. For Löwith, Christian eschatology, in breaking with ancient Greek conceptions of history as a cyclical movement analogous to that of natural phenomena of growth and demise, introduced the predominant conception of historical time that was destined to persevere well into the era of Enlightenment and secularization. For Löwith, the teleological pattern of history that animated Enlightenment ideas of history was a secularized form of Christianity, projecting onto the immanent historical realm the teleological orientation of historical time that the original Christian doctrine had identified with the Providential plan. Hegel's *Phenomenology of the Spirit*, in situating the Divinity in the immanent realm of historical becoming and postulating that each phase of its movement toward self-knowledge supersedes and encompasses the preceding phases, brought this Enlightenment interpretation of historical time to its ultimate expression. Löwith, in accord with this celebrated secularization thesis, tended to consider all modern philosophies of history to be secularized projections of an earlier Christian conception of historical time; and whereas Hans Blumenberg roundly criticized this manner of deriving modern historical conceptions from Christian sources, he nonetheless did not dispute Löwith's central premise concerning the linear, future orientation of historical time embraced on different planes both by traditional Christian eschatology and modern philosophy of history. Whatever relation might be ascribed to the traditional Christian and modern conceptions of historical time, it is an analogous *linear* orientation that comes to expression in modern historical conceptions of progression to ever higher forms of human development as the paradigmatic expression of the philosophy of history. Löwith attributed this model to all forms of "progressive" historical thought, from the Enlightenment and

Hegel onward. Moreover, Löwith considered twentieth-century theories of history as decline, such as in Oswald Spengler's *Decline of the West*, or Martin Heidegger's vision of deepening human historical forgetfulness of Being, to be inversions of the progressive models, which like them assigned to history a unified direction, albeit one of regression, concealment, and obfuscation. All of these visions of history, whether of progress or decline, marshaled for Löwith unwarranted assumptions according to which history might be grasped as a unified linear process that unfolds in the immanent realm.[4]

The more recent work of Reinhart Koselleck presents a third seminal theory of historical time. For Koselleck the great innovation of the Enlightenment lay in its manner of projecting human historical development, on the basis of an existing space of experience (*Erfahrungsraum*), onto a future horizon of historical expectation (*Erwartungshorizont*), toward which it was believed this development was leading. The novelty in this modern approach to history that made its appearance in the eighteenth century lay in its sharp divergence from previous conceptions of history that took long-term continuity between the present and the future for granted. In the modern period, according to Koselleck, a gap emerged between cumulative experiences handed down from the past and expectations for the future, and this gap continued to widen over time. In relation to the space of present experience, modernity could expect a qualitatively different future. Since this difference was in many respects envisioned in the guise of *progress*, it brought forth a specifically modern conception of history. History assumed the form of an immanent process encompassing an overarching, cohesive whole—a "collective singular" in Koselleck's terminology. It introduced the novel modern conception of history as an objective, autonomous agent that, in its manner of providing the temporal structure and essential orientation for human historical development, replaced the providential plan of traditional Christian theology.[5] This orientation opened the way to the assumption shared by different modern ideologies, according to which history as a unified process might be appropriated and subjected to human control. For Koselleck, the illusory character of this assumption reveals itself directly where "human foresight, human plans and their execution always diverge over the course of time." Even where influential people may in a certain sense "make" history, the horizon of the future always remains open, since history as a unified web can never be mastered and subjected to human prevision.[6]

It would reach beyond the limited space of the present study to provide a detailed examination of the three interpretations of historical time proposed at different points of the twentieth century by Wilhelm Dilthey, Karl Löwith, and Reinhart Koselleck. The brief sketch I have drawn suffices, however, to illustrate what I consider to be a salient development in our own early twenty-first century: the distance that separates recent attempts to grapple with the phenomenon of historical time from the earlier models of history that each of these authors described, which shared a conception of history as a unified temporal schema forming an autonomous process moving toward an end. According to my hypothesis, the heightened awareness of contingency and discontinuity that has become a generalized experience in an increasingly globalized historical situation has brought into theoretical view a novel perspective on historical time in the contemporary period.

This hypothesis finds a measure of support in the development of Koselleck's own theoretical orientation in the last period of his production. In the years before his death in 2006, Koselleck turned increasingly toward a less Eurocentric and, indeed, less anthropocentric conception of historical time. This came to poignant expression notably in his speech "The Emergence into Modernity or the End of the Era of the Horse" ("Der Aufbruch in die Moderne oder das Ende des Pferdezeitalters"), presented on the occasion of the reception of the *Historikerpreis* conferred on him in 2003 by the city of Münster. After beginning his speech with the affirmation that "so-called modernity is not indeed a unified, clear, or clearly definable period,"[7] he organized the temporal schema of the modern era in relation to one of its central, if often neglected, consequences: the disappearance of the primary role of the horse, not only as a mode of transport but also as a central aspect of all spheres of human life, from sports, war, agriculture, and art to mythical and religious symbolism. Dividing historical periodization into time before and after the domestication of the horse, leading finally to the devaluation of its role in the modern period, Koselleck situated the advent of the technological era of instantaneous media communication, rapid transit, and automated warfare in a development that avoided purely human categories of progress or decline, for he set the obsolescence of the horse in a temporal framework that has no manifest direction or goal, nor could it be unified in terms of a clear overall orientation. This perspective has been extended and deepened in the more recent work of Ulrich Raulff, *Farewell to the Horse: The Final Century of our Relationship* (*Das letzte Jahrhundert der Pferde: Geschichte einer Trennung*). One of the notable conclusions of this work is that the modern conception of history as a unified process and an autonomous agent, which animated the philosophy of history, generally limited its geographical scope to Europe and Asia Minor and to literate cultures. The end of the age of the horse corresponds to an increasing focus on wider geographical regions and nonanthropological factors that have shaped human history, from archeology and ethnology to paleobiology and other disciplines, and this in turn leads to a broadening of investigation of the historical role of nonhuman factors such as the horse.[8]

The concept of the end of the epoch of the horse permitted Koselleck and Ulrich Raulff to underscore the unprecedented character of the historical situation in which we find ourselves today. This situation may be further qualified in terms of François Hartog's concept of "presentism" as developed in his work *Regimes of Historicity: Presentism and Experiences of Time*, which signals what he takes to be a novel contemporary orientation toward historical time. This concept questioned the ongoing relevance of Koselleck's earlier theory of historical time in terms of a relation between the space of experience (*Erfahrungsraum*) and the horizon of expectation (*Erwartungshorizont*).[9] If for Hartog, Koselleck's model closely corresponded to the emergence of an unprecedented experience of historical time in the eighteenth and nineteenth centuries, it has nonetheless lost its earlier significance in our current world. Hartog's remarks also implicitly question the ongoing significance of models of history, such as those analyzed by Dilthey or Löwith, that took it to be a unified process of development tending toward a goal.

According to Hartog's argument, the experience of history in the current framework of collective life has been propelled beyond its modern form to enter into an era of presentism as a novel "regime of historicity," in which the traditional linear experience of history as a unified movement of past and present toward the future has given way to an increasing contemporary submergence in the present. According to this argument, the linear model of philosophy of history has lost its plausibility in the contemporary world along with modern ideologies that, in terms of class or nation, sought to establish long-term lines of continuity between past and present and provided specific orientations toward the future. In this perspective, moreover, the decline of the philosophy of history and of traditional ideologies that rested on linear models of historical time concerned not only liberal and Marxist ideologies, for traditional conservatism, which sought to maintain the heritage of the past in view of the future, also presupposed the unity of history as a process. Absorbed in present preoccupations, our contemporary societies subordinate both the historical past and the anticipated future to the short-term vision encompassing current projects.[10]

Hartog's concept of presentism provides an important index for assessing a pervasive contemporary experience of historical time as it attends to what is scientifically and technologically up-to-date and accords a privilege to the cognizance of current events, while devaluing what appears to be obsolete in a given present situation. In spite of the merits of Hartog's concept of presentism, it does not, in my opinion, sufficiently account for contemporary attitudes toward the relation between past and present in the articulation of historical time. As I see it, he overlooks above all one of the principal features of the present context: the quest for continuity with the past as a source of group identity and social cohesion. In more extreme forms, this quest has given rise to a nostalgic, quasi-mythical attempt to appropriate a past credo that fuels religious fundamentalism or the new forms of populist nationalism. As our present situation well attests, the accent these extremist movements place on the past by no means excludes the embrace of the latest technologies and the culture of mass communications.[11]

In a contemporary context in which the philosophy of history and traditional ideologies no longer furnish plausible accounts of historical continuity and change, renewed concern for the temporal dynamics of group identity, in a situation of rapid change and dislocation, has inspired investigation into the sources of social continuity and the causes of its evanescence. This to my mind accounts for the fact that the theme of collective memory, not only as a faculty for retaining past experience but above all as an organ for social cohesion and a horizon of plural coexistence in time, has come to the forefront of contemporary discourse. In a world in which the lines of continuity with the past have become tenuous, the question arises concerning how this apparently nebulous function of collective memory might be comprehended. My intention here is not to pass in review the variety of ways in which collective memory has been defined in recent years. I aim to distinguish what I take to be the specific temporal articulations of collective memory from traditional models of historical time. This will permit us to set in relief a deeper source of the experience of historical contingency and finitude that has become an integral aspect of our contemporary world.

Collective Memory and the Finitude of Historical Understanding

My focus on the concept of collective memory as a means of elucidating the finitude and contingency of historical time might seem immediately problematic, due to the difficulty of defining this concept. Previous attempts to interpret "collective memory" have given rise to a panoply of heterogeneous formulations that have been subjected to sharp critique voiced notably, among the numerous examples that might be cited, by Koselleck. I recall in this vein the vehemence with which he rejected the concept of collective memory in his speech commemorating the German capitulation on May 8, 1945, "The 8th of May between Memory and History" ("Der 8. Mai zwischen Erinnerung und Geschichte"), published in the collection of essays *Vom Sinn und Unsinn der Geschichte* (*On the Sense and Nonsense of History*). As he wrote,

> The collective entities that Durkheim, Halbwachs, and other sociologists burdened with shared memory and communal recollection are linguistic constructs, quasi-religious ideological topics, the *unio mystica* of a community of belief that supposedly convey national frames of reference (*Referenzsysteme*). If we subject them to ideological critique, we do not encounter collective memories (for these are always individual), but collective conditions of memories that are each time my own (*der je eigenen Erinnerungen*). These collective conditions are multiple: linguistic, political, economic, religious, mental, social, generational, and so on. These kinds of plural stratified (*abgeschichtete*) conditions call forth experiences and simultaneously limit them, make experiences possible and obstruct them.[12]

Koselleck's statement brings us to the crux of the matter. Might it be possible to admit what he takes to be the originary status of personal memory, in view of the fact that groups as such do not remember, any more than they have a substantial, autonomous being, while insisting on the significance of the concept of collective memory that Koselleck places so strongly in question? Here we must pursue more closely the specific sense I am according to collective memory as an indicator of human temporal finitude.

Let us begin with a reference to the concept of collective memory elaborated by Maurice Halbwachs, who was an explicit target of Koselleck's criticism. The novelty of Halbwachs's theory of collective memory lies in the privilege he accorded to *living* memory as it is shared by groups in their specific milieus of interaction. Collective memory in this sense is deployed at once at the different levels of small groups and of vast collectivities. In dealing with living memory in this sense, Halbwachs recognized the originary status of personal memory based on direct experience in the everyday lifeworld, while he at the same time accorded a fundamental role to remembered experience communicated among members of interwoven living generations. It is at this group level that we uncover the specific *temporal* order of collective memory in relation to historical time.

Halbwachs highlighted the process by which spheres of reminiscence shared by members of living generations gradually fade as these generations disappear. The oldest members in a series of overlapping contemporaneous generations, as long as they survive, are a living testimony to the past that younger contemporaries could not have known. Their modes of existence and the stock of remembered experience they are able to communicate, which are on the verge of disappearing, but which still perdure, resonate in the remembrance of their younger contemporaries. The disappearance of these older generations, beyond the mere loss of individuals and their personal reminiscences, brings about the evanescence of a whole life context of older groups. Their loss brings about a decisive shift in temporal horizon, which for the most part remains unperceived. In this manner Halbwachs set in relief the contours of group *contemporaneity* that, following the demise of living generations, leads to the disappearance of their temporal context, which gradually fades from living memory.[13]

Halbwachs illustrated this movement of collective memory by means of a particularly eloquent example. He cited in this vein the narrative of Stendhal in his autobiographical novel, *La vie de Henri Brulard*, where he recounted Stendhal's reminiscence of his grandfather, born in Grenoble well before the French Revolution. Although Stendhal's reminiscence was personal, it retained words, gestures, and styles that his grandfather shared with a whole prerevolutionary world that had subsequently disappeared. As Halbwachs wrote in commenting on Stendhal's description of his older relative:

> It is not only facts, but previous ways of being and of thinking that become thus fixed in memory.... It is often because the face of an elderly parent is in some sense adorned by all it has revealed to us of a period and of an antiquated society that it is distinguished in our memory not as a somewhat effaced physical appearance, but in the relief and color of a person who is at the center of an entire portrait which he resumes and condenses.[14]

In a more recent epoch, we could indeed invoke in this vein the disappearance of the horse in all of its functions in recent decades as a similar passage of the experience of living generations into the depths of the historical past. It is by no means accidental that Ulrich Raulff begins his book, *Das letzte Jahrhundert der Pferde*, with the words: "To be born in the countryside in the mid-twentieth century meant growing up in an old world."[15]

The profound breach occasioned by the loss of all living remembrance of the past cannot be spanned by collective memory, which extends only so far as its contemporaneously living sources. On this basis, we may establish a radical distinction between collective memory and the historical past. Following the loss of all living sources of collective memory, only the historian's work of deciphering might reconstruct, in an indirect and piecemeal manner, the context of lost time.

My brief depiction of Halbwachs's theory of collective memory suffices to illustrate the distance between the temporal dimension of memory he uncovered and the broad Western conceptions of historical time described by Dilthey, Löwith, and Koselleck that I sketched in the first part of my essay. Dilthey's notion of the unique quality of Western conceptions of historical time as they developed in the wake of Judeo-Christian eschatology, Löwith's conception of Enlightenment and post-Enlightenment philosophies of history that reoriented Christian eschatology by adopting the idea of history's forward movement while projecting it onto the immanent historical realm, Koselleck's theory of the emergence in the eighteenth century of an idea of history as an autonomous self-propelling process, projecting historical time in a given space of experience toward a future horizon of expectation: all of these conceptions belong to an order that contrasts sharply with the temporal schema of collective memory elaborated by Halbwachs. The idea of history in its diversity as a unified, autonomous domain is undermined by the vision of radical discontinuity that intervenes following the loss of living generations and the passage of their horizon of contemporaneity into the depths of the historical past. In the perspective of living memory, the passage of time throws a deepening shroud of opacity over the past. Beyond representations of unity spanning the different epochs of history, we can rely only on prudent historical deliberation and imaginative reconstruction to attain a limited retrieval of the past's remote contours.

Collective Memory, the Contingency of Human History, and Prospects for the Future

My approach to the singular temporal contours of collective memory that distinguish it from the time of history calls for a reformulation of Halbwachs's theory. This reformulation begins by shifting the *level* of analysis on which the concept of collective memory is deployed.[16] Where Koselleck doubted the meaningfulness of the concept of collective memory and was willing to refer at most to "collective conditions of experience that is each time my own" that he enumerated in terms of a heterogeneous collection of transcendental preconditions, including linguistic, religious, political, economic, and other factors, I would ascribe this configurative function more generally to the order of *symbols* and of *symbolic* interaction. Where, moreover, Halbwachs elaborated this concept primarily in relation to the social frameworks of smaller groups, such as families and other associations, my emphasis on the order of symbols requires that we shift the primary focus of investigation to the broad domain of mass social life and of the corresponding public sphere. This shift is based on the consideration that the communication of what is collectively experienced and remembered, far from specific to smaller social frameworks, is conveyed first and foremost through language and other symbolic forms that all publicly intelligible patterns of social interaction presuppose. Symbols in this sense are not mere signs or signals, nor are they secondary additions to what has been given beforehand; they are spontaneous ways of conferring spatiotemporal pattern and logical order on experience. In an urban environment, for example, I immediately familiarize myself with spatial differences between private yards and public parks or semi-public shopping malls, even before I explicitly reflect on them, just as the background music I hear in an airport or supermarket, a restaurant or church, gives me direct clues concerning the surrounding social milieu. In lending spontaneous intelligibility to experience that is interiorized by memory, symbols are communicated in the form of language, gestures, styles, or corporeal attitudes.

What I term collective memory arises from a network of symbolic configurations interwoven at a multitude of different levels of social interaction that are deployed in a contemporaneous framework.

A second reformulation of the concept of collective memory leads us to highlight not only active functions of memory but also the *passive* levels that underlie symbolic networks and confer cohesion to group remembrance in a public world. Beyond reminiscence that is explicitly evoked among groups, the concept of passivity accounts for the implicit strata of shared remembrance. In this framework, collective memory does not only concern commemorations, the display of past vestiges in museums, their storage in archives, or the transmission of a past heritage but first and foremost the vast reservoirs of signification that nourish latent sources of interpretation situated at the basis of group identities. Far from monolithic structures, such collectively retained symbolic configurations that extend into the passive reaches of a given social context are always fragmented, for their interpretation varies according to the group that perceives and recalls them. They are also continually subject to re-elaboration and to gradual effacement, following the demise of living generations and the passage of their traces into the remote reaches of the historical past. Even where language and other symbols retain their general intelligibility over the course of centuries, the nuances that living groups accord to them evoke an intrinsic sense that is specific to their living context. These nuances are subject to a remarkable variability, which is often barely palpable, that ensues with the passage of a contemporary group into the past beyond all living memory.

This constant, if mostly tacit variability in symbolic structures that reach to the deepest passive levels of human experience and remembrance accounts for mutations in perspective through which contemporaneous groups, in spite of all fragmentation in their viewpoints, are interwoven in a common shared context. In linking them to this same context, the contemporaneity of perspective limits their collective grasp of what extends beyond its scope. It characterizes what I have qualified as the *finitude* of collective memory and it is the original matrix of group historicity. Where ambitious claims overlook the specific finite regime of memory, they readily fall prey to the illusion that the historical past might be retrieved, as if it were an object of living remembrance, and placed at the disposal of the present. Nonetheless, changes in the symbolic structures underlying social cohesion that constitute historical perspectives over time, if they render problematic the decipherability of the past, intervene in often imperceptible and unforeseeable ways. Such changes that orient the implicit ways in which we experience and collectively remember, even if they are at times occasioned by palpable influences, hardly conform to the schema of general historical teleologies or other global assumptions concerning history as a unified process. They undermine the basis of a total vision proposed by the philosophy of history and render precarious long-term projects of planification or social control. In the wake of radical and rapid change that brings the limits of human historical understanding into ever sharper focus, the ambitious ideological projects that claim to divine the temporal direction of history and its overarching sense belong to the unfulfillable aspirations of the modern period.

This critical observation by no means contests the possibility of entertaining robust projects for historical development in the future. On the contrary, I emphatically underline the importance of engaging practical principles of collective action in a long-term historical context that can never hope to attain a secure foundation in strictly empirical understanding. This assertion, however, raises a fundamental problem that I will address in conclusion.

If, as I have illustrated, the shifting horizons of collective memory retained by living generations reveal sharp and often unsuspected limits of historical understanding, how might long-term practical principles of collective action be comprehended? Given the radical historicity of human understanding commanded by mutations in the symbolic articulations of group experience and collective memory, how might it be possible to engage transhistorical projects that bridge the life spans of successive generations? It would reach beyond the confines of this brief analysis to answer these questions in detail, and I will limit my remarks to the identification of a model of historical understanding that is to my mind appropriate to our contemporary situation. Indeed, an exemplary practical precept in this sense is suggested to my mind by Hans Jonas's model of understanding of historical time presented by his conception of responsibility to assure the ongoing survival of future generations.

In anticipating the peril to which our continued devastation of the natural ecology of the earth exposes its future inhabitants, this principle calls for present measures to deal with the unprecedented situation that recent abuses have engendered. It engages a novel approach to historical *time*, as Jonas himself recognized, since collective acts in the present, as they involve long-term consequences, require a temporal vision capable of projecting potential dangers imposed on future generations, where irresponsible public policy in the present is not redirected through concerted political action. Here Jonas's historical perspective is characterized by its unprecedented manner of taking into consideration "temporal duration" (*die Zeitspanne*) as it engages long-term anticipation that responsibility commands.[17] It thus differs sharply from the total vision of the philosophy of history and of traditional ideology, since it integrates a view of human precarity and of the vulnerability of nature in the face of an uncertain future corresponding to the finitude of human historical perspective. It must also be distinguished from all forms of illusory enthusiasm that robust projects for the future often inspire, which, in the name of messianic and utopian quests, deflect attention from the modalities of responsible action, since they surpass what we know to be the temporal conditions of existence in an historical world. In the final analysis, it projects a vision of human historical finitude that corroborates and reinforces what I take to be the critical implications of a focus on the finite temporal articulations of collective memory as they lay bare the limited grasp of human historical understanding.

Notes

1 Reinhart Koselleck, "Vom Sinn und Unsinn der Geschichte," in *Vom Sinn und Unsinn der Geschichte. Aufsätze und Vorträge aus vier Jahrzehnten*, ed. Carsten Dutt (Frankfurt am Main: Suhrkamp, 2010), 9–31. Unless otherwise indicated, all translations are my own.

2 Wilhelm Dilthey, "Einleitung in die Geisteswissenschaften: Versuch einer Grundlegung für das Studium der Gesellschaft und der Geschichte," in *Gesammelte Schriften: Vol. 1*, ed. Rolf Tiedemann and Hermann Schweppenhäuser (Göttingen: Teubner, 1973), 234–54, 334.

3 See in this regard Erich Auerbach, "Figura," in *Gesammelte Aufsätze zur romanischen Philologie*, ed. Matthias Bormuth and Martin Vialon (Bern and Munich: Francke, 1967), 84.

4 Karl Löwith, *Meaning in History* (Chicago: University of Chicago Press, 1949), 1–19; Karl Löwith, "Die Dynamik der Geschichte und der Historismus," in *Weltgeschichte und Heilsgeschehen: Zur Kritik der Geschichtsphilosophie, vol. 2 of Sämtliche Schriften*, ed. Klaus Stichweh and Marc B. DeLunay (Stuttgart: Metzler, 1983), 307–23; see also Jeffrey Andrew Barash, "The Sense of History: On the Political Implications of Karl Löwith's Interpretation of Secularization," *History and Theory* 37, no. 1 (1998): 69–82.

5 Reinhart Koselleck, "Über die Verfügbarkeit der Geschichte," and "'Erfahrungsraum' und 'Erwartungshorizont'—Zwei historische Kategorien," in *Vergangene Zukunft: Zur Semantik geschichtlicher Zeiten*, ed. Carsten Dutt (Frankfurt am Main: Suhrkamp, 1979), 260–77, 349–75; English translation, *Futures Past: On the Semantics of Historical Time*, trans. Keith Tribe (New York: Columbia University Press, 2004), 192–204, 255–75.

6 Reinhart Koselleck, "Über die Verfügbarkeit," 272f.; English translation, 201f.

7 Reinhart Koselleck, "Der Aufbruch in die Moderne oder das Ende des Pferdezeitalters," in *Historikerpreis der Stadt Münster 2003: Prof. Reinhart Koselleck: am 18. Juli 2003 im Festsaal des Rathhauses zu Münster* (Münster: Münster Press- und Informationsamt, 2003), 25.

8 Ulrich Raulff, *Das letzte Jahrhundert der Pferde: Geschichte einer Trennung* (Munich: Beck, 2015), 398–9.

9 François Hartog, *Régimes d'historicité: Présentisme et expériences du passé* (Paris: Seuil, 2003), 28–30; and as *Regimes of Historicity: Presentism and Experiences of Time*, trans. Saskia Brown (New York: Columbia University Press, 2015), 17–18.

10 Hartog, *Régimes d'historictié*, 28–9, 119–27.

11 I have analyzed this topic in more detail in my book *Collective Memory and the Historical Past* (Chicago and London: University of Chicago Press, 2016), 115–24; see also Christophe Bouton, "Hartog's Account of Historical Times and the Rise of Presentism," *History: The Journal of the Historical Association* 104, no. 360 (2019): 309–30.

12 "Die von Durkheim, Halbwachs und anderen Soziologen beschworenen Kollektiva mit gemeinsamer Erinnerung oder gemeinschaftlichem Gedächtnis sind sprachliche Konstrukte, quasireligiöse Ideologeme, die die *unio mystica* einer Glaubensgemeinschaft in nationale Referenzsysteme überführen sollen. Befragen wir sie ideologiekritisch stossen wir nicht auf kollektive Erinnerungen (denn diese sind immer individuell), sondern auf kollektive Bedingungen der je eigenen Erinnerungen. Solche kollektiven Bedingungen sind zahlreich: sprachlich, politisch, ökonomisch, religiös, mental, sozial, generationsspezifisch und dergleichen mehr. Derartig plural abgeschichtete Bedingungen rufen Erfahrungen hervor und begrenzen sie zugleich, ermöglichen Erfahrungen und versperren sie . . ." Reinhart Koselleck, "Der 8. Mai zwischen Erinnerung und Geschichte," in *Vom Sinn und Unsinn der Geschichte*, ed. Carsten Dutt (Frankfurt am Main: Suhrkamp, 2010), 257.

13 Maurice Halbwachs, *La mémoire collective* (Paris: Presses Universitaires de France, 1968), 1–79.
14 Halbwachs, *La mémoire collective*, 51.
15 Raulff, *Das Letzte Jahrhundert*, 7.
16 For a detailed theoretical analysis of collective memory, see my book *Collective Memory and the Historical Past*.
17 Hans Jonas, *Das Prinzip Verantwortung: Versuch einer Ethik für die technologische Zivilisation* (Frankfurt am Main: Suhrkamp, 1984), 46.

Bibliography

Auerbach, Erich. "Figura." In *Gesammelte Aufsätze zur romanischen Philologie*, edited by Matthias Bormuth and Martin Vialon, 65–113. Bern and Munich: Francke, 1967.

Barash, Jeffrey Andrew. *Collective Memory and the Historical Past*. Chicago and London: University of Chicago Press, 2016.

Barash, Jeffrey Andrew. "The Sense of History: On the Political Implications of Karl Löwith's Interpretation of Secularization," *History and Theory* 37, no. 1 (1998): 69–82.

Bouton, Christophe. "Hartog's Account of Historical Times and the Rise of Presentism," *History: The Journal of the Historical Association* 104, no. 360 (2019): 309–30.

Dilthey, Wilhelm. "Einleitung in die Geisteswissenschaften: Versuch einer Grundlegung für das Studium der Gesellschaft und der Geschichte." In *Gesammelte Schriften: Vol. 1*, edited by Rolf Tiedemann and Hermann Schweppenhäuser. Göttingen: Teubner, 1973.

Halbwachs, Maurice. *La mémoire collective*. Paris: Presses Universitaires de France, 1968.

Hartog, François. *Régimes d'historicité: Présentisme et expériences du passé*. Paris: Seuil, 2003.

Hartog, François. *Regimes of Historicity: Presentism and Experiences of Time*. Translated by Saskia Brown. New York: Columbia University Press, 2015.

Jonas, Hans. *Das Prinzip Verantwortung: Versuch einer Ethik für die technologische Zivilisation*. Frankfurt am Main: Suhrkamp, 1984.

Koselleck, Reinhart. "Der Aufbruch in die Moderne oder das Ende des Pferdezeitalters." In *Historikerpreis der Stadt Münster 2003: Prof. Reinhart Koselleck: am 18. Juli 2003 im Festsaal des Rathhauses zu Münster*, 23–39. Münster: Münster Press- und Informationsamt, 2003.

Koselleck, Reinhart. "Der 8. Mai zwischen Erinnerung und Geschichte." In *Vom Sinn und Unsinn der Geschichte*, edited by Carsten Dutt, 254–65. Frankfurt am Main: Suhrkamp, 2010.

Koselleck, Reinhart. "'Erfahrungsraum' und 'Erwartungshorizont'—Zwei historische Kategorien." In *Vergangene Zukunft: Zur Semantik geschichtlicher Zeiten*, 349–75. Frankfurt am Main: Suhrkamp, 1979.

Koselleck, Reinhart. *Futures Past: On the Semantics of Historical Time*. Translated by Keith Tribe. New York: Columbia University Press, 2004.

Koselleck, Reinhart. "Über die Verfügbarkeit der Geschichte." In *Vergangene Zukunft: Zur Semantik geschichtlicher Zeiten*, 260–77. Frankfurt am Main: Suhrkamp, 1979.

Koselleck, Reinhart, "Vom Sinn und Unsinn der Geschichte." In *Vom Sinn und Unsinn der Geschichte. Aufsätze und Vorträge aus vier Jahrzehnten*, edited by Carsten Dutt, 9–31. Frankfurt am Main: Suhrkamp, 2010.

Löwith, Karl. "Die Dynamik der Geschichte und der Historismus." In *Weltgeschichte und Heilsgeschehen: Zur Kritik der Geschichtsphilosophie: Sämtliche Schriften: Vol. 2*, edited by Klaus Stichweh and Marc B. DeLunay, 307–23. Stuttgart: Metzler, 1983.

Löwith, Karl. *Meaning in History*. Chicago: University of Chicago Press, 1949.

Raulff, Ulrich. *Das letzte Jahrhundert der Pferde: Geschichte einer Trennung*. Munich: Beck, 2015.

14

The Time of History

Jan-Ivar Lindén

With or without Presence

John McTaggart has a famous distinction between two versions of the temporal series: the A series referring to past, present, and future and the B series referring to the relation between earlier and later.[1] Without discussing the specific quite Platonic views of McTaggart shedding doubt on the reality of time, it is worth reflecting on the difference between these two series. Order in the sense of the B series seems to exist also in structures that are not actual but are only virtual in the sense of determinate sequences that can become actual. We are familiar with this kind of system in using a computer, where the order of commands, corresponding to a possible series, is crucial. The relation between earlier and later can exist in a completely virtual way and does not imply any assumption of presence if somebody or something is not actually triggering the virtual system at a certain moment. This instantaneous present is not part of the virtual order.

The A series is different from the B series and accords an important role precisely to the present. It refers not only to a virtual order but is anchored in presence and divides time accordingly into past and future. This temporal series has an enigmatic character.

In the well-known discussion in the Book XI of the *Confessions* of Augustine, the dilemma presented is that the past is not anymore, the future is not yet, and the present is something extremely difficult to grasp as it disappears into the past as soon as we direct our attention toward it. Additionally, the present is something between two dimensions *that are not*: the past that is *not anymore* and the future that is *not yet*. Augustine turns to the soul in order to find a solution. The past is not anymore and the future not yet, but expectation and hope exist and similarly remembering. Accordingly, the past can be remembered and the future can be anticipated. The *acts* of remembering and of anticipating thus become central, and the tendency of Augustine is indeed to attribute an ontological primacy to the presence of the act. In his theology presence is also the eternal presence of God so that there is thus a certain connection between the omnipresence of the divine and the finite presence of human acts, this latter presence being marked however by the fragmentation of what Augustine calls *dispersio animi*. The challenge is somehow to attain a less fragmentary experience and thus come closer to God. As to what concerns the role of dispositions (habits) in the actualization of the past, Augustine is quite severe and even seems to regard dispositional existence as the opposite of ensouled presence.[2] One could describe his position as anti-Aristotelian insofar as Aristotle to the contrary strongly stresses the important disposing role of habitual and natural organization ("second" and "first" nature), a predetermination that is very different from the Augustinian predestination (which does not have a natural origin) but also different from the total determination that Pierre-Simon de Laplace later intended in stating:

> If it otherwise would be vast enough to analyse these data, an intelligence, which at a certain moment would know all the forces animating nature and the respective situation of the beings constituting nature, would at the same time in a single formula grasp the movements of the biggest bodies of the universe and of the lightest atom: nothing would be uncertain for such an intelligence and the future like the past would be present to its view.[3]

Laplace's omnipresent "intelligence" does not have the personal connotations of its Augustinian equivalent but is equally foreign to the Aristotelian conception of dispositional finitude.

Plato, certainly not a philosopher stressing the temporal world, has an influential image of what time is: the moving image of eternity.[4] This idea of the temporal world as an image of something atemporal corresponds with the mimetic relation between the sensual and the ideal in Plato. Eternity seems however to be something else than a field of atemporal ideas. The eternal is transcendent and ineffable. In Plotinus this relationship between determinate but atemporal ideas and the ineffable eternal One was further elaborated and, especially through Augustine, became an important topic in the Christian monotheistic tradition.

There is indeed a tension between the ideality of the unchanging and the ineffable character of the eternal. For Augustine it was important to assume that both aspects were present in the personal life of the *homo interior*, that is, both the unchanging ideas in the treasury of memory (*thesaurus memoriae*) and the internal eternity (*aeternum internum*) of divine love, which is somehow related to both conscience and consciousness. The so-called Augustinian theory of time even seems to be foremost a theory of eternal presence and, in a privative sense, of human conscience and consciousness. The atemporal and eternal is in Augustine conceived as opposed to the sensual and temporal world of the *homo exterior*—conducting to a dualism even stronger than in Plato. Similarly the emotional theology (and anthropology) of Augustine differs from the rational tendency in Platonism, which is indebted both to the Eleatic school and the Pythagoreans with their stress on mathematical ideality.

The Augustinian idea with its links both to consciousness and moral conscience has been taken up in several modern conceptions: in Luther, in Jansen, in Pascal, in Descartes, and in Husserl. In Søren Kierkegaard's idea of the instant (*øieblicket*) the personal aspects of this presence are developed in a profound manner. Without discussing all these interpretations here, it can be said that presence is indeed decisive if we want to stress how time literally demands involvement, implication, and sometimes direct participation. This can be maintained without sharing the anti-Aristotelian stance of Saint Augustine. In a completely virtual B series world nothing is important and even in the A series it can be said that the past can only be important if it has influence on the present; and similarly the future is troubling, frightening, or bright only if it is related to present anticipations and possible or probable future presence. It is thus understandable that the Augustinian conception of an especially significant present and its corollary, psychic time, has been so influential. Through presence the past and the future can be something that matters. When something matters, there is however always the connected question "to whom?" What is it which in this instance renders time so important? Is it a consciousness, a moral conscience, a soul, a subject, a person, or perhaps only some kind of experience with less clear connotations? One way to tackle this problem is to see historical experience as the ground of significance. This point of departure does not presuppose modern subjectivity (i.e., subjects opposed to objects), even if it seems to need some kind of psychic life, probably also both consciousness and conscience, which is involved in the historical processes. When it comes to human beings, one could perhaps speak of persons (which do not presuppose any opposition between subject and object).[5]

Dispositions and Presence

Without an Aristotelian corollary that revalorizes the temporal and the sensual, Augustinian interiority tends to a radical dualism, which is difficult to combine with an idea of involvement that offers the perspective in the following reflections on historical time.[6] If Aristotle recognizes the validity of the Platonic stress on the atemporal, he at the same time seems to take Heraclitus seriously in developing a profound theory of change, mainly expressed through the concept of *entelecheia*, a principle that governs natural processes. In the *Physics* there is however also a famous definition of time as the number of movement according to the earlier and the later (*arithmos kinêseôs kata to proteron kai hysteron*).[7] One could say that these two conceptions of temporality correspond to the A series (entelechies as actualization of possibilities) and to the B series (the numerical relation of the earlier to the later). The topic also raises questions about the relationship between Aristotelian philosophy of nature and the time of mathematical physics. In the modern epoch the latter orientation has been quite influential, not least because of the dominance of a new conception of nature, conceived without any reference to life and thus quite different from Aristotelian physics with its special interest precisely in vital phenomena (even if there are for Aristotle also nonliving beings in nature). The logic of mathematical science tends to favor the virtual (structural) aspects of nature, whereas actualization is highly problematic in this context as it necessarily involves a presence, which is hard to analyze with the conceptual tools of such a science.[8]

A recurrent difficulty in discussions of temporal influence and causality has been to decide whether the future can influence the past or not. Teleological conceptions are often said to suggest such a possibility. The debate is however somewhat confused as it concerns views stemming from quite different philosophical conceptions. The Aristotelian notion of cause is not the modern one. This is especially evident when modern causality is understood from an experimental point of view. Experience is for Aristotle not an experimental activity but rather the condition of being exposed to things that happen.

Strangely enough, critics of Aristotelian teleology often ground their arguments on the assumption that teleological causes would imply the possibility of retroactive causality. This is problematical not only because of the difference between the modern concept of causality and the Aristotelian causes (*aitia*) but also because this position contradicts explicit statements in Aristotle. That there is a direction of time is for Aristotle evident; and this means precisely that the past is irreversibly given whereas the future is the temporal dimension that admits a certain, even if limited influence upon what is to come.[9]

Modern conceptions of causality are for the most part founded on an idea of causes, which are not only separated from the consequences but also can be identified and generalized. In the words of Francis Bacon, "what appears as the cause from a theoretical point of view, functions as rule in the operation (*quod in contemplatione instar causae est, id in operatione instar regulae est*)."[10] From the Aristotelian, less instrumental point of view, it is difficult to isolate and generalize causes in this way. A cause for Aristotle is rather something like a "because" that renders understandable why something occurs but does not offer strictly limited general causes for instrumental use.[11]

Even if there are some aspects of modern causal theories, such as the generally admitted impossibility of retroactive causality, that are similar to the abovementioned impossibility of changing the past, Aristotle's remarks still need a quite different perspective in order to be understood. The past is irreversibly given, it is true, but not because of a precedence of causes, separated from their consequences, but because of the ontological status of the past, which is precisely what cannot be altered anymore. Without letting itself be influenced, the past can however influence what follows—and heavily does so. This process of actualization is crucial in historical experience with its sufferings and possible interventions.

The Actuality of the Influential

There is a crucial difference between the past and the present. It is possible to defend an influence of the future on the present without claiming any possibility of the future influencing the past. Presence also means actuality, a concept—*actus*—that is extremely important in medieval Aristotelianism and especially in Aquinas. There is thus indeed a quite particular role for the presence when it comes to influence. One could even define presence as *the actuality of the influential*, the influence coming both from the completely determined past and from the partially open future and, perhaps even most important, from the patterns that ground the relation between past and future. This evokes further questions. If past, present, and future are temporal categories, it is not as evident that the patterns that relate these temporal dimensions are temporal. This suggests a certain similarity with McTaggart's B series but differs in stressing the temporally guiding character of the structural element.

Predetermination suggests the existence of some kind of guiding structure behind the processual realization, which is either atemporal or less temporal than the process it guides.[12] In the ancient tradition, most famously in Platonism, this structural element was understood as completely atemporal in the sense of the ideal. This would imply that the structure responsible for the determinate character of temporal processes would somehow be immune to change when it is working in and guiding these processes. This is a very strong thesis and the mechanisms of immunization would have to be clarified. A less radical essentialism can however allow influence through actualization such that the conception is then only that there is some kind of *relatively* stable structure active in the unfolding of time. Predetermination would similarly only be a strong determination, not a completely given destiny. History seems to offer many examples of such a partially open predetermination.

For us, human beings involved in historical processes as we are, it is important to know more about the different possibilities of acting in a relatively free way even if our existence is thoroughly formed by what is already predetermined. One could perhaps say that this is what sense, significance, and meaning are all about. The polysemy of the notion of meaning is understandable in this light: meaning as something that appears more or less clearly to us, but also—like the French word *sens* and the German *Sinn* indicate—as direction. Taking both aspects into account, meaning would then be about finding clarity and orientation in a certain already determined process. The notion is however ambiguous in other ways, too. Gottlob Frege's distinction between *Sinn* and *Bedeutung* is well-known and has been declined in different ways as connotation and denotation and as intension and extension. This is not the place to dwell on these topics, which remain closely linked to the referential functions of language. Meaning is not only a linguistic concept covering semiotic, semantic, and hermeneutic aspects but is also related to *shades of importance*. Let us call this further dimension *significance*—in language often reflected in the adjectival use. (In German one would say *bedeutsam* and *Bedeutsamkeit*.) Significance manifests itself in different forms of experience and is partly affective because of the shades of importance involved (nice, repulsing, pleasant, frightening, indifferent, etc.). All linguistic meaning remains rooted in significance, which is related to life as such and present in every vital interest not only in human experience, even though particularly accessible for us in this human shape.

History is about both meaning and significance, the historical process being closely linked to the latter, whereas the former and especially the linguistic meaning has an important role on several levels but is indispensable when it comes to our possibilities to understand what history is all about. In this sense, the temporal reality of history concerns the relation between significance and meaning.

Animated History

Georg Simmel stated the role of affectivity, which seems to be closely related to significance in historical processes, as follows:

If the theory of knowledge in general begins with the fact that knowing, formally understood, is only a way of representing (*Vorstellen*) and the subject is a soul, the theory of historical knowledge is further characterized by its topic, the representations, volitions and emotions of personalities, of souls. All external events and processes—political and social, economic and religious, legal and technological—would neither be interesting nor possible to understand, were they not rooted in and evoking psychic processes. If history is not a mere puppet show, then it must be the history of psychic processes. So the external events which history describes are merely bridges that link impulses and volitional acts, on the one hand, and the emotional reactions which these external events produce, on the other. Not even the materialist conception of history, which wants to found the movements of history on the physiological needs and the geographic surroundings, can alter this fact. All the hunger in the world would never contribute to world history, if it would not be painful to be hungry and every fight for economic possessions is a combat for sensations of satisfaction and pleasure, which as ends attribute meaning to external possessions. (*Denn zunächst würde aller Hunger niemals die Weltgeschichte in Bewegung setzen, wenn er nicht wehthäte, und aller Kampf um die ökonomischen Güter ist ein Kampf um die Empfindungen der Behaglichkeit und des Genusses, von denen als Zwecke aller äußere Besitz seine Bedeutung entlehnt.*) The properties of soil and climate would have no more bearing upon the course of history than the climate and soil of Sirius if they did not influence—directly or indirectly—the psychological constitution of nations.[13]

This is no psychological reduction of history. It is, instead, a way of indicating how historical relevance is profoundly marked by psychic connotations that give a particular access to those processes and events that we regard as historical. Reality is of course more than access, and access is precisely important as the limitation or particularity enabling us to be involved in reality. Simmel stresses the affective components of this access; and one can indeed say that historical experience is unthinkable without its affective dimension that continuously interacts with other elements, such as chance, predetermination, intellection, reflection, and understanding.

Affective experience is often hard to perceive in other living beings, especially if they are less close to us as is the case with plants, trees, and even some animals. What is left for us to study is, then, more structural elements: behavior, dispositions, different necessary conditions of the experience of these beings, and in general what we can objectify and even sometimes dispose of. In our relation to the nonliving, the objectifying tendency is even stronger and discards the experiential capacity in the objects studied altogether. Such a lifeless sphere of research can in fact be understood as that which is left for us to study when we have no access to the experience of the things studied. Both this lacking access and the limited access to other living beings appear differently in history, which is in a very strong way marked by human affective presence and thus offers an access not only to processes and events but similarly to the emotions involved. The same privileged access also concerns the intellectual and reflective aspects of historical processes. To discard all these dimensions would mean neglecting the richness of experience accorded by our belonging to a certain community (humanity) and thus to reduce historical understanding to a less nuanced epistemic strategy.

From an ontological point of view the differences between these research strategies are rooted in fundamental questions concerning our access to reality and the shades of significance involved.[14] In the present setting reality is understood in the absolute sense of the ontologically given (which does not imply any possibility of absolute knowledge in the Hegelian sense). Ideality stands for differentiating structures in this reality, patterns that are often hidden to us, now and then vaguely perceivable, and sometimes possibly to identify or even to define. In order to understand the significance of the patterns we however need more than only the structural elements. It is here that presence and affectivity come into play. Where reality is understood, it is significant. When it is conceived as structural differentiation, it can be explained and even handled but not—as the following remarks indicate—understood in the full sense of the word.

The modern epistemic tradition has a preference for the useful aspects of reality, which can be called "objective" when they are explained and "material" when they are theoretically or practically possible to handle. As something material in this sense, matter certainly matters *to us*. For the things studied the situation is different. The objective sphere is what appears when hermeneutic access is excluded. Regarding the world as something material is a way of coping with this lack of access, using instead the manipulatory possibilities, offered by materialization. These attitudes of rendering something objective and sometimes material are *as real attitudes* ontologically interesting, but they do not imply any particularly strong ontological status for their intentional (objective) correlates. The objective reality of instrumental reason is useful, not absolute.

When it comes to natural processes, we in our modern age mostly rely on explanations of nature that are founded on culturally very specific strategies of objectivation. It is thus for us hard to grasp other meanings in nature than those that correlate with these quite anthropocentric strategies. Some disciplines, like ethology, are nevertheless capable of catching a glimpse of how other living beings experience their world. However, to one dimension of reality we indeed have privileged access, namely to historical time. In order to understand what temporality, predetermination, influence, and patterns mean, it is thus extremely fruitful to reflect precisely on historical reality. History is that aspect of reality that we can understand better than any other aspect. Through the historical process we are offered experience of a particular mnemic kind. When moving forward, we can compensate for the limitation of freedom stemming from predetermination, that is, we can turn backward and create the movement back and forth in time that constitutes historical phenomena with their inherent cultural memory, that is, mnemically transform linear time into a hermeneutic circle and thus acquire a deeper understanding of our world.

Narration offers one perspective on the past that, even if it cannot alter what has already happened, still can influence how the consequences of the past take shape in the present and live forth in the future.[15] Through our narrative understanding we participate in the temporal process that unfolds more or less vague patterns and we even have a small possibility of contributing to these patterns. The narrative influence is however quite different from foresight, explanation, and the active shaping of the future as it mainly dwells on the past. The widespread consequences of historical understanding are indirect; and one can add: they as much prevent us from doing things as they incite us. This is closely linked to our critical capacity and suggests an important difference in comparison with the striving practical intentionality with its explicit projects. Historical consciousness somehow *grows* through education and historical experience and *generates* consequences without anyone's necessarily intending them.

Affective Presence and Understanding

One characteristic of emotions is their close link to presence. As the present is also the temporal dimension that allows influence in the temporal process, this seems to render emotions quite important. Actualization and affectivity would be closely related in experience in general and in historical experience in particular as we are subjected to history in a way that differs from the detached experience of, for example, experimental science. We do not only observe history but also suffer and profit from it. The suffering is even so strong that some languages stress this pathetic dimension through phrases like "tiden lider" (Swedish for "time passes," but literally "time suffers"). In fact, expressions like "time passes," *le temps passe*, or *es passiert* are all rooted in the Greek *paschein*, which can mean both suffering and experiencing. Historical time is a perfect illustration of this pathetic dimension of time.

Through narration, understanding, and explanation we try to cope with this exposed situation. The influence on the future course of things can be voluntary and precise, whereby our explanatory capacity is extremely helpful. This does not, however, imply any completely autonomous subjectivity. Even in our practical intentionality we are driven forward by our own history in a manner resembling natural teleology. What remains are some open margins, and we try to profit from these. However, a deeper influence is not intentional but indirect and closely linked to our reflective capacities in the literal sense of backward turned acts (*re-flexio*), either narrative or theoretical. The teleology of drives in this case momentarily slows down, or even stops, for us to understand present situations in the light of their significance. This stance is in a continuous interaction with the teleology of drives. Interpretation and understanding of the bygone allow us to (slightly) modify the often strongly felt predetermination given through an unalterable past.

If desire is goal-oriented, affectivity covers sensations (which stand for exposition and not for goal orientation) and further emotions, both momentary affects and enduring emotional states (moods), which tune our experience in a nonteleological manner. Emotions also have a complex relation to the sensitive faculty. Intense emotions tend to increase sensitivity.[16] There are however also moods like boredom that seem to make what we experience less intense. The world has somehow lost its emotional sense. One could even suppose that boredom precisely because of this offers a proficient condition for the relatively detached perception of objectifying science.[17]

Momentary sensations and emotions and also enduring moods are not as such goal-oriented, even if they often are linked to the more teleological desires. Somehow importance is born out of the interaction between drives and affectivity. When we consciously try to influence what is important, desire turns into something we call will. Aristotle expresses this as a deliberation (*bouleusis*) out of which desire or striving (*orexis*) becomes will (*boulêsis*).[18] In historical processes there is a lot of striving interacting with affectivity inside given conditions (historical predetermination and chance) and some voluntary contributions.

Whereas the temporality of striving is advancing in a continuous way, the intensity of affective life is more like a deepening of the temporal experience. Consciousness can profit from this but needs also more stable structures in order to express itself as reflective understanding. In this case the relatively stable patterns for the temporal process are especially helpful. When they somehow improve patterns, we speak of orientation or explanation, when it is for the sake of understanding; it is rather a way of adding experiential richness to the patterns. In the first case experience is subordinated to the teleology of noetic patterns with their orientational goals.[19] In the second case the patterns are exposed to sensual experience or tuned by emotivity instead of giving specific observations. This seems to correspond to some aspects of the classical distinction between explanation (*Erklären*) and understanding (*Verstehen*), but it should then be added that explanatory knowledge also can remain focused solely on patterns, and dispense with experience altogether, that is, when it is priori.

Being Concerned

Differentiation does not figure only in explanatory epistemic strategies but also in the ontologically given, which incites us in all our endeavors. In this case the structural aspect presents itself more as *expression* than as intention and involves the fact of being *concerned*. Reality matters to us but often in a manner that is less manifested through identities than through something that could be called *vagueness*. Vague experience allows recognition, but its distinction is different from the conceptual one. It is more like a persisting sameness, which appears and reappears, than like the definite character of generic identity (general conceptual identity). It has connotations of what used to be called *Erlebnis* in the philosophy of life (*Lebensphilosophie*) and manifests our significant belonging to reality rather than our observation of it. This should, however, not conduct us to any anti-intellectualist conclusions. Conceptual responses to this lived experience are highly natural for us and can also profit from this experience. There is an ongoing interaction between lived experience and conceptions. It is important, however, to add: concepts figure not only in explanatory knowledge but also in reflective and critical understanding. The latter form of conceptual thinking is decisive in an ontological approach to the given reality on which we are so dependent. The aim of our conceptual capacity is here not to define an ideal content, equally applicable to different instances, but rather to grasp persisting sameness in the processual sense of identity.

This is important for the temporality of historical experience because processual sameness (the identity of a person, of an institution, of an epoch, of a tendency) manifests itself as a recurrent character, not as an atemporal conceptual identity. One could call it a *lived sameness*, whose meaning is always significant, too. Even if it is true that there is also a process of concept formation, this historical aspect of conceptuality is not preeminent in rational discourse. When concepts acquire new meanings it is mainly through a metaphorical displacement,[20] which is especially important in poetry, but also present in the use of scientific metaphors and models.[21] Metaphorical concept formation is a certain deviation from established use, and constant deviation is not possible if our utterances aim at distinction. There is a certain priority of the stable in rational discourse. Lived sameness, to the contrary, relies on relatively stable patterns but precisely in exposing them to more or less contingent historical conditions. When patterns become significant in a present situation, past predetermination and future development acquire all the tension this enigmatic mediation comports. Sometimes the moment passes without notice, but at certain occasions the tension can also be perceived and felt in a particularly strong way. This is the essence of perturbations. History is a troubled time, full of perturbations, where meaning and signification cooperate inside a process that transcends our mastery.

Atemporalities—Determinate and Indeterminate

Because of its structural aspects, the historical process is not only temporal, not even if we extend the concept of time to cover the temporality of spatial phenomena. There are atemporal aspects of history, and probably also of nature. In science the interest is often in laws, which do not change in the same way as the phenomena they describe. We use concepts that are quite stable or that we wish to be somewhat more stable than the changing world. In the philosophical tradition the ideal dimension of knowledge and reality is sometimes understood as something general, abstracted from experience—and sometimes, as in Plato and Platonism, rather as a stable structure behind the temporal and sensual phenomena. This kind of atemporal existence is determinate, that is, differentiated in a way that gives the ideas their identity. The Platonist and Neoplatonist tradition has however also stressed another form of atemporality, the eternal.

It would be tempting to describe the atemporal eternity as something indeterminate, and in a sense this is also the meaning of what Plotinus called the One, later so important in monotheistic religions. There was however a great reluctance to describe ineffable eternity as indeterminate (*ahoriston, apeiron*) as this would have been associated with material formlessness, regarded as something low and unworthy. If I still prefer to talk about an indeterminate character of the eternal, it is not in the sense of something lacking form and thus in need of (in)formation but instead as an ineffable instance with *initiative* in real processes, formative and others. There are some possibilities to make sense of this without adhering to a Neoplatonist ontotheology but still linking the eternal to consciousness in a way resembling the Augustinian idea of the *intentio animi*. Consciousness is then defined as ineffable presence, for us a function that—

this time in a less Augustinian way—is a personal equivalent to the actuality that renders the patterns of structural reality present. Consciousness is so to say a way of participating in the actualization of patterns.

As patterns of a historical process, organizing principles are not laws in the modern sense of laws of nature. Such laws depend on generalizations inside a scientific tradition, which already presuppose the historical process, which is singular as there are no alternative pasts, but only the given one. In the beginning of the twentieth century this contributed to the definition of historical sciences and generally understanding (*Verstehen*) through a supposedly idiographic character with focus on the singular and not the general.[22] There are certainly arguments against this characterization as certain phenomena in the natural sciences seem to be singular (like a planet or our moon) and historical sciences also take common and even quite universal aspects into account. Still there is some truth in the stress on the singularity of the historical dimension as history covers the cultural process as a singular whole. Especially when it comes to the irreversibly given character of the past, the singularity is obvious. If there are some possibilities to figure out various scenarios and influence the future, the past only allows various interpretations but not different pasts. Belonging to a historical world has a fundamentally singular character, even when there are some open margins. Our capacity to generalize and find laws is limited to very specific epistemic undertakings inside our historical existence and is not meaningful when it comes to the historical process as such.

This does not mean that history would be only a sum of particular facts. There is something "general" in the historical process, but it is not discovered through successful generalizations in the nomothetic sense. Rather we dwell on what is recurrent in the past and like this understand something about similarity and sameness, which has found expression in historical reality. It is understandable that Wilhelm Dilthey attributes such a great importance precisely to the interpretation of expressions in historical sciences.[23] Interpreting an expression of life (*Ausdruck des Lebens*) is different from the constitution of an intentional object. The interpreter is confronted with something that addresses him, demands in a way similar to the already described demand of present situations. He wants to find out why something was important, find meanings that are significant. In doing so, he navigates between structural patterns with their more or less implicit sameness and the intense actuality of what has been present and reappears in the presence of the interpretative act.[24]

Toward a Historical Ontology

By historical ontology one can understand a philosophical approach that, with the aid of our conceptual capacity, aims at clarifying processual sameness in our historical involvement. Participation and dependence is the starting point, not subjectivity. If this is a relational ground, it is about given relations where the relata are not independent from another—in fact, precisely what is meant with an ontological pattern. The historical aspect of ontology stems from the fact that the past has a predetermining role in our world, that is, in the access to reality that we have. The advantage of this point of view is that it evicts the currently quite common confusion of objective with absolute reality. Similarly, it admits the ontological status of concepts like ideality and meaning, which in our epoch have become far too anthropocentric. Further, it takes into account that there is real indeterminacy, suggesting some parallels with negative theology but without the spiritualistic connotations of this tradition. It surpasses the metaphysical hybris of scientism but stresses the all-encompassing status of reality. For us human beings, it admits a certain freedom, but a freedom, which is real because of its limitations.

Notes

1 John E. McTaggart, "The Unreality of Time," *Mind* 17, no. 4 (1908): 457–74; and *The Nature of Existence* (Cambridge: Cambridge University Press, 1968).
2 Concerning the dualist tendency in Augustine, compare the eleventh book of the *Confessions* with, for example, *Conf.* VII.6.10.
3 "Une intelligence qui, pour un instant donné, connaitrait toutes les forces dont la nature est animée et la situation respective des êtres qui la composent, si d'ailleurs elle était assez vaste pour soumettre ces données à l'analyse, embrasserait dans la même formule les mouvements des plus grands corps de l'univers et ceux du plus léger atome : rien ne serait incertain pour elle, et l'avenir, comme le passé, serait présent à ses yeux." Pierre-Simon de Laplace, *Introduction à la théorie analytique des probabilités* (Paris: Courcier, 1814), 2.
4 Plato, *Timaeus*, 37d.
5 There is an enormous tension between the everyday use of the word "subjective" and its meaning in the modern philosophical tradition, especially its Cartesian and Kantian vein. In everyday use "subjective" often means the particularity of an individual viewpoint, something less real than the "objective" world. The role of the subject in modern epistemology has been quite different, offering an Archimedean point—see René Descartes, *Meditationes de prima philosophia*, ed. Charles Adam and Paul Tannery (Paris: Vrin, 1996)—outside nature and history, which makes it possible to determine the reality of things. The external position of the subject is according to this view precisely what allows us to have objective knowledge. This becomes even more evident when the notion of intersubjectivity is used to explain what objectivity is all about. Objective is then what different subjects can agree upon, when they seriously according to certain criteria study a phenomenon.
6 Concerning historicity in Aristotle, see Jan-Ivar Lindén, "Story and History: Remarks on the *Poetics* of Aristotle and Some Suggestions About a Possible Aristotelian Philosophy of History," in *Aristotle: Timeless and Scientifically Timely*, ed. E. Moutsopoulos and M. Protopapas-Marneli (Athens: Academy of Athens– Research Centre for Greek Philosophy, 2018), where it is argued that Aristotle's remark on the less philosophical character of history in comparison with poetry concerns only a certain kind of historical narration, not the involvement in historical processes.
7 *Physics* 219b.
8 Immanuel Kant, *Kritik der reinen Vernunft* (Hamburg: Meiner, 1990), has as an important ambition to elucidate the new scientific conception (especially Newton) and it is not accidentally that time for him becomes an a priori form of intuition (*Form der Anschauung*). Even if Kant also has some comments on the temporality of

concept formation, it is clear that his perspective on time is linked to mathematical science.
9   For example, *Ethica Nicomachaea*, 1139b.
10 Francis Bacon, *Novum Organum* (Hamburg: Meiner, 1990), I, Aph. III.
11 Cf. Max Hocutt, "Aristotle's Four Becauses," *Philosophy* 9, no. 190 (1974): 385–99. Even if the perspective of Hocutt is different in linking the "because" to explanation. From a hermeneutic point of view one could say that the final cause (or "because") is a presupposed prediction, which we clarify. See Jan-Ivar Lindén, "Intentionnalité et perception: une esquisse aristotélicienne," *Chôra* 9–10 (2011–12): 339–52.
12 Predetermination in the natural sense suggests a temporal movement from the past over the present into the future. The arrow is directed toward the future and not indicating the contrary movement from events first being future possibilities, then present actualizations, and finally past facts.
13 Georg Simmel, *Die Probleme der Geschichtsphilosophie: Eine erkenntnistheoretische Studie, Gesamtausgabe*, Band 2, ed. Otthein Rammstedt (Frankfurt am Main: Suhrkamp, 1989), 303–4. (The first edition is from 1892 and was later modified in 1905 and 1907.) I have translated this passage from the edition of 1892. The English edition *The Problems of the Philosophy of History: An Epistemological Essay*, trans. Guy Oakes (The Free Press: New York, 1977), is based on the later German edition *Die Probleme der Geschichtsphilosophie* (Leipzig: Duncker & Humblot, 1907), where the passage on history and hunger has been replaced with the sentence "Daran ändern auch die Versuche nichts, das historische Geschehen in seinen besonderen Ausgestaltungen auf physikalische Bedingungen zurückzuleiten." (In the English edition: "The various attempts to reconstruct the physical conditions responsible for the peculiarities of historical events do not alter this fact.") One can suppose that Simmel did not through two sentences only want to enter into polemics with contemporary currents of materialism and thus in the later edition suppressed the longer passage. It is a pity that the clarifying comment on hunger and history was left out at the same time.
14 In ontology and in epistemology there have been quite different ways of dealing with these questions, and the concepts are sometimes confusing. "Realism" today figures as for example "scientific realism," that is, a position defending the reality of validated scientific objects. The medieval "realism" of concepts, claiming the reality of universals (like horseness), seems to be something quite different. The counterposition (nominalism), with its stress on the conventional aspects of notions, would be closer to several modern positions and also to some versions of scientific realism, which regard concepts as tools. "Idealism" is no less a problematic term. It has been opposed both to materialism and to realism. Materialism, too, is highly ambiguous. Matter as *hylê* and *materia* is something different in the ancient tradition from what it is in modern materialism and physicalism, which attribute properties to matter that for the ancients would have been forms. With Marxism the notion of materialism acquires a new social and political sense, which has little in common with earlier notions. With such a heterogenous opposite the idealism of the conceptual couple idealism/materialism is anything but clear. Concerning idealism and realism in the modern context, the situation is not better. Idealism is here often regarded as a position denying some kind of reality, for example, the reality of the objects of science. If one takes into account the heavily Platonic and even Pythagorean history of our scientific tradition with its mathematical bent, there would be good reasons to call the highly mathematical reality of modern science ideal. From a Platonic point of view

this would certainly not exclude reality. There are several reasons to be quite prudent in using notions like "realism," "idealism," and "materialism" in order to clarify a philosophical position. This does not mean that ideality, materiality, and reality would be obsolete concepts but only that we have to be clear about their meanings in specific contexts.

15 On narration, see Paul Ricoeur, *Temps et reçit* (Paris: Seuil, 1983–85), especially vol. 1 and 3. Cf. Hayden White, "The Value of Narrativity in the Representation of Reality," *Critical Inquiry* 7, no. 1 (1980): 5–27.

16 Cf. Jan-Ivar Lindén, "Gefühl und Erfahrung," in *Pathos: Affektformationen in Philosophie, Kunst, Literatur und Literaturtheorie*, ed. Giulia Agostini and Herle-Christin Jessen (München: Wilhelm Fink Verlag, 2020), 567–85.

17 This is however not quite evident if something like scientific obsession exists. In her text on scientific attention Lorraine Daston has in a concise way described the selective and emotionally connotated interest that guided early modern scientists when they discovered new fields of study. For this scientific development Daston explicitly uses the expression "auch eine Geschichte der wissenschaftlichen Emotionen," including the traditional Greek amazement (*thaumazein*), but then increasingly centered around attention, so important for Augustine, but especially in the eighteenth century without the church father's condemnation of curiosity (*curiositas*); Lorraine Daston, *Eine kurze Geschichte der wissenschaftlichen Aufmerksamkeit* (München: Carl Friedrich von Siemens Stiftung, 2000), 12. Cf. also this description by her, "Diese Ökonomien der Aufmerksamkeit haben nicht allein die Gegenstände geformt, die von Wissenschaftlern untersucht werden, sondern auch die Leidenschaften, von denen sie, die Wissenschaftler, getrieben werden" (*Eine kurze Geschichte*, 49). Daston also presents the history of science as an "ontological history" (*Geschichte der Ontologie*) and sees the crucial question as follows: "Wie entstehen wissenschaftliche Objekte, und wie vergehen sie irgendwann wieder?" (12). Several examples from early modern science show a certain revalorization of areas that used to be regarded as something less worthy to study: worms, louses, insects, and so on. In this way a science of "the lower things (*die niederen Objekte*)" is born (27). However, one could discuss whether it is completely appropriate here to speak of a new "Wissenschaft vom Gewöhnlichen." The habitual (*das Gewöhnliche*) is a notion with strong Aristotelian connotations, and understanding the habitual seems more closely linked to the reflective activity of the *savant* and the philosopher, who Daston rightly distinguishes from the modern scientists mentioned (Charles Bonnet, Gottlob Schirach, and others). A highly interesting interpretation of boredom is found in Martin Heidegger, *Die Grundbegriffe der Metaphysik: Welt – Endlichkeit – Einsamkeit* (Frankfurt am Main: Klostermann, 1983), especially 117–260. In these lectures from 1929 to 1930 Heidegger seems almost to replace anguish with boredom as the essential mood in our existence, which also modifies the central notion of concern (*Sorge*) in *Being and Time*, the major work published two years earlier. It is noteworthy that the category readiness-to-hand (*Zuhandenheit*) corresponding to the existential concern in the earlier work disappears as key notion in the lectures from 1929 to 1930.

18 See especially the sixth book of Aristotle's *Nicomachean Ethics*.

19 Henri Bergson suggested that our intellectual, conceptual thinking is formed in a vital pragmatics, which finds a more articulate expression in modern natural science, which actively enters nature and acts in and on it. The Bergsonian tendency is however to regard conceptual identity as such as a pragmatic function, a view

that does not sufficiently pay attention to the reflective and hermeneutic capacities of language. See, for example, Henri Bergson, *L'évolution créatrice* (Paris: Presses universitaires de France, 1994).
20 Several references are possible here (Nietzsche, Gadamer, Ricoeur, Derrida, etc.). I mention only one seminal text: Friedrich Nietzsche, "Über Wahrheit und Lüge im aussermoralischen Sinne," in *Kritische Studienausgabe 1*, ed. Giorgio Colli Mazzino Montinar (München: De Gruyter, 2009).
21 See, for example, Max Black, *Models and Metaphors: Studies in Language and Philosophy* (New York: Cornell University Press, 1962); and Mary B. Hesse, *Models and Analogies in Science* (Notre Dame: University of Notre Dame Press, 1966).
22 Wilhelm Windelband, *Präludien. Aufsätze und Reden zur Einleitung in die Philosophie* (Tübingen: J. C. B. Mohr (Paul Siebeck), 1907). The first impression is that Windelband would have wanted to rehabilitate precisely the character of narration, which Aristotle found less philosophical than the poetic representation with its sense for the universally valid.
23 Wilhelm Dilthey, *Der Aufbau der geschichtlichen Welt in den Geisteswissenschaften* (Frankfurt a. M.: Suhrkamp, 1981), 89–272. This edition also contains an important introduction by Manfred Riedel.
24 Cf. Hans-Georg Gadamer on the fusion of horizons, in *Wahrheit und Methode: Grundzüge einer philosophischen Hermeneutik* (Tübingen: J. C. B. Mohr, 1986), II. Teil, 1 d, "Das Prinzip der Wirkungsgeschichte." Gadamer's critique of Dilthey is sometimes exaggerated.

Traditional Sources

Aristotle. *Nicomachean Ethics*.
Aristotle. *Physics*.
Augustine. *Confessions*.
Plato. *Timaeus*.

Bibliography

Bacon, Francis. *Novum Organum*. Hamburg: Meiner, 1990.
Bergson, Henri. *L'évolution créatrice*. Paris: Presses universitaires de France, 1994.
Black, Max. *Models and Metaphors: Studies in Language and Philosophy*. New York: Cornell University Press, 1962.
Daston, Lorraine. *Eine kurze Geschichte der wissenschaftlichen Aufmerksamkeit*. München: Carl Friedrich von Siemens Stiftung, 2000.
Descartes, René. *Meditationes de prima philosophia*. Edited by Charles Adam and Paul Tannery. Paris: Vrin, 1996.
Dilthey, Wilhelm. *Der Aufbau der geschichtlichen Welt in den Geisteswissenschaften*. Frankfurt a. M.: Suhrkamp, 1981.
Gadamer, Hans-Georg. *Wahrheit und Methode: Grundzüge einer philosophischen Hermeneutik*, Tübingen: J. C. B. Mohr, 1986.
Heidegger, Martin. *Die Grundbegriffe der Metaphysik: Welt – Endlichkeit – Einsamkeit (Vorlesungen 1929–30)*. Frankfurt am Main: Klostermann, 1983.

Hesse, Mary B. *Models and Analogies in Science*. Notre Dame: University of Notre Dame Press, 1966.
Hocutt, Max. "Aristotle's Four Becauses." *Philosophy* 9, no. 190 (1974): 385–99.
Kant, Immanuel. *Kritik der reinen Vernunft*. Hamburg: Meiner, 1990.
Laplace, Pierre-Simon de, *Introduction à la théorie analytique des probabilités*. Paris: Courcier, 1814.
Lindén, Jan-Ivar. "Intentionnalité et perception: une esquisse aristotélicienne." *Chôra* 9–10 (2011–12): 339–52.
Lindén, Jan-Ivar. "Story and History: Remarks on the Poetics of Aristotle and Some Suggestions about a Possible Aristotelian Philosophy of History." In *Aristotle: Timeless and Scientifically Timely*, edited by E. Moutsopoulos and M. Protopapas-Marneli, 203–24. Athens: Academy of Athens Research Centre for Greek Philosophy, 2018.
Lindén, Jan-Ivar. "Gefühl und Erfahrung." In *Pathos: Affektformationen in Philosophie, Kunst, Literatur und Literaturtheorie*, edited by Giulia Agostini and Herle-Christin Jessen, 567–85. München: Wilhelm Fink Verlag, 2020.
McTaggart, John E. "The Unreality of Time." *Mind* 17, no. 4 (1908): 457–74.
McTaggart, John E. *The Nature of Existence*. Cambridge: Cambridge University Press, 1968.
Nietzsche, Friedrich. "Über Wahrheit und Lüge im aussermoralischen Sinne." In *Kritische Studienausgabe 1*, edited by Giorgio Colli Mazzino Montinar, 875–90. München: De Gruyter, 2009.
Ricoeur, Paul. *Temps et reçit*. Paris: Seuil, 1983–85.
Simmel, Georg. *Die Probleme der Geschichtsphilosophie: Eine erkenntnistheoretische Studie, Gesamtausgabe, Band 2*. Edited by Otthein Rammstedt. Frankfurt am Main: Suhrkamp, 1989.
Simmel, Georg. *The Problems of the Philosophy of History: An Epistemological Essay*. Translated by Guy Oakes. New York: The Free Press, 1977.
White, Hayden. "The Value of Narrativity in the Representation of Reality." *Critical Inquiry* 7, no. 1 (1980): 5–27.
Windelband, Wilhelm. *Präludien: Aufsätze und Reden zur Einleitung in die Philosophie*. Tübingen: J. C. B. Mohr (Paul Siebeck), 1907.

Section V

Concluding Reflections from Existential Anthropology

15

The Death of the Angel

In Search of a Tango of Temporal Humanity

Ruth Behar

The tango, a form of music, song, and dance, as well as a sensibility, a way of being-in-the-world, was born in Argentina. But I first heard the tango and felt it and fell in love with it in Cuba, my native land.

Daniel Esquenazi Maya, an old and impoverished man who lived in a rooftop apartment in Old Havana, gave me my first introduction to the tango. Daniel was one among a handful of Jews who did not want to be uprooted and stayed in Cuba after the Revolution that brought Fidel Castro to power in 1959. Most Jews left soon afterward. The Communist expropriation of properties, stores, businesses, and miniature enterprises, like door-to-door street peddling, on which many Jews depended for their livelihood, led to a mass exodus from Cuba. As a child of four and a half, I was part of this exodus of fifteen thousand Jews, though I do not remember it. Among the thousand Jews who still remain in Cuba today, most are of mixed heritage and have become converts to Judaism, or "Jews by choice." A few are old-time Jewish atheists and dedicated Communists, still filled with faith in the goals of the Revolution.

Daniel's parents were Sephardic Jews from Turkey. While not religious, when he became elderly and a widower, fearing that the temple of his youth would be shut down if no one took charge of it, Daniel agreed to serve as the president of the oldest synagogue in Cuba, the Chevet Ahim, built by Sephardic Jews in 1914. Eventually it was closed due to the ruined state of the building and the possibility of the roof collapsing. Daniel then attended religious services at Adath Israel, an Orthodox temple a few blocks from his home, where his thunderous singing rose above the others when intoning prayers and chants. Daniel loved to sing, but he never concealed the fact that part of the reason he attended was because the temple gave the elderly a bag of food and an allowance each week. After the fall of the former Soviet Union, the subsidies on which most Cubans depended had been whittled to a little bit of rice and split peas. Hustling and charity were needed to survive. Daniel, like many others, depended on both.

I first met Daniel when I began to travel back and forth to Cuba in the early 1990s. Sitting on the women's side of the temple, I was mesmerized by Daniel's singing. That voice, I learned, had been trained through years of being a tango singer. Daniel spent all his weekends singing tango songs at local cultural clubs in Havana. On several occasions I went with him and saw this world of tango enthusiasts up close. They did not dance the tango, but they sang until they moaned and cried, the lyrics and tunes enough to leave them grief-stricken. Tango was Daniel's great passion. He belted out the songs, in Spanish peppered with Argentine or lunfardo slang, every chance he got, not just at the clubs. His neighbors, he said, thought he was a madman on the roof, singing his tango songs even when no one was listening.

Daniel was one of the most frequently photographed, filmed, and interviewed Jews on the island, where Jews have become an exotic tribe, a rare fauna observed constantly by tourists, anthropologists, and well-wishers. I am guilty of being part of the pack of onlookers who turned Daniel into a celebrity. When I heard he was a tango aficionado, I asked Daniel to sing for my movie, *Adio Kerida/Goodbye Dear Love*.[1] He crooned "Mi Buenos Aires Querido" ("My Beloved Buenos Aires") with the brokenhearted nostalgia of an immigrant, even though he had never been to Buenos Aires. In fact, he had never left Cuba.

He had more than two hundred singles, old 78s, of songs once sung by Carlos Gardel, the great icon of Argentine tango. Enamored of Gardel since his youth, Daniel had an entire wall in his apartment that was an informal shrine to the great Argentine singer, who died young in a plane crash at the height of his international popularity.

When I interviewed Daniel in 2001, his record player, which he had purchased in 1960 for 160 pesos, still worked. He played tangos for me from his collection and they sounded glorious, all their breathy drama intact. But five years later, when I visited him again at his rooftop apartment, he told me he could not play his tango records anymore.

"My record player broke. There isn't a soul in Cuba who knows how to fix it," he said. "It's nobody's fault. They don't make record players like this anymore."

Daniel took a stoical attitude to the loss of his record player. Perhaps, growing older, material possessions were of less use to him. He was gaunt, his hair had thinned, and he struggled to get up the last flight of shaky wooden stairs to his rooftop apartment.

"I still enjoy looking at the records in my collection," he said. "I remember all the tangos. I can hear them in my head."

Later on, in July of 2008, after I finished my book, *An Island Called Home*, which featured a chapter about Daniel, I went to visit him and learned he was recovering from heart surgery.[2] He struggled to get used to a pacemaker while suffering from severe asthma. Barely able to leave his bed, his rooftop home had become a prison—he could not go down the stairs to reach the street. Neighbors who had once ignored him now competed to care for him, hoping to cart away, once he died, whatever meager goods and money Daniel had saved.

I asked Daniel if he would sing a tango. He smiled sadly and half-sung, half-whispered the exilic words that were immortalized by his beloved Gardel:

Mi Buenos Aires querido
Cuando yo te vuelva a ver
No habrá más pena ni olvido.

My beloved Buenos Aires
when I see you again
there will be no pain or forgetting.

Again we were in Havana, in Cuba, and Daniel was singing for a lost Buenos Aires. The moment was worthy of a poem, but I remembered I had to be an anthropologist and snapped a few pictures of him, shirtless, his ribs protruding from his emaciated frame. As I said goodbye, he asked for a dollar. I gave him a couple of dollars and he clutched them tightly in his hand.

This would be the last time I would see the man from whose lips I first heard the tango.

* * *

Thanks to Daniel, I have come to love the tango. I love its melancholy. I love its lyrics, which express an obsession with lost things, lost places, lost passions, and inconsolable goodbyes. I love the dance because you move through space with another person of the opposite gender in a silent yet meaningful conversation, embodying loss and time's inevitable passing in the three or four minutes that a tango lasts. All the while, you stay loyal to the rhythm of the music, haunted with farewells and the longing to return to memories better left forgotten.

I took up dancing the tango at a time in my life that was very painful for me as a mother. My son, Gabriel, then twelve years old, a gifted natural athlete, had seriously injured his knee, tearing his anterior cruciate ligament in a sports accident. It became wrenching to pass a soccer field, to see kids playing basketball at an outdoor court. Those activities were forbidden to Gabriel. He never complained, but I would notice a cloud of sorrow pass over his eyes as we drove past and saw other kids sweating from the strenuous physical activities he loved and once excelled at. My athletic child had developed an invisible disability. He appeared normal, but he was not to jump, run, twist, or turn—and certainly not dare to dance, as the doctor had warned. Gabriel had lost the ability to move freely, to move without thinking.

While my husband was more relaxed about Gabriel's injury and had faith that he would heal, I was very distressed because I also was injured as a child, at the age of nine and was in a body cast for a year due to a complex fracture of my right leg. It took me another year to learn to walk again. My destiny changed afterward. I became sedentary, afraid to fall and hurt myself. I became a girl whose greatest pleasure was reading books. I was not ready yet to see my son's destiny change. I wanted him to be the athlete I had not been.

Who could have predicted that in my forties I would take up the sensual pastime of dancing tango? I had reached the age when I should have been reading the *Kabbalah*. Instead, a couple of times a week, I joined a bunch of strangers who patiently tried to balance each other's bodies in space while listening to sad songs from Buenos Aires. A friend in Michigan had told me about the local tango club, headed by a woman from Argentina who had also recovered from a serious leg injury. "I bet you'll love it," she said. She was right. But they say you can love the tango, though it does not necessarily love you back. That is how it was for me—for years, tango was my greatest unrequited love. I hobbled around the dance floor as heavy as furniture that had to be lifted and carried. Slowly, ever so slowly, I improved. Once I could do basic things, like walking backward in high-heeled stilettos, and keep my posture and embrace from sagging while being led into moves that made me feel I was about to levitate, tango became an essential form of self-expression.

Being led around the dance floor, sometimes with my eyes closed, as I was advised to do in order to enter a "tango trance." I was frequently in tears as I thought about the limitations on my son's movements. Tango became a way to tell, without words, the story of my anguish about Gabriel's loss of his athletic gift. It was an anguish I carried with me from day to day, unable to speak about it because I did not want to sadden him.

It was amazing to me to discover the range of men I could dance with as I got better—tall, short, thin, husky, young, old, it did not matter. I could dance with men, Polish or German, who in another era might have cooperated in my destruction, who would have only seen the Jew in me. I could dance with men, Palestinian and Arab, who in another place might have only seen the enemy in me. Tango, like yoga, could quell unease, quiet the mind of its prejudices and worries and hatreds, and, with regular practice, bring about peace.

* * *

Leopoldo Marechal calls the tango "una posibilidad infinita"—an infinite possibility.[3] According to the musicologist Ramón Pelinski, there are two ideal types of the tango.[4] First, there is the "tango porteño," rooted near the port of Río de la Plata, specifically the city of Buenos Aires, where the tango was born at the turn of the twentieth century in the brothels. Then there is the nomadic tango, the tango that has been dispersed around the world, in diaspora upon diaspora, reterritorialized amidst different skies and seas, as Argentines have moved from place to place taking the tango with them, and as foreigners from everywhere have felt themselves drawn to the tango and have carried it to unexpected locations. These days, with globalization, the two forms of the tango collide and crisscross and are virtually inseparable. But this wasn't always true.

In classical anthropology we focused on cultural diversity and cultural stability; but in contemporary anthropology, in an era of great immigration and displacement, we are aware of culture as mobile, portable, on the move. The mobility of culture is very evident in the history of the tango. The Finnish tango is one example of such cultural mobility. The tango was brought to Finland by seafaring Finnish men (who may have spent time visiting the brothels of Buenos Aires) and was reinvented by them and their descendants in Finland. The Argentine sense of melancholy and longing that is embedded in the tango was reborn in Finland and given a Finnish sense of melancholy and longing.

Probably there is no single musician or composer who has had as strong an influence on the global appreciation for the tango as Astor Piazzolla. Between the 1940s and 1980s Piazzolla struggled to invent a new tango, a tango that came from his feelings, a tango meshing the soul of Argentina with the influences of American jazz and

European symphonic music. The grandson of four Italian immigrants, an Argentine by birth and an immigrant child who grew up in New York, Piazzolla was equally fluent in English and Spanish—having lost his Spanish while growing up and coming of age in New York, he regained it upon returning to Argentina. He was born with a defective right leg and as a small child required several operations, leaving that leg two centimeters shorter than the other.[5] While still a boy in New York, his father bought him a bandoneon at a second-hand shop. The bandoneon, the concertina brought to Argentina by German sailors and Italian workers, is an instrument that breathes in and out with an eerie likeness to the human lungs, joining with the violin, guitar, and piano to create classic tango music. This gift to Piazzolla from his father delivered a strong cultural message: do not forget the tango; do not forget you are Argentine.[6]

Piazzolla did not forget. But he longed for a tango that was neither singable nor danceable, a tango that "appealed to the ear rather than the feet," a tango that belonged not to the world of the cabaret but in concert halls. Like his father, he moved between Argentina and New York throughout his adult life. In addition, he spent many years living in Paris. Piazzolla's first major breakthrough as a composer took place after the death of his father in 1959 while he was performing in Puerto Rico. The loss of his father inspired him to compose, upon his return to New York, a haunting lament, "Adiós Nonino"—"nonino" for grandfather in Italian, the name by which his son and daughter called his father. Composed while weeping as he had never wept in his life, he considered it the "finest tune I have written" and reflected, "Perhaps I was surrounded by angels."[7]

But success did not come easily. Piazzolla's life was one of continual struggle to create his new tangos. He innovated on the style of performing the tango as well. On stage he refused to sit down to play, instead standing tall with his bandoneon, which he opened and stretched to its limits. For this, in Buenos Aires, he was greeted by fury and fervor. In the 1960s, street fights broke out between piazzollistas and anti-piazzollistas. Piazzolla himself was not above throwing a few punches with his strong left hand. There were taxi drivers who would not take him because he had "destroyed the tango," and other taxi drivers who refused payment—"Maestro, please you're offending me."[8] It was said of him that he was for Argentina "what the Beatles were to the world." He transformed "a tradition of popular music into something authentically his own." In the process, "he succeeded in universalizing Argentine tango music."[9]

Still, he kept his Argentine roots and could communicate something unutterable that shone at the core of tango culture: a mode of spirituality that was neither religious nor secular, and yet drew from both, and transcended both. It was the ability to evoke the presence of angels that makes his music like no other. For this knowledge he drew from many sources, including the theater, in particular the plays of Alberto Rodriguez Muñoz. He had the good fortune to compose "The Death of the Angel," a fugue, for *The Tango of the Angel*, the last play in a trilogy by Rodriguez Muñoz. This tango accompanies the story of an angel who attempts to heal broken human spirits in a Buenos Aires tenement, only to die in a knife fight. As the play comes to a close, one of the characters describes the angel as "an angel we created out of the fury of our own impoverished dreams. A true angel, not an angel from God, who is in the heavens, so far from this squalor, but an angel that was ours, made by our desires, birthed by us."[10] This is the angel that inhabits Piazzolla's work: an angel that was once human, still is human, an angel seeking freedom, the angel to whom Piazzolla later gave a different voice in "Libertango." Tango on behalf of liberty, on behalf of freedom—tango to resurrect a dead angel.

* * *

Piazzolla is an inspiration to me in many ways. Since my days as a graduate student, I have come to anthropology wanting to be a writer, an artist, and yet drawn to the philosophical ideas at the heart of this discipline, which mirror so perfectly the twists and turns of post-Enlightenment thinking. I have struggled with my profession, tried to make it something other than what it is, while still calling myself an anthropologist.

The discipline of anthropology took form at the turn of the twentieth century. It was anthropologists, most of them privileged and well-educated white Euro-American men, who brought back dispatches from such places as New Guinea, Africa, Alaska, and South America, places that from a Euro-American perspective appeared to be at the ends of the earth. This was the era in which Robert Flaherty made *Nanook of the North*, a documentary about the Inuit—or Eskimo—premiering his work in Paris to great acclaim at the very moment when the smiling, good-natured man he called Nanook, whom he lauded as a survivor of the wild North, was starving to death after a failed hunt.[11]

Anthropology took it upon itself to give meaning to "the savage slot," constructing an "Other that existed in opposition to the 'West.'"[12] The "Other" had held onto ancient traditions and superstitions, and though mired in poverty, seemed to live contentedly, in a world of "enchantment." In contrast, the anthropologist, and the society he represented, had become modern and scientific. The "enlightened" condition of modernity ought to have guaranteed happiness and peace, but instead civilization had brought about anxiety and discontent. It was the search for an understanding of this paradox that inspired the journeys of the earliest anthropologists. Torn between the world they came from and the world they journeyed to, they justified the superiority of modern life, yet waxed nostalgic for the simpler magical life of "the Noble Savage."

Eventually, the need for anthropological dispatches from the ends of the earth became obsolete. Following two brutal European world wars, the entire world became accessible to a much larger number of people than at any other time in human history. After decolonization, the old distinction between the "civilized West" and the "barbaric non-Western Other" ceased to make sense. Though the connection is rarely made in histories of anthropology, the testimonies of the Holocaust revealed the savagery nestled in the very heart of the Western world. Who, then, was calling whom a savage? Was the price of enlightenment a greater ability to do evil in the world?

In the 1960s and 1970s, American anthropology was further challenged in the wake of the civil rights movement, the anti-war movement, the feminist movement, the Native American movement, and the Chicano movement. Gender, race, and class, the trinity of categories that have become so central to the way we analyze the world, exploded the social theories anthropologists had previously worked with. These enormous transformations might have spelled the end of anthropology, but instead a range of new anthropologies emerged that sought redemption for the discipline and restored history, agency, and geographic mobility to ethnographic subjects. Feminist anthropology, activist anthropology, reflexive anthropology, and native anthropology were born from the ashes of a disgraced anthropology. Miraculously, the most seemingly antiquated of the social science disciplines became one of the most provocative and progressive. Now cultural anthropology, as a profession, is more inclusive of women, people of Latin American, Asian, and African descent, Native Americans, and people of working-class background—scholars who in the past would have been anthropological "Others" but are now anthropologists in their own right. The presence of these post-anthropological "Others" has brought about a necessary rethinking of ethnographic authority and subjectivity and put issues of "love and rescue," in the words of Virginia Dominguez, at the forefront of our practice.[13]

Many of us feel that at the core of what cultural anthropologists do is ethnography, which is both a method for entering into the lives of others and an artistic form of expression, a way of telling a story.[14] Ethnography emerges from a unique and fleeting encounter between an ethnographer and the individuals who choose to become the subjects of the ethnography. Like dancing a tango, where two people become one in their movements, ethnographies can lead us to a border where the story of the observer and the story of the observed threaten to blur and dissolve. Our lives become wound up in the lives of others and we form messy, awkward, uncertain bonds. Somehow from these bonds we piece together a science . . . a social science . . . a human science . . . . In my case, ethnography is a blurred genre, which permits me to mix ethnographic stories that emerge from fieldwork with analysis, commentary, cultural criticism, family history, and personal reflections.

The life of an ethnographer is a haunted life. We spend so much time listening to the stories of others that we can hear all those voices in our heads. We are constant witnesses to human agony and hope. And we are worriers, asking ourselves over and over if there was more we could have done to be present, to be compassionate, to give back to those who gave to us. We work with people who are usually total strangers at first, but as we get to know them, through the close bonds created by ethnography, we come to feel inextricably tied to one another.

I find that even strangers I have no interest in knowing will confess their hopes and sorrows to me when I sit next to them on the plane or the train or wait together on a long checkout line at the grocery store. Somehow, without saying a word, I communicate my capacity to listen, my willingness to listen, wherever I go. And the thing is most of the time I really am "all ears," and my accidental listening will do that other person so much good he or she will actually thank me and be sorry to part ways with me. But sometimes I just want to be off duty as an anthropologist and I will try hard to look the other way or crack open a book, but even then someone insists on baring his or her broken heart to me. There is an aura about those of us who are professional listeners that there is no escaping from.

In addition to this predisposition toward being listeners, we have another quality we cannot let go of. While we cherish each individual life and believe that every person has a story to tell, a story that is a world unto itself and deserves to be heard and honored, we also have great confidence in communities, and believe the work we do must serve a bigger world. We are tense observers of the boundaries between the individual and society. That is why we are drawn to people at risk, people on the border, people on the margins, people who are outcasts, people on the edge between life and death, people who can push us to think about how to be independent and connected to others at the same time. We feel not just concern, but shame, about the inequalities in our society and around the globe. We dedicate most of our energy to bringing attention to those who lack the power and the means to make themselves be seen and heard.

We care about those whom no one else cares about. We love those who are unloved and rescue those who do not even realize they are lost and need a map to find their way home. In the process we learn to love and rescue ourselves and come closer to creating the homes that we need in order to be able to nourish our own spirits and intellects so that we can go on being such intensely caring listeners. Our research projects can and should open the doors of the soul.

Ours is a world that is humane in unprecedented ways. There is more awareness of individual needs and the potential for personal fulfillment is at an all-time high. As our world grows smaller and more homogeneous, there is a greater appreciation for the heritage that each community brings to our vast human mosaic, greater tolerance overall of cultural differences. There is a heightened consciousness that language that is sexist, racist, and homophobic is wounding and will not be tolerated. We have made our streets and buildings accessible to all sorts of people, able-bodied and disabled alike. Whatever its shortcomings, the internet revolution, which brought us Google and YouTube, has made more of the world's knowledge available to more people. We should not shy away from taking pride in the spirit of greater empathy and understanding that has come about in our post-Enlightenment era. As Rebecca Solnit puts it, "we inhabit, in ordinary daylight, a future that was unimaginably dark a few decades ago."[15]

At the same time, there are terrible, violent divisions around the world, and it is perhaps those who occupy spaces "in between" that can help to bring about understanding and cooperation. As Amin Maalouf points out, there is the danger of reducing identity to a single affiliation, which "encourages people to adopt an attitude that is partial, sectarian, intolerant, domineering, sometimes suicidal, and frequently even changes them into killers or supporters of killers."[16] The recognition of mixed identity, on the other hand, helps to promote peace. As he notes,

> a man with a Serbian mother and a Croatian father, and who manages to accept his dual affiliation, will never take part in any form of ethnic "cleansing." A man with a Hutu mother and a Tutsi father, if he can accept the two "tributaries" that brought him into the world, will never be a party to butchery or genocide.[17]

Air travel, the media, the web, and globalization have brought human beings closer, making possible numerous intercultural encounters that would have been inconceivable in the past. If tragedy strikes anywhere, we learn about it instantly. All of us are unwitting experts on genocides, wars, rapes, disasters, plagues, cancers, tsunamis, famines, and earthquakes. Our capacity to feel compassion for another's suffering is put to the test each and every day, in a way that earlier generations never knew.

Much of the horror in the world that we experience comes to us in a virtual format. We are exquisite spectators, watching human sorrows unfold on a computer or TV screen. When we tire of it all, we can power off. The fact that we can power off is both terrible and fortunate. We would go crazy if we did not power off and enjoy life. But it is also possible to be driven crazy by thinking about all the horror in the world that we are doing nothing about. It is overwhelming to know so much about what is happening in the world and to recognize that we can do so little.

What a challenge it is for us, then, to continue to be caring listeners, for us to continue doing our work, slowly building an understanding of just a few human beings at a time, slowly learning in detail the dilemmas those human beings face in sustaining their own humanity. Our work can at times seem so small, so miniature; no more than a grain of sand that will not make a difference, will not make things better. But we know that every act of kindness counts; and the more we multiply kindness, the greater our chance of challenging the heartless rationality of evil with the heart-filled irrationality of the good.

Most of the world does not understand the work we do. We are not doctors who can fix broken bones or remove cancers from anyone's brain, nor are we novelists who can sweep you off your feet with a story about an adulteress who cannot decide whether it is her husband or her lover who makes her more miserable. And yet, though it may seem surprising, we have only a little bit of the doctor and a lot of the novelist in us.[18] Our greatest asset is our compassion, our ability to enter the stories of others with such thoroughness that they come to haunt not just our waking lives but our dreams as well. Unlike novelists, our imaginations are in service to real individuals and real communities that we come to know firsthand.

But we incur a debt to the people who consent to work with us that can never be paid back. In fact, this contractual metaphor is wholly inadequate to describe the relationships we form with our subjects. While we are helping them by providing a sensitive ear to their stories, they give us something greater—the gift of their trust. We promise to listen faithfully to what they have to tell us and to share their stories truthfully with the rest of the world, while trying to make sure we do not cause any harm or hurt or humiliation. That is a huge responsibility we take on. I do not know if it is humanly possible to really make good on our promise. We try our best. I think it is amazing we can sleep at night.

* * *

Another thing ethnography has in common with the tango is sorrow. The soul of the tango is sorrow. There is sorrow, too, at the soul of ethnography. Let us not forget Lévi-Strauss and his *Tristes Tropiques* of 1955, his sad tropics.[19] Loss is a classical trope of the ethnographic imagination. The practice of ethnography originated in the desire to salvage fragments of societies that appeared to be on the verge of extinction. Ethnography engaged in a language of loss—of preventing loss, mourning loss, arriving just in time to save cultures from oblivion.

Sorrow and loss were emotions I felt strongly when I started out in my career. Working in a village in León, in northern Spain, I found myself in the company of aging farmers who had an intimate relationship to the earth. I was very young when I first knew them, in my early twenties, and they took me in as a kind of granddaughter and they showed me how it hurt your kidneys to pick potatoes and how it hurt to be left behind by everyone. People kept rabbits, chickens, pigs, sheep, and cows in stables adjoining their houses. The summer months were occupied with gathering hay, harvesting wheat and rye, caring for vegetable gardens, and picking pears, cherries, and apples. Winters, besides being long, were bitterly cold, and you stayed in the kitchen most of the day, because it was the only heated room. It was the late 1970s and early 1980s. The post-Franco transition had just begun. These farmers felt abandoned by their children and grandchildren, who had left the countryside for the city as part of a mass exodus. Out of nowhere, I appeared, sent there by a professor, mysteriously, like an angel, to ask them for their stories, to bear witness to their poignant efforts to remain on the land at a moment when urbanization, the growth of commodity culture, and corporate globalization made it seem foolish and backward to continue to grow your own food in absurdly little villages where everyone knew each other. It would take years for the organic food movement to arise, and for there to develop awareness about protecting the beauty of local spaces and customs. Back then, the villagers I met felt no pride; they were ashamed and humiliated to be working "like brutes" on the land.

Although I had never lived in the countryside before, I was not a total stranger to the reality I was witnessing. I spoke Spanish, even if it was Cuban Spanish rather than Castilian Spanish. And the more time I spent in Spain, the more I thought about how, as a Sephardic Jew, I had a connection to this land and this people that went way back. My ancestors, five hundred years ago, before the expulsion, had thought of Spain as home. But all this felt unspeakable to me. Living with farmers who were devout Catholics, I kept my Jewish claim to a connection to Spain quiet. I went to mass every Sunday with everyone in the village. In the bedroom where I slept, I took down the crucifix each night and put it back in its place on the wall the following morning.

Why did I act in this way? People had taken me in and come to accept me. I worried about losing their protection and love. I worried about being expelled, like my ancestors. And so I hid. Hid from them, hid from myself.

The dissertation I wrote about the village was serious and scholarly, and it led to my getting a job as a professor at the University of Michigan. But I was disappointed with it. I wished it had had more heart, more feeling. It was only when my lie exploded in my own face, after my grandfather died in Miami while I was back in Spain doing additional research on death customs, that I began to do the writing I considered meaningful. I had learned through fieldwork to recite the rosary in Spanish and had come to know the mass by heart, but I did not know how to mourn for my grandfather as a Jew. I was an anthropologist who was woefully ignorant about my own traditions. Writing about that realization, in an essay I entitled "Death and Memory" was my first stab at being a vulnerable observer. This writing was still an act of cowardice. I never told anyone from the village I was Jewish until decades after I completed my fieldwork.

Now, so many years later, the grandchildren and great-grandchildren of the people I knew in Santa María have found me on the internet, and they've written to thank me. The book that came from the dissertation, *The Presence of the Past in a Spanish Village*, that I so desperately wished could have been better, for this younger generation has become a crucial document about the traditions and way of life of their ancestors, whom I was blessed to know.[20] Recently, a young man from one of the neighboring villages, who studied anthropology, has taken it upon himself to translate my book into Spanish. His dedication has moved me deeply; his attention to detail has been meticulous. He did it, he says, for his father; so his father can read my book. This act of love is huge; it has reminded me that always at the core of ethnography is the gift—the gift of stories given, received, and written down, not knowing who will need them. As Rebecca Solnit says, writing is

> an intimate talk with the dead, with the unborn, with the absent, with strangers, with the readers who may never come to be and who, even if they do read you, will do so weeks, years, decades later. An essay, a book, is one statement in a long conversation you could call culture or history; you are answering something or questioning something that may have fallen silent long ago, and the response to your words may come long after you're gone and never reach your ears—if anyone hears you in the first place. . . . No one is more hopeful than a writer, no one is a bigger gambler.[21]

* * *

After the years in Spain, I went on to Mexico, and now it was a desire for feminist solidarity that drew me into a complex relationship with a Mexican street peddler named Esperanza. Ethnography, like the tango, is an effort to find a connection between human beings. But I soon discovered that not I but Esperanza was the one who would establish the terms of our connection. She never let me forget that I, though a Cuban immigrant, could cross the border easily between the United States and Mexico, but she could not because she was poor; I was the one who could write her story, not she, she was illiterate. She forced me to reflect on my privilege as a writer and ethnographer, and in that way, she helped me to write a daring book that questioned the very act of writing another woman's life story as I still attempted to tell her life story.[22]

Our relationship was based on an unspoken but very real contract, an exchange of desires and longings, in which she told me her story in the presence of her younger children, so I might validate the decisions she had made in her life, and I listened to her story so I could write a book that would help me to become the feminist ethnographer I did not yet know how to be. Her story was given to me in the context of the spiritual kinship we'd formed as comadres ("co-mothers"), and there were real things Esperanza expected and wanted from me, which included a television, a VCR, and financial support when her luck was down. She did not ask for it, but I also gave her shares of the royalties. Was that enough to give back to her after she had given me the gift of her story—a story that helped me rise up in my academic career? I did not know. I would never know.

Esperanza did not realize that through her life, and the *historias* (the "histories" or life story) she told about her yearning for freedom as a woman, she was helping to tell a larger story than her own: the story and the history of modern feminism. She knew she suffered seeing her mother suffer from violence. She knew that she, like her mother, also endured the pain of beatings, and that the beatings left scars on her body. Long before feminism reached her small town in northern Mexico, she refused to live a life she found intolerable. She left her abusive husband and went to work as a street peddler to support her children. She understood in her heart, though there was no official confirmation of it anywhere in her social world, that her *historias* mattered. Alone and wretched, but she had her *historias*. No one could take them from her. Her *historias*, she rightly believed, were her capital, her riches.

When Esperanza was a young woman, struggling to find her way out of the soul-crushing cycle of domestic violence, there were no resources to support her, no experts to counsel her. The feminist movement and the discourse of women's equal rights had not yet universalized the idea that women are full human beings who deserve to have the same opportunities as men to develop their intellectual and creative gifts without fear of discrimination, abuse, and oppression. But before feminism existed, there were brave women. Esperanza was one of these brave women. Although disparaged as a *bruja*, a "witch," she had been unafraid to speak out and protest the injustice of her condition. We recognize now that it was through the struggles of many women like Esperanza that feminism came into being.

There is now a new office in Esperanza's hometown dedicated to solving problems of *violencia intrafamiliar* (intrafamilial violence). A lawyer and a psychologist are available on a daily basis to provide services, at no cost, to women and children in need, and to help sustain *una Vida sin violencia* (a life without violence). Esperanza's voice as well as the voices of so many women who have suffered in similar ways are being heard, at last, in Mexico. And *Translated Woman*, which I thought would mainly be of interest to people who cared about Mexico, is now read by women prisoners in American jails, who find in Esperanza's story relevant clues to understand how violence in their own lives has led them to face imprisonment and diminished futures. As Rebecca Solnit says: "History is full of small acts that changed the world in surprising ways."[23]

* * *

There is always one more story to tell after the last story has been told. Here it is. Long before Daniel Esquenazi Maya died, I went to Buenos Aires. I saw the city he sang about so passionately, the city he never saw with his own eyes. I showed *Adio Kerida* to many people there, and everyone loved the scene of Daniel singing "Mi Buenos Aires Querido." I kept meaning to tell him I had gone to Buenos Aires, but I never got around to it. A part of me was afraid it was not fair that I had been able to go rather than he. Perhaps that was why I never told him.

In Buenos Aires, I had a strange feeling I belonged in that city that felt so distant, so southern, so far from everything and everybody. I reasoned it had to do with the fact that my maternal grandfather, a Russian Jew, was supposed to have met his older sister there, back in the 1920s, but he had somehow gotten on the wrong boat in Europe and disembarked in Havana, thinking he had arrived in Buenos Aires. Afterward, neither he nor his sister had enough money to be reunited. Many years later, after my grandfather was old, and his sister even older, he got on a plane in Miami with my grandmother and went to see her. Then, until the day he died, he sent packages every month with clothes, shoes, anything he envisioned his sister and her family could use.

My great-aunt's daughter and two of her grandchildren, who are close to me in age, are still in Buenos Aires, so I can say I have family there in that city that might have belonged to me. I take comfort in that. I am left to wonder about the turns of destiny that made me born in Cuba rather than in Argentina.

Late at night, my cousins do not know this, but all by myself I go to the milonga in hopes of dancing. As a woman, you never know if you will be asked to dance. But you hope. You can love the tango; it does not necessarily love you back. I am older, I am a woman of a certain age, I understand that very well, though Marta Savigliano, an expert on the tango, says that the *milonga* environment "defies accepted parameters of old and young, and mature women are still in the running . . . because what matters is the confidence with which the milonguera moves her body on the dance floor."[24] I find that this is true enough of the time to encourage me, as well as other women my age, and even older, to keep going back.

They do not play Piazzolla's tangos at the *milongas* in Buenos Aires. They play the tangos from before his time, before his revolution, as if Piazzolla had not existed. His music still is not viewed as danceable—it is for listening, for the shows, or for acrobatic tango dancers, not for the ordinary insomniacs who want to dance away their evenings, and in the best of situations, reach a point of such strong connection that both the follower and the leader are dancing with their eyes closed. But I like to think that Piazzolla's angel is always there at the milongas, keeping watch over all of us, a little sad, but very patient.

* * *

Do I need a conclusion? A friend read this essay in advance of my presentation and said I did. What do you think? Yes? Well, I will try to do my best to conclude.

Having gone with me on this journey, with so many stops and starts, how do I tie it all together for you? What did I want you to learn along the way? Yes, tango is like anthropology, and anthropology is like tango. Anthropologists are always desperately trying to save the present before it is past and over. We can learn from the tango to dwell in the moment, even as the music pushes us to contemplate the eventual loss of everything we love. And the symbol of the angel—what is the angel?

Enlightenment? Yes, because the angel has been present every time we, as human beings, have expanded our notions of freedom and justice.

Enchantment? Yes, because the angel is in us when we create, tell stories, play music, make art, dance, meditate, and love the world more than ourselves.

So the angel is a bit of both—enlightenment and enchantment. Not at all a rosy cherub but the human angel of Piazzolla's tangos.

It is impossible to speak of the angel without mentioning Walter Benjamin. He famously wrote, "the face of the angel of history is turned toward the past. . . . The angel would like to stay, awaken the dead, and make whole what has been smashed. But a storm is blowing from Paradise; it has got caught in his wings with such violence that the angel can no longer close them."[25] These bleak words were set down on paper in

1940. Expecting to be turned over to the Nazis by the Spaniards, Benjamin committed suicide only a few months later, an act of courage and resistance.

But these are different times, are they not? Have we learned from history? Dare we now imagine an angel of hope, with its face turned toward the present? And even toward the future? More than ever, we need faith in the future, the kind of faith called upon to bring about change for the sake of the long term, change we might not benefit from in our own lifetime, change we want those who come after us to enjoy and cherish and pass on to those who will come still later. Let us have faith in those tangos no one can yet sing, or dance, or hear, or even begin to imagine.

Notes

1. Ruth Behar, dir., *Adio Kerida/Goodbye Dear Love: A Cuban Sephardic Journey* (New York: Women Make Movies, 2002).
2. Ruth Behar, *An Island Called Home: Returning to Jewish Cuba* (New Brunswick, NJ: Rutgers University Press, 2007).
3. Leopoldo Marechal, "Narración con espía obligado," in *Crónicas con espías*, ed. Juan-Jacobo Bajarlía et al. (Buenos Aires: Editorial Jorge Alvarez, 1966), 73.
4. Ramón Pelinski, *El tango nómade: ensayos sobre la diáspora del tango* (Buenos Aires: Corregidor, 2000).
5. María Susana Azzi and Simon Collier, *Le Grand Tango: The Life and Music of Astor Piazzolla* (Oxford: Oxford University Press, 2000), 5.
6. Azzi and Collier, *Le Grand Tango*, 134.
7. Azzi and Collier, *Le Grand Tango*, 76.
8. Azzi and Collier, *Le Grand Tango*, 79–80.
9. Azzi and Collier, *Le Grand Tango*, 282–3.
10. Alberto Rodriguez Muñoz, *Melenita de Oro: los tangos de Orfeo, y el tango del Angel* (Buenos Aires: Editorial Sudamericana, 1965), 208.
11. Robert J. Flaherty, dir., *Nanook of the North* (France: Les Frères Revillon, 1922).
12. Michele-Rolph Trouillot, "Anthropology and the Savage Slot: The Poetics and Politics of Other-ness," in *Global Transformations: Anthropology and The Modern World* (New York: Palgrave Macmillan, 2003), 19.
13. Virginia Dominguez, "For a Politics of Love and Rescue," *Cultural Anthropology* 15, no. 3 (2000): 361–93.
14. Ruth Behar, "Ethnography and the Book That Was Lost," *Ethnography* 4, no. 1 (2003): 15–39.
15. Rebecca Solnit, *Hope in the Dark: Untold Histories, Wild Possibilities* (New York: Nation Books, 2004), 28.
16. Amin Maalouf, *In the Name of Identity: Violence and The Need to Belong* (New York: Arcade Publishing, 2001), 4.
17. Maalouf, *In the Name*, 4.
18. Ruth Behar, "Believing in Anthropology as Literature," in *Anthropology Off the Shelf: Anthropologists on Writing*, ed. Alisse Waterston and Maria D. Vesperi (Malden, MA: Wiley-Blackwell, 2009), 106–16.
19. Claude Lévi-Strauss, *Tristes Tropiques* (New York: Penguin Books, 1992).
20. Ruth Behar, *The Presence of the Past in a Spanish Village* (Princeton: Princeton University Press, 1986).

21 Solnit, *Hope in the Dark*, 64.
22 Ruth Behar, *Translated Woman: Crossing the Border with Esperanza's Story* (Boston: Beacon Press, 1993).
23 Solnit, *Hope in the Dark*, 66.
24 Marta Savigliano, *Angora Matta: Fatal Acts of North-South Translation = actos fatales de traduccion norte-sur* (Middletown, CT: Wesleyan University Press, 2003), 141–66.
25 Walter Benjamin, "Theses on the Philosophy of History," in *Illuminations*, trans. Harry Zohn (New York: Harcourt, Brace, and World, 1968), 257–8.

Bibliography

Azzi, María Susana and Simon Collier. *Le Grand Tango: The Life and Music of Astor Piazzolla*. Oxford: Oxford University Press, 2000.

Behar, Ruth. *Adio Kerida/Goodbye Dear Love: A Cuban Sephardic Journey*. New York: Women Make Movies, 2002.

Behar, Ruth. "Believing in Anthropology as Literature." In *Anthropology Off the Shelf: Anthropologists on Writing*, edited by Alisse Waterston and Maria D. Vesperi, 106–16. Malden, MA: Wiley-Blackwell, 2009.

Behar, Ruth. "Ethnography and the Book That Was Lost." *Ethnography* 4, no. 1 (2003): 15–39.

Behar, Ruth. *An Island Called Home: Returning to Jewish Cuba*. New Brunswick, NJ: Rutgers University Press, 2007.

Behar, Ruth. *The Presence of the Past in a Spanish Village*. Princeton: Princeton University Press, 1986.

Behar, Ruth. *Translated Woman: Crossing the Border with Esperanza's Story*. Boston: Beacon Press, 1993.

Benjamin, Walter. "Theses on the Philosophy of History." In *Illuminations*, translated by Harry Zohn, 253–64. New York: Harcourt, Brace, and World, 1968.

Dominguez, Virginia. "For a Politics of Love and Rescue." *Cultural Anthropology* 15, no. 3 (2000), 361–93.

Lévi-Strauss, Claude. *Tristes Tropiques*. New York: Penguin Books, 1992.

Maalouf, Amin. *In the Name of Identity: Violence and The Need to Belong*. New York: Arcade Publishing, 2001.

Marechal, Leopoldo. "Narración con espía obligado." In *Crónicas con espías*, edited by Juan-Jacobo Bajarlía et al., 69–96. Buenos Aires: Editorial Jorge Alvarez, 1966.

Muñoz, Alberto Rodriguez. *Melenita de Oro: los tangos de Orfeo, y el tango del Angel*. Buenos Aires: Editorial Sudamericana, 1965.

Pelinski, Ramón. *El tango nómade: ensayos sobre la diáspora del tango*. Buenos Aires: Corregidor, 2000.

Savigliano, Marta. *Angora Matta: Fatal Acts of North-South Translation = actos fatales de traduccion norte-sur*. Middletown, CT: Wesleyan University Press, 2003.

Solnit, Rebecca. *Hope in the Dark: Untold Histories, Wild Possibilities*. New York: Nation Books, 2005.

Trouillot, Michele-Rolph. "Anthropology and the Savage Slot: The Poetics and Politics of Other-ness." In *Global Transformations: Anthropology and The Modern World*, 7–28. New York: Palgrave Macmillan, 2003.

Index

"The 8th of May between Memory and History" ("Der 8. Mai zwischen Erinnerung und Geschichte")   231

Abe Yoshishige   154
absolute dialectic   148
absolute negation   148, 149
absolute nothingness   148–50, 152, 154
Absolute Spirit   226
absolute transcendence   126, 148
accent   25
acceptance   108
acedia   76
action (*Handlung*)   105, 106, 110, 114
activist anthropology   263
actuality   242–3
actus   242
Adath Israel   257
Adio Kerida/Goodbye Dear Love (2002)   258, 268
aesthetic(s)   28
    choices   31, 32
    constructive appeal to   31–2
    engagement   33
    framing   31
    reframing   31
affect   11, 13, 89, 90, 92, 97, 100, 117, 161, 173, 221
affective experience   244
affective presence   246–7
affectivity   16, 216, 217, 219–21, 243–7
Affleck, Casey   111
afterlife   164, 166
agape   149
agency   6, 10, 13, 60, 89, 100, 105–17, 118 n.25, 119 n.30, 120 n.55, 195, 202, 204, 213, 220, 263
agent   106–17
age of death   143–5, 150, 152
akleros   54
Alcott, Louisa May   93

alterity   122–8, 130, 132, 133, 213, 218–20
American anthropology   262
American Civil War (1864)   10
Améry, Jean   12, 72, 74–6, 80
Amino Kiku   153
Amnesty Law (1979)   131
Amstuzt, Mark   71
anachronisms   94
analytic metaphysics   179
analytic philosophy   169
Anatomy of Melancholy, The (Burton)   77
ancestor(s)   12, 59, 79, 198, 200, 201, 266, 267
ancient Greeks   115, 117
Angelus Novus (Benjamin)   76
animated history   243–6
Ankersmit, Frank   29, 30
Anne and *Emily* (Montgomery)   93
Anne of Green Gables (Montgomery)   92
Anne with an E (2017–20)   92–4
anthropological artifacts   60
anthropological studies   205
anthropology, histories of   262–3
anti-Aristotelian stance   240–1
anticipatory resoluteness (*vorlaufende Entschlossenheit*)   184
Antigone   107–9, 114
Antigone (Sophocles)   107, 158
antiquity   109, 111–14
Aotearoa New Zealand   195–8, 200
Apartheid   69
Aquinas   242
A. Raghuramaraju   4
Archbishop of Saint-Boniface   25, 26
Arendt, Hannah   123
Argentina   131, 257, 259–61, 269
Aristophanes   160–1
Aristotelian philosophy of nature   241
Aristotelian physics   241
Aristotelian teleology   241, 242
Aristotle   4, 76, 141, 240–2, 247

aroha 198, 204
Assmann, Aleida 44, 65
Assmann, Jan 65
atemporalities 248–9
At the Mind's Limits (Améry) 74
Auerbach, Erich 227
Augenblick 212
Augustinian theory of time 240
Australian aborigines 60
authentic historicity (*eigentliche Geschichtlichkeit*) 57
authenticity 183
authentic (*eigentlich*) mode 174, 182
authentic self 151
authoritarian dictatorships 69
authoritativeness 30
"average everydayness" (*durchschnittliche Alltäglichkeit*) 180

Backhouse, Stephen 165
Bacon, Francis 242
Barth, Fredrik 3
Bartra, Roger 78
Baudelaire, Charles 76
Bedeutung 243
"*Begriffgeschichte* and Social History" (Koselleck) 43
Being and Time (Heidegger) 53, 55, 56, 129, 133 n.1, 144, 174–7
being/Being 126, 129, 130, 174–6, 178, 181, 211
being concerned 247–8
being-in-the-world 124, 176–8, 181, 183, 184
being of beings 177
being of non-Dasein-like beings 176
being of other beings 176, 178
being-with (*Mitsein*) 53
Being with the Dead (Ruin) 53
being with this being 176, 183
belligerence 30
Benjamin, Walter 12, 43–5, 58, 72, 74, 76–80, 269, 270
Bérard, Réal 29
Bergson, Henri 45, 46, 252 n.19
Bernstein, Jeffrey 77
Best, Elsdon 202
Bevernage, Berber 72
bewältigung 74

binary concept 197
biological identity 184
biotechnology 64
Black Sun (Kristeva) 78
Blue Cliff Record, The 146, 151
Blumenberg, Hans 227
Blyton, Enid 93
Boddhisattva 149, 151
Brandom, Robert 106, 107, 113, 115–17
Brazil 131
British colonization 205
British history 61
Brothers Karamazov, The (Dostoyevsky) 152
Brudholm, Thomas 71, 72, 74, 76
Buddha 150–1
Bumsted, J. M. 30, 31
Burnett, Frances Hodgson 93
Burton, Robert 77
Butler, Joseph 173
Butler, Judith 79

Canada 27
Canadian government 35
capitalism 60
capitalist economy 61
care (*Sorge*) 177
Carlos de Oliveira, Antonio 131
Castro, Fidel 257
catharsis 108
causality 242
Cavell, Stanley 95, 97, 98
censorship 142
ceremonies 167, 168
Chakrabarty, Dipesh 43
Chevet Ahim 257
Chile 78, 131
chōi 146
Christ 165, 166, 167, 226–17
Christensen, Anne-Marie Søndergaard 95
Christian faith 165
Christianity 149, 151, 165, 226, 227
Christian philosophical tradition 161
chronological inconsistency 210–11, 219–20
chronopathologies 7, 221–2
chronophobia 221
chronopolitics 199, 205–6

Index

circumspective interpretation (*umsichtige Auslegung*) 177
Cleary, Thomas 146
climate 64
clock and calendar time (CCT) 4, 204–6
Cohen, Richard 219
Cold War 144
collective destiny 55
collective identities 226
collective memory 40, 59, 226, 230–5
collective trauma 72, 79, 80
collective violence 69, 76
Collingwood, R. G. 123
colonial warfare 69
commemorations 44, 53, 61, 64
commodification 60–2
communal norms 113, 114, 116
communio sanctorum 151
compassion 147, 149, 152
Complex View 173, 179, 183
Comte, Auguste 226
Confessions (Augustine) 4, 168, 239
connective structures 65
conscience (*Gewissen*) 111–15, 119 n.39, 240, 241
conscientious agent 113–14
consciousness 240, 241, 247–9
conservatism 230
conservative identity politics 61
constructive approach 31–3
constructivist model 61
contemporaneity 163–167
contemporary anthropology 260
continental philosophy 144
"Convention Concerning the Protection of the World Cultural and Natural Heritage (*patrimoine mondiale*, 1972)" 60
corruption 113
COVID-19 105
Crary, Alice 95
creative imagination 32
Creon 107, 108, 114
Crimp, Douglas 79
Critchley, Simon 3
critical discourse analysis 196
critical-historical approach 59
critical rethinking 74
critical theory 59

cross-cultural philosophy 4
Cuba 257, 259
Cultural Memory and Western Civilization (Assmann) 65
culture(al)
  anthropology 263
  continuity 65
  of death 53
  discourse 58
  geography 59
  heritage 59, 60, 63, 64
  memory 65, 245
  politics 54, 58, 61
  practices 53
  property 65
  totality 124

Daniel Esquenazi Maya 257–9, 268
Daodejing 146
Darwin, Charles 55
Das, Veena 90, 95–8
Dasein (Being-there) 56–7, 129, 173–84, 190 nn.80, 85, 212
Daston, Lorraine 252 n.17
Davidson, Donald 123, 133 n.2
Davis, Kathleen 43
dead 141, 146, 151, 152, 155, 159–63, 166
death 55–7, 64, 65, 141–3, 146–9, 151, 152, 155, 159, 162, 163, 166, 167, 169, 170, 177, 181, 182, 184, 212–14
"Death and Memory" (Behar) 266
death-and-resurrection 145–52, 155, 214–15
"The Death of the Angel" (Rodriguez Muñoz) 261
Decline of the West (Spengler) 228
deconstruction 11, 18 n.6, 28, 33–6, 53, 57, 58, 64, 174, 179, 183, 197
deconstructive approach 33–4, 36
deconstructive hermeneutics 58
deed (*Tat*) 105, 106, 114
dèja-vu 45, 46
Delhi 90
democracy 69, 71, 142
Derrida, Jacques 33, 47, 49, 53, 55–8, 63, 65, 122–5, 133 n.1
Derrida and the Inheritance of Democracy (Haddad) 57

de Saussure, Ferdinand   127
Descartes, René   127
desire   27, 46, 47, 54–6, 58, 63, 65, 73, 75, 76, 161, 164, 219, 221, 246, 247, 261, 265, 267
determinate atemporal existence   248–9
diachronic dissonance   42
diachronic identity   181
diachrony   127, 216, 218
dialectical nothingness   148
Dialectic of Christianity (Tanabe)   145, 146, 149
dialectic of death   145
Diamond, Cora   95
Dickinson, Emily   10
dilemmas   69–72
Dilthey, Wilhelm   226–9, 232, 249
discontinuity   7, 206, 215, 216, 218, 220, 225, 228, 233
disinterested knowledge   28
disorder   113
dispersio animi   239
dispositions   239–42
divine   114
divine law   107, 108, 115, 118 n.14
Divinity   226, 227
dogmatism   125
domestic violence   268
Dostoyevsky, Fyodor   152
Durkheimian sociology   59

ecstatic   176, 178, 184, 219
ego   214, 217
Ego and the Id, The (Freud)   77
"The Eighteenth Century as Beginning of Modernity" (Koselleck)   42
Einleitung in die Geisteswissenschaften (Dilthey)   226
Einstein, Albert   169
"The Emergence into Modernity or the End of the Era of the Horse" ("Der Aufbruch in die Moderne oder das Ende des Pferdezeitalters")   229
emotional theology   240
emotions   17, 28, 71–3, 77, 78, 143, 154, 159, 163, 240, 244, 246, 247, 252 n.17, 265
empirical relations   173
empowerment   61

endless mourning   43–6
England   43
English language   195–8
Enlightenment   227, 228, 232
entelecheia   241
epistemology(ical)   29
  character   30
  commitment   31, 33, 34
  questions   27–8
Erlebnis   247
eschatology   215
  Christian   227, 232, 233
  time   215–16
"Essential constitution of Historicity" (Heidegger)   57
eternalism   179, 187 n.49
eternity   164, 167, 240
ethical life (*Sittlichkeit*)   27–8, 30, 31, 113
ethics(al)   29, 47
  character   31
  decisions   72, 74
  metaphysics   211, 219, 221
  philosophy   217
  relations   28, 34, 48
  risk   221–2
  time and whakapapa   203–5
  value   141
ethnic cultures   195
ethnic minorities   60
ethnographer   263
ethnography   90, 263, 265, 267
ethology   245
ethos   113
Euripides   106
European modernity   144
European philosophy   141, 142, 148
European tradition   78
Eversmeyer, Bernd   154, 155
exapropriation (*exapropriation*)   55, 56
Existence, Love and Practice (Tanabe)   145, 146, 149
existential analytic   175, 180
existential communion   141, 148, 150–2
existential hermeneutics   58
existential immanence   190 n.85
existential ontology   55, 57
existential phenomenology   54
existential relativity   9
existential structure   176, 177

exorcism 49
expectation 93, 101, 228, 229, 233, 239
experience 4, 5, 8–18, 25, 42, 45, 46, 58, 65, 66, 70–5, 77, 80, 81, 90, 96, 97, 99, 100, 101, 124, 127–30, 132, 133, 160, 162, 171 n.28, 179–83, 187 n.49, 188 n.62, 195, 198–200, 206, 210, 214, 215, 218, 221, 228–35, 239, 241–8, 265
experimental science 246
expressive events 123–4

face (*Visage*) 126
facticity 133 n.2, 176–8, 181, 184
false memories 160
fama 65
Farewell to the Horse: The Final Century of our Relationship (*Das letzte Jahrhundert der Pferde: Geschichte einer Trennung*, Raulff) 229, 232
farness 129–32
fate (*Schicksal*) 108, 110, 159, 184
fear (*phobos*) 108
Fear and Trembling (Kierkegaard) 163–6
fecundity 214, 215, 220
feminism 268
feminist anthropology 263
feminist ethnographer 267
feminist movement 268
fiction 92–5
Fieldwork in Familiar Places (Moody-Adams) 89
Finnish tango 260
fireside tales 202
First World War 77
Firth, Raymond 202
Flaherty, Robert 262
Flanagan, Thomas 35
Flatley, Jonnathan 79
folk culture 60, 62
forgiveness 69, 71–3, 78, 80, 116
France 142
Francoism victims 78
Frankl, Viktor 162, 163, 169
Frege, Gottlob 243
French Revolution 59
Freud, Sigmund 77, 78
From Violence to Speaking Out (Lawlor) 26

fundamental ontology 126
future 28, 34–6, 41, 44–9, 212–14, 233–5, 239, 241, 242

Gadamer, Hans-Georg 8, 9, 123, 127, 132
Gaia (the Greek ancestral deity, the personified Earth mother) 204
Gardel, Carlos 258
Geist 106, 116
genealogy 63, 200–3
general relativity 169
generation(s) 5, 9, 10, 15, 54, 56, 60, 62, 64, 92, 196, 199–202, 204, 231–5, 264, 266
genocide 34
gensō movement 154
German idealism 144
German society 74, 75
Germany 74, 142
"Getting on With Life" (Villa-Vicencio) 71
ghosts of time 40–2, 44–9
Gleichzeitigkeit des Ungleichzeitigen (synchronicity of the non-synchronous) 42, 43, 45
global economic system 60
Google 264
Goulet, Elzéar 26–7, 30
Goulet, Maxime 26
Goulet Street 26
Greek tragedy 106, 108, 109, 112
grief 160, 162, 163
Grief Observed, A (Lewis) 158
group histories 226
group identities 226, 230, 234
Gumbrecht, Hans Ulrich 44, 45

Haddad, Samir 57
Halbwachs, Maurice 59, 231–3
Hamlet (Shakespeare) 40–1, 43–5, 49
Hartog, François 16, 44, 45, 58, 59, 62, 64, 229, 230
Harvey, David C. 61, 62
haunting 12, 17, 27, 32–4, 40, 43, 46, 48, 49, 55, 69, 70, 72, 73, 78, 166, 220, 259, 261, 263, 265
Haunting History (Kleinberg) 46, 47
Healing of Nations, The (Amstuzt) 71

Hegel, G. W. F. 6, 13, 105–9, 111–17, 118 n.14, 119 n.39, 227, 228
hegemonic ontology 127
Heidegger, Martin 15, 53, 55–8, 63, 123, 126, 127, 129, 133 n.1, 173, 174, 176–84, 189 n.74, 190 n.80, 212, 228
Heideggerian legacy 55–8
Heisig, James 146
Heraclitus 241
Herder, Johann Gottfried 6
heritage (inheritance) 54–7
  industry 58
  inheriting 63–6
  process 62
  studies 54, 59, 61–3, 65
Heritage Crusade, The (Lowenthal) 59
heritage-ification 54, 58, 60, 62, 63
hermeneutic orientation 128
hermeneutic(s) 4, 9, 10, 16, 58, 62, 63, 122, 126–8, 135 n.9, 175, 177, 243, 245, 251 n.11, 253 n.19
heroic deeds 106, 109–11, 115
heroic self-conscious agency/agent 109–12, 114
heroism 117
hierarchical order 33
higher times 167, 168, 170
historical consciousness 53, 246
historical continuity and discontinuity 225, 230
historical culture 53, 62
historical debts 69, 70, 75
historical existence 54, 64
historical fiction 90, 94
historicality (*Geschichtlichkeit*) 182
historical justice 75
historical material 32
historical materialism 79
historical narratives 32, 44
historical ontology 249–50
historical process 241, 243, 245, 248, 249
historical relativity 6
historical sciences 249
historical studies 32, 63, 123
historical temporality 58
historical time 44, 57, 58, 64, 70, 75, 76, 225–31, 235, 241, 245, 246
historical trajectories 100

historical understanding 10, 42, 45, 234–5, 245, 246
  in contemporary era 225–6
  finitude of 231–3
historicity 4, 6, 7, 11, 13, 15, 47, 48, 55–7, 63, 93, 123, 126, 133 n.2, 230, 234, 235, 250 n.6
Historikerpreis 229
historiography 27, 90
historization of ethics 6, 7
history and heritage 58–63
History of the Peloponnesian War, The (Thucydides) 45
Hobbes, Thomas 6
Hollywood golden age cinema 98
Holocaust 69, 74, 75, 262
Holy Spirit 166
homo economicus 204
homo exterior 240
homo interior 240
Hudson's Bay Company 27, 29
human civilization 64
human existence 57, 148
human existential condition 210
human history, contingency of 233–5
humanity 4, 5, 48–9, 64
human law 114
human life 8, 64
human persons 184
human sciences 8, 10
Hume, David 173
Husserl, Edmund 55, 127, 129, 217, 218

idealism 251–2 n.14
identity-politics 63
identity-shaping processes 61
ideology 4, 48, 62, 100, 142, 198, 206, 228, 230, 231, 234, 235
immanence 145, 148, 151, 184, 211
immemorial past 125, 127, 217, 218, 221
immemorial time 122, 128–33
Imperial University of Kyoto 143
inauthentic Dasein 180
inauthenticity 180, 182, 183
inauthentic (*uneigentlich*) mode 174, 177, 182
inauthentic self-affirmation 151
indeterminate (*ahoriston, apeiron*) 248

India-Pakistan partition   96
Indigenous knowledge   202
Indigenous people   26, 27, 30, 34, 36, 205
indigenous rights   62
individual mortality   55
Industrial Revolution   206
infinity   130, 132
instant (*øieblicket*)   240
intentio animi   248
intention   13, 35, 105–7, 109–12, 115, 117, 117 n.4, 119 n.30, 129, 135 n.12, 167, 168, 176, 217, 230, 245–7, 249
intentional actions   106, 107, 109–11, 115, 117
interactive existential self-stabilization   178–84
intergenerational   54, 55
interpretive engagement   102
Introduction to the Human Sciences (Dilthey)   226
Inuit   60
Island Called Home, An (Behar)   258

Japan/Japanese   43, 142–4
  imperialism   142
  military   143
  philosophy   141, 142
  religions   146
  society   142
Jefferson, Thomas   90
Jews   257, 258
Jonas, Hans   235
Journal of Heritage Studies   59
Jun, Tosaka   142
Justice and Reconciliation (Rigby)   71, 80
justice of suffering   107–9

Kant, Immanuel   6, 76, 127, 250 n.8
Kaupapa Māori   196, 197, 205
Kierkegaard, Søren (Johannes de Silentio)   14, 159, 163–7, 170, 240
Kiyoshi, Miki   142
Kleinberg, Ethan   33
kleronomos/kleros   54
koan   146, 151
Koselleck, Reinhart   16, 42, 43, 45, 225, 228, 229, 231–3
Kristeva, Julia   78

Kulla-Gulla (Burnett)   93
Kyoto   153
Kyoto School   142–3

LaCapra, Dominick   79
Lacou-Labarthe, Philippe   55
landscape   59, 61
Landwehr, Achim   42, 43
language narratives   32
languages   26, 32, 56
Laplace, Pierre-Simon de   240
Latin America   131
La vie de Henri Brulard (Stendhal)   232
Lawlor, Leonard   26, 28, 35, 36
Laws (Plato)   54
least violence   28, 36
"Left-Wing Melancholia" (Traverso)   78
legacy   55–8, 63, 69, 80, 105, 132, 227
legitimacy   34, 41, 60, 61, 65
Leibniz's Law   188 n.50
Lepenies, Wolf   77
le trace (vestige, trace)   126
Levinas, Emmanuel   16, 122–4, 126–8, 134 n.4, 210–21
Lévi-Strauss, Claude   265
Lewis, C. S.   158–61, 166
liberation   61
Lieux du Mémoire (Nora)   58
life   56, 146–9, 151, 152, 155, 170
life-affirming science   144
ligature   65
ligature of history   54
Lin, Yael   221
linear model   221, 230
linear temporality   70, 72–4, 75, 79, 80
Little House on the Prairie (Wilder)   93, 94
Little Women (Alcott)   93
lived sameness   248
living   141, 151, 160, 166, 170
living anachronism   72, 75
living in two worlds   195, 197, 200
Locke, John   173
Løgstrup, Knud Ejler   6, 7
loss   158, 159, 162–4, 265
love   150–5, 160–5, 170
love-as-union view   161, 163
Lovelock, James   204
Lowenthal, David   59, 61, 62
Löwith, Karl   227–9, 232

Maalouf, Amin 264
McTaggart, John 169, 239, 242
Madres de la Plaza de Mayo 78
magnanimous (*edelmütige*) 116
magnanimous character 116, 117
Mahayana Buddhism 149, 151
mana (prestige/power) 203, 204
Manchester by the Sea (2016) 111, 115
Manitoba 25, 27, 29, 35, 36
Manitoba Legislature 26
Man's Search for Meaning (Frankl) 162
Mantel, Hilary 94
Māori 195–7, 199–203, 205
   cosmogenic narratives 201–3
   creation stories 200–1
   iconography 201
   identity 197
   knowledge 196, 197, 200–2, 206
   language 197, 198, 206
   myths and legends 202
   nature narratives 201
   philosophy 196, 200–2, 204, 206, 207
   society 204
Māori-English translations 198
Māori-Pākehā cultural binary 195, 196
"Māori time" 205
Marechal, Leopoldo 260
Marion Street 26
Marxism 57, 251 n.14
Marxist sociology 59
Marx, Karl 57
Masakazu, Nakai 142
mass crimes 70
material conditions 100
material culture 65
materialism 251–2 n.14
materialization 244
material transformation 60
mathematical physics 241
mathematical science 241
Matter and Memory (Bergson) 45
Meaning in History (Löwith) 227
Meiji Japan 153
melancholia 72–4, 76–81
Melancholy and Society (Lepenies) 77
"Memento Mori" (Tanabe) 141, 143
Memorandum on Mallarmé, A (Tanabe) 141
memorialization 58

memory/ies 58, 60
   culture 65
   false 158, 160
   studies 59
messianic consciousness 22
messianic time 215, 220
metaphorical concept formation 248
metaphysicians 173
metaphysics(al) 125, 126, 174, 183
   commitments 123
   interpretation 126
   thinking 148
Métis 25, 27, 29, 33, 34, 36
"Mi Buenos Aires Querido" ("My Beloved Buenos Aires," song) 258, 268
military dictatorships 131
Mills, Charles W. 206
mineness (*Jemeinigkeit*) 173, 176, 183
Minkowski, Hermann 169
Mirror and The Light, The (Mantel) 94
Mitvorhandensein 179
modern agency 106, 107, 109–12, 114–16, 115
modern epistemology 123
modernity (*Neuzeit*) 42, 61, 106, 107, 111–13, 115, 116, 145, 150, 205, 228, 229, 262
modernization 60
modern Japanese philosophy 141, 142
modern self-conscious agency 107, 111, 112
momentary sensations 246, 247
Montgomery, L. M. 92–4
Moody, Jessica 62
Moody-Adams, Michele 89–92, 94, 95, 99–102
moral agency 100
moral beliefs 91
moral courage 97
moral crimes 92
moral criticism 90, 102
moral cultures 91
moral idealism 154
morality 91, 92, 98, 100, 101, 108, 113, 114
moralization 75
moral judgment 89, 90, 93–5, 101, 102, 114
moral life 91, 95–102

moral perfectionism 98
moral philosophy 90, 95, 98
moral principles 101, 154
moral relativism 91
moral world 94
mourning 55, 77–80, 97
"Mourning and Melancholia" (Freud) 77
multiple historical events 124
Munslow, Alun 28, 29
Murdoch, Iris 98
"murmur" 26–8, 32, 35
museums 53, 64
"My Interpretation of the Zen Foundation" (Tanabe) 141
mystery 156 n.16, 161, 164, 182, 212–14, 220, 266
mythology/ies 59, 61, 151, 226

Nancy, Jean-Luc 55
Nanook of the North (1922) 262
Napoleon Bonaparte 60
national heritage politics 64
nationalism 63
national memory 60
national patrimony 59
national socialism 55, 74
Native Americans 60
native anthropology 263
natural attitude 129
natural processes 76, 241, 245
Nazism 92
necropolitics 53, 64
negative emotions 71
neo-Kantian and Nishidian philosophy of culture 144
Neoplatonist ontotheology 248
New Zealand 205, 206
New Zealand English 196
Nicomachean Ethics (Aristotle) 141
Nietzsche, Friedrich 41
nihilism 145
Nishitani Keiji 154
noa (unrestricted) 203
No Future Without Forgiveness (Tutu) 71
nomadic tango 260
nomos 54
nonsense (*Unsinn*) 225
nonteleological conception 215
non-Western cultures 205

Nora, Pierre 58, 59
nothingness-qua-love 149, 152
"not to be" 142, 152
nuclear destructions 144
nuclear energy 143–5
nuclear power plants 144
nuclear wastes 144

objectivation 244
Oedipus 106–11, 114, 115
Oedipus the King (Sophocles) 110, 115
Oedipus Trilogy, The (Sophocles) 106
Of Grammatology (Derrida) 55
Old Testament 226, 227
On Escape (Levinas) 219
"one-seventh", principle of 36
"On the Concept of History" (Benjamin) 78
ontology(ical) 29, 129, 217
  characteristics 176
  difference 175, 182
  of history 123
  of life 145
  priority 29, 124
  space 56
  structure 180
  values 141
  of vestiges 122
"Ontology of Life or Dialectic of Death" (Tanabe) 141
Orange Order 30
"ordinary concept of time" (*vulgäre Zeit*) 178
ordinary ethics 90
Origin of the German Trauerspiel (Benjamin) 78
Ōshima Yasumasa 154
Other 211–14, 217–21, 263
otherness 41, 47, 129, 217, 218
Otherwise Than Being or Beyond Essence (Levinas) 212, 216–19
Our Broad Present (Gumbrecht) 44
our selves 160–3

Pacific War 142
Pakistan 96
Panofsky, Erwin 227
pardon 215, 220
passivity 234

past 44, 45, 47, 48, 63, 70, 71, 73–5, 76, 89, 94, 100, 126, 127, 130–2, 159, 217, 239, 241, 242
Past is a Foreign Country, The (Lowenthal) 59
patrimony 58
Pelinski, Ramón 260
periodization 206
permanent structures 46
personal identity 173, 174, 178–84
personal memory 231
personal non-identity 179–81
personhood 174, 183, 184
persons 3, 5, 7, 8–10, 13, 14, 16, 31, 41, 48, 54, 75, 93, 98, 105, 108, 114, 116, 129, 135 n.12, 146, 147, 158, 161–6, 168, 170, 173–6, 179, 180, 183, 184, 185 n.3, 185 n.4, 186 n.8, 195, 198, 199, 203–5, 211–14, 216, 219, 222, 232, 241, 248, 259, 263
"the phantom" (*le fantôme*) 56
phenomenological ethics 95
phenomenology 144, 145
Phenomenology of Spirit (Hegel) 114, 118 n.14, 227
philosophical anthropology 5
philosophical ethics 3, 10
philosophical legacy 56
Philosophy as Metanoetics (Tanabe) 143, 145, 146, 154
philosophy of death 142–3, 145, 146, 148, 149, 151, 152, 155
philosophy of history 6, 9, 225–30, 234, 235
philosophy of idealism 144
philosophy of life (*Lebensphilosophie*) 144, 145, 148, 247
philosophy of religion 141, 145, 149, 154
Philosophy of Right (Hegel) 105, 106, 111, 114
philosophy of science 202
Phoenician Women, The (Euripides) 106
physical properties 41
Physics (Aristotle) 241
Piazzolla, Astor 260–2, 269
Pihlainen, Kalle 32, 33
pity (*eleos*) 108
Plato 54, 160, 240, 248

Platonism 167, 240, 243, 248
Plotinus 167, 240, 248
political burials 64
political debates 69
political-ideological space 62
political struggles 60, 65
politics of heritage 61
pono 198, 204
positivism 226
postcolonial critique 4
postcolonial struggles 60
post-Enlightenment 232, 264
post-Franco transition 266
Postill, John 205
post-partition India 90
post-structuralism 221
postwar philosophy 141
power 10, 41, 45, 46, 61, 69, 70, 75, 79, 100, 108, 120 n.53, 133, 143, 144, 145, 149, 160, 169, 195, 198, 203–6, 213, 216, 219, 220, 257, 264, 265
pre-Christian monuments 62
predetermination 16, 98, 240, 243, 244–9, 251 n.12
premodern agency 106, 109–11, 113–16
premodern self-conscious agency 107, 111, 112
presence 239–42
presence-at-hand (*Vorhandenheit*) 175
Presence of the Past in a Spanish Village, The (Behar) 266
present 44–6, 71, 94, 126, 127, 130, 242
present-at-hand 123–6, 128–33, 176, 177, 179, 181, 182
present-centered operations 129
presentism 58, 169, 187 n.49, 221, 229, 230
presentist ontology 125
prestige 203
primordial identity 180
principle of values 145
process, definition 173–4
"processes of heritageisation" 61
process metaphysics 184
process ontology 174
processual 15, 174, 175, 178, 180, 184, 185 n.4, 243, 247–9
processual animalism 184
profane time 167

prophet Jonah 227
prospective acts 65
Provencher Boulevard 26
Providential plan 227
provisional government 27, 29, 30, 31
psychic processes 244
psychoanalytic discourse 78
psychological processes 41
"pure expression of Being" (*ein reiner Seinsausdruck*) 175
Pure Land/Shin Buddhism 149

racism 30
Radden, Jennifer 76
radioactive elements 144
Raulff, Ulrich 229, 232
ready-at-hand 177, 180
realism 251–2 n.14
real union 159, 161, 164, 167, 169, 170
reciprocity 56
recognition 4, 7, 10, 16, 27, 29, 30, 31, 37 n.6, 46, 48, 60, 65, 69, 91, 92, 94, 101, 105, 113, 116, 117, 119 nn.31, 39, 127, 143, 148, 151, 155, 174, 199, 206, 231, 235, 241, 247, 264, 265, 268
reconstructive approach 31, 33
reconstructive lure 29–32
redemption 45–7, 75
Red River 25–7
reflexive anthropology 263
Regimes of Historicity: Presentism and Experiences of Time (Hartog) 44, 58, 229
Reid, Thomas 173
relationships 5–8, 16, 61, 77, 79, 95, 97, 100, 150, 153, 156 n.31, 158–66, 169, 170, 195, 211–14, 216–18, 220, 229, 240, 241, 265–7
relative being 148–51
relative immanence 148
relativism of historical distance 89–92, 99, 102
religious fundamentalism 230
Renaissance period 144
repetition (*Wiederholung*) 56
re-presentation 29–31
representing (*Vorstellen*) 244
resentment 72–6, 78, 80–1

Resentment's Virtues (Brudholm) 74
resignation 164–6, 168, 170
responsibility (*Schuld*) 4, 7–9, 11–13, 16, 20 n.26, 31–4, 54, 57, 60, 64, 65, 69, 89, 96, 100, 105–12, 114–17, 118 n.25, 119 n.39, 120 n.56, 123, 127, 128, 134 n.5, 135 n.12, 204, 213, 216, 217, 219, 220, 222, 235, 243, 251 n.13, 265
resurrection 145–53, 155, 211, 212, 214, 215, 218, 220, 227, 262
retribution 108
retrospective acts 65
Reynolds, Jack 221
Ricoeur, Paul 4, 5, 127
Riel, Louis 11, 25, 28–9, 33–6
Rigby, Andrew 71, 80
right of intention 105, 106
right-wing nationalism 142
rituals 167–8
robotics 64
Rodriguez Muñoz, Alberto 261
Roman-Christian times 61
Roman Empire 124
romantic love 161
Rosa, Hartmut 44

Saint Augustine 4, 167–70, 239–41
Saint-Boniface Cathedral 33
Saint-Boniface Museum 28, 33
Salmond, Anne 197, 198, 202, 203
salvation 150, 216, 220
Sami 60
sapience 18
Sartre, Jean-Paul 213
Savigliano, Marta 269
science knowledge 202
scientific realism 251 n.14
scientism 250
Scott, Thomas 27, 30, 31
Scruton, Roger 161
Second World War 142–5, 153, 225
Secret Garden, The (Burnett) 93
Secular Age, A (Taylor) 167
secular time 167, 168
Sein und Zeit (Heidegger) 173
self 141, 147, 148, 150–2, 155, 159, 163, 164, 174, 179, 195, 211, 214, 217, 219, 220

self-alienation   176
self-awareness   147–9, 152
self-conscious agency   106, 107, 116
self-conscious approval   115, 116
self-conscious Spirit   116
self-determination/self-legislation   112
selfhood   174, 176, 183
self-negation   150, 152
self-stability (*Selbst-ständigkeit*)   182
self-transparency (*Durchsichtigkeit*)   176
sensation(s)   46, 244, 246, 247
Sephardic Jews   257
settlement   26, 27, 30, 32, 33, 36
Shakespeare, William   40
Shimomura Taratarō   155
sign   55, 124, 129, 143, 148, 181, 200, 233
significance   25, 29, 30, 33, 34, 41, 53, 54, 91, 92, 98, 124, 125, 127, 129–31, 144, 145, 147, 149, 151, 152, 155, 156 n.16, 195, 202, 205–7, 211, 217, 218, 221, 226, 229, 231, 241, 243, 245–9
Simmel, Georg   243
Simple View   173, 179, 181, 183
Sinn   243
situatedness   4, 5, 8, 10, 99, 101
slavery   92, 99, 101
Social Acceleration (Rosa)   44
social conflicts   71
social constructivism   59
social Darwinism   205
social justice   92, 93, 97
social ontology   54
social processes   76, 79
social-psychological processes   45
social reconciliation   71–4, 78, 80, 81, 108
social relations   100
society   4, 9–12, 15, 16, 65, 69–75, 77, 79, 89, 101, 109, 115, 116, 120, 142, 143, 197, 201, 202, 204–6, 230, 232, 262, 264, 265
sociobiology   55
sociolinguistics   196
socio-ontological category   53
sociopolitical process   60
Solnit, Rebecca   264, 267
Solomon, Robert   161
Sophocles   107, 110

spatial justice   206
spatiotemporal categories   41
spectrality (*spectralité*)   56
Spectres of Marx (Derrida)   47, 56, 57
Spengler, Oswald   228
spirit of trust   115–17
Spirit of Trust, A (Brandom)   106
spiritual realm   164
state-sponsored violence   69, 71, 80
Stauffer, Jill   70
Stendhal   232
Stewart, Georgina Tuari   4
Strasbourg   55, 56
Strasbourg conversation   55, 56, 58
stretching-along   134 n.5, 181
subjective freedom   112–16
subjectivity   113, 123, 124, 174, 195
subject-object scheme   123
substance metaphysics   175
substance ontology   174, 178
suffering   162, 163, 212, 213, 246
Surge   46–9
symbolic structures   234
symbols   233
Symposium (Plato)   160
synchrony   127, 217
systematic violence   69, 71, 79, 80
systemic racism   206

Taché Avenue   25, 26, 28, 29, 32, 33, 36
Tanabe, Hajime   14, 141–55, 156 n.31
Tanabean philosophy   141, 143
Tanabe Chiyo   143, 153–5, 156 n.31
Tango of the Angel, The (Rodriguez Muñoz)   261–2
"tango porteño"   260
tangos   257–62, 269, 270
taonga whānau (family heirlooms)   202
"Tao Wu's Condolence Call" (Cleary)   146
tapu (restricted)   203, 204
Taylor, Charles   167–9
te ao Māori (Māori worldview)   197–203, 206
te ao Pākehā (Western worldview)   198, 199
technology(ical)   144, 145
   artifacts   64
   transformation   60

techno-scientific culture 8
Teitel, Ruti 70
teleology 48, 150, 216, 220, 227, 234, 246, 247
temporal anarchy 41, 42, 45, 47, 48
temporal dimension 25, 40
temporal duration (*die Zeitspanne*) 235
temporal humanity 7, 16, 17, 257–70
temporality 56, 69–78, 122–4, 126–30, 132, 167, 177, 178, 181, 182, 210, 221, 241, 248
temporal process 178–82, 243, 246, 247
temporal series 239
te reo Māori 195–8, 204
Teresina-PI 131
testamentary desire 55, 56, 63, 65
Te Tiriti o Waitangi (Treaty of Waitangi, 1840) 195, 206
theology 6, 228, 239, 240, 248, 250
Theses on History (Benjamin) 58
thing, definition 173
thing identity 182
thing ontological self-misunderstanding 175–8
thing ontology 174, 178
Thucydides 45
tika 198, 204
time 167–9, 240
  completed 214–15
  death, future, and 212–14
  diachronic 216–19
  eschatological 215–16
  of ghosts 40–3, 47–9
  of history 70, 71, 75
  infinite 214–15
  of justice 70
  Levinas on 211–12
Time and the Other (Levinas) 217, 219, 220
time map concept 204, 206
time-sicknesses. *See* chronopathologies
"to be" 142, 152
Tokyo Electronic Power Company 144
Totality and Infinity (Levinas) 214, 215
totalizing union 161, 164, 165
traces 124–5, 218
traditional conservatism 230
traditional ideology 230, 235
traditionalisms 63

traditional metaphysics 174
traditional pilgrimage sites 62
tragedy 107–10, 111, 114, 117
transcendence 128, 148, 149, 181, 184, 211, 213, 214, 220
transgenerational 7, 10, 12, 15, 16
transitional justice 69–81
transitional process 69–72, 78, 80
Translated Woman (Behar) 268
transnational justice 72
trauma 40, 73
traumatic effects 75
traumatic past 71–6, 80
Traverso, Enzo 79
true self 166
trust 93, 106, 115–17, 265
Tutu, Desmond 71

Ueda Yasuharu 154
Ueda Yasuji 155
uncooperative and unforgiving victims 72–4
understanding (*Verstehen*) 246–7, 249
UNESCO 58, 60
Union Theory 160, 161, 170
United Nations 60
United States 43
universalism 89
"The Unreality of Time" (McTaggart) 169
Ursprung Des Deutschen Trauerspiels (Benjamin) 43

vagueness 247
Van der Weyden, Rogier 227
Vattimo, Gianni 127
Vergangenheitsbewältigung 12, 74–6
vestiges 122, 124
  elusive phenomena, challenges of 127–8
  farness and immemorial time 129–32
  overview 124–5
  temporality 125–7
victims' rights 70, 71
Villa-Vicencio, Charles 71
violencia intrafamiliar (intrafamilial violence) 268
virtue ethics 95

Vivaldi, Jean-Marie 75
Volk 55
Vom Sinn und Unsinn der Geschichte (*On the Sense and Nonsense of History*, Koselleck) 231

Walker, Margaret 71
war-campaigns 60
"we" 161, 163, 170
Weltanschauung 226
Western culture 196, 205, 226, 227
Western metaphysics 174, 178, 183
Western painting 227
Western philosophical traditions 4
Western thought 226
whakapapa 201–6
White New Zealand 205, 206
Wilder, Ingalls 93

wildlife 60
Williams, Bernard 90, 107, 117
Winnipeg 26, 27
Winnipeg's "French Quarter" 25–6
wisdom 112
"within-time-ness" (*Innerzeitigkeit*) 178
Wittgenstein, Ludwig 95
work of history 28
world heritage 60
world-time (*Weltzeit*) 178
worst violence 34–6

Yin Yang 202
YouTube 264

Zen Buddhism 146, 147, 149
Zerubavel, Eviatar 204
Zusammenvorhandensein 179

www.ingramcontent.com/pod-product-compliance
Lightning Source LLC
Chambersburg PA
CBHW052214300426
44115CB00011B/1674